Shulamit Volkov
Interpreting Antisemitism

Perspectives on Jewish Texts and Contexts

Edited by
Vivian Liska

Editorial Board
Robert Alter, Steven E. Aschheim, Leora Batnitzky, Richard I. Cohen,
Mark H. Gelber, Moshe Halbertal, Christine Hayes, Moshe Idel,
Menachem Lorberbaum, Samuel Moyn, Ilana Pardes, Alvin Rosenfeld,
David Ruderman

Volume 23

Shulamit Volkov

Interpreting Antisemitism

—

Studies and Essays on the German Case

DE GRUYTER

ISBN 978-3-11-221400-8
e-ISBN (PDF) 978-3-11-076228-0
e-ISBN (EPUB) 978-3-11-076230-3
ISSN 2199-6962

Library of Congress Control Number: 2023937354

Bibliographic information published by the Deutsche Nationalbibliothek
The Deutsche Nationalbibliothek lists this publication in the Deutsche Nationalbibliografie;
detailed bibliographic data are available on the internet at http://dnb.dnb.de.

© 2025 Walter de Gruyter GmbH, Berlin/Boston
This volume is text- and page-identical with the hardback published in 2023.
Cover image: picture alliance/dpa/Monika Skolimowska/Holocaust-Mahnmal
Typesetting: Integra Software Services Pvt. Ltd.
Printing and binding: CPI books GmbH, Leck

www.degruyter.com

Preface

The hope of having a Europe free of Antisemitism after the Second World War proved to be no more than wishful thinking. The same was specifically true with regard to Germany. However, when the impact of Nazi propaganda weakened and the country – particularly its western part – began to enjoy long years of prosperity and an ever better functioning democracy, liberal anti-Antisemitic forces appeared to have gained the upper hand. It was later on, following the most recent wave of refugees, who were crossing the borders into Germany in 2015, that the far Right began to agitate as it had never done for decades and predictably, Antisemitism followed suit. At the same time, critics of Israel on the Left often seemed to cross the fine line separating this critique from sheer Antisemitism and one wondered how far would such criticism – legitimate, though sometimes excessive or disproportionate – be still considered decent in post-Nazi Germany.

Meanwhile, the debate was also manifested in a growing interest in the *history* of Antisemitism. It is in this context that I thought to contribute to the discussion by offering a collection of my studies and essays on this topic, written during the last fifty years. I hoped that by presenting them together, old insights would be recovered and new ones gained. This book includes works dealing with various aspects of Antisemitism in Germany since the late 1870s. It documents the way I have proceeded in studying this phenomenon and brings to the reader the fruits of my efforts in an orderly way, usually though not always chronologically.

As I was preparing this volume for publication, I quickly realized that I could not possibly update such a corpus, considering the huge bibliography that has meanwhile been assembled and the changes that have occurred in my own interests and my own views on this theme during the last fifty years. Instead, I decided to leave the collected pieces as they were with only few corrections and some stylistic improvements. This does create a certain amount of repetition, but it seems to me unavoidable. In addition, I have also left the notes practically unchanged and only slightly shortened. Naturally, these notes refer to literature that may now seem outdated. But this is not always the case. Having seen how even outstanding masterpieces are being forgotten in the face of so much new research, I hope that younger historians will find useful and interesting material in my somewhat antiquated apparat. Hebrew and German texts have been translated by me, unless otherwise indicated, and the sources for all previously published texts are given, with thanks, at the end of the book. As for the term Antisemitism: I am using it despite recent efforts to provide ever more precise definitions of this term and even suggestions to avoid it altogether. I find the discussion on terminology more distracting than productive. Moreover, I do not believe it is in our hands, as historians, to dispose of the term even when we wish to do so. Here, in any case, I have decided to use the unhyphenated form, since in this way it clearly denotes hatred of or opposition to Jews and to Judaism, not to some undefined Semites. For the sake of uniformity, I have replaced other ways of spelling it everywhere, even in my own previous texts.

Naturally, during a period of so many years, I have been helped by innumerable colleagues and profited from discussions with many of them or from reading their related works. Equally important for me were my many graduate students in four decades of intense teaching at Tel Aviv University. A few of them are mentioned in the notes, but I am deeply thankful to all of them. In preparing this book, I was helped by the editor of the series in which it appears, Professor Vivian Liska, who accepted the book with warmth and followed its progress throughout with useful advice. Dr. Ulrike Krauss and Mrs. Katja Lehming from the DeGruyter publishing house, were likewise welcoming and helpful. I am deeply grateful to all three of them. The careful work done by Ms. Anna Leah Berstein Simpson, my English language editor, and by Mr. Luis Gruhler in Munich, who did some translating and much too much proofreading and technical work, was indispensable. I thank them both most especially.

In working on this book, realizing its auto-biographical sub-text, I am often reminded of my esteemed teacher at Berkeley, an outstanding historian, a friend and mentor, Hans Rosenberg. Everything of value that I know about history I have learned from him. This book is dedicated to his memory.

Tel Aviv, 2023

Contents

Preface —— V

Introduction —— 1

I Preliminaries

1 What's Wrong with the Historiography of Antisemitism? Two Reviews and Two Unanswered Questions —— 17

2 The Social and Political Function of Late Nineteenth Century Antisemitism: The Case of the Small Handicraft Masters —— 25

3 The Immunization of Social Democracy against Antisemitism in Imperial Germany —— 43

II Cultural Code and its Derivatives

4 Antisemitism as a Cultural Code: Reflections on the History and Historiography of Antisemitism in Imperial Germany —— 61

5 The Written Matter and the Spoken Word: On the Gap Between Pre-1914 and Nazi Antisemitism —— 85

6 Antisemitism and Anti-Feminism: Cultural Code or Social Norm —— 107

7 Readjusting Cultural Codes: Reflections on Antisemitism, Anti-Zionism and the Critique of Israel —— 121

III Revisions and Related Themes

8 Nationalism, Antisemitism and German Historiography —— 137

9 Language as a Locus of Confronting Jews and Judaism in Germany —— 147

10 German Jews: The Temptation of Racism —— 159

11 Interim Balance: Continuity and Discontinuity in the History of German Antisemitism —— 173

IV In the Context of National Socialism

12 Old and New Approaches to the History of National Socialism: The Double Perspective of Jews and Germans —— 189

13 Antisemitism as Explanation: For and against —— 207

14 A Comment on Brutal Antisemites and Brutal Antisemitism —— 221

15 Revisiting Friedländer on Nazi Antisemitism —— 225

16 Historiography in the Loop: Explaining Nazi Antisemitism —— 233

Epilogue

Germany after 1945 or the Return of Cultural Code —— 245

Acknowledgements —— 253

Introduction
On Interpreting Antisemitism: An Autobiographical Sketch

I never intended to study or work on Antisemitism. Although hating Jews is clearly, though perhaps not exclusively, a matter for non-Jews, the topic has traditionally been studied by Jewish historians, or, more precisely, historians who write about Jews and Judaism. At the Hebrew University in Jerusalem, where I began my studies in 1963, it was taught, of course, in the Department of Jewish History. I, however, chose to study what was then and is today still being called in Israeli universities "general history."[1] It was in observing the struggle among states and nations that one confronted the drama of world history, I thought. And after all, it was also in that Department that one could attend lectures given by renowned historians such as Yaakov Talmon, Yehushua Arieli and Michael Confino. The first, by then already world-famous for his book *The Origins of Totalitarian Democracy*, lectured in the largest hall on the university campus in West Jerusalem, where students crammed onto window sills and stairs to hear his performances.[2] I, too, listened excitedly, fascinated by what Talmon had to say as well as by the way he said it. He was a brilliant lecturer and an eloquent orator.

When I moved to Berkeley, California a year later, there was not even the *option* of studying Jewish History, and in any case Berkeley's Department of History provided sufficient intellectual nourishment. Moreover, outside the classroom, the so-called Free Speech Movement was taking shape and, though as a foreign student I always remained an observer rather than an active participant, there could be no better schooling for a beginning historian. It was only there and then that history began to interest me in earnest. I heard Karl Schorske on European Intellectual History, a course in which he surely provided no less eloquence and passion than Talmon had in Jerusalem. I took Richard Herr's seminar on Tocqueville and Wolfgang Sauer's course on Germany in the nineteenth century. I wrote seminar papers for Gerald Feldman on the revolution of 1918 and the early Weimar Republic, and then, significantly, participated in Hans Rosenberg's graduate seminar on the social history of the *Kaiserreich*. At the same time, I was learning German, though not diligently enough, preparing myself for a

---
1 On this division see [in Hebrew], Ariel Rein, "History and Jewish History: Together or Separate? The Definition of Historical Studies at the Hebrew University, 1925–1935," in: *History of the Hebrew University in Jerusalem*, vol. 1: *Origins and Beginnings*, eds. Shaul Katz and Michael Heyd, Jerusalem (2nd edition) 2000, 516–537.
2 See Jacob L. Talmon, *The Origins of Totalitarian Democracy*, London 1952, printed later in numerous editions.

career in *social* history, as befits a young scholar who sought to be politically aware, socially engaged, and intellectually daring.

Antisemitism was not on the curriculum. But as I was galloping towards my Ph.D., preparing a dissertation on the handicraft masters in the later years of the nineteenth century, I was rather unexpectedly confronted with it. To be sure, Rosenberg's opus magnum on the *Kaiserreich* did include a short and illuminating chapter on Antisemitism, but at first its significance was completely lost on me.[3] By then I was focused on what had been Rosenberg's main topics: economic cycles, class relationships and – further on the horizon – the preconditions for Fascism. However, reading documents on the masters' assemblies during the 1848 revolution and later in the late 19th century, I could no longer avoid addressing their Antisemitism.

Then in 1972, as I was busy completing my dissertation, I was asked to contribute to a *Festschrift* for Hans Rosenberg's 70th birthday. It was an extraordinary honor for me at that stage in my career and feeling indebted to him in many ways, I readily agreed. The volume eventually included thirty-three contributions, written mostly by far more experienced scholars than I; many more men than women. The essay I submitted was, in fact, my first truly independent academic work, and the topic was the social and political function of Antisemitism among handicraft masters in late nineteenth century Germany.[4] It is included in this volume as no. 2, despite the fact that it is by no means a ripe piece of work. Like more than a few other essays reprinted here, I would have written it differently today.

To be sure, studying the master-artisans' history, regardless of their Antisemitism, seemed fitting at the time. It was a typical case of research on a lower social stratum, neglected by previous historiography, a group composed of men, whose voices were previously lost to later generations. In addition, this topic allowed me to inch beyond the evolving social history at the time, in the direction of E.P. Thompson's *The Making of the English Working Class*, a greatly influential book at the time.[5] Thompson presented a mixture of social and what could already be called cultural history. While as students of Hans Rosenberg, we learned to write a history that was above all linked to economics, Thompson's approach called for the inclusion of more social and anthropological considerations. Moreover, the urge to contribute to the understanding of *political* events, above all to matters

---

3 Hans Rosenberg, *Grosse Depression und Bismarckzeit. Wirtschafatsablauf. Gesellachaft und Politik in Mitteleuropa*, Berlin 1967, and see especially 88–117.
4 See *Sozialgeschichte Heute*, ed. Hans-Ulrich Wehler, Göttingen 1974, and in it my essay: 416–431.
5 The book appeared in New York, 1963.

concerning the rise of National Socialism, had remained present as well. After all, politics is always an important aspect of writing history and at that time the riddle of Nazism was never far from our minds. Soon it would become apparent, of course, that social history based on the economy alone did not suffice to accomplish political tasks. I was ready to move on and use other analytical tools for my purposes.

In the meantime, the sense of intellectual-cum-political excitement so prevalent in Berkeley during the late 1960s followed me to London, where I then lived with my small family, as well as to the different German towns I visited during my archival research trips. I was still acutely aware of this sense when I returned to Israel in 1972, although just here, at home, I now felt like a complete stranger. In the aftermath of the Six Day War, Israel became triumphant and complacent. Preoccupied with its own problems, it was oblivious to the revolutionary waves that shook the campuses of North America or England and the boulevards of Paris. At the University of Tel Aviv these were still the heydays of the "second-generation scholars."[6] The Institute for German History had been established shortly before my arrival and its faculty members were all men in their late fifties, some of whom had even studied in pre-Nazi Germany or Austria, and I – not yet 30 and a woman to boot – did not fit in at all. I felt somewhat disoriented, not sure how to handle the situation and above all confused as to the direction I ought to be taking in my further academic work.

Early in 1974, I was approached by Shlomo Na'aman and asked to contribute to a symposium he was organizing on *Jews and Jewish Aspects of the German Working-class movement*.[7] Other participants were renowned experts in the field. It was an honor. Once again, I agreed, and even if they were not too impressed by my performance, the work I did in preparation for this conference proved to be important in moving me forward. In fact, the building blocks for my later piece, namely "Antisemitism as a Cultural Code," were by then almost all there, and in this case, too, one piece proved to be more crucial than others. Just as Thompson's book was instrumental for my thinking about the master artisans, now an article by the German sociologist Mario Rainer Lepsius, under the English title "Party-System and Social

---

[6] For this expression see *The Second Generation. Émigrés from Nazi Germany as Historians*, eds. Andreas W. Daum, Hartmut Lehmann and James J. Sheehan, New York – Oxford 2016. My essay on Israel: 261–270.

[7] See Beiheft 2 of the *Jahrbuch des Instituts für Deutsche Geschichte*, ed. Walter Grab, Tel Aviv 1977.

Structure: On the Problem of Democratization in German Society," gave me the clue I needed.[8] Lepsius suggested a division of German society since the late nineteenth century into "blocks" based on socio-economic characteristics, but each representing a cultural milieu as well, supported by a more or less outspoken *Weltanschauung*. The Social-Democratic workers' "block," the inner structure of which had been previously analyzed by Gunther Roth in an English-language thesis published in 1963, seemed ready-made for this kind of analysis. Dieter Groh added another important layer to this edifice by describing the way in which this unique block had managed to be integrated into the overall social web of the Kaiserreich, namely through a process he had named "negative integration."[9] I referred to all of these in my lecture (here appearing as number 3), while I was trying to say something new, not so much about Social Democracy, but on the role of Antisemitism within it; something beyond the bare facts and the familiar quotes brought forward by other historians. Now it became clear: Antisemitism was an interesting topic; more importantly, perhaps – it was relevant to my life. After all, it was present as a concept and major historical component of the Zionist ideology, constantly used in the Israeli political discourse, for me often an irritant for the way it had been used or rather manipulated. At first, I tried my hand in a lecture on what was often named, following a memorable book published as early as 1930 by the German Jewish philosopher and publicist Theodor Lessing, Jewish "Self-Hate."[10] The main motivation was my objection to the branding of all radical political critics as self-hating Jews. More generally, the stress on the presumed fact that "the whole world was always against us" seemed excessive to me, making improper usage of a much more complicated and many-sided history. By then my interest narrowed on this history.

At this point, I began to sense not only what *kind* of history I wished to apply to the study of Antisemitism in pre-Nazi Germany, which I now considered my field of expertise, but also what kind of history was *not* appropriate to the handling of this topic. It was then that in attempting to scrutinize the Israeli literature

---

8 Mario Rainer Lepsius, "Parteiensystem und Sozialstruktur. Zum Problem der Demokratisierung der deutschen Gesellschaft," in: *Festschrift F. Lütge*, ed. Wilhelm Abel et al., Stuttgart 1966, 371–393.
9 See Gunther Roth, *Social Democrats in Imperial Germany*, Ottawa 1963, and Dieter Groh, *Negative Integration und revolutionärer Attentismus. Die deutsche Sozialdemokratie am Vorabend des 1. Weltkrieges, 1909–1914*, Berlin 1973.
10 Theodor Lessing, *Der Jüdische Selbsthass*, Berlin 1930 and my "Selbstgefälligkeit und Selbsthaß: Die deutschen Juden zu Beginn des 20. Jahrhunderts," in: *Geschichte in Wissenschaft und Unterricht*, 1986, no.1, 1–13. This essay appeared earlier in Hebrew in: *Zemanim. A Hisorical Quarterly*, no. 14, 1984, 28–41. Another version was included in Shulamit Volkov, *Germans, Jews and Antisemites. Trials in Emancipation*, New York 2006, 33–46.

on Antisemitism, I was preparing a review-essay for the new Hebrew-language periodical of the School of History at Tel Aviv University, *Zemanim* (Times), that was later published in 1982. It was based on two new books in Hebrew. One was a collection of essays by the doyen of Jewish history at the Hebrew University, Shmuel Ettinger, and the other, a modern history of Central European Antisemitism by another highly respected professor at the Hebrew University, Jacob Katz.[11] Here I tried to combine my appreciation of the two elder scholars with a fundamental critique of both their books, concentrating on two aspects of their oeuvre. Above all, I was irked by their insistence on the permanence and continuity of Antisemitism all the way to National Socialism and beyond.[12] I myself focused on the novelty of Antisemitism in modern times, stressing change over permanence. Furthermore, I thought of the two scholars as intellectual historians; Ettinger in a principled way and Katz, known in fact as a social historian even a sociologist, despite himself. Identifying what I thought was wrong with the actual study of Antisemitism helped me define the way I wished to proceed in revising its history. Thus, although chronologically it belongs slightly later than the two following pieces, I decided to place this essay as number 1 in this volume.

In parallel, I set out to write a piece on Antisemitism for the Leo Baeck Institute Yearbook. However, while a few building blocks for the new essay were already there, the theoretical framework was still missing; its elements were still hanging unattached.

What happened next was fairly typical of my haphazard modus operandi. One sunny afternoon, on my way to the university library, I met a colleague and friend of mine, Haggai Horowitz, a historian of the United States, who has since sadly passed away. I told him of my predicament, and he asked if I knew the work of Clifford Geertz. I do not remember whether Horowitz ever explained why he suggested just that, but in any case, I hurried and got myself a copy of Geertz's collected essays.[13] This was an eye-opener. I read some of the essays again and again and felt that I found here the clue to my new essay. To be sure, quite a lot of

---

11 Shmuel Ettinger, *Modern Antisemitism. Studies and Essays,* {Hebrew} Tel Aviv 1978; Jacob Katz, *From Prejudice to Destruction. Antisemitism 1700–1933*, Cambridge Mass. 1982. The Hebrew edition was published in Tel Aviv 1979.
12 For a useful and concise review of the present historiography of Antisemitism, albeit in Hebrew, see Scott Ury and Guy Miron, "Antisemitism: On the Dialectical Relationship between a Historical Concept and contemporary Debates," in: *Antisemitism. Historical Concept, Public Discourse* [Hebrew], edited by the authors above, and published as volume LXXXV, 1–4, 2020 of the journal *Zion*, 7–30.
13 See Clifford Geertz, *The Interpretation of cultures*, New York 1973, especially "Ideology as a Cultural System", 193–233, printed earlier in: *Ideology and Discontent,* ed. David E. Apter, New York 1964, 47–60.

additional thinking and extra work was needed before the piece was completed, and early in 1978 I presented the final draft of my "Antisemitism as a Cultural Code" (appearing in this book as number 4), to a small crowd assembled at St. Antony's College, Oxford. The reception was cool. Historian Geoff Eley was unconvinced. Above all, he found fault with my analysis of German society during the late Kaiserreich; it was too schematic and thus, unjustifiably too negative. He was adamant and no support was coming from other colleagues in the hall. In hindsight, much of their criticism was correct. The same aspects of this essay would be contested by later reviewers, too.[14] But in the end, perhaps it was the tone, rather than the content of the critique, that made the feedback so painful.

Walking to 'high-table' in college later on, Reinhard Rürup, in private, was far more complementary. He liked the idea of a cultural code, but he thought it was more fitting to see *anti*-Antisemitism as a code for the liberal Left and Center in Germany and not Antisemitism as a code for the anti-modern, anti-democratic, imperialist and colonialist Right. Could both be applied, I then wondered, but at the time it did not seem to matter, though later on, using anti-Antisemitism as code often seemed enlightening, too.

The critique and the atmosphere in that hall in Oxford unsettled me. It was not an easy trial, but in the end I was sure that by using the cultural code metaphor as I did, I would be able to both sustain the novelty of so-called modern Antisemitism and explain the gap between it and Nazi Antisemitism. This last point seemed crucial to me, and soon I would have the opportunity to stress it again, in preparing a lecture for a conference dedicated to National Socialism and the Holocaust, organized by the well-known historian of the French Revolution, Francois Furet, in Paris. Surprisingly, in contrast to my embarrassment in Oxford, the new paper was received with enthusiasm by a number of my French colleagues and by at least some of the other participants from Israel, Germany and the United-States. To be sure, I was no expert in the field of Nazi history; I spoke mainly on the pre-Nazi period. In addition, I was, once again, one of two women among twenty-five older men. Nevertheless, this was definitely an encouraging experience.

It seems that in the years between 1978 and 1982, the scholarly community, perhaps especially in France, became more open to what would be later known as "the cultural turn," and therefore my approach better fitted the overall historiographical discourse of the day. The Paris essay (here reprinted as number 5)

---

[14] See Eley's critique of both my and especially Hans Rosenberg's work in his, *From Unification to Nazism. Reinterpreting the German Past*, Cambridge Mass, 1986, 23–41. And from among later commentators see Gideon Reuveny, "'Productivists' and 'Consumerist' Narrative regarding Jews in German History," in *German History from the Margins*, eds. Neil Gregor, Nils Roemer and Mark Roseman, Bloomington 2006, 165–184.

opened with the usual review of the existing writings on Antisemitism in modern Germany, while I then proceeded to list the various functions of Jew-Hating during the *pre*-Nazi era: The strengthening of a new German national identity in the Kaiserreich; the channeling of fear, anxiety, and hate vis-à-vis rapid industrialization away from the capitalist system and the new state towards the Jews; the role all of these played in transferring voters to the Right, and finally, the function of Antisemitism as a code of belonging to the anti-modern camp. Section 3 dealt with Antisemitism in France and gave me the opportunity to show that it had had similar functions there as in Germany, namely strengthening Nationalism, channeling anxiety concerning economic hardships in times of industrialization, and helping lower middle-class elements move from the Left to the Right. Most importantly, in France, too, it served as a cultural code, I argued, a code of belonging to the anti-republican camp.

Having expanded upon the situation in France during the Dreyfus affair, I reached the most important section of this essay, arguing that both in France and in pre-Nazi Germany, Antisemitism had remained a matter of the "written word," a literary affair. Hitler diagnosed its limits. *His* Antisemitism was instead a matter of speech – in the open, in the larger city-squares, and in crowded Beer-halls. The force of his attack was in hateful rhetoric, in the "spoken word," an action in itself, soon to be turned into violence and finally into expulsion and extermination. In Nazi culture, to put it differently, spoken Antisemitism was clearly *intended* to lead to action, and this made it, I claimed, different than nearly all previous kinds of Jew-hating.

As in previous articles, new readings lead me to some of the ideas and formulations in this essay, too. This time, it was above all Victor Klemperer's brilliant book of 1947, *LTI* [Lingua Tertii Imperii] *Notizbuch eines Philolgen*, and George Steiner's essays on what he called the "Language Revolution."[15] These sources allowed me to stress once more the break with the past in reaching National Socialism and the fact that Nazi Antisemitism was neither yet another chapter in the history of an old phenomenon, nor the final peak of its prolonged procession.

It was ten years later, in 1993, that I once again assessed the merits and weaknesses of the idea of Antisemitism as a cultural code. Shortly before, I wrote an essay for *Zemanim*, this time on the differences between Antisemitism and anti-

---

15 I noticed especially his "The Hollow Miracle" (1959), in George Steiner, *Language and Silence*, London 1967, 117–132, and "The Language Animal" (1969), in his, *Exterritorial Papers on Language and the Language Revolution*, London 1972, 71–88.

Feminism, of which a somewhat shorter English version (reprinted here as essay number 6) was later re-printed in my Cambridge University Press book of 2006.[16] In contrasting cultural codes with social norms, I was able to show from another standpoint that Antisemitism had not been particularly central or widespread in Imperial Germany, and was surely not as central or widespread as anti-Feminism. The latter was the *norm* against which feminists had to struggle in order to gain greater equality for women, while the former was unique for a particular section, the Right and perhaps segments of the Center-Right. *Because* it was not so central or widespread, I added, it could well serve as a code of belonging to one camp and not to another. At the same time, the argument in this piece weakened the option of using anti-Antisemitism as a proper code, an issue that has been still unclear in my mind. Furthermore, presenting this contrast made clearer the nature of a code, any code, and at the same time, it enabled me to acknowledge that there were also autobiographical sources, as opposed to academic or intellectual ones, for my enthusiasm vis-à-vis this concept.

It was during my time in Berkeley, where I had first confronted the anti-Zionism of the New Left on campus, and now I realized that in fact their anti-Israel rhetoric had served them as a cultural code. In my contribution to a conference at Brandeis University in 2004 (reprinted here as number 7), I recounted this experience. Usually it is the study of the past that informs events and experiences in the present, I argued. Here it was the other way around. Events and experiences at the time informed my study of the past and prepared me to grasp Geertz's ideas and make use of them in my own work. Having observed the role of Antisemitism and anti-Israel sentiments on the contemporary Left, I only needed to find the correct concept for characterizing and then applying it to events in the past.

Meanwhile, in parallel to working on my ideas concerning Antisemitism, I continued to work on various aspects of German social history, gradually moving to intellectual and political history, as well. And while I was lecturing and writing on these topics, I often revisited and revised my view on Antisemitism. The third section of this book brings together a number of essays in this category, under the heading 'Revisions and Related Themes'.

The essay on the link between Nationalism and Antisemitism (here reprinted as number 8), was written for a conference celebrating the 65th birthday of Hans-Ulrich Wehler, a friend from my early research visits to Germany. The conference was a festive occasion and the resulting volume brought together articles written

---

[16] See my *Germans, Jews, and Antisemites* (note 10 above), and for this section especially: 129–144.

by a whole generation of mostly German scholars, by then experienced social historians.[17] Going over the list, it was impossible not to notice the old pattern: these were largely scholars older than myself, among them – yet again – only two women. Still, it was a pleasant reunion, in which I felt warmly accepted, despite the many aspects of my otherness. My contribution pointed to what, at that time, seemed to me an exaggerated attack on the *Sonderweg*-thesis. Like many historians at the time, I too tended to minimize Germany's uniqueness all the way up to the Nazi era. But of late, I was beginning to feel that negating *all* uniqueness cost us the few tools we had had for explaining modern German history, most particularly National Socialism and the vicious Nazi attacks on the Jews. Furthermore, minimizing the role of Antisemitism in the pre-Nazi years and disregarding its link to nationalism – first allied to liberalism on the left and then increasingly bound up with a new kind of conservatism on the right – was particularly misleading. Not only did this approach obscure the history of modern Antisemitism, it also blurred the overall picture of the Kaiserreich – progressive, indeed, in some respects but surely containing the seeds of the approaching catastrophe.

The piece on "language as a site for confronting Jews and Judaism" was written for another conference, this time at the German *Literaturarchiv* in Marbach (and it appears as number 9 in this book). Most of the participants chose to speak on one figure in this context, as the title of the printed book suggests.[18] But the occasion gave me the opportunity to return to some aspects of language and of discourse that I had touched upon before, especially in my Paris paper of 1982. Clearly, my concentration on Jewish history during the years in between made all the difference. Although some Jews spoke German previously, I explained, it was only starting in the mid-eighteenth century that the educated among them learned German and some even made it their only tongue. They soon excelled in all its facets, though the degree of their proficiency never stopped being a matter of controversy, even among themselves. In the Marbach piece, while I did address the Antisemitic attacks against Jewish achievements and failures on this account, I focused on the position of some Jews on this matter.

The next essay goes a step further. I wrote it for the series *Lessons and Legacies*, dedicated to the study of the Holocaust in North America. I travelled to Florida and delivered a lecture entitled "German Jews: The Temptation of Racism"

---

[17] See *Nation und Gesellschaft in Deutschland. Historische Essays*, ed. Manfred Hettling and Paul Nolte, Munich 1996. My essay: 208–219.
[18] *Jüdische Intellektuelle und die Philologien in Deutschland 1871–1933*, eds. Wilfried Barner and Christoph König, Göttingen 2001.

(here reprinted as number 10) to a large audience of teachers and scholars.[19] Once again, I hardly belonged. While the other participants were experts on the Holocaust, I specialized in the late nineteenth and early twentieth centuries. What's more, I mainly treated the German *Jews* and their attitudes toward late nineteenth century racial theories. As I was then deeply involved in work on my Rathenau biography, I took the narrative all the way to the early decades of the twentieth century and into the early years of the Weimar Republic. I tried to demonstrate, as the title suggests, the temptation of racism not only for educated Germans in general, but also for many German Jews, despite the danger inherent in racism for themselves and despite the fact they were always potential and sometimes actual targets of the hateful discourse involved. The tensions at play in this topic are reason enough, I think, for including this essay in the present volume.

Next comes an essay (number 11 in this book) in which I finally revisit the question of continuity vs. discontinuity in German Antisemitism. A year or so earlier, I had written an article on Anti-Semitism (so spelled in this case) for a renewed edition of the *Encyclopedia of the Social and Behavioral Sciences*.[20] Naturally, it was not limited to *modern* Antisemitism and so, in preparing it, I had to read the latest literature on earlier periods and other regions, all the way back to antiquity, update my general knowledge of the subject, and gain a new perspective on the issue of continuity. In fact, I have here clearly reformulated the balance between continuity and discontinuity, even more than I had done before in the paper on nationalism, allowing more room for traditional forms of Jew-hating and somewhat relaxing the stress on the fundamental change occurring with the rise of National Socialism. This piece, which I have here entitled 'Interim Balance', documents the way I had been gradually nuancing and refining my original position, and how nevertheless, the same basic themes have preoccupied me all along. In addition, this essay seems to be a fitting opening to the next section of this book, dealing directly with National-Socialism.

In introducing it, a few more general comments are needed. It may seem strange today that historians of my generation only rarely treated the Nazi era. There were exceptions, of course. Saul Friedländer, ten years my elder, made it his main topic of research, though not before the mid-1980s. Moshe Zimmermann, at the Hebrew University, more or less my age, wrote about Nazism in the same series in which I wrote on the nineteenth century. But Reinhard Rürup and Monika Richarz in Berlin, and certainly Steven Aschheim in Jerusalem and the older Jacob

---

[19] See *Expanding Perspectives on the Holocaust in a Changing World*, eds. Hilary Earl and Karl Schleunes, *Lessons and Legacies*, Volume XI, Evanson Ill. 2014. My essay: 211–228.
[20] See, "Antisemitism", in the new edition of the *Encyclopedia of the Social and Behavioural Sciences*, 2002, vol. 1, 542–549.

Toury in Tel Aviv, who all studied the history of German-Jewry and the relationships between Jews and non-Jews in Germany, made sure to end their studies with 1933. Likewise, this was also the endpoint for the Leo Baeck Yearbook, established 1956, and for most lecture-courses on Germany at the universities at which we have all studied and taught. To be sure, there were also historians, whose research focused on the Holocaust, but we considered them specialists, dealing with a single topic, and tended to stress their ideological and political motivations, at times even doubting their professional objectivity. Even those, who, unlike myself, believed in the continuity of Antisemitism from some undefined past into the 'years of extermination,' like Jacob Katz, for instance, normally stopped at 1933 and in any case proceeded no later than 1938/9 – always short of the Holocaust itself.

With time, this avoidance became increasingly obsolete. It no longer had any professional justification. The archives – even in the countries of the one-time Soviet Union – were usually open to all after the fall of Communism and at the same time, most of us began to be involved in one way or another in the controversies associated with the history of National Socialism. Although I always remained on the margin of these debates, my skepticism toward the centrality of ideology, for instance, may have drawn me more to the "functionalist" than to the "intentionalist" school. Likewise, my longstanding emphasis on discontinuity clearly positioned me against historian Daniel Goldhagen in the debate over his 1996 book, *Hitler's Willing Executioners*. However, I was never too outspoken in such debates. Here and there, I felt the need to express my views but always on the historiography rather than on the actual history of Nazism; more on the way we ought to think about it than in practically researching it. A number of the resulting interventions are collected here.

The first deals with the differences between non-Jewish historians and their Jewish colleagues regarding their attitudes toward Nazism and the Holocaust, a divide that was brought to the fore by Martin Broszat, especially in his exchange of letters with Saul Friedländer in 1987.[21] In another context and without discrediting either group, historian Dan Diner attempted to show that same gap by using the metaphor of a courtroom with prosecutors on the one side and defense attorneys on the other.[22] I chose to discuss the matter when contributing for a book of

---

21 For the English translation, see Martin Broszat and Saul Friedländer, "A Controversy about the Historicization of National Socialism," *Yad Vashem Studies*, XIX (1988), 1–47.
22 See Dan Diner, "Varieties of Interpretation: The Holocaust in Historical Memory," in: *Language and Revolution. Making Modern Political Identities*, ed. Igal Halfin, London 2002, 379–391. Diner delivered a very similar presentation in a conference at the Hebrew University in Jerusalem in 1995. See *The Third Reich. A historical Reassessment* [Hebrew], ed. Moshe Zimmermann, Jerusalem 2000, 40–51.

essays in honor of Monika Richarz, herself an author of books and essays on various topics of German-Jewish history, whom I knew as colleague and friend for over thirty years. In what appears here as number 12, I disagreed with Diner's analysis, arguing that by then we had managed to create an international community of scholars dedicated to the study of National Socialism, a community in which it was possible to present various, even contrasting, views, without necessarily falling into opposing groups defined by nationality. Clearly, each of us depended on his or her personal experience, and perhaps the fact that Diner lived mainly in Germany and I mainly in Israel affected our different views.

The next essay (number 13 in this book), had been written a couple of years earlier, for a conference that took place in Chicago in the fall of 2001. It remains fixed in my memory because I was on a plane back to Tel Aviv while the catastrophe that closed the twentieth century, 9/11, took place. By sheer coincidence, it seems, the subtitle of the book in which the lectures of this conference were collected was "The Holocaust and the Twentieth Century." Although it was intended to close a chapter in one century, it unintentionally opened a new one, belonging to the next century.[23] In my own essay, I came back to the question of explanation that had preoccupied me since my "Antisemitism as a Cultural Code," some twenty-five years earlier. Here, I argued again for the limited explanatory potential of Antisemitism as an ideology, especially with regard to Nazism. Above all, I stressed the importance of the interaction between ideology and praxis, demonstrating that certain plans and ideas for action became relevant only in particular real situations and that they are in themselves insufficient for explaining the run of events. It was an argument in a losing battle against the over-emphasis on ideology in the study of Nazism, especially in Israel.

In fact, it was once again my lived experience, this time in present-day Israel, that now influenced my thinking on Antisemitism and the Holocaust. By then, I was becoming aware of how the ideology of the so-called "Greater Israel," almost non-existent in the public sphere before the Six Day War, was quickly revived after the conquest of the West Bank. Suddenly, even some of its most ardent former opponents joined its traditional propagators in an orgy of nationalistic victory and overwhelming power. Just as my experiences observing the U.S. New Left of the late '60s informed my study of "Antisemitism as a Cultural Code" in the late nineteenth century, I found myself now once more convinced that one could learn not only from the past about the present but also from the present

---

23 The title of the book in question was: *Catastrophe and Meaning. The Holocaust and the Twentieth Century*, eds. Moishe Postone and Eric Sautner, Chicago and London 2003.

about the past. It was certainly this belief that inspired the writing of "Antisemitism as Explanation: For and Against."

In 2008, Jonathan Little's novel, *Les Bienveillantes*, (*The Kindly Ones* in English), describing the life of a fictional SS officer in some 900 pages, came out in Hebrew. In a newspaper exchange on this book, I took the opportunity to draw more attention to the brutal, neurotic side of Nazi Antisemitism and Antisemites. I bring this short piece here (number 14) as an interlude, and it is followed by a much later piece, written for a special issue of the *Journal of Holocaust Research* printed as an homage to Saul Friedländer on his 90th birthday. In organizing the present volume, it has occurred to me that this recent essay supports my somewhat hesitant argument of almost fifteen years ago. In fact, Friedländer was the first to apply psychoanalytical tools to the study of Antisemitism with respect to both individuals and groups. He saw in Jew-hatred a symptom of neurosis, and though later he emphatically rejected this approach, it seems that he never altogether denied its relevance for understanding the decisions and the behavior of at least the core of rabid Antisemites within the Nazi elite. My own essay deals with *his* stance on the matter, not mine, but I find that the piece (appearing here as number 15), contributes to an understanding of that important aspect of Nazi Antisemitism, which I stressed in my literary review. Indeed, I still believe that seeing Antisemitism, especially Nazi Antisemitism, as an individual or collective "craze," to quote Friedländer,[24] has been too often and far too rashly rejected, since we have become accustomed to treating it wholly in terms of an organized, bureaucratic project. The matter is too important to leave to novelists.

Finally, a piece first published in 2011 (number 15 in this book), the last in this volume, deals again with the historiography of Antisemitism. This, too, was written as an homage to another historian, namely Shmuel Ettinger, who died twenty years earlier, in the fall of 1988. Ettinger was one of the two historians I had severely criticized in the first essay reprinted in this book and was not a very likely subject for an homage coming from my pen. But, being invited to participate in a conference in his memory, twenty years later, it seemed like a good idea to write a piece that would acknowledge the changes in my position as a sign of appreciation for his important contribution to the field. In so doing, I observed the circular movement of an entire historiographical school, acknowledging the significance of long term Anti-Jewish views, including religious Antisemitism, the focus of Ettinger's writings. In translating this essay for publication here, I have shortened the parts that re-evaluate Ettinger's writings, though the principle

---

[24] See Saul Friedländer, *History and Psychoanalysis: An Inquiry into the Possibilities and Limits of Psychohistory*, New York 1978, 92.

argument of "Historiography in the Loop" remains intact and is still valid, I think, even today.

Finally, in reviewing the collected pieces in this book I became once more and with particular emphasis aware of the changes that I have made in my interpretation of Antisemitism. I began in rejecting the purely intellectual-history approach to the study of Antisemitism. Soon, however, my alternative, namely the social-history approach proved insufficient and likewise unsatisfactory. I was then groping in the direction of cultural history, before the actual 'cultural turn', and it felt right indeed for a long time. Later on, freed from the dogmatism of my earlier years, I came back to some of the notions I had so energetically rejected before: re-introducing the notion of long term hatred, its religious roots, its deep-seated preview of the Jew as the quintessence of evil, feeding phantasies of extinction and redemption, conspiracy theories, sometimes perhaps and in unexpected contexts, functioning as a cultural code.

Preparing this book for publication almost felt like writing an autobiography.[25] I hope that beyond the attempt to handle an interesting, significant, and politically relevant topic, something could also be learned from a peek into the life of one single historian during these eventful years. In a recent article in Hebrew, entitled "What do we do when we talk about Antisemitism?" historian Yair Mintzker reminds us that "when we talk about Antisemitism we do many things, one of them – doubtlessly – is also to talk about ourselves."[26] Doubtlessly, indeed. This book is a proof of it. The book deals with Antisemitism, yes, but also with myself, though perhaps not exactly in the sense intended by Mintzker. Did I also write about Antisemitism in the sense intended by him, namely out of the pain suffered by all Jews, or rather out of the memory of that pain? Probably. Despite the distance required by academic writing and despite the pretense to objectivity. Perhaps I chose this topic not only because it incidentally presented itself to me but because it was relevant to my life as an Israeli-Jewish historian writing on German history. In fact, this topic chose me, so to speak. It was relevant at the time I began my journey as a historian fifty years ago and unfortunately it is still relevant today.

---

25 For the form of this introduction and the overall concept of this book I have taken as examples George L. Mosse, *Confronting the Nation. Jewish and Western Nationalism*, Hanover and London 1993, and the more recent James J. Sheehan, *Essays on German History and Historians*, Palo Alto Cal. 2022.
26 *Zemanim*, no. 147, 114–119.

I Preliminaries

1 What's Wrong with the Historiography of Antisemitism? Two Reviews and Two Unanswered Questions

Four ways of conceptualizing Jewish history competed with each other roughly between the end of the nineteenth century and the Nazi accession to power in Germany. The first, and surely the least regarded framework when dealing with the modern period, is the old religious view, radical and self-contained, central not only for the lives of Orthodox Jews in Eastern Europe, but also in this continent's Central and Western parts. The second was the so-called Liberal framework, supporting Jewish efforts at full integration in the surrounding societies by using the opportunities opened to individual Jews through their legal emancipation, aiming at as full a participation in non-Jewish society, economy and culture as possible. The third framework was part of the overall Socialist view of modern history, skeptical with regard to the possibilities of integration within the old, capitalist bourgeois order, hopeful of a new world in which all age old barriers among ethnic, national and religious groups would collapse and be replaced by their sense of human brotherhood and peaceful co-existence. And finally, a new Jewish national history had meanwhile emerged, in parallel with and under the auspices of the new Jewish national movement, which in its Zionist version endeavored to establish an independent and separate cultural and political center for all Jews in Eretz-Ysrael, namely in Palestine.

Each one of these conceptions presumed to be an overall ideology, providing answers to the Jewish existence as a whole, and each had a view of its own concerning Antisemitism. Perhaps with the exception of the orthodox conception, all of these views were shaped in an on-going dispute concerning the meaning of Antisemitism, its sources and its functions. For liberal Jews, Jew-hating was a kind of ancient social disease, a residue of a disappearing world, an expression of temporary social unease or cultural distress. Some considered it a remnant of an age-old Christian obsession that is slowly disappearing as a result of ongoing progress and secularization, and some saw in it a painful but meaningless phenomenon, characteristic of marginal and frustrated social groups or neurotic individuals. Others explained the persistence of Antisemitism by pointing out the deficiencies of bourgeois society and still others stressed the role of the particular abnormal position of Jews in this society, which ought to be overcome in a process of self-critique and self-rejuvenation. Jewish Socialists, too, saw in Antisemitism a reaction to the presumably parasitic existence of Jews in society, a symptom of a general social illness that could be healed only by a change in the overall social structure and the creation of an egalitarian one. Zionists, in their turn, insisted on seeing Antisemitism as an imminent component of the European consciousness that could be extinguished only by a radical exodus of the Jewish element from this continent and its settlement elsewhere, preferably in the old Jewish homeland, in Palestine.

The controversy among these views of history became ever deeper during the years prior to the Second World War. Intuitively, one would expect a reshuffle of the relationships among them as a result of experiencing an unimaginable expansion and brutalization of Antisemitism under Nazi rule, first in Germany and then in the occupied countries – east and west. One could expect an overhaul of all the established historical narratives, perhaps even a new breakthrough. In fact, however, nothing happened. The four basic conceptions of Jewish existence among the nations as well as the relevant interpretations of Antisemitism remained unchanged. And if, indeed, the balance among them slightly shifted, the last word has not yet been spoken.

Undoubtedly, the Zionist interpretation slightly gained in influence. In a way, Jewish life in the diaspora was proven impossible, and the potential danger of Antisemitism could no longer be denied. The need to reorganize in a separate national territory and to create an independent state, capable of protecting not only the Jews living within it but, in a way, Jews everywhere in the world; this need, too, seemed now undeniable. But interestingly, the other forms of Jewish existence retained their validity, reasserted old *Weltanschauungen* and historical views, and developed new categories for holding on to old communal ties and lifestyles. For many men and women, religiosity remained intact or strengthened even during the years of the holocaust. They continued to find solace in their faith and in their traditional living habits. They even found religious ways of living with the memory of the Shoah. The horrors of the Nazi era strengthened the Jewish Socialists and Communists in their belief that the world had to be changed according to their doctrine. To be sure, they soon had to come to terms with the claims of totalitarianism, bringing them together with the Fascist world, and even more concretely, with the new Antisemitism in the Soviet Union. But true believers withstood this test, too.

No less difficult to uphold was the Liberal position. The strengthening of the Jewish communities in the United States and the revival of Jewish life in the "new" Europe, reconstructed after the war, gave their argument a new thrust. Now it was possible to claim that following the experience of National Socialism and the confrontation with the holocaust, a comprehensive recovery of the Western, Liberal countries from the Antisemitic affliction, and a secure Jewish existence in that part of the world became a hopeful solution once again. The memory of Nazism served as a vaccine against Antisemitism, it was claimed. For those who held on to the belief in human progress, the holocaust was a catastrophic set-back, no doubt, but not a proof of necessary failure in the future. Early in the 1950s, a new liberal historiography began to take shape. One was ready to refashion the old narrative but not to give up its basic principles. Hannah Arendt, in her book on the origins of Totalitarianism, did so with the help of two assumptions: The one was the negation of continuity in the history of European Antisemitism; the other was shifting the focus of investigation from the general society to the role of the Jews in it and their part in sustaining Jew-hatred throughout the ages – the modern age included. Her book, though surely befitting the *Zeitgeist* of the early Cold War, caused a veritable storm among Jewish scholars, especially in Israel. And indeed, Arendt's two assumptions remain at the heart of the historiography of Antisemitism, expressing the main ideological split within contemporary Jewry.

Let us attempt to formulate the two questions defined by Arendt in the following way: (1) Is Jew-hating a permanent feature of the non-Jewish world that only takes various forms since Antiquity and till today, or are the differences among its various manifestations greater and more important than the similarity among them? And (2) What ought to be the focus of the ongoing research effort in this field: The Antisemitic society which hosts the Jews or the unique diasporic life-style of the Jews and their behavior while living among the nations? In other words: What is it that we ought to investigate: the pains and hardships experienced by the members of the host society, their ideologies, *Weltanschauungen* and psyche, or the Jewish object of their fear and antipathy, its uniqueness on the one hand and the transformations that it underwent, on the other hand?

Liberal historians tend to stress in their studies the uniqueness of *modern* Antisemitism. Usually, they begin either early in the nineteenth century or in the late 1870s. Sometimes it seems that they accept the Antisemites' own narrative, when they insist on the role of the Jews in the advance of modern Capitalism or in propagating and executing a world revolution. Jewish prominence in some specific areas of culture could turn into envy and then to total rejection and even hatred. Zionist historiography in its turn tends to stress the continuity of Antisemitism and to minimize the role of the Jews themselves in reinforcing Antisemitism. In its primitive version, this approach reiterates the claim that "the whole world is against us" and sees in every critique – mild or radical – a sign of a revived Antisemitism. One version of this approach blames the non-Jewish society only, while the other stresses the misery of Jewish existence in the *Golah*. In both it seems unnecessary to take into consideration the unique and changing Jewish place in the host society and the complex interactions between Jews and non-Jews. The force of every new history of Antisemitism would be in rejecting every easy solution, even if one's own ideology depends on it. Today we need, more than ever, a level-headed and balanced historiography.

In realizing this need, two of the best Israeli historians recently published (1984) the sum total of their research and reflections on this subject. Shmuel Ettinger republished his relevant articles on Antisemitism and added an extensive introduction that expands upon his overall view of this phenomenon, while Jacob Katz's book, *From Prejudice to Destruction. Antisemitism 1700–1933*, presents a more continuous overview of some two hundred years and implicitly presents his own conception, too, even if – indeed – in a very different way. Ettinger does not offer a full picture, nor does he presume to do so. Nevertheless, he obviously has a clear opinion concerning both the essence of Antisemitism and the reasons for its continuous and obstinate nature. Jacob Katz's book is more comprehensive and well-constructed but he has no final answers. His argument, both with regard to the main topic and with regard to approach and methodology, is complex and in the end rather open and not entirely decided.

Let us examine, then, how the two authors relate to the two basic questions we have posed above; how do they conceive of the continuity of Antisemitism and what exactly is, according to them, the direct object of their investigation. Here, in short, is Ettinger's position: Antisemitism is for him a constant element in European society – East and West. It is a cultural constant everywhere in this continent ever since the Hellenistic time. It's ideological reasoning has undergone many changes, but underneath, what has been always preserved is the negative stereotype of the Jew, sometimes on the surface and sometimes in an implicit sense. Even when this stereotype is hidden, in periods of relative calm, Antisemitism continues to exist as a latent phenomenon everywhere and in all strata of society.

Katz's answer is less clear cut but no less interesting. The continuity theme is very much present in his interpretation, but he makes sure to qualify it repeatedly. Jew hatred in Antiquity, he explains, is a separate phenomenon. Only Christianity has given it a metaphysical dimension, made it a part of its overall theology and thereby introduced it to all parts of Christian society. Katz opens his book with a chapter that summarizes the anti-Jewish Christian tradition and in fact, the religious motive is preserved in all its forms and transformations throughout his narrative. Even the Rationalists, the Deists and the Atheists could not escape this anti-Jewish tradition, he claims, nor the early preachers of race-theory, who in fact did no longer need this motive for their anti-Jewish argumentation, but nonetheless always made ample use of it. The 'peak' of the nineteenth century Antisemitic movement was, in the end, National Socialism, but from this point onward – once again – we must move very cautiously. The historical constellation that has made the growth of this radical movement possible was "a unique one – as every constellation depending on many factors always is," Katz explains.¹ In the post-Shoah world and while confronting another kind of Jewish existence, it is still unclear, he thinks, whether the new animosity is a link in the ancient chain or not. The Question is legitimate, but the experience of the past provides no answer for it.

Let us, then, try to find out the answer of our two historians to the second question that we have posed before, namely their attitudes towards the exact object of the relevant investigation in this field. Here, too, Ettinger takes a clearer view. According to him, we are no doubt treating an issue, in which both material reality and spiritual context are interwoven, but the primacy of the latter is unquestionable. Throughout his essays the history of Antisemitism is the history of the stand taken by generations of non-Jewish intellectuals towards Judaism and the Jews. This is being especially clear in his essay on the English Deists in the eighteenth century and the German young Hegelians in the nineteenth. But overall in this book the history of Antisemitism is that of the ideational arguments against the Jews. The material reality – the economical and the social – plays only a minor role. And although the Jews had a considerable influence in activating latent Antisemitism, and although sometimes material changes – like population growth or an escalation of economic competition – constitute an important background for new waves of Antisemitism, they always remain on the margin. Antisemitism is the product of an ancient tradition and it necessarily re-emerges, each time in a different form and shape, according to circumstances.

In the introduction to his book, Katz expresses unease vis-à-vis this approach. Ideology is important, he admits, "[h]owever, the more significant question is," according to him, "what were the social intentions and political goals that motivated the ideologues to use these ideas, and how did they adapt them to the needs of the situation at each particular time."² Nevertheless, Katz too upholds the primacy of intellectual history. Between Voltaire and Chamberlain, we analyze with him books and pamphlets on Jews and Judaism; a long parade of the relevant writings and publications – some of them sophisticated and some rather primitive. It seems that despite his intentions, Katz finds himself again and again applying the very method he claims to oppose. He tries to explain this paradox, perhaps to himself too, in an interesting chapter dedicated to methodology, arguing that after all, one could only find evidence for anti-Jewish positions by using certain thoughts expressed by concrete individuals.

---

1 The quotes from Katz here and below refer to the English translation of the Hebrew book (published 1979): *From Prejudice to Destruction. Antisemitism 1700–1933*, Cambridge Mass. 1982. For the quote here see 325. The second book to which I refer is Shmuel Ettinger, *Modern Antisemitism* [Hebrew], Tel Aviv 1978.
2 Katz, 9.

But in fact, it is possible to find plenty of historical evidence for Antisemitism outside the writings of more or less prominent intellectuals, by studying directly the attitudes of various social groups – high and low. Katz prefers not to do so. For him, turning points in the history of Antisemitism were caused by ideational changes. Thus, the modern era opens with the rise of Rationalism and not with new capitalist forms of production and the growth of industry. The effects of economic, social and political change on the position of Jews in the early eighteenth century, he explains, depended on simultaneous change on the ideational level. And it is these later change that preoccupies him in this book. He does describe the history of emancipation in France, for instance, or the situation of the Jews in Germany at the beginning of the nineteen century; he also mentions the main events along the road from that time to the era of National Socialism, e.g. the position of the Frankfurt Jews between the French occupation and the establishment of the new German Bund, including the Hep-Hep riots in the summer of 1819, but here too the narrative quickly goes back to the ideological debate and the literary activity of the time, assuming that "the continuous incitement would end in violence against Jews", just as Rahel Levin had privately warned at the time.[3]

Finally, Katz comes back close enough to Ettinger's Conclusion. We are confronting here, he says, a chain of ideological arguments, in the background of which remains an "irrational revulsion" from Jews and from everything Jewish, based on age-old "emotional layers" of resentment, envy and fear.[4] Katz, like Ettinger, stresses the ongoing story of Antisemitism in the *spiritual* world, so to speak, adapting to a changing intellectual environment and arguing according to changing intellectual fashions.

These books are so comprehensive that they seem to have brought to completion the discussion concerning the intellectual justifications of Antisemitism. But now we must ask again: did we receive satisfactory answers to the questions we have initially posed? Is the issue of continuity settled? Are we clear concerning the legitimate object of research in trying to explain Antisemitism?

Ettinger's answer to the question of continuity is, no doubt, clear, but nonetheless very complex, perhaps too complex. In fact, he suggests to combine the permanent feature, that is the negative stereotype of the Jew, with the changing rationalizations of Jew-hatred and with the changing external conditions that help explain its decline into latency and its explosion into new life again and again. This is a brilliant solution to the dilemma of continuity and change, always so unsettling for historians. But while the analysis of the various ideological

---

3 Katz, 97.
4 Katz, 320.

positions in his book is deep and convincing, the social issues remain all too often on the margin and the questions concerning the *nature* of the stereotype, that permanent element, lying at the basis of its apparently changing justifications remains vague.

In order to understand this stereotype one could apply a psychological, or even psychoanalytical approach, explaining the permanent human need served by it or use what we may call an anthropological approach, searching for the dynamics of this very stereotype. We must ask then: How is this stereotype constructed? Which were the linguistic and the symbolic tools used for its construction and how were they transformed along the time axis and in their various geographical locations? And finally, was the medieval stereotype, in which all the anti-Christian trends were combined, the same as that of the early modern one, representing the growing Capitalism and the emerging modern world? In both cases, to be sure, the negative image is preserved, but the image itself changes and fulfills different functions within a different cultural context. After all, the process of shaping this stereotype is dynamic. It is a complex cognitive procedure, in which the relevant worldview moves ever further from reality and in which symbolic tools are being applied for its completion.

Possibly, when we observe this procedure closely, we would discover that not only the social and cultural *circumstances* have been changing with time but the presumably permanent element too, the Stereotype of the Jew, is part of the ongoing transformation. A measure of continuity is being upheld, no doubt, so that the Stereotype remains negative, but even in this respect one needs a clearer and more careful periodization. The fact that various Antisemitic authors tended to apply old linguistic forms is interesting but can also be mistakenly interpreted. They themselves may have not always been aware of the changes inherent in their appreciation of the Jew that was expressed in their writings; of the ambivalence, in which their own linguistic formulations undermined the permanence of the Stereotype that they were making use of. This stereotype is itself, after all, a historical product and as historians we ought to see not only its permanent features but also its transformations. Side by side with its permanence, we also ought to realize its unstable place and its contradictory roles.

Finally, an exaggerated stress on continuity and on the permanent components of Antisemitism is particularly damaging when we deal with Nazi Antisemitism. Both Ettinger and Katz consider it a continuation of previous forms of Jew-hating, in fact – their peak or completion. To be sure, Katz is clearly uneasy with such simple continuity, and that despite the titles he had given to the last part of his book: "Culmination", and to the relevant chapter within it: "Racism and the Nazi Climax". Furthermore, although he generally discards psychological explanations, he does apply terms and concepts from this field in dealing with Hitler and the Nazis in order to show and stress their uniqueness. They have had a special "mentality" and "their own kind of impulses", he claims. Despite the fact that their ideology was practically ready-made and the social foundation of their movement had been supplied by previous Antisemites, Nazi Antisemitism was a new phenomenon, and thus, the emergence and development of National Socialism, including its radical Antisemitism, were essentially different from earlier Antisemitic manifestations.

Now, that the history of anti-Jewish ideas has been summarized and properly set forth in the books before us, it is time to see the overall phenomenon in its full social and cultural context. We need to identify precisely the social characteristics of the active Antisemites in various periods, as well as the social conditions that allowed their movement to flourish. We need to present the Antisemitic claims vis a vis precise data on Jewish life, not for apologetic purposes that are no longer relevant but in order to understand them better and see how fiction and reality were mixed within them. Uriel Tal, in dealing with "Territory and Space in Nazi ideology", has begun to explain the unique inversion of meaning applied by the Nazis.[5] Like "Blood" and "Space", the "Jew", too, has lost his position as representative of a special world-view within their ideology, he explained. The symbolic meaning of the Jew has vanished, according to him. "The symbol itself has undergone a reversal of meaning and of function. From now on, the symbol and the symbolized became identical . . .". It is time, indeed, to take a new look at what we thought as fully explained. We need to take the next step for achieving just such an explanation.

---

[5] For this article see *Zemanim* [Hebrew], 1979, no. 1.

2 The Social and Political Function of Late Nineteenth Century Antisemitism: The Case of the Small Handicraft Masters

It is one of today's standard historical 'truths' that among the various social groups and classes in Germany the *Mittelstand* has always been most susceptible to Antisemitic propaganda and most active in Antisemitic political organizations. In broad outlines this has been argued, and partially demonstrated, at least for the interwar period when *Mittelstand* voters were among the most persistent supporters of the Nazi Party.[1] Less convincingly the same has been said of the last quarter of the 19th century, when the *Mittelstand* allegedly nurtured the first political Antisemitic movement in Germany.[2] But while the sociology of the Nazi party has been under serious investigation for some time, the social composition and the peculiar social character of late 19th century Antisemitism has largely remained a matter for speculation. Most of what has been said about it is couched in general terms and appears to be largely intuitive, although often intelligent and plausible.[3] Some remarks on the frustration of the middle-class in the face of rapid industrialization and social change are invariably included in all attempted explanations of the intensity of anti-

---

1 See, for example, Rudolf Heberle, *Landbevölkerung und Nationalsozialismus. Eine soziologische Untersuchung der politischen Willensbildung in Schleswig-Holstein 1918–1932*, Stuttgart 1963; Heinrich-August Winkler, *Mittelstand, Demokratie und Nationalsozialismus. Die politische Entwicklung von Handwerk und Kleinhandel in der Weimarer Republik*, Cologne 1972; Arthur Schweitzer, "The Nazification of the Lower Middle-Class and Peasants," in: *The Third Reich*, UNESCO, London 1955; David Schoenbaum, *Hitler's Social Revolution. Class and Status in Nazi Germany*, New York 1966.
2 The literature on early political Antisemitism is surprisingly limited. The major works are Paul W. Massing, *Rehearsal for Destruction. A Study of Political Antisemitism in Imperial Germany*, New York 1949; Peter G. J. Pulzer, *The Rise of Political Antisemitism in Germany and Austria*, New York 1964; still indispensable is the work by Kurt Wawrzinek, *Die Entstehung der deutschen Antisemitenparteien 1873 bis 1890*, Berlin 1927. Much additional information and an interesting analysis has been provided by Hans Jürgen Puhle in his *Agrarische Interessenpolitik und Preussischer Konservativismus*, Hannover 1966, 2nd ed. 1974, esp. 111–140, 298–302. Insight into the problem of modern antisemitism can also be gained from Eva G. Reichmann, *Hostages of Civilization: The Social Sources of National Socialist Antisemitism*, Westport, Conn., 1949; Hannah Arendt, *The Origins of Totalitarianism*, New York 1951; and from a recent contribution in Hebrew: Uriel Tai, *Christians and Jews in the 'Second Reich' 1870–1914. A Study in the Rise of German Totalitarianism* [Hebrew], Jerusalem 1969.
3 Characteristic are the two spirited and inspiring studies of modern Antisemitism by Hannah Arendt and Eva Reichmann, which are full of interesting but unsupported suggestions. See Arendt, *Totalitasianism*, chap. II. and Reichmann, *Hostages*, chap. I and II.

Jewish sentiment. But the transition from wide-spread resentment of Jews to the emergence of an organized political Antisemitic movement has rarely been analyzed. Discussions of the causes and the effects of Antisemitism leave untouched the social and the political functions of the movement, and neglect to examine in depth the unique environment in which it grew.

These deficiencies have resulted from the preoccupation of the research with the nature of Antisemitism, with the theoretical and ideological aspects of the movement; from its tendency to perceive Antisemitism in general as a chapter in world-wide Jewish history; and from and the efforts to reveal the socio- psychological roots of this phenomenon, while avoiding its social and especially its political functions. All three directions of research have by no means been exhausted, but they all seem to have arrived at something of a dead end. Since the end of the Second World War surprisingly little new ground has been gained in the study of modern Antisemitism – so crucial a topic for the understanding of our age and for the self-evaluation of an entire civilization. Recent historiographical trends in the study of mass movements have left the subject of Antisemitism virtually untouched. They do, however, suggest the need for a new direction in the treatment of this problem, which will begin to ask new questions and apply new tools and new conceptions to old ones.

Thus, even if we accept the thesis that the German *Mittelstand* constituted the social basis of the Antisemitic parties in Germany, we still ought to seek answers to a host of additional questions: Which elements within the *Mittelstand* were more, and which were less, susceptible to Antisemitism? Was the old *Mittelstand* of artisans and shopkeepers more anti-Jewish than the new *Mittelstand* of white-collar employees and managerial staff? Was it the educated *Mittelstand* consisting of teachers and bureaucrats, which led the Antisemitic movement? Was it led perhaps by the small industrial producers, or by the small tradesmen? Where in Germany was Antisemitism among *Mittelständler* more rampant – in rural or in urban areas? In Catholic or in Protestant regions? In the east or in the west? In industrial Germany or in its traditional regions? Only when answers to these and other questions begin to emerge can we hope to be able to examine anew the motivation for Antisemitism, its socio-psychological sources, its social meaning and its political function.

We shall attempt to investigate the extent of Antisemitic sentiment among traditional handicraft masters in Germany during the two distinct waves of political Antisemitism in the last quarter of the 19th century. We shall then proceed to examine the specific social and political role of Antisemitism during each of these waves and attempt to offer an analysis of their peculiar characteristics.

The economic nature of Antisemitism during these years has often been stressed. Hans Rosenberg has suggested a specific approach to the analysis of the relationship between the Antisemitic movement and the periodic fluctuations of the German economy during the so-called "Great Depression".[4] Recognition of the link between the two spheres is indeed essential for studying the emergence of Antisemitism in Germany among certain social elements and at certain points in time. It is also relevant for an explanation of the changing character of the movement. Nevertheless, we shall intentionally attempt to keep away from this issue.[5] We shall instead concentrate on the handicraft-masters' place in the social and the political structure of the German Reich, leaving aside their peculiar economic history. We shall focus on the role which political Antisemitism played in forming the masters' political allegiances and in shaping their character as a group.

I. As the anti-liberal campaign got off the ground in 1874/75, Antisemitism immediately became popular. A host of newspaper articles, pamphlets and books argued the connection between the operation of Jewish capitalists and the collapse of the Viennese stock-exchange.[6] The Jews and the "Jew-like Germans", ran the argument, were responsible for the economic catastrophe.

It was at best a result of their irresponsible behavior, and at worst an outcome of their sinister scheming. In fact, Antisemitism was an old ally of anti-liberalism. The two views were often held simultaneously and in conjunction during the pre-March years and became increasingly intertwined in 1848. Both those who opposed liberalism on political grounds, and those who objected to its economic doctrines revealed intense Antisemitic sentiments. They all objected to the emancipation of the Jews as an attack on traditional privileges and on the old socio-economic order.[7] Although no open Antisemitic pronouncements were heard in the two major master-artisans' congresses in Hamburg and in Frankfurt a. M. during the eventful summer of 1848, there is enough evidence to show the prevalence of

---

4 Hans Rosenberg, *Große Depression und Bismarckzeit. Wirtschaftsablauf Gesellschaft und Politik in Mitteleuropa*, Berlin 1967, 88–117.
5 For this and other aspects of the handicraft-masters' history see Winkler, *Mittelstand*, 21–64, and the author's, *The Rise of Popular Anti-Modernism in Germany. The Urban Master Artisans 1873–1896*, Princeton NJ, 1978.
6 The Antisemitism of the 'Era-Articles' which opened the anti-liberal campaign in the Kreuzzeitung in July 1875 was strong and apparent. Sec also C. Franz, *Der Nationalliberalismus und die Juden-Herrschaft*, Munich 1874; Otto Glagau, *Der Bankrott des Nationalliberalismus und die 'Reaktion'*, Berlin 1878; *Die Gartenlaube*, December 1874–December 1875; *Die Deutsche Wacht*, Berlin 1879–1880; G. Wilmanns, *Die Goldene Internationale und die Notwendigkeit einer sozialen Reformpartei*, Berlin 1876; E. Henrici, *Was ist der Kern der Judenfrage*, Berlin 1881.
7 For the Pre-March period, by far the best study of Antisemitism is Eleonore Sterling, *Die Anfänge des politischen Antisemitismus in Deutschland 1815–1850*, Frankfurt 1969, (first published in 1956 under the title *'Er ist wie Du'*), esp. 115–130.

Antisemitic sentiment among master-artisans during that time.[8] Thus, for example, a group of masters from Leipzig sent out a circular letter to all guild-members in Germany, closing a tirade of anti-liberal rhetoric with an attack on the emancipation of Jews, the greatest enemies of the honest German *Bürgertum*, of the workingmen and of society at large, the hated "strangers, who are nowhere at home and have no heart for the Volk, where (sic) they live."[9]

During the following years of rapid industrialization in Germany some masters continued to associate their material difficulties with the activities of the Jews. In their daily life, however, master craftsmen could have only rarely encountered direct Jewish competition. In the old territories of the German Reich Jews were barred from the practice of most handicrafts.[10] In Prussia in 1817 only 4.6% of the Jews were occupied in handicrafts, while over 90% were employed in various commercial enterprises.[11] The number of Jewish craftsmen undoubtedly increased considerably during the 19th century, first under the influence of the French occupation and then through the effects of the liberal state legislations. The Jews all over Germany were entering new professions as a sign of their growing emancipation. However, centuries-old customs, both among Jews and among Christians, slowed down the entry of Jews into the traditional crafts and most new legislations left untouched a host of previous restrictions.[12] Even by 1895 less than 20% of the Jewish labor force in the country was occupied in industry and the handicrafts together, as compared with over 35% of the general population.[13] Striking is the fact that the ratio of independent handicraftsmen among the Jews was far greater than among Christians. Thus, it was reported that in Berlin only 1.05% of all the men employed in the various wood crafts were Jews, but that among them 35% were employers, 19% self-employed artisans and 45% wage-earners. Among the Protestant artisans in the same crafts only 9.4% were independent employers, 6.6% were self-employed artisans and as many as 84%

---

8 See the protocols of these meetings: *Verhandlungen des ersten deutschen Handwerker- und Gewerbestandes zu Hamburg*, 2.-6. Juni 1848, ed. G. Schirges, Hamburg 1848; and idem., *Verhandlungen des ersten deutschen Handwerker- und Gewerbekongresses zu Frankfurt am Main*, 14. Juli-18. August 1848, Darmstadt 1848.
9 *Offener Brief an alle Innungsgenossen Deutschlands so wie zugleich an alle Bürger und Hausväter von Zweiundzwanzig Innungen zu Leipzig*, Leipzig 1848, 21–22.
10 See Mark Wischnitzer, *A History of Jewish Crafts and Guilds*, New York 1965, 197–205.
11 Hans Martin Klinkenberg, "Zwischen Liberalismus und Nationalismus im 2. Kaiserreich 1870–1918" in: *Monumenta Judaica*, ed. Konrad Schilling, Cologne 1963, 366.
12 See Jacob Toury, *Prolegomena to the Entrance of Jews into German Citizenry* [Hebrew], Tel Aviv 1972, 94–111.
13 Klinkenberg, "Zwischen Liberalismus," 368.

were wage-earners.[14] This picture is confirmed by a study based on the general statistical survey of 1912, in which over 17.000 independent Jewish craftsmen were counted among 40.000 Jewish artisans. The Jews, however, concentrated in a limited number of trades only, and were mostly tailors, shoemakers, bakers and butchers.[15] Moreover, the great increase in the number of Jewish craftsmen which was noticeable towards the end of the 19th century was a direct result of the growing immigration of Jews from the previously acquired Polish territories of Prussia. These constituted as late as 1880, at the time of the first Antisemitic wave, only 3.9% of the total Jewish population of the Reich.[16] Thus, at that time Jewish competition in the handicrafts, although not entirely unknown, certainly was not a widespread phenomenon.

Equally unrelated to actual economic circumstances was the association of peddlers, among the alleged competitors of the established small masters, with the Jews. Research has shown here, too, that in 1852 77.5% of all peddlers in Germany were non-Jews, and that this percentage rose to over 95% by 1895.[17] Nevertheless, the emancipated Jews were easily noticeable in the growing German towns. The small peasants and agricultural laborers who found their way into these cities usually encountered there a far larger proportion of Jews than in their previous communities.[18] Jews, intermingling in gentile society and often showing outstanding energy and resourcefulness in enhancing their social and economic position, were an unpleasant novelty for these new arrivals.[19] With the help of demagogues and rabble-rousers, Antisemitism became increasingly popular in the German urban environment, attracting struggling new immigrants as well as a segment of the established community.

What gave the Antisemitic sentiment and the emerging Antisemitic movement of mid 70's its unique character was the assertion which was first coined and made public in the notorious, and then endlessly paraphrased, *Gartenlaube* articles, that "the social question is the Jewish question". Otto Glagau himself, the author of these articles, is an interesting example of the role which his brand of

---

14 See Bernard Dov Weinryb, "The Economic and Social Background of Modern Antisemitism," in: *Essays on Antisemitism*, ed. Koppel S. Pinson, New York 1946, 29.
15 For these data see Jacob Segall, *Die beruflichen und sozialen Verhältnisse der Juden in Deutschland*, Berlin 1912.
16 Klinkenberg, "Zwischen Liberalismus . . .", 366.
17 See Bernard Dov Weinryb, "The Economic and Social Background," 29.
18 The rate of urbanization was much more rapid among Jews than among non-Jews in Germany. By 1900 48,5% of the Jews lived in cities classified as large, while only 16,2% of the non-Jewish population lived in them. See Weinryb, "The Economic and Social Background", 25.
19 Nowhere is this encounter more vividly described than in Adolf Hider's, *Mein Kampf*, Munich 1942, 54–62.

Antisemitism had played in the 1875–1882 years.[20] Glagau had previously been an economic correspondent of the *Nationalzeitung*, one of the leading liberal dailies of Berlin. His desertion of liberalism, although partially motivated by his own personal failure, became characteristic of many among his *Mittelstand* readers. Like him, they too finally broke their former liberal allegiance, and like him they sought a new political home for themselves. It was indicative of the mood among the master-artisans during these years that Glagau, who was a shrewd if not always an original political observer, dedicated one of his popular books to the fate of the small traditional handicraft-masters.[21] His peculiar brand of ideology did indeed appeal to them. His new anti-liberalism was based upon a principled opposition to the economic measures introduced by the liberals at the creation of the German Reich. These were blamed for the alleged misery and the impoverishment of his *Mittelstand* readers. His Antisemitism helped to explain the 'degeneration of German liberalism', which he, as well as the majority of the small masters, had previously supported. If it was embarrassing for them to attack their previous allies, the attack became comprehensible as a defense against the progressive *Verjudung* of the German liberal movement. If it was unpleasant to attack the patriotic German liberals as a whole, it was easy enough to attack the Jews among them. Thus, it was not capitalism which was to be blamed but Jewish capitalism; not liberalism but Jewish 'Manchesterism'; not the 'national' government but its Jewish advisers. F. Perrot, an old *Kreuzzeitung* reactionary could publish his anti-liberal history of the handicrafts without any open Antisemitic overtones.[22] Glagau, the former liberal, apparently could not. For him, as for many *Mittelständler* Antisemitism appeared to serve as a necessary stage of transition between a traditional, though often contradictory, liberalism, and an increasingly entrenched conservatism.

The master-artisans' organizations in the early 1870's were still liberal in their overall political leanings. They followed the pattern which had evolved among the majority of the handicraft masters after the events of 1848/49, and which combined political liberalism, sometimes of the radical democratic type, with specific economic demands having strong anti-liberal connotations. During the 70's, when both liberals and conservatives fortified their ideologies and made their social alliances more explicit and more binding, the masters' political position

---

20 On Otto Glagau see the brief but illuminating comments in Hellmut von Gerlach, *Von Rechts nach Links*, Zürich 1937, 110; also Pulzer, *The Rise of Political Antisemitism*, 88–90, and Massing, *Rehearsal for Destruction*, 10–14.
21 *Deutsches Handwerk und Historisches Bürgertum*, Osnabrück 1879.
22 *Das Handwerk, seine Reorganisation und seine Befreiung von der Übermacht des Großkapitals*, Leipzig 1876.

appeared increasingly untenable, and gradually they resolved their ties with liberalism. But while the alliance with liberalism was slowly deteriorating, no clear political alternative was yet available. The leaders of the master-artisans' movement repeatedly attempted to fill the vacuum by establishing a separate artisans' party. Their desire to avoid a full-scale shift of artisan's votes into the established conservative camp was predominant in all these efforts. Not surprisingly, however, none of these organizations survived the planning stage, and by the time of the election-campaign of 1879 they were all long forgotten.[23]

All the existing parties at the time attempted to appeal to the small handicraftsmen. Most vocal among them were the various Antisemitic associations, parading their social-conservatism, their support for state-protection, and above all their ardent opposition to all the manifestations of the liberal political and economic doctrine. The *Soziale Reichspartei*, led by the "progressive" and ex-liberal Ernst Henrici, the *Deutsche Volksverein* organized by the conservative Max Liebermann von Sonnenberg, the Saxonian *Deutsche Reformpartei* and the various Antisemitic leagues and conferences all wished to appear as allies of the small handicraft masters in their economic struggle against liberal state economic measures, and against the competition of big capital and modern industry. Each in its peculiar style supported the master-artisans' limited demands for compulsory guild-membership, for reintroduction of masters' qualifying examinations, for restriction on prison work-shop production, reorganization of the bidding system and the like.[24]

In spite of these propaganda efforts, one encounters little open Antisemitism in the masters' own pronouncements during the late 1870's. The masters showed little anti-Jewish feelings but seem to have nevertheless joined, in growing numbers, the organized Antisemitic movement. There is no way to assess the number of handicraft-masters who actually voted for Antisemitic candidates in national and local elections. Undoubtedly, they accounted for a considerable segment of the 46.000 Antisemitic votes cast in Berlin during the 1881 election.[25] In Dresden, another center of handicraft production, a building-master won the Reichstag seat on the ticket of the Antisemitic *Deutsche Reformpartei*. But only a detailed analysis of local voting could perhaps overcome some of the difficulties in investigating the voting behavior of a group whose members were scattered in all German towns and throughout the

---

[23] For the sources and the bibliography on the handicraft-masters' organizations during the 1870's see Volkov, *The Rise of popular Antimodernism*, 220–248, 264–273.
[24] See Massing, *Rehearsal for Destruction*, 77–89; and for some of the Antisemitic party programs Fritz Specht, *Die Reichstagswahlen 1867–97*, Berlin 1898, 66.
[25] Pulzer, *The Rise of Political Antisemitism*, 99.

country. But if, indeed, precise numbers cannot as yet be provided, a general trend can certainly be observed.

In May of 1880, the two most prominent leaders of the Berlin master artisans' movement took part in a public meeting organized by Adolf Stöcker's Social Conservative Party. The formerly liberal leaders of the masters' *Nationalverein* were ceremoniously seated at platform. They had indeed travelled a long way since their days of political activism on behalf of the Progressive Party in Berlin and their repeated efforts during the 1870's to preserve the general liberal character of the artisans' movement.[26]

The story of Adolf Stöcker has been told many a time.[27] [. . .] During the years of his political experimentation, primarily but not exclusively in Berlin, Stöcker became aware of the need to supply his potential supporters with an emotional battle-cry, stronger than the negative attitude towards liberalism and the nostalgic view of past society. Antisemitism, by then already practiced by other social-conservatives, seemed to be the obvious choice, and Stöcker enthusiastically seized upon it. He was operating in the spirit of Liebermann v. Sonnenberg, the Junker among the local Antisemitic social conservatives, who had shocked the young Helmuth v. Gerlach when he casually remarked to him in a street-side cafe in Berlin: "First we want to become a political power; then we shall seek the scientific evidence for Antisemitism."[28]

In the same way that a militant social-conservative, Antisemitic movement was needed in Prussia and Saxony in order to finally sever the ties of the small master-artisans with the Liberals, so was it also needed in the mixed Protestant-Catholic areas of Western Germany. The small master-artisans in the Rheinland and in Westphalia were the first to demand the repeal of *Gewerbefreiheit* and a reconstitution of the guild system. It was they who introduced a strong anti-liberal tone into the discussions of the otherwise liberal *Verein selbständiger Handwerker*. They too, however, needed a transition through militant social-conservatism and vocal Antisemitism before they could finally join the established Conservative forces.

---

26 See the report in Wilhelm Marr's Antisemitic publication, *Die Deutsche Wacht*, July 1880.
27 The most detailed story is by the official Nazi historian Walter Frank, *Adolf Stöcker und die Christlich-Soziale Bewegung*, Hamburg 1935. See also the remarks in von Gerlach, *Von Rechts nach Links*, 102, and Wanda Kampmann, "Stöcker und die Berliner Bewegung," in: *Geschichte in Wissenschaft und* Unterricht 13, 1962; Wawrzinek, *Die Entstehung der deutschen Antisemitenparteien.*,18–29; Massing.*Rehearsal for Destruction,* 21–47; Pulzer, *The Rise of Political Antisemitism.*, 88–101.
28 von Gerlach, *Von Rechts nach Links,* 112.

Freiherr Friedrich Carl v. Fechenbach was a landowner from Hesse, who started his political career in the National-Liberal Party, and eventually joined the *Deutschkonservative Partei* in 1878.²⁹ Towards the end of the 70's he had evolved his own political program and was, for several years, stormily engaged in publicizing it and in attempting to give it an organizational backbone. Living in a mixed Catholic-Protestant area, he visualized a social conservatism which would be capable of uniting Protestants and Catholics into a mighty political force, jointly withstanding the tide of socialism. Fechenbach's political objectives were the abolition of the *Kulturkampf*, far-reaching social legislation particularly for peasants and artisans, and the institution of strong anti-capitalist and Antisemitic legal measures. Early in 1880 he attempted to reach an agreement with Stöcker, Perrot, and a number of other South-German Protestant social-conservatives. When these efforts failed, he convened in Frankfurt a. M. a joint meeting of Protestant and Catholic celebrities interested in the social question, at which a *Verein fur conservative Sozialreform* was established. The program of the new Verein urged an end to the anti-Catholic campaign, restrictions on the power of *Geldkapital*, a break with the policy of *'unlauterer Wettbewerb'*, a return to the joint silver-gold money standard, a 'healthy' colonial policy, an expulsion of all non-Christians from the German legislative bodies, and the establishment of "a representative system, based on occupational estates."³⁰

In striking parallelism with the development of Adolf Stöcker's career, v. Fechenbach sought to create, side by side with his organization of conservative notables, a powerful grass-root movement. Operating after Stöcker, and no doubt learning from his mistakes, v. Fechenbach immediately concentrated his efforts on the recruitment of *Mittelstand* elements, especially master-artisans and peasants. For the former his program included a demand for the establishment of compulsory guilds with legal corporative rights, and a replacement of taxation on industrial enterprises with taxes on stock profits, inheritance and luxury-articles. Like Stöcker in Berlin, v. Fechenbach in the Rheine area combined a strong anti-liberal campaign with fervent Antisemitism and with a conservative nostalgia for the past. It was a mixture specifically designed to appeal to the small ex-liberal master-artisans in the rapidly industrializing regions of western Germany, who were increasingly clinging to the old social-industrial structure as a remedy for all their

---

29 Hans Joachim Schoeps, "CDU vor 75 Jahren. Die sozialpolitischen Bestrebungen des Reichsfreiherrn F. von Fechenbach 1836–1907," in: *Zeitschrift für Religion und Geistesgeschichte* 9, 1957, 266–277.
30 *Die Post*, 13 November 1880; see also Hugo Böttger, *Das Programm der Handwerker*, Braunschweig 1893, 137–138; and Eugen Jäger, *Geschichte der Handwerkerbewegung bis zum Jahre 1884*, Berlin 1887, 166.

present hardships. By 1881, v. Fechenbach had established some 50 branches of his *Verein zum Schutze des Handwerks*, mainly in south-western Germany, but also as far as Hamburg and Breslau.[31] In Cologne, v. Fechenbach prepared the ground for establishing a new master-artisans' organization. For several years he managed to run a special two-monthly artisans' journal, *Die Innung*, subtitled *"Organ der Sozialkonservativen Vereinigung fur das deutsche Handwerk"*.[32] Fechenbach's movement was short-lived. The tireless Freiherr toyed with the prospects of a national Antisemitic movement for a while, and participated in drafting the program for the *Deutsche Reformpartei*, established in Dresden in September 1881. By 1885, however, he finally joined the Center Party. Many of his previous supporters followed the same route. By the middle of the 80's both the Protestant social-conservatives and their Catholic counterparts had joined their respective established conservative parties. Their separate political existence was of transitory nature. It had filled a temporary political vacuum during a period of radical shift in the popular pattern of political allegiances. It served to smooth the transfer of a segment of the German *Mittelstand* population, including numerous small handicraft-masters, from the Liberal to the Conservative camp.

II. The early beginnings of the second wave of political Antisemitism among small handicraft masters in Germany can be dated to 1887. By that time the majority of the politically minded masters had settled for consistent, though often unenthusiastic support of the established Conservative parties. They probably voted for the *Deutschkonservative Partei* in the Protestant north, and for the Catholic Zentrum in the south and in much of south-western Germany. The masters' conservatism was rooted in their anti-liberalism and in their growing opposition to all the manifestations of modem industrial society. While the alliance of the Catholic master-artisans with the Zentrum has proven relatively unproblematic and lasting, the Protestant support of Junker-conservatism, increasingly in alliance with big business, often remained half-hearted. Anti-liberalism and a romantic nostalgia for the past did not

---

[31] Jäger, *Geschichte der Handwerkerbewegung*, 176; and a propaganda pamphlet entitled *Die Demokratische Partei und die Handwerker*, Munich 1883, which describes in detail von Fechenbach's acitivities among small handicraft-masters.

[32] On the degree of von Fechenbach's appeal one can judge from reports on the master-artisan's national congress. For 1881 see *Die Handwerkerfrage, Kölnische Zeitung*, 5 August 1881, for 1882 and 1883 the protocols of the meetings: *Verhandlungen des allgemeinen deutschen Handwerkertages zu Magdeburg 1882*, 25–36, and the *Verhandlungen des allgemeinen deutschen Handwerkertages zu Hannover 1883*, 23–25. The most ardent supporters of von Fechenbach during these years in the masters' organizations were the master-tailors Fasshauer from Cologne and Möller from Dortmund. Both remained until well into the 1890's among the most militant antisemitic and radical leaders of the master-artisans in Germany.

quite suffice to make the small urban master-artisans at ease within the party of aristocratic owners and cultivators of big agricultural estates.

The Liberal-Conservative cartel policy which crystallized before the 1887 Reichstag election dramatically brought into the open the ambivalence of the masters' position vis a vis the Conservatives. They were suddenly faced with a coalition between those who claimed to be their most loyal supporters and those who had been their allies and were therefore all the more objectionable as their present opponents. The organ of the handicraft masters in southern Germany, the mouthpiece of the masters' Bund, mourned the alliance between the Conservatives and the Liberals, and predicted with apprehension the end of the parliamentary cooperation between the Conservative party and the Zentrum on all social and economic matters – a cooperation which had lasted since the beginning of the decade. It saw in the new political constellation "a sad picture of our present parliamentarism" and immediately proceeded to launch a doubly heated campaign against liberalism and the liberal parties.[33] This was sprinkled with occasional Antisemitism. But with some significant exceptions, master-artisans' meetings during the late 80's and successive issues of their journals were very restrained in the expression of anti-Jewish sentiments. Open and radical Antisemitism can be detected among them only from around 1892. From that time on it seemed to be on the increase. It reached unprecedented proportions and was pursued with previously unknown determination and passion. By then it had developed all the characteristics of racial Antisemitism, and its connection with anti-liberalism, while certainly present, had lost its predominance. The Antisemitic movement of 1892–97 was a new phenomenon. Whereas it had been a by-product of political re-grouping during the late 1870's, it had become by the 90's an expression of a structural crisis in German society and its relationship with the state.

The late 1870's and early 1880's had been years of reorganization of the social and the political forces in the Reich.[34] By 1890 a new structure had clearly emerged. Within it the master-artisans had a peculiar position. Regardless of their actual material standing, the new industrializing economy always remained basically alien to them. By the end of the 19th century little if anything had been preserved of their old handicraft community. Masters and journeymen were by then aligned in opposite and hostile camps. The craft apprenticeship had lost the last vestiges of its

---

33 *Die Allgemeine Handwerkerzeitung*, 25 January 1887, and a barrage of articles in every issue throughout 1887.
34 The Reichstag election results between 1877 and 1884 offer a glimpse into this period of political instability. Specht, *Die Reichstagswahlen*, 88–104, provides a series of useful tables combining changes in the relative power of the various parties with the shifts in the political allegiance within the various German states and provinces.

traditional image, and apprentices were often no more than a source of cheap labor. No other community emerged to replace the disintegrating one. The *Mittelstand* was a conglomeration of elements with objectively conflicting interests and with fierce internal fights. During the 19th century it was often no more than a slogan. The bond among retail shopkeepers, master craftsmen, white collar employees, teachers and low-echelon bureaucrats always remained tenuous. The master-artisan's position inside this heterogeneous social unit was particularly ambivalent. As manual workers they remained outsiders in a group whose members were normally engaged in non-manual occupations, and as small industrial producers they were outsiders in a group whose members were primarily consumers. Their relationships with all the segment of the *Mittelstand*, with their workers, with larger entrepreneurs and with the bourgeoisie of Besitz and of Bildung, were characterized by envy and estrangement.[35]

The isolation of the small handicraft-masters was not merely a social and cultural phenomenon. By the 1890's it had been extended into the political sphere. Without much enthusiasm, but nevertheless in a consistent fashion, the central Reich government had accepted a great number of the masters' reform demands.[36] These were passed in the Reichstag throughout the 1880's, supported by the Center party and the Conservatives, with occasional help from the Free Conservatives and segments of the National-Liberal Party. At a time of relative economic recovery, the consistent, though often slow, move of the Reich government towards the social reform demands of the masters, gave the latter reason for optimism and time for consolidating their own interest-group organizations. In 1890 the German economy suffered a renewed cyclical crisis. At the same time, in response to the growth of the Social-Democratic Party and the Socialist Trade-Unions after the repeal of the anti-socialist legislation, the government embarked upon a new reform program for master-artisans. It wished, so it had repeatedly claimed, to give legislative expression to its concern for the needs of the state supporting elements in German society.[37] The government was ready to meet representatives of the handicraft-masters' national organizations in order to hear from them directly their specific reform demands. Soon, however, it became clear that the Ministry of the Interior

---

[35] For a fuller treatment of this problem see Volkov, *The Rise of Antimodernism*, 117–188.

[36] Legislation for the reorganization of the handicrafts was passed in 1881, late in 1884, 1886, 1887, and 1889. For a summary see "Gewerbegesetzgebung", in: *Handwörterbuch der Staatswissenschaften* IV, 1910.

[37] See, for instance, the speech by the State Secretary of the Interior von Boetticher in the Reichstag on 24 November 1891. Also Karl Erich Born, *Staat und Sozialpolitik seit Bismarcks Sturz.*, Wiesbaden 1957, 90–112; and Hans Rothfels, *T. Lohmann und die Kampfjahre der staatlichen Sozialppolitik 1871–1905*, Berlin 1927, 123–125.

was intent on pursuing its own reform program, and the masters' hopes for finally achieving their major objectives, above all a compulsory guild-system and an obligatory masters' examination, were once more shattered.[38] During the following years of government procrastination, the masters lost their initial confidence in it, and became bitter and hostile towards it.

At the same time, the support of government social legislation by both the Center and the Conservative parties in the Reichstag was increasingly resented by the masters. What had previously been the source of their pressure power, became an obstacle to their further plans. They suddenly remembered that as late as 1890 the *Deutschkonservative Partei* had no representative of the handicraft-masters among its Reichstag members, and that the Catholic Center included only three master-artisans among its parliamentary fraction of over 100 men. The two most loyal supporters of the master-artisans appeared to have easily accepted government legislation, which was vehemently opposed, both for its details and for its general concept, by the organized master-artisans' movement.[39] The masters felt increasingly neglected by the government and scorned by their former political supporters. Their 1892 national congress gave ample expression to their rage, their feeling of helplessness and their growing defiance. They claimed to have been treated as "step-children of the nation", and as "Pariah of the legislation."[40] Their repeated organizational failures, their political disillusions, and above all their feeling of social and political homelessness created a mood of lonely despair among them which gave their pronouncements a threatening overtone. "Wir deutsche Handwerker" – exclaimed the *Deutsche Handwerkerzeitung* – "fühlen uns als eine der festesten Stützen eines geordneten Staatswesens; wir deutsche Handwerker fürchten aber Niemanden in der Welt als Gott, den unerbittlichen sicheren Rächer alles Unrechtes auf Erden."[41]

As in the late 70's, the severing of ties with previous allies forced the masters to attempt the organization of a separate political party. Once again, however, they found themselves unable to overcome the opposition and the active sabotage of the existing parties, the numerous organizational and financial difficulties and their

---

38 See the fierce argument in: *Protokoll über die Verhandlungen am 15., 16. und 17. Juni 1891 mit Vertretern des Centralausschusses der Vereinigten Innungsverbände Deutschlands und des Allgemeinen Deutschen Handwerkerbundes zu München*, Bayerisches Hauptstaatsarchiv MH-14661, and in the Reichstag on 24 November 1891.
39 *Protokoll über die Verhandlungen des deutschen Innungs- und allgemeinen Handwerkertages zu Berlin 1892, passim.*
40 Ibid, 42, 46.
41 *Protokoll über die Verhandlungen des XIII. Allgemeinen Deutschen Handwerkertages zu Halle 1895*, 4.

endless internal disputes. At the same time the newly organized Antisemitic parties made strong efforts to turn the masters' general hostility and their political isolation into electoral capital. The Antisemitic propaganda during the 1890's was explicitly directed at the various *Mittelstand* elements in Germany. It emphasized the urgent need for state intervention in the running of the economy, the demands for progressive income tax, inheritance and capital tax, a supervision of the stock-exchange and the protection of agriculture, handicraft and small business. It was essentially anti-liberal and anti-capitalist, reformist and nationalist. The endorsement of the specific reform demands of the master-artisans' interest-organizations by the various Antisemitic parties, however, was initially no more emphatic than the endorsement offered by the Conservatives or by the Catholic Center Party.

In the 1890 Bochum program of the *Deutschsoziale Partei*, article 13 unfolded the party's plan for reform of the handicrafts.[42] It included a call for the restriction of the *Gewerbefreiheit*, for the introduction of official examinations of master-employers, for shorter terms of limitations, and for the institution of Handicraft Chambers with jurisdiction over matters of professional ethics. It further demanded the improvement of tender regulations and the prohibition of all handicraft production in prison workshops. While these were, indeed, all part of the master-artisans' standard reform demands, the Antisemitic plan did not mention compulsory membership in the guilds, nor was it explicit on the matter of a comprehensive and obligatory masters' examination. The *Antisemitische Volkspartei* was even more elusive on these two essential points. In its 1890 program it demanded assistance for the handicrafts by means of putting an end to the "schrankenlose Gewerbefreiheit", and to the competition of state-prison workshops. It then proclaimed the need to expand the rights of, and the support for, handicraft organizations.[43] Thus, during the early years of the decade, the Antisemitic parties in their intense recruitment efforts preferred to follow a cautious line on the handicraft question, in order not to alienate any potential supporters. But in spite of these hesitations and the lukewarm attitudes of the Antisemitic leadership towards the essential demands of the master-artisans' interest organizations, the latter were showing growing enthusiasm for these parties. This time it was not merely a passing phenomenon, but an expression of a social and political crisis manifested in an outburst of intense anti-Jewish sentiments.

At the masters' 1892 national congress, Adolf Stöcker, again on the podium to express the Antisemitism of his audience, was warmly applauded. A string of speakers from all parts of the country voiced their Antisemitism in extreme and

---

42 Specht, *Die Reichstagswahlen*, 503.
43 Ibid, 504.

often vulgar terms to the general approval of the delegates.[44] Eventually the Antisemitic parties, forced by the aridity of their own programs, and apparently impressed by the masters' enthusiasm, came closer to the position of the master-artisans' interest-groups on matters related to the reform of the handicrafts. By 1895 the reconstituted Deutschsoziale Reformpartei introduced the masters' demand for compulsory guilds and obligatory masters examinations into its new official program.[45] The alliance between the small handicraft masters and the Antisemitic political movement was thus fortified and publicly acknowledged.

At the artisans' congress in April of 1893, the Catholic master-shoemaker Beutel from Munich was still apologetic, and was far from being unanimously applauded, when he stated that "we are all a little Antisemitic, even if not exactly in Ahlwardt's sense."[46] But in May of the same year the Bavarian *Allgemeine Handwerkerzeitung* openly called upon its readers to vote for Antisemitic candidates in all cases where they could not in good conscience continue to vote for Conservative or Center party representatives.[47] Early in 1894 the two major artisan newspapers, in Munich and in Berlin, were inundated with Antisemitic articles, reprinted public speeches, letters to the editors and even occasional verses. The Jews were made responsible for everything that was objectionable to the craft masters: for liberalism, capitalism, socialism, trade-unionism, industrialism. They were presented as the main exploiters of the small masters, and as the cause of their alleged misery. Issue after issue of these papers was filled with articles providing additional evidence to prove the moral degeneration and the utter ruthlessness of the Jews.[48] By the 1890's the small independent handicraft-masters had joined the political Antisemitic movement as "true believers".

It has been often noted that Antisemitism served to bring together various ideological positions, unrelated and often openly contradictory. Thus, for the unsophisticated, anti-liberalism, anti-capitalism and anti-socialism could all be expressed by opposition to the Jews – as the social element responsible for the corruption and subversion of all three. Likewise, Antisemitism permitted the expression of repressed hostility by disoriented men and channeled it into an acceptable, and in some circles even respectable, direction. For small master artisans, however, Antisemitism had an additional function: It provided this isolated and unintegrated group of men with a much needed negative identity.

---

44 *Protokoll*, 1892, passim.
45 Specht, *Die Reichstagswahlen*, 507.
46 *Allgemeine Handwerkerzeitung*, 28 April 1893.
47 Ibid, 26 May 1893.
48 See, for instance, the *Deutsche Handwerker-Zeitung*, 6 January, 24 February, 3 March and 7 June 1894; and die *Allgemeine Handwerkerzeitung*, 5 and 12 May 1894.

A sense of social isolation was not unique to the small master-artisans in German society of the 1890's. Rainer Lepsius has suggested a rough model for understanding the structure of this society from the turn of the century until the Nazi seizure of power.[49] German society, he argues, was divided by the early 1890's into four major social 'milieus', each representing a unique sub-culture, an overall *Weltanschauung*, and a specific political direction. Within each of these blocks, culture and life-style, ideology and political organization coincided, overlapped and enforced each other. The four were the Conservative, the Liberal, the Socialist and the Catholic milieus. Each developed a strong cohesion within itself and evolved a pattern of interaction with the others. In addition, however, a fifth social element in Germany became increasingly discernible. It was composed of the various groups of individuals who, for a variety of reasons, did not succeed in becoming associated with any of the major blocks in the country. This 'left-over' mixture of men from different walks of life normally constituted about 10% of Germany's voters – a small but flexible and susceptible body. Among them one can easily identify a large segment of the master-artisans' population. The Catholic masters normally managed to be integrated within the general, and increasingly influential, Catholic 'milieu'. It was the traditional masters in the Protestant north and in the mixed areas who were chronically unattached and isolated. It was these men who responded to the lore of demagogues and rabble-rousers; who in the face of their isolation clung to distorted historical memories and cultivated generalized resentment and hostility.

Bismarck had correctly appreciated the extent of the centrifugal forces within German society. For years he had practiced tactics for internal cohesion based upon the permanent availability of a national enemy. Antisemitism can be easily perceived within this context. It provided the necessary internal enemy in the years between the repeal of the anti-socialist legislation and the embankment of the Reich government upon an aggressive Weltpolitik. In addition, the Jews served as an object for contempt and hatred in contrast to whom the belonging of small masters and other isolated social groups to the glorious German nation was indisputable. The European tradition of Antisemitism made the Jews a perfect target for the hatred of the unattached.[50] Small master artisans, outside the mainstream of German social and political development, identified themselves negatively as non-Jews and thus hoped to achieve a greater sense of belonging within Christian society. The

---

[49] Rainer Lepsius, "Parteiensystem und Sozialstruktur. Zum Problem der Demokratisierung der deutschen Gesellschaft," in *Wirtschaft, Geschichte und Wirtschaftsgeschichte. Festschrift Friedrich Lütge*, ed. Wilhelm Abel et.al., Stuttgart 1966, 371–393.
[50] From this point of view modern Antisemitism, in spite of its unique character, is nevertheless a chapter within the general history of European Antisemitism.

existence of a group which was so apparently outside the social fabric of the Christian German Reich made their belonging to it – both as Christians and as Germans – more secure. Positively, extreme nationalism helped these men to identify themselves as members of the proud and indivisible German nation. Antisemitism thus served a complementary function to nationalism, and it is only within this context that the affinity between the two becomes comprehensible.

Our efforts to investigate the social and the political functions of the Antisemitic movement for the small master-artisans in Germany of the late 19th century have brought into sharp focus the distinct nature of the two Antisemitic waves during these years. In many ways the first wave, between 1875 and 1882, was characteristic of the 19th century, and expressed the major ideological and social conflicts associated with liberalism and the process of industrialization. During these years, master-artisans who had little if any contact with Jews at all, showed sporadic anti-Jewish sentiments and were only temporarily attracted to the anti-liberal, Antisemitic political organizations. It was only during the 1890's that Antisemitism became a major and permanent feature of their *Weltanschauung*. Together with extreme nationalism it served to alleviate a crisis of identity for men who otherwise felt isolated, rejected and even scorned by all other elements in German society and by the spokesmen of the German state. Political Antisemitism was a phenomenon unique to Germany, drawing its strength from its particular integrative function in a specific sociopolitical situation. As such it was close to the political Antisemitism in Germany of the 20th century. On the basis of our analysis, it can perhaps be suggested that another crisis of belonging was at the root of the great appeal of Antisemitism during the years of the Weimar Republic. Even by the 1920's the master-artisans in Germany had not succeeded in becoming a part of any of the major social milieus in the country. They still felt as outsiders vis a vis the modern market economy. The *Mittelstand* was as far from being a social community or a base for a unified political force as it had ever been. The masters had even less confidence in the government of the new republic than they had had in the Imperial Reich government. Indeed, the Nazi's initial popular support came from an assorted mixture of declasses and isolated social groups. They all had in common the desire to find a way – indeed any way – for escaping their sense of social and political homelessness.

3 The Immunization of Social Democracy against Antisemitism in Imperial Germany

The history of Antisemitism and anti-Jewish sentiment in Germany is, and bound to remain for some time, a highly sensitive topic. It may therefore be suitable to open by laying out explicitly what it is that I do not wish to do here. First, I do not intend to take you along onto a journey across the published and unpublished writings of German socialist thinkers and party-leaders from Marx and Engels through Lassalle, Bebel, and others from among the prominent figures of Social Democracy in late 19th century Germany. I shall not weary you with an exposition of their pro and anti-Jewish pronouncements, their witticisms concerning Jews, their direct and indirect references to the Jewish question, etc. There is no great difficulty in thus producing a rather embarrassing set of quotations which are, or which could be construed as anti-Jewish. Such a course of action, however, is both misleading and fruitless. It is misleading because as a study in the history of ideas it is bound to remain one-sided and to lead to an interpretation of socialist thinking on Jews and on Antisemitism which is too narrow and dangerously out of context. It is, furthermore, fruitless because it tends to reduce the study of the position of the socialist movement in Germany on the Jewish question to an examination of sporadic statements made by its more or less prominent leaders. It therefore evades the real issue at hand, namely the analysis of the views adopted by a unique social movement in which the leadership was in fact often being led, and ideological discussion, although of great significance, nevertheless played only a limited role in determining even the official posture of the movement in relation to the actual problems of the day.

Surrendering this course of action, I believe, implies the abandonment of any attempt to present socialism and Social Democracy as Antisemitic by their very nature. Flying in the face of later events, this thesis, more often put forward in anti-socialist polemics than in serious historical writings, tends to begin with an exposition of Karl Marx's essay *Zur Judenfrage*.[1] This early piece, written in 1843, is often made to stand as a proof for the basic, inborn Antisemitism inherent in socialist thought, and represents *"the source of the Antisemitic tradition in modern socialism"*.[2] This is not the proper place for elaborating upon Marx's controversial essay, defending or criticizing it. A short comment, however, appears to be almost indispensable in our context. Above all it is important to indicate the limitations

---

1 *Marx-Engels-Werke (MEW)*, vol. 1, part 1, 576–606.
2 Edmund Silberner, *Sozialisten zur Judenfrage*, Berlin 1962, 142; 119–27.

of an interpretation that isolates Marx's position on the Jewish question from his other concerns at the time. Marx's *Zur Judenfrage* was to remain his only elaborate statement on this subject. He had written it at the age of 25 and never returned to it. But even at that stage of his intellectual development it had merely served him as a point of departure for touching upon a wider sphere of philosophical speculation. To begin with, Marx's controversy with Bruno Bauer must be taken into account in examining this essay. It must then be read together with some of his sporadic comments on the matter written slightly later in *Die Heilige Familie*.³ Above all, Marx's predominant concern to develop a new analysis of the relationship between the political state and civil society under the conditions of capitalism must be firmly kept in mind. Within this context, I believe, the charge of Antisemitism must appear unwarranted. An abstract Judaism, stripped of religious content, did indeed represent for the young Marx the single most articulated manifestation of the profit-seeking spirit, and served him as a symbol for the unavoidable moral degeneration of bourgeois society brought about by capitalism, At the same time, Marx considered the degree to which the Jews as individual members of society enjoyed political and civil rights to be the most telling indicator of a country's level of modernity, and demanded unequivocally a full civil and political emancipation for the Jews as a logical consequence of the very premises of bourgeois society. True to his assertion of the inherent limitations set upon human freedom by the nature of society, he argued that the full and final emancipation of Jews and Christians alike could be finally achieved only through the complete overthrow of the present social order.⁴

But while a philosopher may be content to expose the true nature of Marx's argument, the historian's task does not end there. Marx's writings are historically important not only for what he had actually meant to convey, but also for what it had been possible for others to deduce from them. Ambiguities and potential misinterpretations are often of primary significance in determining the historical role of social thought. Undoubtedly, Marx's extreme language directed at Judaism and the Jews, in this essay and in some of his other writings, could have been used as a justification for a more or less overt Antisemitic position on the part of the international socialist movement. Under certain social circumstances, the tone of his polemics could have easily been made an excuse for tolerating Antisemitism or for encouraging its latent forms and averting attention from its dangerous open expression. That this did not happen in a society as thoroughly

---

3 *MEW*, vol. 2, 91–95; 99–104; 122–25. See also: Shlomo Avineri, "Marx and Jewish Emancipation," in: *Journal of the History of Ideas*, vol. 25, 1965, 445–50.
4 *MEW*, vol. 1, 580–86, 599–606.

infected by Antisemitism as that of Imperial Germany cannot be explained by an analysis of Marx's thought alone.

This brings me to the second line of argument which I have chosen to discard, namely the a priori assertion that socialism in general, and German Social Democracy in particular, were by their very nature *immune* to Antisemitism. This thesis was often put forward by historians in the DDR,[5] but it is not uncommon among Western historians – Marxists and non-Marxists alike. On the whole, this is a subtler and more powerful thesis than its reverse and includes philosophic-ideological arguments as well as sociological ones. Thus, for instance, Peter Pulzer in his *The Rise of Political Anti-Semitism in Germany and Austria* (London, 1964) argues that Marxian Socialism, of the kind that had finally taken hold of the Social Democratic Movement in Germany was "clearly related to 19th century Liberalism," and therefore inspired by "a revulsion against tyranny and poverty, by optimism and a belief in progress, by the assumption that if a formula could be found to explain how society worked, spread by education and applied, the world's evils could be abolished." As such, runs Pulzer's argument, Social Democracy was diametrically opposed to Antisemitism, which was concerned "not with more emancipation but with less," and which "set forth the primacy of the national and the integral over the universal".[6] There is, no doubt, a great deal of truth in this view, but in its present formulation it too may become both misleading and fruitless, as it tends to disregard the strong element of anti-liberalism in modern socialist thinking, and once again restrict the debate to the sphere of ideologies.

The inborn immunity thesis, however, has yet another aspect, sociological rather than ideological. The proletariat, it asserts, due to the specific socio-economic conditions of its life and the consequent mental structure of its individual members, is incapable of sustaining Antisemitic attitudes. This argument too is common among Marxist historians.[7] It is also strongly supported, for instance, by no less an authority than Jean Paul Sartre. "We find hardly any anti-Semites among the workers" – he wrote in 'Anti-Semite and Jew'. ". . . Shaped by the daily influence of the materials he works with, the workman sees society as the product of real forces acting in accordance with rigorous laws. His dialectical 'materialism' signifies that he envisages the social world in the same way as the material

---

5 See. e.g. Walter Mohrmann, *Antisemitismusideologie und Geschichte im Kaiserreich und in der Weimarer Republik*, Berlin (Ost) 1972.
6 Pulzer, *The Rise of Political Anti-Semitism*, 259.
7 Mohrmann, *Antisemitismusideologie*, 8. See also R. Rürup, "Antisemitismus", in: *Sowjetsystem und demokratische Gesellschaft*, vol. 3, Freiburg 1970, 381–408.

world . . .".⁸ Based on a given situation at the post World War II period, this argument neglects to consider over half a century of intensive educational activity, directed by the European socialist movement. Even if the incidence of Antisemitism is indeed rare among workers in some societies, this does not *have* to be a direct result of the circumstances of their life and work, but may be and is to a great extent an outcome of a specific historical process, directed by human efforts. Moreover, this view usually disregards ample evidence presented by a great number of recent studies establishing the particular propensity of individuals in the working class to entertain social prejudices, Antisemitism included.⁹

It appears that the immunity to Antisemitism which the Social Democratic movement in Germany had exhibited from about the mid-1890's must be explained by other than *a priori* notions. It must be studied historically, within the particular context of German Society during the last quarter of the 19th century, and can be made clear only through a historical understanding of the nature of both Antisemitism and Social Democracy at the time.

Having discarded the *a priori* theses about the relationships between socialism and Antisemitism, we can now turn to examine the ways in which these relationships grew and developed in Germany of the 19th century. Methodologically, a combination of ideological and social factors will serve us as a guiding line. Without postulating any causal link between the two spheres, I shall attempt to present to you their independent effects as well as some of the intricacies of their relationship. Chronologically, I have chosen the early years of the 1890's as the decisive years of transformation, in which eventual immunity of Social Democracy to political Antisemitism was being established.

That the early 1890's were a turning point in the history of Social Democracy needs hardly be explained.¹⁰ The year 1890 brought the end of the legal oppression

---

8 English translation, New York 1973, 35–36.

9 See Seymour Martin Lipset, *Political Man*, Garden City, 1960, chap. 4, and the bibliography cited there. More directly on working-class Antisemitism see the comments in: Gertrud J. Selznick and Stephan Steinberg, *The Tenacity of Prejudice. Anti-Semitism in Contemporary America*, New York 1969, 70–71, 93; and James H. Raab, *Working Class Anti-Semites*, London 1954; W.G. Runciman, *Relative Deprivation and Social Justice*, London 1966.

10 Fort the history of Social Democracy at that time Franz Mehring's *Geschichte der deutschen Sozialdemokratie*, Berlin 1960 (first complete edition 1903/04), is still useful. From the available modern literature see especially: G. A. Ritter, *Die Arbeiterbewegung im Wilhelminischen Reich*, Berlin 1959; Vernon L. Lidtke, *The Outlawed Pary. Social Democracy in Germany, 1878–1890*, Princeton 1966; Dieter Groh, *Negative Integration und revolutionärer Attentismus. Die deutsche Sozialdemokratie am Vorabend des 1. Weltkrieges, 1909–1914*, Berlin 1973; Gunter Roth, *Social Democrats in Imperial Germany*, Ottawa 1963; Susanne Miller, *Burgfrieden und Klassenkampf: Die deutsche Sozialdemokratie im Ersten Weltkrieg*, Düsseldorf 1974.

of the socialist movement under the Bismarckian anti-socialist legislation. Furthermore, the early nineties saw the completion and intensification of important changes both in the ideology of the German labor movement and in its sociological composition. With the acceptance of the Erfurt program in 1891, Marxism was officially endorsed as the party ideology. This by no means brought an end to ideological controversies within the party. It did, however, signify the end of previous feuds and helped clear the ground for new ones. Simultaneously Social Democracy increasingly became a proletarian movement. German industry grew rapidly even during the years of the so-called Great Depression, and took on a fresh start with improved conditions around 1894/95. The socialist trade unions, free at last from police supervision and government repression, while overcoming a number of difficult years at the beginning of the decade, grew by leaps and bounds. The characteristic feature of this growth was the recruitment of the unskilled and of workers in heavy and large-scale industry.[11] This was also reflected in the composition of the Social Democratic membership and in its voting public. By the mid-90's, the SPD became a party of industrial workers, drawing its strength from the overwhelmingly Protestant industrial regions in big towns.[12] Thus, in spite of sporadic evidence for a continuing bourgeois support of Social Democracy throughout the pre-war years, it had apparently emerged during this first period of expansion as a class party, a Marxist proletarian movement.

That the early 1890's also signify an important turning point in the development of political Antisemitism in Germany is not a generally accepted thesis. Research into the nature of 19th century Antisemitism has established a periodization based on a demarcating line sometime during the 1870's, either in the beginning of the decade with the achievement of legal emancipation, or towards its end with the emergence of the new Antisemitic political organizations.[13] For our purposes, however, the early 1890's represent perhaps a more crucial turning point.[14] Although

---

11 See Ritter, Die Arbeiterbewegung, 113.
12 Ritter, Die Arbeiterbewegung, 74–78. See also R. Blank, "Die soziale Zusammensetzung der sozialdemokratischen Wählerschaft Deutschlands", in: *Archiv für Sozialwissenschaft und Sozialpolitik*, vol. 20, 1905, 507–50, and R. Michels, "Die deutsche Sozialdemokratie. Parteimitgliederschaft und soziale Zusammensetzung", in: *Archiv für Sozialwissenschaft und Sozialppolitik*, vol. 23, 1906, 471–556.
13 See Paul Massing, *Rehearsal for Destruction. A study of Political Anti-Semitism in Imperial Germany*, New York 1949, and P.G.J. Pulzer, *The Rise of Antisemitism in Germany and Austria*, New York 1964, both of whom begin their investigation in the mid-1870's. For another approach see: R. Rürup, "Kontinuität und Diskontinuität der 'Judenfrage' im 19. Jahrhundert. Zur Entstehung des modernen Antisemitismus," in: *Sozialgeschichte Heute, Festschrift für Hans Rosenberg*, ed. H.-U. Wehler, Göttingen 1974, 338–415.
14 On this see the author's "The Social and Political Function of Late 19th Century Antisemitism: The Case of the Small Handicraft Masters", in: *Sozialgeschichte Heute*, 416–431 (Here no.2.).

Antisemitism necessarily changed its face after 1869 and had by the late 1870's indeed found some new institutional expressions, the motive force behind it at that time was essentially similar to that which had been operating throughout the so-called period of emancipation, since the early 19th century. Antisemitism was then a common and familiar companion of anti-liberalism. It accompanied the political anti-liberalism of the Prussian conservative Junkers on the one hand, and the economic anti-liberalism of various lower-class elements in German society on the other.[15] Anti-Jewish pronouncements at the age of emancipation were invariably a part of the attack against liberalism and the capitalist economy. Civil and political emancipation of the Jews symbolized for the conservatives the "absurdities" of the liberal political doctrine; and the urban, commercial activities of the Jews stood in the eyes of a large segment of the German population for all the "atrocities" of the new industrial system.

The combination of Antisemitism with anti-liberalism and anti-capitalism still characterized the wave of political Antisemitism in the second half of the 1870's. The movement was launched simultaneously with a new campaign against liberalism, following the economic crash of 1873, and grew during the years of general economic set-back culminating in 1879.[16] Popular Antisemitism during the 1870's was primarily a by-product of a virulent attack on liberalism, and was used politically by the anti-liberal forces in the Reich. The *Kreuzzeitung* which publicly opened the attack on liberalism in its "Era articles" in the summer of 1874 was quick to inject the Antisemitic overtones, and it was promptly followed by the catholic *Germania*, capitalizing on the embarrassment of its liberal enemies. It was then joined by deserters from the liberal camp itself, (such as the journalist Otto Glagau, the ex-liberal agitator Ernst Henrici and others), who became self-appointed prophets of the groups most badly hit by the downward swing of the capitalist economy.[17] Stöcker's Berlin campaign was also primarily motivated by anti-liberalism, although it had some peculiar features to which we shall soon have to return.

The 1880's were years of transition and experimentation for the political Antisemitic movement. Re-emerging in the early 1890's, it was of a different hue, showing a far greater vitality and power of attraction. By 1893 the various Antisemitic

---

15 On pre-1848 Antisemitism see especially: Eleonore Sterling, *Judenhaß. Die Anfänge des politischen Antisemitismus in Deutschland, 1815–1850*, Frankfurt a. M. ²1969.
16 Hans Rosenberg, *Große Depression und Bismarckzeit*, Berlin 1967, 62–78.
17 On the various Antisemitic political groups see in addition to the books by Massing, *Rehearsal for Destruction*, and Pulzer, *The Rise of Antisemitism*, also K. Wawrzineck, *Die Entstehung der deutschen Antisemitenparteien*, Berlin 1926; and Richard S. Levy, *The Downfall of the Anti-Semitic Political Parties in Imperial Germany*, New Haven 1975.

groups managed to send 16 deputies to the Reichstag, and kept an impressive voting public throughout the 1890's. Antisemitism became for a while a mass movement. It remained of course strongly anti-liberal, but its anti-liberalism ceased to be the only, nor even the main motivating force behind it. The Antisemitic movement of the 1890's combined its anti-liberalism with a dose of democratic rhetoric and a cautious anti-capitalism. It was struggling to combine all of these with an increasingly pronounced anti-socialism. The force behind these confused ideological tenets was a deep-seated anti-modern sentiment, rejecting every manifestation of modernity in city-life, in large-scale industry, in technological advance, in the rapidly changing social hierarchy, in the developing parliamentarism, etc.[18] Anti-liberalism was by then only one, and not the most outspoken element of this general anti-modernism.

Socially, the Antisemitic movement of the 1890's attracted a mixture of social groups no longer united by their common hostility to liberalism alone but by their undifferentiated negation of modern society and economy, and their growing disappointment with all existing political institutions in Germany. Antisemitism was by then an indispensable element in the *Weltanschauung* of a specific social stratum in German society, an independent structural phenomenon.

The changes and transformations in both the nature and character of the Social Democratic Party and the ideological and social momentum of the Antisemitic movement, are at the root of the incompatibility which had developed between them by the mid-1890's. Up to about 1980, socialism and Antisemitism had much in common. They shared above all an anti-liberal, or at least an anti-capitalist conviction, and they recruited their support from similar social elements. This is particularly true of the Lassallean branch of the developing labor party. Lassalle had distanced himself early in life from Judaism, and although he must have occasionally experienced the awkwardness of his position as a Jew in a predominantly gentile society, he did not shy away from injecting a fair amount of Antisemitic verbiage into his agitation among the workers.[19] From the very beginning of Lassalle's political and organizational activity, he had conceived of the liberals as his major enemies, and made it quite clear, early in his career, that he preferred an alliance with the leading forces of the authoritarian Prussian state to any dealing with the liberals of his day. Anti-liberalism was the main impetus in Lassalle's thought and action, and he freely used Antisemitic rhetoric in order to degrade and abuse his liberal opponents. Jews, and not only Judaism in the

---

18 On popular anti-modernism see the author's "Popular Anti-Modernism. Ideology and Sentiments among Handircraft Masters in the 1890's", in: *Jahrbuch des Instituts für deutsche Geschichte*, vol. 3, Tel-Aviv 1974, 203–225.
19 Shlomo Na'aman, *Ferdinand Lassalle. Deutscher und Jude*, Hannover 1968, 39.

abstract, were for him a symbol of liberal hypocrisy and capitalist exploitation.[20] As has been noted by his biographer, Lassalle had readily identified the bourgeoisie with Jewish bourgeoisie, and everything that appeared rotten to him in the modern world with Judaism.[21]

In the early 1860's, however, Lassalle was not alone in making use of this convenient equation. It was by that time an indispensable element in the writings of a growing number of conservative, state-socialist thinkers. These politically reactionary men had belatedly begun to take notice of the *Soziale Frage* in Germany, and soon concluded that it was urgent for the conservatives to concern themselves with the problems of the so-called fourth estate and to make concrete proposals for the improvement of its lot.[22] There is no need here to go into the details of the state-socialist theories of these men, but it is of interest to note that without exception they had all been making use of Antisemitism, in a more or less overt and articulated form.[23] Lassalle had some personal contacts with these men. He carried on a correspondence with their intellectual leader, Karl Rodbertus, and exchanged views publicly with the catholic bishop von Ketteler and with the conservative proponent of the cooperative movement, Victor Aimé Huber. Lassalle shared with all of them a virulent anti-liberalism mingled with Antisemitism, and some of his followers inherited this combination from him. It was in any case quite apparent in the agitation, as well as in the literary work of Johann Baptist von Schweitzer, or in the journalism of Wilhelm Hasselmann in the early part of the 1870's.[24] The combination of state-socialism, anti-liberalism and Antisemitism was a part of Lassalle's legacy to the new Social Democratic Party. During the 1870's, however, it received an additional impetus from other sources as well.

The economic collapse of 1873 helped to spread anti-liberalism and Antisemitism among a growing segment of the German population. State-socialism, too, was invigorated by the obvious failure of the liberal economic policies during the *Gründerjahre*. The writings of Rodbertus became particularly popular, and with

---

20 Ibid, 85–86.
21 Ibid, 41–42.
22 See William O. Shanahan, *German Protestants Face the Social-Question*, Indiana, 1954; Ralph Bowen, *German Theories of the Corporative State 1870–1919*, New York ²1961; Vernon L. Lidtke, "German Social Democracy and German State-Socialism, 1871–1884," in: *Int. Rev. of Social History*, 9, 1964.
23 See especially Rudolf Meyer, *Der Emancipationskampf des vierten Standes*, Berlin 1874–1875, and his *Was heißt conservativ sein?* Berlin 1873. Meyer was particularly esteemed by the socialists and in the 1890's contributed regularly to the *Neue Zeit* articles on agrarian issues.
24 See Massing, *Rehearsal for Destruction*, 155–57, and Silberner, *Sozialisten zur Judenfrage*, 198–99.

them those of Adolf Wagner, Hermann Wagener, Rudolf Meyer and others. At the same time Social Democracy suffered from a lack of a unified and coherent economic theory. While the Lassalleans tended naturally to borrow from the arsenal of state socialist writings, the Eisenachers too, by then possessing only a very rudimentary knowledge of Marx's work, were drawn towards these theories. A considerable number of prominent Social Democratic leaders and journalists, especially in Berlin, were then attracted by various versions of state-socialism. Among them were Karl Hochberg and Carl August Schramm, and through the influence of Eugen Dühring the young Eduard Bernstein was also drawn into this circle.[25] In Dühring's thought Antisemitism played a particularly decisive role, but it was apparently his personal idiosyncrasies and not his Antisemitism which had first shaken Bernstein's early admiration.[26] When in Zürich he later became the editor of the official Social Democratic organ, the *Sozialdemokrat*, Bernstein allowed an assortment of Antisemitic comments to be published in it through the early 1880's.[27]

At the same time, Antisemitism had also crept into the rhetoric of another branch of the Social Democratic movement. The agitation of Johann Most, the energetic opponent of Stöcker in Berlin of the late 1870's, the later anarchist, was infused with Antisemitic overtones.[28] His anti-Jewish comments, however, can best be traced not to the anti-liberalism of the Social Democrats but to their suspicion of intellectuals and of the educated, yet another legacy of Ferdinand Lassalle.[29] To Most, and to some of the other contributors to the radical *Freiheit*, the Jews were associated less with liberal economic practices, and more with the liberal press and the so-called intellectual professions.

The ideological sources of Antisemitism in the early years of the socialist movement were diverse and powerful. Furthermore, it was then appealing mainly to social strata which were also most susceptible to Antisemitic propaganda. A true industrial proletariat was hardly in existence in Germany of the 1860's. Both the *ADAV* and the Eisenacher socialists recruited their support mainly from among working men in small industry and in the traditional handicraft trades. The lines of division between self-employed and hired men or even between small employers and skilled employees dictated by these forms of production were very unclear. The socialists, like the Antisemitic agitators later on, and like some of the more

---

25 Lidtke, *The Outlawed Party*, chap. 6.
26 Ibid, pp. 61–6. Also Peter Gay, *The Dilemma of Democratic Socialism*, New York 1962, 94–103.
27 Der *Sozialdemokrat*, 16.2. and 26.10.1882.
28 On Most see Lidtke, *The Outlawed Party*, chap. 4, and Massing, *Rehearsal for Destruction*, 251–252.
29 Na'aman, Lassalle, 86.

active social-conservatives even as early as the 1860's, appealed to masters and men alike, and the original nucleus of their supporters came from among the previous adherents of the liberal-democratic movement, including many self-employed and independent tradesmen. By the 1860's the social process of separation between *Mittelstand* and Proletariat had been in progress for some time, but it was certainly far from being completed. Anti-liberalism mingled with Antisemitism was singularly attractive to this mixed social stratum.

This became particularly clear from about 1878 to 1884 during Adolf Stöcker's campaign in Berlin.[30] Stöcker, who was influenced earlier in the decade by the state-socialism of Rudolf Meyer and Alfred Todt, began in 1878 to agitate among the working-men of Berlin for the creation of a *Christlich-Soziale Arbeiterpartei*. Acting simultaneously with the worst repression of the labor movement by the government through legislation and administrative police action, he naturally found little enthusiasm among the workers for his appeal on behalf of Crown and Church. The workers of Berlin, asserted Bernstein later, had proven that they were not to be easily dragged out of the socialist camp, not even by the rhetoric of the energetic *Hofprediger*.[31] Franz Mehring later reported that the class-conscious Proletariat immediately distanced themselves from Stöcker and eventually caused the final collapse of his efforts.[32] Stöcker was indeed greatly disappointed by the response of the Berlin workers to his appeal. He then changed tactics and began to campaign almost exclusively among the *Mittelstand* elements in town. By doing so, however, he did not cease to pose a threat to Social Democracy. He was still appealing to its potential supporters.

In Berlin itself, developing into a center of large industrial enterprises, this fact might have not been as apparent and as acute as it was in Vienna. In 1884, Karl Kautsky wrote to Engels of the serious danger which the oppositional Antisemitic movement posed for the budding Social Democratic Party there. He was clearly aware of the fact that the Antisemites managed to attract elements, including some very radical ones, which had previously supported the socialists.[33] Bernstein himself admitted that there had been at the time a great number of men who "without actually disliking the Jews, considered the Antisemitic phrases as an unavoidable element in the struggle, since they did see the Jews as the main

---

[30] In addition to the general literature on political Antisemitism, see also: S. Kaehlwe, "Stöckers Versuch, eine christlich-soziale Arbeiterpartei in Berlin zu begründen", in: *Deutscher Staat und deutsche Parteien*, ed. P. Wentzke, Munich 1922, 227–265.
[31] Eduard Bernstein, *Die Geschichte der Berliner Arbeiterbewegung*, Berlin 1907, vol. II, 58–61.
[32] Mehring, *Geschichte der deutschen Sozialdemokratie*, Stuttgart 1897/98, 491.
[33] Quoted in Pulzer, *The Rise of Political Anti-Semitism*, 265.

representatives of Capitalism and the excesses of commerce."[34] Thus, while the 1881 election was a disappointment to Stöcker and the other Antisemitic social-conservatives in Berlin, it was a sign of danger to Social Democracy too. In the 2nd Berlin voting district, where Stöcker was campaigning himself, the Social Democratic vote dropped from 26.3 percent in 1878 to 9.5 percent in 1881. This, however, was not a typical workers' district. It may not have indicated a desertion of Social Democracy by the Proletariat. It did, no doubt, show the tendency of *Mittelstand* voters to abandon Social Democracy for social-conservatism in Stöcker's style. But the socialist vote in more typical working class areas of Berlin also dropped considerably in the 1881 election. In the 4th district, where August Bebel was the Social Democratic candidate, the socialist vote dropped from almost 50 to 32 percent, and in the 6th district from 41 to 27. This was clearly a result of a *number* of factors. Yet, significantly, by the time of the second poll, when the social-conservatives were withdrawn from the contest and the socialists faced only their traditional left-liberal opponents, they managed to pick up some of their losses.[35] In a letter to Engels in November 1881 Louis Viereck wrote that he was convinced the majority of the 47,000 Antisemitic votes in Berlin had been recruited from among previous supporters of Social Democracy.[36] While this assertion is difficult to verify in quantitative terms, it appears unquestionable that Antisemitism was by the early 1880's still appealing to men who under other circumstances might have retained their allegiance to the socialists or even transferred it to them.

Considering this fact, it is all the more remarkable that the socialists made no use of Antisemitic propaganda in their election campaigns, and indeed often took an outspoken anti-Antisemitic line. Already in 1881 the SPD refused to cooperate with the Antisemitic candidates in run-off elections, and by 1884 in a contest between Rudolf Virchow and Stöcker all the Social Democratic leaders in Berlin made it quite clear that they preferred a left-liberal Jew to the Antisemitic pastor. With one or two exceptions this remained the policy followed by the Social Democratic leadership from the mid-1880's onward.[37] By that time, Marxism became increasingly influential among prominent socialists in Germany, providing them with a powerful alternative to state-socialism and increasingly making Antisemitism unnecessary and irrelevant for them. Simultaneously, the social and political process of separation between *Mittelstand* and Proletariat was carried on and accentuated by continuing industrialization. This provided an ample recruiting

---

[34] Bernstein, *Die Geschichte der Berliner Arbeiterbewegung*, 76–77 (translation S.V.).
[35] The numbers are given by Lidtke, *The Outlawed Party*, 163.
[36] Ibid, 163–164.
[37] Bernstein, 75–76. Also Massing, pp. 173–174, and Levy, 174.

ground for Social Democracy among the increasingly class-conscious proletariat, and made the loss of *Mittelstand* vote relatively less important.

It was this combination of ideological and social factors which then dictated the response of the socialist movement to the new Antisemitism of the 1890's. During much of the 1880's the socialists' position on Antisemitism was mainly a by-product of ideological controversies only indirectly related to Antisemitism, and as the Antisemitic movement of that time was weak and ineffective, they did not feel called upon to take an explicit stand in relation to it. With the transformation of the Antisemitic movement into a veritable mass party, the Social Democrats were again forced to take a direct interest in it, and form an explicit position in response to its unexpected success.[38] In May 1890, Friedrich Engels set the tone by allowing the publication of one of his private letters in the Viennese *Arbeiterzeitung*.[39] This was perhaps the most unambiguous socialist statement on Antisemitism to be found in the socialist literature of the time. Writing from London, Engels was not inhibited by any practical, party-political consideration which must have affected the Social Democratic leadership in Germany in one way or another. Indeed, Bernstein, Kautsky and Bebel were never able to match Engel's outspoken and decisive stand. They did, however, participate in developing and propagating an analysis of Antisemitism which both corresponded with their inner conviction and served their practical needs.

The content of the Social Democratic analysis of the phenomenon of Antisemitism has often been investigated, and a short summary will serve our purposes here.[40] The analysis was notable for the following points: 1. It offered a complete sociological breakdown of the Antisemitic movement, sensing its special attraction for the so-called "decaying *Mittelstand*", the small peasantry, a part of the Junker aristocracy and the unsuccessful among the educated. 2. It regarded the Antisemitism of these groups as mistaken but essentially understandable in view of the special role played by the Jews in the capitalist economy. 3. It assumed, therefore, that in due course the elements now attracted to Antisemitism would transfer their allegiance to Social Democracy, as they would gradually come to realize the true nature of their misery and the only course of action realistically open to them. And 4. It emphasized the historical causes of the alleged exploitative role of Jews in contemporary society, and viewed it as a result of age-old discriminations and not as a proof for their intrinsic evil nature.

---

[38] In the 1880's the *Neue Zeit* published no article directly related to Antisemitism. In the 1890's, however, more than 30 pieces discussed this matter.

[39] *MEW*, vol. 22, 49–51.

[40] The best available summary is still Massing's, chap. X.

The application of this analysis in the battle against Antisemitism often had a curiously ambiguous effect. In the early 1890's the Social Democrats still considered the liberals their worst political enemies. It was particularly Franz Mehring, a belated Marxist and a long-time anti-liberal campaigner, who remained particularly careful to keep the proper balance between the attack on Antisemitism and on the so-called philo-Semitism of the Progressive Liberals. In his *History of German Social Democracy*, written in the mid-90's Mehring still asserted, for instance, that "compared with an Eugen Richter, (Stöcker) could still be an example of truthfulness".[41] And in his *Neue Zeit* articles he repeatedly came back to the hypocrisy of the left-liberal protectors of the Jews and saw in their campaign nothing but a battle for the defense of capitalism.[42] By 1893, when the danger of Antisemitism became more apparent, Eduard Bernstein attempted to draw a new balance between the opposition to anti and philo-Semitism.[43] He too, however, shared Mehring's distaste for the philo-Semitic stand, which according to him set out to defend Jewish capitalism, chauvinism and some of the *"häßliche Eigenschaften"* of the Jews. Nevertheless, since the battle had become one of slogans, Bernstein continued, special care had to be taken to prevent too close an identification of Social Democracy with Antisemitism through an overt emphasis on opposition to philo-Semitism.

In the early 1890's then, one can still detect a degree of ambiguity in the Social Democratic pronouncements on Antisemitism. In fact, even the resolution brought forth by Bebel and accepted by the 1893 party-congress in Köln reads today as a strangely watered-down document.[44] After stating in brief the social basis of Antisemitism and its reactionary purposes, the resolution declared the fight against Jewish exploitation to be basically irrelevant, and the determination of Social Democracy not to spend its energy on fighting a mere by-product of bourgeois society. It ended with an optimistic expression of hope that Antisemites would eventually join the socialist struggle against capitalism and for the realization of a new socialist society. The resolution says nothing about the moral content of Antisemitism and wastes no words in defending German Jews against the Antisemitic slander. In his *Referat* Bebel essentially accepted the thesis asserting the exploitative nature or Jewish activity in town and countryside, and this theme

---

[41] Mehring, *Geschichte der deutschen Sozialdemokratie*, 490.
[42] *Neue Zeit*, 1890–91, IX, 2; 1891–92, X, 2.
[43] Ibid, 1893–94, XI, 2.
[44] *Protokoll über die Verhandlungen des Parteitages der Sozialdemokratischen Partei Deutschlands abgehalten zu Köln am Rhein*, Berlin 1893, 223–224. There is also a reprint of Bebel's speech, which was later distributed as a separate pamphlet in a slightly amended version.

was reiterated even a decade later in a series of articles in the *Neue Zeit*, mostly written by Karl Kautsky.[45]

It is, however, important to remember that during the early 1890's the SPD was still making some serious efforts to gain electoral support from rural and urban *Mittelständler*. In 1893 Bebel reported to Engels of the unsuccessful attempts made by the Social Democrats to convince small craftsmen of the folly of the Antisemitic promise of salvation.[46] At that time the socialists also renewed their efforts to win over elements of the small peasantry in the countryside.[47] These efforts may have in part influenced the cautious stand of the Social Democratic leadership with regard to Antisemitism. As late as 1906 a note of admiration and envy could still be detected in Philip Scheidemann's description of the Antisemites' easy success in the Hessian countryside during the early 1890's.[48] The Antisemitic politicians, he recalled, knew how to make politics appealing even to those elements of the population which could not be moved by any other political force at the time. Scheidemann, who had then been a socialist organizer in Hesse, stressed the democratic impulse in Böckel's agitation among the peasantry and his parliamentary stand against the military and the naval bills. Only after Böckel's decline, Scheidemann explained, did the Antisemitic movement become an appendage to the conservative, reactionary parties of the right. Thus, in spite of its ideological stand against Antisemitism, the Social Democratic leadership during the early 1890's often found it somewhat embarrassing to come out unequivocally against the essentially democratic and anti-capitalist version of Antisemitism. Only when by the middle of the decade, the SPD finally gave up its efforts to win *Mittelstand* support, could it also reach a real immunity against Antisemitism.

Under the social and political conditions of Imperial Germany, Antisemitism was increasingly attractive to some groups and not to others. The Social Democrats usually attributed *Mittelstand* support of Antisemitism to the economic misery of this 'declining class' and its resentment of Jewish competition. But Antisemitism was not only the creed of the impoverished and the desperate. In addition, it fulfilled two other functions for the various elements of the *Mittelstand*: an ideological function and a social one.

To begin with, Antisemitism offered a way for achieving a degree of integration among conflicting beliefs. The men who gradually evolved a general hostility towards

---

[45] *Neue Zeit*, 1903–4, XXI, 2. See also his *Rasse und Judentum* (Ergänzungsheft zu *Neue Zeit*, no. 20, 1914).
[46] Quoted in Hans-Georg Lehmann, *Die Agrarfrage in der Theorie und Praxis der deutschen und internationalen Sozialdemokratie*, Tübingen 1970, 61.
[47] Ibid, 62–63.
[48] *Neue Zeit*, 1905–6, XXIV, 2.

everything modern, were not only, nor even primarily, Antisemitic. They were opponents of liberalism, of the capitalist economic system in its modern industrial version, of industrialization, secularization, and last but not least of Social Democracy. Antisemitism allowed them to remain both anti-capitalist and anti-socialist, since it was in fact not capitalism as such which they opposed but Jewish capitalism; not liberalism but its corruption by the Jews; not even the labor movement but the Jewish intellectuals who stood at its head. Antisemitism was a force of ideological coherence for men whose concept of the world was dictated by resentment, suspicion and fear.

Socially and psychologically Antisemitism fulfilled another important function for these men. By the 1890's German society was clearly divided into a number of separate social milieus, roughly corresponding to a division of classes and of parties.[49] The integration of the Reich was in fact based on the ability of these bodies to co-exist. The upper-class conservatives formed one of these socio-political and cultural blocks; the Catholics – united in spite of class divisions – formed another. Recent literature on pre-war Social Democracy suggests that the Social Democratic workers also constituted such a milieu, which became a part of the social fabric of the Reich through a process of "negative integration".[50] By creating a Social Democratic subculture, the workers were able to attain a clear sense of identity. As individuals the socialist workers did not merely belong to a specific political party, but were also supplied with a coherent ideology with which to evaluate their conditions and with a network of social institutions, in which they could act on the political, economic and social levels.

The *Mittelstand* did not belong to any of these social milieus. It never managed to overcome the conflicting interests among its various elements, nor to substitute the overall social function of the old guilds with any other viable institutional structure. For this social stratum, therefore, the unity of the glorious German nation and a sense of belonging to it were of particular psychological significance. For them, Antisemitism was the other side of extreme nationalism, both helping to provide them with a sense of identity and belonging which they seemed to have lost in the process of modernization. They negatively identified themselves as non-Jews, and this negative self-definition became for them a powerful and comforting tool.

In contrast, the working-class possessed by that time a coherent ideology which, even in its primitive popular form, supplied an analysis of past and

---

[49] The basis for this analysis is M.R. Lepsius, "Parteiensystem und Sozialstruktur. Zum Problem der Demokratisierung der deutschen Gesellschaft", in: *Festschrift F. Lütge*, ed. Wilhelm Abel et al., Stuttgart 1966, 371–393.
[50] For a short exposition of this concept see: Dieter Groh, "Die Sozialdemokratie im Verfassungssystem des 2. Reiches," in: *Sozialdemokratie zwischen Klassenbewegung und Volkspartei*, ed. Hans Mommsen, Frankfurt a. M. 1974.

present and a hopeful perspective for the future. Socially and psychologically, workers identified themselves with the Social Democratic Party, the trade unions and the socialist clubs and societies. The working-class was negatively defined vis-à-vis the bourgeoisie, and positively by its own international movement. Thus, while anti-Jewish Feelings could have certainly been found among individual workers in imperial Germany, Antisemitism had no function to fulfil within the context of the Marxist Social Democratic, working-class movement.

II **Cultural Code and its Derivatives**

4 Antisemitism as a Cultural Code: Reflections on the History and Historiography of Antisemitism in Imperial Germany

I. The problem of continuity preoccupies historians of Germany for a long time. Rejecting the view of Nazism as a mere aberration in the normal flow of German history, representatives of various schools have tried to reconstruct the traditional view of Bismarckian Germany and the Wilhelminian period in order to demonstrate the links that join pre-1914 Germany with the inter-war years, or rather Imperial society with the Nazi era. Continuity in the development of Antisemitism, however, remained a relatively insignificant sideline in most of these general studies. Few observations have been suggested – some pertinent and illuminating, no doubt – but the task of treating the problem in depth has been left for the specialists.[1]

Historians of Antisemitism have dealt with the problem in a variety of other ways. To be sure, they have had to come to terms not only with the question of continuity in *German* history but also with the equally baffling one of continuity in the history of anti-Jewish sentiments and action over time and, of course, not only in Germany. In the immediate post-war years Hannah Arendt warned historians against a conception of *modern* Antisemitism as yet another manifestation of an "eternal hatred", prevalent in the Christian world from times immemorial, or at least an heir to medieval anti-Jewish prejudices and oppression. It was to a large extent their deep ignorance of the past, she argued, that had been responsible for the miscomprehension of later, concrete dangers.[2] But while Arendt drew a sharp distinction between old and modern Antisemitism, she perceived a clear line of continuity in what she singled out as "modern Antisemitism" itself. This, she claimed, emerged with the birth of the modern nation-state as a response to the unique role of the Jews within it. For Arendt, Antisemitism was a reflection, though undeniably a distorted one, of the specific, "abnormal" position of the Jews in society, and the break she saw was not inherent in the anti-Jewish forces

---

[1] See especially Hans Rosenberg, *Grosse Depression und Bismarckzeit. Wirtschaflsablauf, Gesellschaft und Politik in Mitteleuropa*, Berlin 1967, 88–117; Hans-Ulrich Wehler, *Das Deutsche Kaiserreich*, Göttingen 1973, 105–118.

[2] Hannah Arendt, *The Burden of our Time*, London 1951, 8. (The American editions of Arendt's book appeared under the title *The Origins of Totalitarianism*.) The following historiographical remarks are not intended as a comprehensive review of the literature. For this see Ismar Schorsch, "German Antisemitism in the Light of Post-War Historiography", in: *LBI year Book XIX* (1974), 257–271.

themselves but in Jewish history as such. She reaffirms the unique role of Jews in the modern world, but not the novelty of modern Antisemitism or even of its Nazi exterminatory version.[3]

Other studies offer a different view and another periodization. Both Paul Massing and Peter G. J. Pulzer distinguished between the various anti-Jewish views and actions during the so-called "century of emancipation" and the precise era of modern, *political* Antisemitism, since the 1870s.[4] Thus, the emergence of Antisemitic political parties signaled for them a radical departure, and it was the continuity of modern Antisemitism from Adolf Stöcker to Adolf Hitler that was repeatedly affirmed by them. In more or less explicit terms, the assertion of this continuity underlines both the conception of Imperial Germany as a "rehearsal for destruction" (Massing), and the final chapter in the history of a modern, liberal Germany.

Somewhat later contributions to the history of Antisemitism have thrown further light on the problem of continuity. In a book on political Antisemitism in Imperial Germany, Richard S. Levy challenged the often assumed link between the Antisemitic movement in Imperial Germany and National–Socialism.[5] He questioned this continuity by stressing the complete failure of political Antisemitism in pre-war Germany. Levy provides a detailed analysis of the various Antisemitic organizations in the *Kaiserreich* and describes their internal conflicts, the clashes of personalities within them, their failing parliamentary tactics, methods of recruitment, and their final disintegration. He did not claim to settle the question of continuity, yet his view on the matter, though always phrased with due caution, was as evident as its reverse, implicit in Massing's work and slightly qualified in Pulzer's. The legacy of the Antisemitic political parties in Imperial Germany, Levy argues, was one of discord and incompetence, of endless internal haggling, followed by disillusionment everywhere in Germany, inevitably culminating in a final and total loss of electoral support. A new political party dedicated to Antisemitism would have had to make a fresh start, he argued.[6]

While Levy's conclusion was well demonstrated, it was perhaps not as novel as it may have seemed. More than a decade earlier, Pulzer had already shown the decline of the Antisemitic political parties in pre-world war I Germany. In the end of his book he stressed, although admittedly failed to demonstrate in detail, the

---

3 Ibid, 3–10.
4 See Paul Massing's book carrying this title, first published in New York 1949, and see Peter G. J. Pulzer, *The Rise of Political Antisemitism* in *Germany and Austria,* London 1964.
5 Richard S. Levy, *The Downfall of the Anti-Semitic Political Parties in Imperial Germany,* New Haven 1975.
6 Ibid, 1–7, 254–265.

infiltration of Antisemitism into many of the political and semi-political associations in the *Kaierreich*, particularly during the last pre-war years.[7] The momentum of political Antisemitism in Imperial Germany, he argued, had indeed been slackened, but it nevertheless remained conspicuous and pervasive. What was at issue here, therefore, was not whether or not the Antisemitic parties lost popular support, not even why they suffered such total collapse at the polls, but whether and to what degree that final collapse was a reflection of a slackening Antisemitism as a whole.

Levy's book has had its own inner logic. It was the parliamentary political Antisemitic parties, emerging during the late 1870s, that represented a uniquely new phenomenon, ran his argument. They occupied center-stage and "their agitation was uppermost in the minds of contemporary Germans".[8] Moreover, their leaders and membership were the only true, authentic Antisemites, preaching their hatred of Jews regardless of changing circumstances. Among the other political bodies that professed more or less open Antisemitism, Levy's attention focuses on the groups "whose primary purpose was to enact anti-Jewish legislation", relegating to a second order of importance those who were "willing to foster and use Antisemitism in order to marshal support for other aims not directly touching upon Jewish life".[9] Having asserted the centrality of the "sincere" Antisemitic parties, Levy described their downfall as a direct reflection of the overall decline of Antisemitism in Imperial Germany. Pulzer, on the other hand, likewise dedicating his major effort to the study of the Antisemitic political parties, concluded by limiting their overall historical significance. Accordingly, Antisemitism remained a constant in Germany even if the decline of the parliamentary Antisemitic political parties in Imperial Germany appeared to be a closed issue. It was time for historians to divert their attention to other aspects of the problem.

In an essay on the structure and function of Antisemitism in Wilhelminian Germany, Werner Jochmann has taken another route.[10] Relying on a wealth of material previously unused, he has examined the degree to which Antisemitism did indeed penetrate into the various social and political associations in Imperial Germany and was widely accepted by the different social groups in Wilhelminian society. *Because* of the fragmentation of organized political Antisemitism, Jochmann argued, the direction *it* represented had not been taken seriously by its opponents

---

7 Pulzcr, *The Rise of Political Antisemitism*, 219–292.
8 Levy, *The Downfall of the Antisemitic political Parties*, 2–3.
9 For this see Ibid, 427, 460.
10 See Werner Jochmann, "Struktur und Funktion des deutschen Antisemitismus", in: *Juden im Wilhelminischen Deutschland 1890–1914*, eds. Werner E. Mosse and Arnold Paucker, Tübingen 1976 (Schriftenreihe wissenschaftlicher Abhandlungen des Leo Baeck Instituts 33), 389–477.

and its force was generally underestimated. Antisemitism was thus allowed to spread into students' organizations, into teachers', judges' and officials' unions, slowly finding its way into the ranks of the Protestant and, to a lesser extent, the Catholic clergy, and finally, during the 1890s, it gained ground in smaller *Bürgervereine, Heimatsvereine* and a variety of local cultural groupings. Antisemitism became endemic. It was to be found in occupational interest organizations and in many of the political pressure groups. Local authorities were infected and central governments rarely escaped open admission of Antisemitism as they had to take the mood of the country increasingly into consideration. Even in the Social Democratic camp, particularly in some of the trade unions, Antisemitic views were not altogether absent. The weakness of the Antisemitic political parties, ran Jochmann's argument, should not cover up the *growing* strength of Antisemitism in Imperial society, and it was perhaps just this weakness that made possible the wide-scale infiltration of Antisemitic sentiment and verbiage within it.[11]

The decline of the Antisemitic political parties can therefore be considered not as a sign for the overall slackening of German Antisemitism but merely as an indication of its changing form. Antisemitism had spread from the "sincere" groups to other organizations and it was no less significant or potent for that change of face. In fact, even the most "sincere" Antisemitic parties had always fought for more than the introduction of Antisemitic legal measures. Levy himself clearly shows their weakness in pushing through precisely this part of their program.[12] From Adolf Stöcker to the various Antisemitic leagues and combinations of the 1880s and 1890s, these groups campaigned for a variety of social reforms and political changes, using Antisemitic propaganda by linking it to the disparate tenets of their programs as well as for sheer recruitment purposes. In fact, from the early appearance of political Antisemitism, the distinction between "sincere" and "tactical" motives figured highly in internal controversies among the Antisemites themselves, but in itself had little meaning in reality.[13] Sincerity and opportunism were inseparably mixed in the use of Antisemitism by all groups.[14] Stöcker's position on Antisemitism may be still debated, and it is unlikely that historians will ever be able to decide the inner motives of this one man. The distinction between true and pretended Antisemitism therefore seems untenable and perhaps even misleading.

---

[11] For this thesis see Ibid, 427, 460.
[12] Levy, *The Downfall of the Antisemitic political Parties*, 166–172.
[13] According to Levy, 14, who used this distinction to explain some of the problems of parliamentary Antisemitism. The distinction was first introduced by Otto Glagau, attacking the conservatives for their "demagogic" Antisemitism.
[14] On this problem see Hellmut von Gerlach's interesting comments in his memoirs, *Von Rechts nach Links*, Zürich 1937, 102–112.

Extending our view to include not only these "sincere" Antisemites but all individuals and organized bodies that in one way or another professed resentment of Jews, the problem of continuity takes another form. Although one cannot point out any direct link between the Antisemitic *parties* of Imperial Germany and Nazism, one can easily trace a more or less continuous line between them. In yet another essay Werner Jochmann provided some of the material for establishing this continuity. He investigated the various organized expressions of Antisemitism during the war years, and although many of the original Antisemitic associations had disintegrated, others took their place in rapid succession.[15] There seems to have been no appreciable slackening of Antisemitism in Germany during the pre-war years, nor during the war itself. Continuity is thus clearly established. Nazi Antisemitism took yet another form and showed unparalleled intensity, but it grew upon the institutional and ideational building blocks provided by Wilhelminian society.

But the problem of continuity refuses to disappear. When one declines to limit the investigation of modern Antisemitism to what has for some time appeared as its true essence, namely the growth of Antisemitic political parties; when the study of Antisemitism once more encompasses other institutions that were, often covertly, susceptible to Antisemitism, and when we are again seeking individual pronouncements of socialist and trade-union officials concerning Jews and Judaism; when we view Antisemitism as the sum total of anti-Jewish statements and actions, are we not back with the concept of "eternal hatred"? What is, after all, unique or modern about this basic antipathy to Jews in Western society in general and in German society in particular? Having established the continuity between Imperial Germany and the post-war variety of Antisemitism, have we not resurrected the ghost of that "eternal hatred"? Is modern Antisemitism ultimately not yet another expression of an age-old hatred, taking on some relatively new and some more traditional forms? *Was* there a distinguishable *modern* Antisemitism beginning in the 1870s?

II. Historians of modern Antisemitism have, without exception, dealt with its novelty in terms that transcend the normal political vocabulary, and when links between Antisemitism and other ideas and attitudes became increasingly apparent, further conceptualization seemed unavoidable. For some time, with the focus on *Ideengeschichte*, emphasis was placed on the role of Antisemitism within the so-

---

[15] Werner Jochmann, "Die Ausbreitung des Antisemitismus", in: *Deutsches Judentum in Krieg und Revolution, 1916–1923*, eds. Werner E. Mosse and Arnold Paucker, Tübingen 1971, 409–510.

called "German Ideology".[16] George L. Mosse has shown the intellectual links between Antisemitism and racism, *völkisch* ideas and aggressive nationalism. He repeatedly warns us against treating Antisemitism in isolation, and asserts it was "a part of German intellectual history".[17] In *The Politics of Cultural Despair* Fritz Stern too enlarged our conception of the intellectual environment of Antisemitism in Germany. Not only racism and *folkish* nationalism were related to it, he claimed, but the whole complex which he chose to term "cultural pessimism". Stern's sources were those of intellectual history, but his book remains on the interesting borderline between the study of ideas and of mentality. His analysis portrays not a rational system of ideas but a *Weltanschauung*.[18]

It is indeed as a *Weltanschauung* that later historians have characterized Antisemitism. In an article on continuity and discontinuity of the Jewish question in nineteenth-century Germany, Reinhard Rürup, reasserting the importance of the new political parties and the use of Antisemitism as a political tool, suggested an additional line of approach:

> Expressions of hate in the age of emancipation . . . were almost always related concretely to the Jews and their position in the bourgeois society . . . Since the second half of the seventies, however, radical Antisemitism became a 'Weltanschauung', and even the moderate Antisemitism of the Conservatives showed a clear tendency to become a 'Weltanschauung'.[19]

Cautiously placing *Weltanschauung* in quotation marks, Rürup goes on to define it as an "Erklärungsmodell" for comprehending a rapidly changing world, combining an analysis of existing circumstances with a blueprint for the solution of all pressing problems in the future.

Other authors have taken a slightly different line. They do not *identify* Antisemitism as a substitute *Weltanschauung*, but tend to see in it one aspect of a more inclusive alternative world-view. Antisemitism, argues Jochmann, has become a constitutive element of nationalism, an integral part of a new imperialist

---

16 Sec especially George L. Mosse, *The Crisis of German Ideology. Intellectual Origins of the Third Reich*, New York 1964; and his "Culture, Civilization and German Antisemitism," in: *Judaism: A Quarterly Journal of Jewish Life and Thought*, VII (1958), 1–11.
17 George L. Mosse's essay above, 11.
18 See Fritz Stern, *The Politics of Cultural Despair. A Study* in *the Rise of the Germanic Ideology*, Berkeley 1961. A somewhat different view of Antisemitism during the Bismarckian years emerges from his biography of Bismarck's private banker, *Gold and Iron. Bismarck, Bleichröder, and the Building of the German Empire*, New York 1977, especially 461–54.
19 Reinhard Rürup, "Die 'Judenfrage' der bürgerlichen Gesellschaft und die Entstehung des modernen Antisemitismus", in *Emanzipation und Antisemitismus. Studien zur 'Judenfrage' der bürgerlichen Gesellschaft*, Göttingen 1975, 91.

drive in Germany, bound together with conservatism and *Kulturpessimismus*.[20] In his study of the myth of the "Elders of Zion", Norman Cohn suggested that the Jews became a "symbol of the modern world" and Antisemitism an immediate companion to a variety of anti-modern attitudes, joined to permanent nostalgia for a pre-industrial past.[21] For Hans-Jürgen Puhle Antisemitism was an element of the "weltanschauliche Allgemeingut" of the agrarians,[22] and Andrew G. Whiteside diagnosed it as part of the syndrome of the Viennese students' movement, "a working form" for other ideas.[23]

Following the pioneering work of Theodor W. Adorno and his California collaborators, we have all begun to associate Antisemitism with the so-called "authoritarian personality".[24] Despite many objections and a prolonged scholarly controversy, it appeared that there was an increasing amount of evidence to support Adorno's conclusions. The argument on the precise make-up of the authoritarian personality continued, and the diagnosis of the authoritarian personality structure as a case of psychopathology was bound to be repeatedly disputed. But the existence of a unique authoritarian *syndrome* was accepted even by many of the staunchest opponents of Adorno's work.[25] The literature reveals the two levels at which this syndrome operates: the level of intellectual choice and ideology and that of the individual's inner personality, behavior pattern, automatic responses, and associative meaning.[26]

---

[20] Jochmann, Werner: "Struktur und Funktion des deutschen Antisemitismus", in: *Juden in Wilhelminischen Deutschland 1890–1914*, eds. Werner E. Mosse and Arnold Paucker, Tübingen 1976, 460–462, 472–474.
[21] Norman Cohn, *Warrant for Genocide. The Myth of the Jewish World-Conspiracy and the Protocols of the Elders of Zion*, London 1967, 23–24, 164–179. In my own work on master-artisans in Imperial Germany I, too, have indicated Antisemitism as an aspect of an overall anti-modern mentality, stressing the rising popular *Weltanschauung* distinct from and independent of the writings of philosophers and ideologues. See also Shulamit Volkov, "Popular Anti-Modernism: Ideology and Sentiment among Master-Artisans during the 1890s", in: *Jahrbuch des Instituts für Deutsche Geschichte*, Tel-Aviv, Ill (1974).
[22] Hans-Jürgen Puhle, *Agrarische Interessenpolitik und preussischer Konservatismus im wilhelminischen Reich (1890–1914)*, Hannover 1966, 133.
[23] Andrew G. Whiteside, *Socialism of Fools. Georg Ritter von Schönerer and Austrian Pan-Germanism*, Berkeley 1975, 84–85.
[24] See Theodor W. Adorno, *The Authoritarian Personality*, New York 1950. For a good summary of the discussion see Newitt Sanford, "The Roots of Prejudice: Emotional Dynamics," in: *Psychology and Race*, ed. Peter Watson, Harmondsworth 1973, 57–75, and the bibliography cited there.
[25] See for example: John J. Ray, "Is Antisemitism a Cognitive Simplification? Some Observations on Australian Neo-Nazis", in: *The Jewish Journal of Sociology*, XIV (1972), 207–213.
[26] Adorno., *The Authoritarian Personality*, especially 151–288. Sec also *Studies in the Scope and Method of the Authoritarian Personality*, eds. R. Chrisitie and M. Jahoda, New York 1954.

Towards the turn of the century a segment of German society disclosed a cultural pattern *analogous* to the authoritarian personality syndrome, similarly operating both on the level of rationality and on that of implicit values and norms, style of life and thought, common ambitions and emotions. The cluster of ideas, sentiments and public behavior patterns that characterized this syndrome cannot be subsumed under the title "ideology", as this term was and is commonly understood. If it included a systematic philosophy with direct implications for social and political action at all, this remained only a part of a larger whole.[27] A *Weltanschauung* can properly define this phenomenon only when it is understood in the widest sense.[28] Perhaps a better term, more easily associated with basic human needs, while not excluding philosophy, science or the arts, is culture, "the total interconnected set of ways of thinking, feeling and acting". Both ideology and *Weltanschauung* are subsumed under this conception of culture, seen as "a great symbolic unit", shared and learned by individuals and serving to unite them in "a particular and distinct collectivity".[29]

The unique German culture emerging in the 1890s was expressed in the "German ideology", to use Mosse's terminology again, in a radical anti-modern mentality, rejecting Liberalism, Capitalism, and Socialism, in a nostalgic passion for a long-lost world. It implied a series of political views including an opposition to Democracy and a call for the re-establishment of a just and harmonious national community. It was associated with extreme Nationalism, a colonial and imperial drive, an enthusiasm for war and an advocacy of a pre-industrial moral code, all tinged with more than a trace of hypocrisy. In one way or another it was always combined with Antisemitism.

---

[27] For the meaning of ideology see Clifford Geertz, "Ideology as a Cultural System", in: *Ideology and Discontent,* ed. David E. Apter, New York 1964, 47–60. I have used here what appears to be the most common definition of ideology. See, for example, the discussion in Carl J. Friedrich and Zbigniew Brzezinski, *Totalitarian Dictatorship and Autocracy,* Cambridge Mass. 1956, 73–75.

[28] The term *Weltanschauung,* apparently untranslatable, is used very loosely in historical writing, often indeed too loosely to be of any explanatory value. It was given a critical but limited philosophical interpretation by Wilhelm Dilthey in "Die Typen der Weltanschauung und ihre Ausbildung in den metaphysischen Systemen", in: *Gesammelte Schriften,* vol. VIII, Berlin 1931. Karl Mannheim provided the best available theoretical treatment in his "On the Interpretation of Weltanschauung", in: *Essays on the Sociology of Knowledge,* London 1952, 33–88, as well as the best case-study, "Conservative Thought", in: *Essays on Sociology and Social Psychology,* London 1903, 74–164. Admittedly the word "Culture" is equally ambiguous. For the reasons I preferred it and for much of the following discussion see Clifford Geertz above, on which I have relied very heavily.

[29] Guy Rocher, *A General Introduction to Sociology. A Theoretical Perspective,* London 1972, 89–92.

The variations on this general pattern were many. Particularly significant were the diverging views on Christianity and on the role of the Junker aristocracy.[30] A comparison of the attitudes of men in the Pan-German League, the *Bund der Landwirte*, and the *Deutschnationaler Handlungsgehilfenverband* is bound to bring forth numerous variations and significant shifts of accent.[31] Undoubtedly these ought to be kept in mind, but they should not be allowed to obstruct our view of the whole. Despite all these there was much in common in the beliefs, ideas and style of life and thought of many Germans at the time. They shared a common pattern of values and norms, an unmistakable culture. To be sure, some individuals rejected it altogether and many conformed passively. A few consciously espoused it with a full knowledge of its meaning and implications.

The range of this culture can be grasped by reviewing the huge amount of literature produced by its advocates. In 1914 the G. Hedeler publishing house in Leipzig published a small guide to the literature of the *"Deutschbewegung"*.[32] It listed some 800 titles and more than 80 periodicals. The subject-matters encompassed religion and philosophy, biology and the natural sciences, anthropology, history, heraldry and genealogy, language, art and literature, economics, politics and law. Significantly no special section in the list was exclusively concerned with Jews or the "Jewish Question", but a look at the list of titles and authors confirms the impression that many of the "highly recommended" items dealt extensively, if indeed rarely in isolation, with Jews. Antisemitism was an i n t e g r a l aspect of this world-view, a fitting element in a complex and many-sided culture.

In an unusually perceptive passage Friedrich Lange, a rabid Antisemite writing in 1893, asserted that Antisemitism had to be ". . . Ein Element und keineswegs das wichtigste einer viel weiter und höher greifenden nationalen Weltanschauung und Politik."[33] His "broader and higher" ideal was "pure Germanism", upon which he endlessly elaborated in his journal and pamphlets. These included a high-pitched Nationalism, an elevation of war and conflict, an insistence on the need for German

---

30 For the distinction between Christian and anti-Christian Antisemitism see Uriel Tal, *Christians and Jews* in *Germany. Religion, Politics and Ideology* in the *Second Reich, 1871–1914*, Ithaca 1975, especially 223–289. On pro and anti-Junker Antisemitism see Pulzer, *The Rise of Political Antisemitism*, 106–117, in contrast to Puhle, *Agrarische Interessenpolitik*, 125–140.

31 See Puhle, *Agrarische Interessenpolitik*, 72–140; Iris Hamel, *Völkischer Verband und Nationale Gewerkschaft. Der Deutschnationale Handlungsgehilfen-Verband 1893–1933*, Frankfurt a. Main 1967; Mildred S. Wertheimer, *The Pan-German League 1830–1914*, New York 1924; and Alfred Krück, *Geschichte des Alldeutschen Verbandes, 1890–1939*, Wiesbaden 1954.

32 *Was tut not? Ein Führer durch die gesamte Literatur der Deutschbewegung*, ed. Rudolf Rusten, Leipzig 1914.

33 Friedrich Lange, *Reines Deutschtum. Grundzüge einer nationalen Weltanschauung*, 5th edn., Berlin 1905, 109. The title article quoted here was first published on 11th April 1893.

expansion, a view of the required economic reforms to achieve autarchy and social ones to preserve the *Mittelstand*. It provided treatment of the various aspects of the "Social Question", labor legislation and the so-called *Frauenfrage*.[34]

On the eve of war a fuller exposition of this "Germanic" world-view was put forward by Heinrich Class in a book entitled *'Wenn ich der Kaiser wär'*.[35] Class is known for his Antisemitism, but few historians have seriously concerned themselves with his views on other matters, although contemporaries showed considerable interest precisely in them.[36] Class developed a critique of the Imperial government's foreign policy that rejected the concept of a "saturated Germany" and the values of a "just peace". He demanded expansion to the East and colonies across the sea, and protested against what he saw as the presumed humiliation of Germany in Serbia and Morocco. He called for a rejuvenating war, and campaigned for a new type of social and economic legislation to reverse the trend of urbanization and put an end to racial intermingling, which together posed a grave danger to the true "German soul". He pleaded for agrarian reforms, constitutional changes and new educational programs. No major issue of the day was left untouched by him, and his various demands were strongly tied together, not by the irrefutable logic of the argument or the force of his didactic thought, but by an underlying set of basic values, easily discernible behind them: worship of power identified with manliness and virility; search for uniformity conceived as harmony and for authority seen as leadership; anti-egalitarianism expressed in racism, anti-feminism, opposition to democracy and finally, of course, Antisemitism. Hatred of Jews neatly fitted into this whole. Nevertheless, Class's book can be accurately described as an Antisemitic tract only if one chooses to name the entire *Weltanschauung* expressed in it "Antisemitic". In many ways this is not an unfair judgment; it was one frequently made by contemporaries; but here it must be made more explicit.

The *Alldeutscher Verband*, headed by Class since 1907, was not originally an openly Antisemitic organization. The "Germanic syndrome" was all there but Antisemitism did not as yet seem unavoidable within it. Significantly, it was the Berlin chapter which pressed for a more outspoken stand on the "Jewish question". At the heart of the Empire the association between Antisemitism and pan-Germanism,

---

34 Ibid, 135–187.
35 The book was published under a pseudonym: Daniel Frymann, *'Wenn ich der Kaiser war' - Politische Wahrheiten und Notwendigkeiten*, Leipzig 1912. By 1914 the book sold about 25,000 copies. See Levy, *The Downfall of the Antisemitic political Parties*, 262.
36 See Franz Guntram Schultheiss, *Deutschnationales Vereinswesen. Ein Beitrag zur Geschichte des deutschen Nationalgefühls*, Munich 1897, 77; Pulzer, *The Rise of political Antissemitism*, 226–228.

militarism and authoritarianism had become apparent long before it was realized elsewhere in the country. Gradually, however, the *Alldeutscher Verband* became increasingly Antisemitic, combining its distaste and resentment of Jews with militant anti-Slavism and repeated diatribes against the Poles.[37]

From about 1892/93 onwards Antisemitism was professed by all groups and associations that propagated militant Nationalism, imperial expansion, racism, anti-Socialism, militarism and support for a strong, authoritarian government.[38] The 1892 convention of the *Deutschkonservative Partei* in Tivoli was also indicative of this. There was no doubt an element of opportunism in the party's conversion to open Antisemitism at this stage. But a decision had to be taken. Antisemitism was by then strongly associated with everything the conservatives stood for. It became increasingly inseparable from their anti-modernism and the social and economic program of their party. With or without the "Antisemitic clause", so to speak, the Conservatives were clearly a part of the Antisemitic sentiment in the country, and their own initial lack of enthusiasm was soon compensated by the establishment of the militant *Bund der Landwirte,* savagely propagating its Antisemitic views.[39]

Antisemitism was not only associated with nationalist foreign policy, protectionist economic policies, or corporative social reform demands. It was also a part of an ethos, an element of a moral outlook. A good example is the Antisemites' views on women and on women's rights. *Deutschtum* was a virile cult, and while German women were likewise expected to manifest a proper German spirit in fulfilling their various roles, they could not possibly be regarded as equals or take any part in the political life of the nation. Women, like Jews, ran the argument, lacked the required ethical consciousness and moral vigor characteristic of German men. Thus, Antisemitism and Antifeminism were almost invariably combined in Imperial Germany. Both were elements of an anti-emancipatory culture shared by a majority of German men in the pre-war years.[40]

---

37 Wertheimer, *The Pan-German League,* 90–110.
38 Lcvy chooses to take at face value both the attacks of extreme Antisemites on these associations and the reservations of several of their leaders *vis-a-vis* the politics of the Antisemitic political parties. See his *The Downfall of the Antisemitic political Parties,* 127–129. He seems to disregard the antisemitic tones and overtones in these organizations as shown by Pulzer, *The Rise of political Antisemitism,* 226–228, and Jochmann, "Struktur und Funktion des Antisemitismus", 444–445, 464–472.
39 See Pulzer, *The Rise of Political Antisemitism,* 118–126; and Puhle, *Agrarische Interessenpolitik,* 111–140.
40 For the position of Antisemites on the *Frauenfrage* see, for example, Lange, *Reines Deutschtum,* 166; Frymann, 'Wenn ich der Kaiser war', 118–122. Willy Haas, 'Die Frauenhasser und der Antisemitismus', in *Eckart Jahrbuch,* 1964/1965, 68–80; Richard J. Evans, *The Feminist Movement*

Thus, Antisemitism was neither identical with the overall "Germanic culture" of the *Reich*, nor was it merely an element within it. Being mainly verbal and of little *practical* importance in deciding the more crucial issues of the day, it was particularly well placed to take on a symbolic value. By the end of the nineteenth century it had become a cultural code. Professing Antisemitism became a sign of identity, of one's belonging to a specific cultural camp. It was a way of communicating an acceptance of a particular set of ideas and a preference for specific social, political and moral norms. Contemporaries, living and acting in Imperial Germany, learned to decode the message. It became a part of their language, a familiar and convenient symbol.

III. How did Antisemitism come to play so central a role in the culture of Imperial Germany? What was the process by which it was transferred into a symbol, a short-hand label for an entire set of ideas and attitudes, having little if anything to do with direct affection or dislike of Jews? A focus on the tedious question *how*, for once neglecting the far more inspiring search for origins and causes, may help to provide a clue for understanding the Antisemitism of the day. "True believers" can perhaps only be dealt with by applying the tools of psychology. But the majority of followers were not of the fanatical type. Their commitment to Antisemitism ranged from enthusiasm to sheer conformity. For the study of these men, on both the personal and the social level, sidestepping the question of motives and concentrating on the dynamics of the cultural processes involved may prove more relevant and perhaps more fruitful.

Seeking the causes of Antisemitism is bound to bring forth concepts of pathology, associated with the vocabulary of fear and anxiety. Literature on Antisemitism, indeed, tends to dwell on "social psychology", on "cultural" or "collective psychopathology", expounding upon the distress of the pre-capitalist classes of society in the age of industrialization.[41] Both the psychological diagnosis and the social and economic analysis may be correct, but the link between disease and symptoms remains obscure. Andrew G. Whiteside, for example, in a biography of Georg Ritter von Schönerer, assures us that "for the artisans, Antisemitism was a derivation of their economic experience".[42] This type of argumentation has become stock in trade for the social historians of Imperial Germany, too. It must,

---

in *Germany 1894–1933*, London 1976, 175–182; and Pulzer, *The Rise of Political Antisemitism*, 221–222.

41 See Saul Friedlaender, *L'Antisemitisme Nazi. Histoire d'une Psychose collectiv*, Paris 1971; Norman Cohn, *Warrant for Genocide*, especially the concluding chapter, "A Case-Study in Collective Psychopathology", 251–268; G. M. Gilbert, *The Psychology of Dictatorship*, New York 1950.

42 Whiteside, *Socialism of Fools*, 81.

however, be stressed that not all artisans seemed to derive Antisemitism from their economic experience, nor did they all go through a similar ordeal during the process of industrialization. Furthermore, there was nothing in their so-called "economic experience" that could by itself provide an explanation for Antisemitism. There was no real clash of interests between artisans and Jews as such, although of course some Jews did come into conflict with some artisans.[43] Even when Antisemitism is considered a particular therapy against generalized distress, there still remains a missing link.[44]

In a classic study of prejudice Gordon W. Allport suggested a series of elements that must all be considered as part of a satisfactory "theory of prejudice".[45] He has constructed a pyramid, placing at its base the wide historical background of conflict between two social, racial or ethnic groups. Proceeding upward he then arrived at an analysis of the socio-economic factors at a concrete time and place, providing the information about specific strains in a particular society. But between this level and the peak of the pyramid, where Allport located the "stimulus object", he has introduced an additional level, that of the cognition process mediating between actual conditions and a particular target of hatred and prejudice. Phenomenology has often been neglected in the study of ideology, and it is a negligence that the research into the nature of Antisemitism can ill afford. Having provided the historical background for the anti-Jewish feelings endemic in the Christian world, having analyzed the particular circumstances in Germany of the late nineteenth century, having disclosed the strains within German society at the time, there still remains the task of explaining the process by which a particular social element in this society first came to blame the Jews for all hardship, for everything evil in its environment, and then gradually to identify their resentment of Jews with an overall worldview and accept Antisemitism as a cognitive label for it.

There is only one way by which this complex task can be avoided. Only if one assumes that the Antisemites' claims were truthful, that Jews were in fact identical with exploitative capitalism and the decline of the pre-industrial modes of production and the moral code associated with it, and finally with corruption and social disintegration. Only then is one exempt from the effort to show how men, who were perhaps not sufficiently alert to the dangers of indoctrination but who were not necessarily psychopaths or morally inept, succumbed to the patently

---

[43] See essay no. 2. above.
[44] Dealing with ideology in general, Clifford Geertz has shown the insufficiency of both the "interest theory" and the "strain theory" in explaining the rise of a particular ideology in a concrete historical situation. See his "Ideology as a Cultural System", 47–57.
[45] Gordon W. Allport, *The Nature of Prejudice,* 2nd edn., New York 1958. See for the following, 201–208.

false world-view of Antisemitism. Even assertion of the partial accuracy of this view, questionable and unproven, does not provide a sufficient explanation.[46]

Antisemitism was not a direct reaction to actual circumstances. In fact, men do not react directly to events. Through a process of conceptualization and verbalization men construct an interpretation of their experience, and it is only to this man-made conception of reality that they are then capable of responding. Any interpretation of reality is an independent, creative product of the human mind, and it is often all the more powerful for being partially or entirely false.[47] In order to provide the link between conditions of stress and the particular response of many Germans to these condition during the late nineteenth century, we must probe not only into the actual circumstances of the time but also into the process of cognition which helped interpret, and in its own way also create these circumstances. We must probe into the process of symbolic formulation that produced the Antisemitic ideology and gave it its cultural role.

The association between hatred of Jews and other social or political views can be easily traced back to the first half of the nineteenth century, and many such links existed much earlier, too. In her unsurpassed work on the beginning of political Antisemitism in Germany between 1815 and 1850, Eleonore Sterling has shown the various ways by which anti-Jewish attitudes were combined with a variety of social and political positions. By the first half of the nineteenth century, she claims, *Judenhass* was made a part of a special brand of liberalism, and was congruous with the most extreme left-wing radicalism as well as with "*christlich-germanischer Kons*ervatismus" and an emerging "Germanomanie".[48] After the middle of the century Antisemitism was increasingly linked to anti-emancipatory attitudes, and became almost a permanent ally of *anti*-liberalism and anti-capitalism. It remained, however, ambiguous and diffused in character. In the 1850s Wilhelm Riehl detested Jews because he saw them as a proletarian element, a rootless unattached horde.

---

[46] No serious historian of Antisemitism has argued in this vein, although Arendt's arguments occasionally seem to point in this direction. Partially this is accepted by Stern, *Gold and Iron*, 461–531, concerning the role of the Jews in the development and practice of finance capitalism, and by Saul Friedlander, *Some Aspects of the Historical Significance of the Holocaust*, Institute of Contemporary Jewry, Jerusalem 1977, 29–38, concerning the Jews as revolutionaries.

[47] This view of human action and thought was put forward in a detailed form by Ernst Cassirer in *Die Philosophie der symbolischen Form*, 3 vols., Berlin 1923–1929. In a concise form Cassirer's theory is given in his *Language and Myth*, New York 1946. See also Susan Langer, *Philosophy in a New Key*, 4th edn., Cambridge Mass. 1960. The theory of symbolic form has affected a number of disciplines, but although anthropological thought is profoundly influenced by it, history remained virtually untouched.

[48] Eleonore Sterling, *Judenhass. Die Anfänge des politischen Antisemitismus in Deutschland (1815–1850)*, 2nd edn., Frankfurt a. Main 1969, especially 77–129.

At about the same time Gustav Freytag depicted the selfish, calculating Jewish merchant and Wilhelm Raabe the cynical, destructive Jewish intellectual.[49] Jews were hated because they were different and poor and because they were different and rich. Some dreaded the impoverished Jewish peddler, others the wealthy Jewish banker. During the century of emancipation Jew-baiting was often but by no means always related to anti-emancipatory views. Later in the century, and well into the twentieth, anti-Jewish feelings remained endemic and ambivalent, but a pattern was made increasingly clear. It was after emancipation had been achieved that Antisemitism gradually came to be inseparable from its negation. The necessary climate was created with the onset of economic depression in 1873, and the process itself was then detected and exploited by a number of successful publicists especially in the late 1870s. By correctly assessing the atmosphere in the *Reich*, they managed to formulate the cognitive link between anti-Jewish sentiment and an emerging Germanic ideology, a nationalist anti-modern *Weltanschauung*, a unique *Staatskultur* in a new *Kulturstaat*.[50] It was the strength of this cognitive link that at a later stage made possible the transfer of Antisemitism into a shorthand substitute for an entire culture.

IV. Wilhelm Marr is known in the historiography of nineteenth-century Germany as the man who first launched the term *"Antisemitismus"* and popularized it.[51] The new term was enormously successful. Within a few months it had acquired a complex meaning, far exceeding its direct communicative value. It became an important element in the *creation* and *formulation* of a unique world-view. Initially, Marr and his associates sensed the need for a term that would supply a substitute for *Judenhass*, *Judenverfolgung* and *Judenfeindlichkeit*. Significantly, the new term did not refer directly to Jews or to Judaism. It spelled an opposition to "Semitism" – an abstraction of all the presumed qualities of the presumed Semitic race. The Jews, according to all authorities, constituted only one segment of the Semites, and scientific knowledge of Semitic qualities was meagre enough to allow the term a full measure of ambiguity.

---

[49] See George L. Mosse, "The Image of the Jew in German Popular Culture: Felix Dahn and Gustav Freytag", in: *LBJ Year Book II* (1957) 218–227; and Ernst Kohn-Bramstedt, *Aristocracy and the Middle Classes in Germany. Social Types in German Literature 1830–1900*, London 1937, 132–149.
[50] The best account of the economic depression of the 1870s is Rosenberg, *Bismarckzeit*, 22–57.
[51] On Marr see Moshe Zimmermann, *Wilhelm Marr: the patriarch of Anti-Semitism*, New York 1986. See also the discussion in Alexander Bein, "Der moderne Anti-Semitismus und seine Bedeutung für die Judenfrage", in: *Vieteljahrshefte für Zeitgeschichte*, VI (1958), 340–360; Reinhard Rürup and Thomas Nipperdey, "Antisemitismus", in: *Geschichtliche Grundbegriffe. Historisches Lexikon zur politisch-sozialen Sprache*, ed. Otto Brunner et al., vol. I, Stuttgart 1972, 129.

Marr's first "Antisemitic" publication was entitled: D e r *Sieg des Judenthums über das Germanenthum* and its content suggests some of the qualities of the cognitive abstraction which culminated in the later use of the new term. Marr had agitated against Jews as early as the 1850s, while he was still a left-liberal member of the Hamburg legislature.[52] By 1879, choosing new tactics, he wrote:

> I am neither inspired by the remotest hatred of Jews, nor by any confessional hatred against them, or by any national or racial hate . . . I too have violently polemicized against Judasim, but I admit my mistake . . . My politics was an anachronism[53]

Regardless of the way we choose to explain the psychological make-up of a Wilhelm Marr, his repeated assertion that "I cherish not the slightest animosity against the Jews" is not only ludicrous but also indicative.[54] It may hint at the nature of his personal pathology, but it also tells us something about the social atmosphere in which he operated. A direct attack on Jews, as individuals or as a community, had proven ineffective in the fight to prevent emancipation. In a society that professed a general liberal attitude, such "medieval" superstitions were bound to arouse contempt and opposition. Marr sought to launch a new kind of attack by suggesting a new name for an old phenomenon, but by doing so he in effect *created* a new one.

The first stage in the process of abstraction was quite familiar to nineteenth century readers of various schools and persuasions. It was achieved by shifting the center of attentions from Jews to Judaism.[55] In order to avoid misunderstanding, Marr was quick to declare his *"nicht confessioneller Standpunkt"*, and secure himself against any religious or theological interpretation of his views. Judaism for him was more than a collective name for Jews. It was an abstraction of everything he abhorred, the opposite of another, equally ambiguous abstraction – *Deutschtum*. Even so, *Judentum* was still too specific. Its link with living Jews was too immediate, and it was therefore inappropriate for Marr's purposes. Semitism provided sufficient, though indirect indication of Marr's real target, but it was also conveniently inaccurate, enabling him to infuse it with meaning that transcended hatred of Jews yet elegantly became identical with it. A new term was needed to express the symbolic process through which anti-Jewish attitudes were made analogous for a whole series of other views.

---

52 See Levy, *The Downfall of the Antisemitic political Parties*, 19–20.
53 Wilhelm Marr, *Der Sieg des Judenthums über das Germanenthum. Vom nicht-confessionellen Standpunkt aus betrachtet*, 8th edn., Berlin 1879, 38–39.
54 Ibid, 40.
55 This had often been done as early as the 1840s by the left Hegelians as well as by Karl Marx himself. See his "Zur Judenfrage", in *Marx-Engels-Werk*, vol. I, 576–606.

The term had, of course, other advantages that made it attractive to contemporaries. Above all, it implied a pretentious scientific theory of race, and carried with it the prestige of scientific terminology. At the outset, a link between Antisemitism and racism has been established, together with a claim for scientific objectivity and truth. The construction "ismus" suggested an affinity, in scope if not indeed in content, with "Liberalismus", "Konservatismus" or "Sozialismus". Like them Antisemitism was expected to provide a total philosophy, a full and elaborated world-view. The tenacity of the term and the various ways it has been used, outside its original context in late nineteenth-century Europe, eventually reduced it to a synonym of *Judenhass*. This, however, was not its original meaning. At the very least Antisemitism did not mean *only* hatred of Jews. It was not Jew-baiting made respectable, but hatred of Jews made symbolical.

The first stage of development, therefore, was at the level of name-giving. The next was achieved by supplying the appropriate slogans. Otto Glagau had been a journalist with liberal preferences even more comprehensive than in Marr's case. His reasons for deserting the liberal camp and for developing a passionate hatred of Jews are of little interest in our context.[56] He began as an independent pamphleteer in 1876, writing a series of articles for the *Gartenlaube* under the title: *Der Börsen- und Gründungsschwindel in Berlin,* and followed it up in 1878 with *Der Bankerott des Nationalliberalismus und die 'Reaktion'.* In both pamphlets the collapse of the stock-exchange as well as the entire operation of banking and capitalism was blamed upon the Jews, and as Glagau was more involved in the daily social and economic events of his day than Marr, he soon seized upon a theme which had been present but remained marginal in Marr's analysis. First, linking Jews with the hated "Manchesterism", Glagau then singled out the Jewish question as the center of a far more general *soziale Frage*, and ended by triumphantly identifying the two.

The label "social question" was a generalized way of referring to a variety of social issues debated in Germany from the early nineteenth century onwards, with the focus of public attention shifting from one to another according to circumstances. For men who were disillusioned with both the promises of liberalism and the inaction of government, and who refused to adopt Socialism, the *soziale Frage* increasingly became the focus of their unease and a source of confusion and disorientation. In 1879 Glagau's third pamphlet was published dealing with

---

56 On Otto Glagau see Pulzer, *The Rise of Political Antisemitism,* 88–90; Massing, *Rehearsal for Destruction,* 10–14; Levy, *The Downfall of the Antisemitic political Parties,* 13–16. On Glagau see also the following essay by Henry Wassermann, "Jews and Judaism in the Gartenlaube", in: *Leo Baeck Year Book*, XXX, 47–60.

Deutsches Handwerk und Historisches Burgertum.[57] In it he managed to coin the slogan that contributed more than anything to his reputation as the leading Antisemite of his time. This work, dealing primarily with the history and possible future of the craftsmen in Germany, ended with a call to *all* working men to unite against the degradation of human labor and particularly against the dominance of a certain "foreign race". "Die soziale Frage ist die Judenfrage" (The social question is the Jewish question), he concluded, and apparently the slogan was placed in the right context and launched at the right time. It soon became a cornerstone of modern Antisemitism, linking a specific view of social reality and a particular method in attempting to improve it with open and virulent antagonism to Jews.

The combination was not new, but this successful slogan made it far more powerful and lasting. Glagau sensed the cultural disorientation of craftsmen and other *Mittelständler* in Germany and diagnosed their dilemma.[58] In their search for a new direction Glagau's Antisemitism came at an opportune moment. It offered a simple context within which distress and hardship could be perceived and it proved stronger than the evidence of reality.

Glagau had produced an analogy; he created a metaphor. As in poetry, so too in the language of politics, it is the *"wrong* metaphor" that may prove most potent.[59] Clearly, the social question in Germany was not and had never been identical with the so-called Jewish question. If Otto Glagau himself was not aware of his "mistake", artisans, retailers and other lower middle-class men certainly knew better. Nevertheless, it worked. It was endlessly repeated and eventually helped to achieve, by a process which Kenneth Burke has called an "associative merger", the link between the social critique prevalent in *Mittelstand* circles and Antisemitism.[60]

Writing of another metaphor in a different context, Clifford Geertz commented:

> The power of metaphor derives precisely from the interplay between the discordant meaning it symbolically coerces into a unitary conceptual framework and from the degree to which that coercion is successful in overcoming the psychic resistance such semantic tension inevitably generates in anyone in a position to perceive it. When it works, a metaphor transforms a *false* identification into an apt analogy; when it misfires it is a mere extravagance.[61]

---

[57] 5th edn., Osnabrück 1879.
[58] On the situation of the master-artisans see my book, *The Rise of Popular Anti-modernism* in *Germany. The Urban Master Artisans, 1873–1896*, Princeton 1978.
[59] See Walker Percey, "Metaphor as Mistake", in: *Sewanee Review*, LXVI (1958), 79–99; and Geertz's discussion of the "slave-labour act", 57–70.
[60] Kenneth Burke, "The Rhetoric of Hitler's Battle", in: *The Philosophy of Literary Form*, 3rd edn., Berkeley 1973, 200–207; See also H. D. Lasswell, "The Language of Politics", in Lasswell et al., *Language of Politics*, New York 1949, 12–13.
[61] Geertz, 59.

For many in Glagau's Germany his metaphor was clearly a misguided extravagance, "demagogy" in the language of the time.[62] But for segments of the *Mittelstand* and for others who were in search of a conceptual framework within which to comprehend unwanted social and economic change it could provide the much sought-after clue. For them overcoming the "psychic resistance" created by Glagau's patently false metaphor was amply rewarded by a relaxation of other tensions, by providing a solution to far more pressing needs.

In his memoirs Hellmut von Gerlach recalled Glagau's influence upon his intellectual development:

> His slogan was: 'The social Question is the Jewish Question'. 'The social Question' stood for me in the forefront of my interests. Glagau had invented an ingenious medicine for solving it: Get rid of the Jews and the social question is solved! Well then, I went to him in order to absorb this social wisdom from the source.[63]

Glagau's slogan was "wrong", but it was simple, elegant and extremely suggestive. It was the very stuff of propaganda, and it was effective.

Another measure of the success of this slogan can be gained by a look at an interview given by the aged Adolph Wagner to Hermann Bahr in 1893. Wagner, himself among the first to link Antisemitism with Social Conservatism, repeatedly sought to dissociate himself from the popular identification of the social question with the Jewish question. He thought it necessary to stress that: "I consider the Antisemitism which mixes up the social question with the Jewish question as false."[64] But by then, through endless repetition, its truthfulness was taken for granted by many. Virulent attacks on Capitalism, on Socialism and the demands for social reforms along corporatist lines were invariably associated with Antisemitism. The slogan replaced reality. The link was made as a matter of course. It became part of the prevailing culture.

V. Marr and Glagau were instrumental in creating the vocabulary of this culture, but it was historian Heinrich von Treitschke who first achieved the integration of all its elements. The significance of Treitschke's writings on the Jewish question has often been noted. It has been rightly claimed that Treitschke made Antisemitism *"salonfähig"* in bourgeois society and openly introduced it into German universities. On the cultural, phenomenological level Treitschke's contribution was equally significant.

---

62 See the anti-antisemitic declaration of notables in the *National-Zeitung*, Berlin, 14th November 1880; and *Preussische Jahrbücher*, LXXXI (1893), 385–387.
63 Hellmut von Gerlach, *Von Rechts nach Links*, 110–111.
64 Hermann Bahr, *Der Antisemitismus. Ein internationales Interview*, Berlin 1893, 76.

In his *History of the German People in the Nineteenth Century*, his lecture courses on politics and his articles in the *Preussische Jahrbücher* Treitschke built up a complex of ideas which were to constitute the essence of a unique German ideology for decades to come. His popularity derived from his unfailing ability to sense the mood of his audience and his talent for bringing together the different issues uppermost in their minds. He gave the best available expression to a cluster of attitudes that was then gradually crystallizing into a unique world-view. Treitschke succeeded in indicating the intellectual, political and moral boundaries of a new ideology and in sketching the contours of a culture within which it was to flourish. Unlike most of the publicists who wrote in the same tradition and had arrived at a similar position by the late 1870s, Treitschke had the intellectual stature needed to link the German idealist and historicist tradition with a new nationalism, applying a philosophy of history and a unique ethical system in an attempt to provide a suitable interpretation of German history, an outline of a program for the present and an inspiring vision of the future.[65]

Treitschke's first article dealing with Jews and Antisemitism gives an excellent exposition of his overall social, political and cultural position.[66] It is dated 15th November 1879, and opens with an analysis of world affairs. Treitschke reiterates the familiar theme of German isolation in world politics and denounces the suspiciousness of other nations. This state of affairs, Treitschke believed, made the need for a strong state all the more urgent; a state based upon a "true harmony between the Crown and the Volk", as he put it.[67] A debating parliament was not only an unnecessary luxury, it was entirely foreign to the Germans, arousing only contempt among them. Instead of democratic demagogism Treitschke offered a therapy in the form of a rising consciousness of the *Volk*, which alone could withstand the tide of a "weichliche Philanthropie" and devastating cosmopolitanism.[68] Continuing in the same vein Treitschke turned to the genuine mass antagonism towards Jews, characterizing it as an encouraging "Symptom der Zeit". Praising the instincts of the masses he had so often derided himself, Treitschke himself was perhaps intuitively made aware of the immense potential of anti-Jewish propaganda and its

---

[65] For an anthology of the controversy around Treitschke's articles on the Jewish question see *Der Berliner Antisemitismusstreit*, ed. Walter Boehlich et al., Frankfurt a. Main 1965. On the development of Treitschke's historical and political views see Andreas Dorpalen, *Heinrich van Treitschke*, New Haven 1957; and Georg Iggers, "Heinrich von Treitschke", in: *Deutsche Historiker*, vol. II, ed. H. U. Wehler, Göttingen 1971.
[66] "Unsere Aussichten", reprinted in Treitschke's *Deutsche Kämpfe. Schriften zur Tagespolitik*, Leipzig 1896, 1–28.
[67] Ibid, 18.
[68] Ibid, 22–23.

possible link with other components of his world-view. The Jews, Treitschke explained, were a danger to the "new German life, correctly realized". They were the opposite of everything German, and in their very presence a danger to German culture. Jews stood for *"Lug und Trug"* and for sheer materialism in opposition to the "Joy of Labor, [characteristic] of our Volk." The entire intellectual community in Germany, Treitschke declared, had arrived at the unavoidable conclusion: *"Die Juden sind unser Unglülck"*.[69]

Treitschke not only achieved the "associative merger" necessary for creating the link between Antisemitism and *his* special brand of Nationalism, he also applied the familiar propaganda technique of the "wrong metaphor". The Jewish question was not one problem among others, according to him, but simply the essence of all evil. A quick turn of the pen made a single problem stand for all others. The Jews were made identical with every negative aspect of German life, or were seen as a mere symptom of far more serious ills. By a simple technique an unsatisfactory situation was at least made comprehensible. A strong opposition to government policies could now be coupled with an idolizing of the state. The responsibility for weakness of character, for folly and failure, was placed where it hurt the least – at the margin, upon the outcast, on the Jews.

The effect of Treitschke's writing on the *Judenfrage* was all the more striking because he had not been previously known as an Antisemite. During the 1860s he repeatedly complained in his letters of the blatant intolerance towards Jews that he had encountered in academic and student circles, and like his liberal colleagues objected to coarse anti-Jewish propaganda. Later, the anti-Bismarck anti-Jewish campaign of the mid 1870s appeared dangerously unpatriotic to him. But with the turn to conservatism in the years 1878/1879, Treitschke, too, began to "see the light". He left the National Liberal Party, supported Bismarck's anti-Socialist legislations and adopted an openly Antisemitic stand.[70] It was not an anti-Jewish passion which made him defend his Antisemitic views in so many polemical articles, but the realization of the link between it and his overall social, political and moral stand. He perceived the affinity, and in turn helped in making it more "natural" and self-evident. Treitschke joined Antisemitism with the emerging ideology of German Nationalism. He sensed not merely the tactical advantage of this merger but its intrinsic logic. His anti-Socialist, anti-democratic, anti-emancipatory ideology in Germany of the late 1870s was not complete without Antisemitism.

---

69 Ibid, 28.
70 Dorpalen, *Heinrich van Treitschke*, XX.

By the late 1870s the entire arsenal of this ideology was forged. The combination of elements barely apparent in 1848 gained a clear expression in the works of Marr, Glagau, Treitschke, as well as in the writings of Paul de Lagarde, Eugen Dühring and a host of lesser publicists in the late 1870s and early 1880s. By the mid-1890s the cluster of ideas, values and norms created during the first decade of the *Reich* was absorbed by a society predisposed to it, and became a unique popular culture. What was forged in the heat of passion in the 1870s became a matter of course by the 1890s. Antisemitism was preached with true passionate hate in the earlier period, while it became a part of a whole cultural cluster towards the end of the century. Thus, it is interesting to compare Lagarde's anti-Jewish feelings with Langbehn's attitude only twelve years later.[71] Lagarde's Antisemitism had been intense and fanatical. Langbehn's could be proclaimed with composure and what seemed like a measure of indifference. The worst social and economic crisis of the 1870s was by then over. The possible therapeutic function of Antisemitism was losing significance. Meanwhile, however, it became a part of the new Imperial culture, a permanent companion of aggressive Nationalism and anti-modernism.

The link was made so self-evident that even men of Jewish origin often succumbed to its internal logic. Maximilian Harden is an interesting case in point. While he only rarely criticized political Antisemitism, anti-Jewish comments were rather common on the pages of *Die Zukunft*.[72] During the Dreyfus affair Harden distinguished himself by a series of articles, fiercely attacking the Dreyfusards.[73] His attitude gave rise to two conflicting interpretations. Theodor Lessing, in a book on Jewish self-hatred, used Harden as an example of this peculiar Jewish pathology, grouping him with Walther Rathenau and Otto Weininger. Others have defended Harden against this charge by stressing his consistent fight for justice and his independent, free-thinking individuality.[74] Commentators agree, however, that Harden's attitude to Jews was primarily an outgrowth of the way in which he conceived the struggle between the so-called forces of light and darkness. The Dreyfus affair was for him – surely, not only for him – symbolic of this fight; an indication of a historic battle between "traders" and "warriors". He took sides against Dreyfus

---

[71] See Paul de Lagarde, *Deutsche Schriften*, 3rd edn., Munich 1937, 30, 41, 421–422; and Julius Langbehn, *Rembrandt als Erzieher*, Leipzig 1922, 36–37, 242–244. See also Stern, *The Politics of Cultural Despair*, 61–64, 139–145.
[72] *Die Zukunft*, 1892, 447–460; 1893, 93–96.
[73] Ibid, 1898, 369–379, 417–436; 1899, 481–487, 521–529.
[74] Sec Theodor Lessing, *Der jüdische Selbsthass*, Berlin 1930,167–194; Harry F. Young, *Maximilian Harden. Censor Germaniae. The Critic in Opposition from Bismarck to the Rise of Nazism*, The Hague 1959, 6.

because he sensed that in France too, the Jewish question had become a symbol of the struggle between two political directions, two trends of thought, indeed two cultures.[75] The analogy to German conditions was all too obvious. The Dreyfusards were republicans, democrats, modernists. Harden was not, and he could not therefore support them. Lessing himself indicated that there was nothing more sacred for Harden than Germany.[76] During the following war years he became an annexationist and a pan-German. His attitude towards Jews was a corollary of his other views. He felt compelled to take what under the circumstances amounted to an Antisemitic stand, despite its embarrassing and eventually tragic consequences. Harden sensed the dilemma when he complained to Hermann Bahr of being labelled an Antisemite only "because I am against the intermediary commercial spirit, against the mob in the stock exchange market, and against the lazy Egotism of the bourgeoisie!" And he then added:

> Am I responsible for the fact that one is therefore immediately labelled an Antisemite? Am I responsible for the fact that the Jews always declare solidarity with the Wolffs, the Leipziger and the Sommerfelds? Am I responsible for the fact that one is not allowed to say anything against the mercantile spirit without immediately being counted among the Ahlwardts?[77]

Such a separation of issues seemed by then no longer possible. The lines of conflict were clearly drawn, and one had to accept either modernism with emancipation or a n t i - m o d e r n i s m with Antisemitism. This was taken for granted by most Germans, but often posed a particular problem for many patriotic, nationalist Jews, as well as for a minority of Germans in the emancipatory camp. The role of Antisemitism as a cultural signifier was gradually realized by contemporaries during the 1890s. In Bahr's interviews this became a repeated theme. Theodor Barth himself, a progressive politician, asserted that Jews were taken as a general symbol of the time, and the aged Theodor Mommsen, surprisingly optimistic in his hope for the inevitable disappearance of Antisemitism, characterized it as a hatred not of Jews but of *"Bildung, Freiheit und Menschlichkeit"*.[78] Eduard Bernstein in an article in the *Neue Zeit* warned against the simplification of considering the opposition to Antisemitism as *philo*-semitism. Mehring's analysis of the Jewish question, he claimed, was no longer appropriate. Since the battle had become one of slogans, he added, it was urgent to take special precautions to avoid any possible identification of Social Democracy with the Antisemitic camp.[79] Just as an Antisemitic stand in

---

75 This is emphasized by Arendt, *Totalitarianism*, 89–120.
76 Lessing, *Der jüdische Selbsthass*, 189, 194–197.
77 Bahr, *Der Antisemitismus*, 50–51.
78 Ibid, 13, 28–29.
79 *Die Neue Zeit*, XI, 2 (1893–1894).

Wilhelminian Germany meant in effect a generally anti-emancipatory position and a resistance to the various manifestations of "the modern social and political struggle for freedom", so did an opposition to Antisemitism meant a stand *for* emancipation, not of Jews alone but of society at large.[80] The nationalist, state-supporting patriot could hardly afford to remain neutral on the Jewish question and almost invariably professed his Antisemitism. His opponents could not in good conscience afford to comply with it.

Emancipation and Antisemitism became the signposts of two sub-cultures, co-existing in Imperial Germany. Wilhelminian society preserved some hope of a compromise, but during the Weimar years the gulf between the two became ever deeper. Meanwhile, Hitler and his associates began to infuse the milder "Germanic culture" with a new radical meaning. For them Antisemitism first gained in intensity and political significance, and was then fundamentally transformed. It ceased to denote the acceptance of the old nationalist, conservative, anti-emancipatory world-view of pre-war Germany and came to be associated with the politics of violence, terror and extermination. Cultural symbols, however, have a curious tenacity. These continued to be circulated within the new social, political and cultural context. Indeed, the continuity between Imperial Germany and the post-war years was not primarily based on the existence of old political parties and social associations, but above all on the persistence of culture and its unique vocabulary. While the Nazis revolutionized the so-called "Germanic ideology", they continued to use old terms and concepts. Antisemitism for them meant a battle cry with direct implications for action, a program of intimidation and final annihilation. But for millions of Germans and for the majority of German Jews it remained for too long no more than a cultural signal. Decoding it they felt secure, although often uneasy, within a familiar cluster of views and attitudes. They were unaware that the language had changed and that they were no longer in a position to decipher the message.

---

80 On the concept of emancipation see Jacob Katz, "The Term 'Jewish Emancipation': Its Origins and Historical Impact", in: *Emancipation and Assimilation. Studies in Modem Jewish History*, Cambridge Mass. 1964, 1–16; and Reinhard Koselleck, "Emanzipation", in: *Geschichtliche Grundbegriffe*, vol. II, 153–170.

5 The Written Matter and the Spoken Word: On the Gap Between Pre-1914 and Nazi Antisemitism

I. Almost without exception, general histories of National Socialism and especially of the Nazi policies concerning the "Jewish question" begin with the story of nineteenth-century Antisemitism. Conversely, most works on Antisemitism in pre-Nazi Germany see in it a prelude to the Holocaust. Modern German history is then scrutinized for the manifestations of Antisemitism, always unique in their radicalism and pregnant with destructive implications. For some, continuity is established by perceiving the history of Antisemitism as a circular phenomenon, a series of historical repetitions, reenacting in different guises one permanent, central theme. For others, the link is made through the paradigm of a dynamic process, an acceleration inevitably culminating in catastrophe. The fanaticism and finality of the Nazi case is always acknowledged, but it is rarely studied apart from its so-called "origins."

Historians are, of course, repeatedly confronted with the issue of continuity versus change, and it would be banal to repeat the simple truth that these are always bound together. Nevertheless, the balance is perpetually a matter of controversy; and the balance normally established between continuity and change in the case before us is, I believe, inadequate. By practically obliterating the elements of novelty and overestimating the forces of continuity, we have too often obscured important issues. Both the study of the pre-Nazi tradition of German Antisemitism and the issue of the Nazi attitudes and behavior toward the Jews have thus been forced into preconceived patterns, missing, so it appears to me, much of the essence of historical developments. It is the proper balance between continuity and change, permanence and novelty, that must be sought; and it is this balance that I would here like to try and redress – yet once again.

The stress on permanence and continuity is especially evident among Jewish historians.[1] The most extreme position was taken by Benzion Dinur, writing during the Second World War and perhaps before the magnitude of the Holocaust had been fully realized. In "Exiles and Annihilation," Dinur offered a circular view of Jewish history, in which each center of Jewish life and culture was in its turn destroyed, only to be reconstituted elsewhere – another heir to an awesome tradition,

---

[1] See the essays on Antisemitism from Antiquity till today, edited by Shmuel Almog, *Jew-Hatred through the Ages* [Hebrew], Jerusalem 1980; in it especially Israel Guttman, "On the Character of Antisemitism according to the Nazi Version," 353–387.

a link in a perpetual chain. Within this view the Holocaust repeated, admittedly in a modern and unusually efficient manner, the pattern of the past.[2] For Shmuel Ettinger, the explanation of the permanence of Antisemitism lies not in the uniqueness of Jewish history, but in the existence of a Jewish stereotype as a permanent feature of Western culture. Reappearing in times of crisis, it transforms a latent hatred into the various forms of active persecution.[3] Salo Baron, to take another example, used both the permanent peculiarity of Jewish status among the nations and the others' inevitable "dislike of the unlike" in his "theory of Antisemitism."[4] In all these versions Nazi performance, despite its totality and scope, is yet another chapter in the history of anti-Jewish measures – a modern version of old pogroms, expulsions, mass executions. Other historians prefer development, dynamism, growth, to repetition and permanence. For Yaakov Talmon, Nazi Antisemitism was not yet another Antisemitic episode but the culmination of a long development. He traced the links between Richard Wagner and Houston Stewart Chamberlain on the one hand, and Alfred Rosenberg or Adolf Hitler on the other, and followed the intensification of anti-Jewish sentiments and the ripening of the "exterminatory ideology." It was the development of a radical ideology which, according to him, systematized the wishes and the ideas of the Antisemites and made them a basis for the eventual Nazi policy of annihilation. In his last book, Talmon restated in a slightly different form his diagnosis of over twenty-five years before: Antisemitism, he concluded, was a "centuries-old neurosis culminating in a demonic and murderous madness."[5]

Using a culturally more diffused view, taking into account more than the highlights of the Antisemitic literary ideology, George Mosse too presented the Nazi case as the end result of a long acceleration. Antisemitism, he explained, was the center of the "German Ideology," an institutionalized part of the *völkisch* movement, and finally the basic reality of Nazism. Conversely, National Socialism was fulfillment of a promise, the realization of a dream.[6] Yaakov Katz, in his own book on Antisemitism, reached a similar conclusion, despite some reservations and an explicit admission of unease. The theories of racial Antisemitism, he

---

[2] See *Kneset* [Hebrew] 8, 1943–44, 46–60.
[3] See Shmuel Ettinger, *Modern Antisemitism: Studies and Essays* [Hebrew], Tel Aviv 1978.
[4] See his "Changing Patterns of Antisemitism: A Survey," in: *Jewish Social Studies*, XXXVIII, 1, 1976, 5–38.
[5] See especially his essay on the universal significance of Antisemitism, in: Jacob Talmon, *The Unique and the Universal. Some Historical Reflections*, London 1965 and compare with Part 9 in his *The Myth of the Nation and the Vision of Revolution. The Origins of Ideological Polarization in the 20th Century*, London 1981. I am quoting from the Hebrew Edition, 633.
[6] George L. Mosse, *The Crisis of German Ideology: Intellectual Origins of the Third Reich*, New York 1964, 294–311.

finally agreed, "helped to consolidate ideas by making clear thought out of them, transforming them into a plan of execution, eventually carried out by the Nazis."[7]

The sense of self-evidence, characterizing these presentations of the link between pre-Nazi Antisemitism and the extermination of the European Jews is also prevalent among historians outside the Zionist tradition. These, however, usually pay only lip service to the age-old tradition of Antisemitism in Christian Europe, and concentrate instead on the period beginning in the 1870s.[8] Typical, and by now of textbook significance, are Paul Massing's *Rehearsal for Destruction*, and Peter Pulzer's history of *Political Anti-Semitism in Germany and Austria*; but even Hannah Arendt, pointedly stressing the uniqueness of what she introduced as "modern Antisemitism," does not draw a clear line between it and the Nazi phenomenon.[9] In her *Origins of Totalitarianism* she examined the general nature of Antisemitism in post-emancipation, modern Europe, presenting it clearly as a prelude to Nazism. The by now standard work of Helmut Krausnick on the persecution of the Jews in the Third Reich opens characteristically with a review of pre-Nazi Antisemitism in imperial Germany.[10] Thus, while sometimes rejecting the search for roots in the very remote past, most historians accept, almost intuitively, the "origins thesis."

I would like to begin my critique of these positions by quoting at some length from Marc Bloch's *Métier d'historien:*

> The explanation of the very recent in terms of the remotest past, naturally attractive to men who have made of this past their chief subject of research, has sometimes dominated our studies to the point of a hypnosis . . . However, the word "origins" is disturbing, because it is ambiguous. Does it mean simply "beginnings"? That would be relatively clear except that for most historical realities the very notion of a starting-point remains singularly elusive. It is doubtless a matter of definition, but of a definition which it is unfortunately all too easy to forget to give. On the other hand, is "origins" taken to mean the causes? In that case, there will be no difficulties other than those which are always inherent in the nature of causal

---

[7] Jacob Katz, *From Prejudice to Destruction. Antisemitism 1700–1933*, Cambridge Mass. 1982. I quote from the earlier Hebrew edition, 306.

[8] Compare in this context: Reinhard Rürup and Thomas Nipperdey, "Antisemitismus," in: *Geschichtliche Grundbegriffe. Historisches Lexikon zur politisch-sozialen Sprache*, vol. 1, ed. Otto Brunner et al., Stuttgart 1972. For a full bibliography, see the yearly lists in the Leo Baeck Institute Yearbooks (LBIYB), since 1956. See also Ismar Schorsch, "German Antisemitism in the Light of Post-War Bibliography," in: *LBIYB* 1974, 257–271.

[9] Massing's book was first published in New York, 1946, and its title is somewhat misleading. The book treats the continuity issue very carefully. See also Peter Pulzer, *The Rise of Political Antisemitism*, London 1964 and the first edition of Arendt's book, *Totalitarianism*, New York 1951, 3–10.

[10] See especially Krausnick's introduction for his part in H. Krausnick and Martin Broszat, *Anatomy des SS Staat*, Munich 1965.

inquiry (and even more so, no doubt, in the sciences of man.) But there is a frequent cross-contamination of the two meanings, the more formidable in that it is seldom very clearly recognized. In popular usage, an origin is a beginning which explains. Worse still, a beginning which is a complete explanation. There lies the ambiguity, and there the danger![11]

In the post-1945 historiography, German Antisemitism before 1914 has become "a beginning which explains," and too often, indeed, "a beginning which is a complete explanation." It is presented as a necessary condition for the Nazi 'Final Solution and sometimes, though usually not explicitly, as a necessary and sufficient condition – "a complete explanation" in Marc Bloch's terminology.

Allow me to approach the problem from this perspective. In what follows I would like to argue that while on the basis of demonstrable continuity pre-Nazi antisemitism can serve as a useful *background* to the National Socialist rise to power and the Nazi Jewish policies, it should not be construed as an explanation, let alone a *complete explanation*, of these phenomena. The Nazi policy of extermination took shape during the years of the Second World War and never before, within the bounds of the Third German Reich and not elsewhere. If pre-Nazi German Antisemitism actually brought it about, it must have been in itself significantly different from all previous forms of Antisemitism, and unique for its time and its place. But what was novel in the Antisemitism of late nineteenth and early twentieth century Germany, I would attempt to argue, was time specific and grew out of the particular needs and problems of that era. It had little relevance for later events, and in comparison with the contemporary French case even its characteristic features seem to lose much of their uniqueness. Pre-Nazi Antisemitism in Germany, in all its peculiarities, was more akin to the French version of the time than to the later Nazi positions. It can, therefore, serve as a loose "beginning" for National Socialism but not as an explanation for it, as its background but not as its cause. A special "turnabout of meaning," a growth of a new language, and an all-important transition from words into action was required in moving from Marr, Stöcker, and Dühring to Hitler, Goebbels, and Himmler.[12] The explanation of Nazism, therefore, I believe, lies not in the analysis of its so-called origins, but in a fuller and better understanding of its total present.

II. In order to present nineteenth century Antisemitism in Germany as a "beginning" of Nazi Antisemitism, the establishing of any kind of continuity is sufficient.

---

11 Quoted from the English translation: Marc Bloch, *The Historian's Craft*, New York 1953, 29–30.
12 See especially Uriel Tal, "Political faith of Nazism prior to the Holocaust," printed separately by the Chair for Contemporary Jewish History at Tel Aviv University, Tel Aviv 1978, and see above my article "Antisemitism as a Cultural Code,". Here no. 4.

Nazi Antisemitism ought to be shown as touching somehow upon the last link in the chain of earlier forms of anti-Jewish manifestations, through personal contacts, organizational developments, or some apparent ideological borrowing. All these have been exposed by historians, with a fair amount of success. In the realm of ideas historians showed the affinity between Hitler's diatribes against the Jews and the pronouncements of men from Paul de Lagarde to Heinrich Class. It will probably remain unclear how much of these men's works was actually read by Hitler, though his early reliance on Theodor Fritsch is presumably certain. Operating within the postwar context, Hitler employed some new, if not original, themes, especially concerning the links between Jews and bolshevism, or Jews and the revolution in Germany. But with some shifts in emphasis, old Antisemitic claims and prejudices were all there, too. His was a mixture not unlike those dished out to the Munich crowd by other Antisemitic orators.[13]

From a wider perspective, a line of continuous development is likewise not difficult to establish. The old Antisemitic political parties were virtually extinct on the eve of the First World War. But Antisemitism in associations and trade societies, in student organizations and in groups of organized officials, teachers, lawyers, or medical doctors, was rampant. This socially diffused form of Antisemitism, characteristic of the prewar years, can be seen as an early stage in the preparation of popular support of, and compliance with, first the vigorous anti-Jewish tone of the early Nazi propaganda and then with later Nazi actions.[14]

But once this kind of continuity is established, the thread begins to unravel. With similar methods the line of development can easily be traced back to earlier periods and other national environments. Why not, after all, go back to the time of the Black Death or to the writings of Martin Luther? And proceeding through the time of pietism, why not stretch the line to the many-sided manifestations of Antisemitism in nineteenth-century German society? And what about the often latent, but occasionally erupting Antisemitism elsewhere in Europe? Are these not all chapters in the long story of the rise of Nazism?

---

13 See comments in Reginals H. Phelps's introduction to the reprint of his article "Hitler's grundlegende Rede über den Antisemitismus," in: *Vierteljahreshefte für Zeitgeschichte*, 1968, 395–399. And see also Uwe Lohalm, *Völkischer Radikalismus: Die Geschichte des deutschvölkischen Schutz- und Trutzbundes 1919–1923*, Hamburg 1970, 298–301. On Fritsch's influence see also Phelps, "Theodor Fritsch und der Antisemitismus," in: *Deutsche Rundschau* 87, 1961, 442–449.

14 See, above all, Werner Jochmann's two large essays: "Struktur und Funktion des deutschen antisemitismus," in: *Juden in Wilheminischen Deutschland 1890–1914*, eds. Werner Mosse and Arnold Paucker, Tübingen 1976, 389–477, and "Die Ausbreitung des Antisemitismus," in: *Deutsches Judentum in Krieg und Revolution*, eds. Werner Mosse and Arnold Paucker, Tübingen 1971, 409–510.

Historians of Antisemitism do indeed look back to the distant past and beyond the borders of Germany.[15] If the search is for a beginning, there is then little justification in stopping at the establishment of the Bismarckian Reich or in remaining within its borders. If, however, *a beginning* is to be made *an explanation*, then a thousand years of such a beginning, spread across an entire continent, is particularly inappropriate for the task. If modern pre-Nazi Antisemitism is to become the *explanation* of the unique horrors of the Holocaust, not merely its prolonged prelude, then it must be shown as a phenomenon *sui generis*. If German Antisemitism before the First World War is to *explain* the unequaled case of Auschwitz, then it must itself be perceived as unique – both in relation to previous anti-Jewish manifestations and in comparison with contemporary Antisemitism elsewhere. History must seek to account not just – perhaps not even primarily – for the very existence of situations or the actual occurrence of events, but for their existence or occurrence *then and there*.

Much of the historiography of nineteenth-century Antisemitism strives, indeed, to establish the uniqueness of this so-called "modern Antisemitism." Hannah Arendt went so far as to consider the disregard of its peculiarities a cause for the blindness of Jews and non-Jews alike in the face of the approaching Nazi danger.[16] But while for Arendt change resulted from the transformed position of emancipated Jews within the new context of the modern nation-states, most historians diagnose the new beginning in the mid-1870s, when Antisemitism presumably began to show two new traits: it became a platform for political organization, and it was ideologically transformed by the introduction of racial theory. From Stöcker, Böckel and Ahlwardt, through Zimmermann and Förster, modern Antisemitism was operating as a political force, used for the mobilization of the social elements responsive to its manipulation. With Gobineau, Chamberlain, and the biologists, it was finally able to dispense with its religious rationale, and pose as a modern, scientifically based theory, with legitimate constitutional, social, and political implications.

Now, without extensively going into the matter, I would like to suggest that not much can be made of the novelty of modern Antisemitism on these two counts. A political though not a strictly party-political use of Antisemitism was widespread before the 1870s, both in Germany and elsewhere. In an important and little-known book on 1848, Jacob Toury has conclusively shown the force of *political* Antisemitism during the months of this mid-century revolution.[17] Though Antisemitism at the time was spontaneous and popular, usually not reaching the

---

15 See the books mentioned above in notes 1,3,5,7.
16 In her *Origins of Totalitarianism*, New York 1951, 8.
17 Jacob Toury, *Turmoil and Confusion in the Revolution of 1848. The anti-Jewish Riots in the 'Year of Freedom' and their Influence on Modern Antisemitism* [Hebrew] Tel Aviv 1968, and Eleonore

organizational form of a proper political party, its political usefulness was never in doubt after the turbulent revolutionary experience.[18] Neither did political parties in their full modern sense exist under the particular constitutional arrangement of imperial Germany. None of the existing parties by then, including the so-called Antisemitic parties, was entirely devoted to the Jewish issue, and to some degree all were willing to employ the Antisemitic idiom to attract potential voters.[19]

Furthermore, it is sobering to remember that the small Antisemitic parties, all taken together, constituted less than 2.5 percent of the electorate in 1893, and less than 2 percent by 1907, the two peak years of their success. The parties themselves have been grossly overestimated by historians, partly due to the slanted perspective of the post-Nazi era, and partly because of the often eccentric and scandalous behavior of their leading figures.[20] Antisemitism in various social associations and half-political groups was far more important for the fabric of social life in imperial Germany, and of greater importance for later developments. But Antisemitism in these forms was not essentially different from its varied manifestations throughout the century, and indeed even before. Antisemitism, diffused in the various social elements and expressed in their organizations, was not new in the immediate prewar years, nor was it unique to Germany.

Second, racism is often cited as a peculiar trait of German Antisemitism beginning with the last quarter of the nineteenth century – a central heritage to be absorbed by Nazism. But as in the case of the Antisemitic political parties, this aspect too has grown out of proportion. Racism, as a biologically founded social theory, claiming the support of modern science, was indeed a novelty of these years, but its importance for the development of contemporary Antisemitism was overestimated. A reexamination of the writings of the main ideologues of Antisemitism – and here we are primarily dealing with matters of ideology – throws grave doubts on the significance of the purely racial element for their thought processes and the essence of their message. It is true that the vocabulary of Antisemitism had been changing, but only rarely did this entail a corresponding change in content.[21] It was Marc Bloch, again, who commented that, to the great

---

Sterling, *Judenhass. Die Anfänge des politischen Antisemitismus in Deutschland (1815–1850)*, Frankfurt a. M. 1969.
18 Toury, Ibid, 115–119.
19 See in Fritz Specht, *Die Reichstagwahlen von 1867–1897*, Berlin 1898, esp. 503–507; D. Fricke, *Die bürgerlichen Parteien und andere bürgerliche Interessenorganisationen vom Vormärz bis zum Jahre 1914*, vol. 1, (East) Berlin 1968, 36–40, 245–55, 429–31, 754–756, 759–762.
20 Richard S. Levy, *The Downfall of the Antisemitic Political Parties in Imperial Germany*, New Haven 1975.
21 Despite the transition to Racism, the reliance on the religious roots, as well as on the social, economic and cultural motives of Antisemitism continued during the late nineteenth century.

despair of the historian, "men fail to change their vocabulary every time they change their customs."[22] But to add further confusion, men also often *preserve* their customs while changing their vocabulary.

Richard Wagner is an interesting case in point. Wagner's writings are diffused with nationalist-racist concepts. In an interesting interpretation of his anti-Jewish works, Jacob Katz has reargued that, despite this usage, Wagner was never a true racist, though he clearly was an extreme and venomous Antisemite. He apparently was willing to consider, albeit grudgingly, the possibility of the eventual assimilation of the Jews in their environment, thus not sharing a belief in the basic tenet of racism: the incurable, permanent, inborn inferiority of the Jew. But Wagner, like the majority of the Antisemitic ideologues, was not a systematic thinker. He adopted the racist vocabulary when it suited his purpose, and abandoned it as he saw fit.[23] This was the way racism was used by other Antisemites throughout the century: it was no more than a useful instrument for them, an additional weapon in their arsenal of anti-Jewish arguments – a convenient but not indispensable substitute for the outdated categories of religion.

Among the Antisemites, Lagarde explicitly ridiculed the idea of race as "a crude form of materialism, scientifically meaningless."[24] But for the others, too, moral and cultural questions seemed always to have been more crucial than the racial-biological perspective. Even Eugen Düring, who in the title of his main Antisemitic publication claimed to treat the Jewish question as a racial problem, used the term quite arbitrarily. Volk, Nation, and Kultur were all used by him interchangeably with Rasse, and his application of the term *Judenhaftigkeit* virtually emptied the racial argument of all meaning.[25] Wilhelm Marr and Otto Glagau too occasionally vented their rage against the *"verjudeten"* elements in German society, as

---

See Uriel Tal, *Christians and Jews in Germany. Religion, Politics and Ideology in the Second Reich 1870–1914*, Ithaca 1977, and Katz, *From Prejudice to Destruction*, especially Chapter 27 and passim.

22 Bloch, *The Historian's Craft*, 34.
23 For the debate concerning Wagner's racism, see Leon Stein, *The Radical Thinking of Richard Wagner*, New York 1950; R.E. Herzstein, "Richard Wagner at a Crossroad of German Antisemitism," in: *Zeitschrift für die Geschichte der Juden*, no. 2–3, 1967; Dov Kulka, "Richard Wagner und die Anfänge des deutschen Antisemitismus," in: *Bulletin des Leo Baeck Instituts* 19, 1961; Toury, *Turmoil and Confusion*, 153–160; Katz, *From Prejudice to Destruction*, Chapter 15.
24 Quoted by Fritz Stern, *The Politics of Cultural Despair: A Study in the Rise of the Germanic Ideology*, New York 1961, 91–92.
25 Eugen Dühring, *Die Judenfrage als Rassen-, Sitten- und Kulturfrage*, Karlsruhe 1880; Christoph Cobet, *Der Wortschatz des Antisemitismus in der Bismarckzeit*, Munich 1973, 82–94.

despicable and as dangerous as the real, "racial" Jews.²⁶ Finally, here is a passage from the 1910 edition of Theodor Fritsch's *Antisemiten-Katechismus*, the main handbook of the presumably new type of racial Antisemites:

> Thus, it is a superficial and misleading conception to consider the opposition against the Jews as if it merely represents the discharge of a stupid religious or race hatred, while in fact it is a selfless defense, carried out by the highest ideals against an enemy of humanity, respectability and culture.²⁷

III. The uniqueness of late nineteenth-century and early twentieth-century Antisemitism lies neither in its forms of political organization nor in its ideological characteristics. The novel elements in the Antisemitism of this period depended upon the particular needs and difficulties of the time. The significantly new aspects of this Antisemitism were the roles which it had grown to fulfill within the social, political, and cultural systems of imperial Germany. Its functions developed in response to the main issues of late nineteenth-century Germany, and were time-specific – to be explained only by an analysis of the context in which they had emerged.

First, Antisemitism played a constitutive role in the definition of the German self-image, and in rebuilding a German sense of identity after the crisis of unification. A series of basically internal wars, and a reshuffling of borders and constitutional structures created the need for a new type of integration. In the new Bismarckian Reich, Antisemitism was a welcome weapon in welding together the geographically, historically, and socially disparate elements of the German nation. It is, therefore, hardly surprising that the most influential representative of the new Antisemitism was Heinrich von Treitschke, the fervent nationalist and prominent spokesman of German unity under the power domination and the class rule of the Prussian Junker. Treitschke was above all concerned to achieve an internal cohesion in Germany, based on a common consciousness of a unique nationality and culture. He did not hesitate to use anti-Jewish sentiments for the task. Thus, he warned against the undue influence of *Judentum* on "our national life," and the approach of a *"Zeitalter deutsch-jüdischer Mischkultur."* He called for the creation of a *"gekräftigtes Nationalgefühl,"* rejecting any form of *"Doppelnationalität,"* particularly that of the "Jewish-cosmopolitan" type.²⁸ These themes, bound up with Treitschke's contempt for parliamentarism and democratization, had a

---

26 Wilhelm Marr, *Der Sieg des Judenthums über das Germanenthum*, Bern 1897; Otto Glagau, *Der Bankrott des Nationalliberalismus und die Reaktion*, 8th edition, Berlin 1878, passim.
27 The quote is from the 1919 printing of this edition, 20 (The Underlining is mine).
28 The quotes from "Unsere Aussichten" (15th November 1878), reprinted in his book, *Deutsche Kämpfe: Schriften zur Tagesppolitik*, Leipzig 1896, 17–28. See Andreas Dorpalen, *Heinrich von Treitschke*, New Haven 1957.

lasting effect upon a generation of students who were later to become the leadership of the nationalist-imperialist, and almost invariably Antisemitic, movement in the early years of the twentieth century.[29] That was a time of another crisis of self-consciousness and national identity, clumsily covered up by a pompous and irresponsible Weltpolitik. At that time, once again, Antisemitism proved its usefulness as a convenient tool for integration, a complementary sentiment to national pride, an effective addition to a communal sense of uniqueness and superiority.[30]

Second, Antisemitism channeled a growing social malaise and discontent engendered by rapid industrialization and the disappointment with the liberal-capitalist economic system. This was particularly needed following the crash of 1873 and during the following period of deflation and instability up to the mid-1890s.[31] Presenting the Jew as the corrupter of capitalism, and the real destructive force behind liberalism, the new economic order could be attacked without fear of revolution and without inciting class struggle or civil strife. Otto Glagau, who coined the slogan *"Die soziale Frage ist die Judenfrage,"* was second in popularity and influence only to Treitschke. Adolf Stöcker, an eager imitator, was soon to roam the streets of Berlin with a similar message. At a time of economic insecurity and social disorientation it was such slogans that appealed to the German urban *Mittelstand*, providing it with a proper target for venting its anxiety and rage.[32]

Third, Antisemitism had a political role to fulfill, too. Many prominent Antisemites in Bismarckian Germany were trustworthy conservatives, though Stöcker's tactics in Berlin were always suspect in Bismarck's eyes, and even the old Kaiser, whose court chaplain Stöcker was for some years, remained cautious and aloof. But the Antisemitic movement of this early period also included a group of ex-liberals, sometimes even old radicals, with a revolutionary past. Wilhelm Marr was an old forty-eighter, but Glagau and Henrici too had had a previous liberal record. These men represented a considerable segment of German society, especially from among the *Mittelstand*, who were by this time seeking a new political allegiance. After the events of 1848, crafts masters, shop-keepers, small officials, and perhaps also elements of rural Germany, tended to combine political liberalism with a set

---

[29] Compare Helmut von Gerlach, *Von Rechts nach Links*, Zürich 1937, 110ff. and Heinrich Class, *Wider den Strom*, Leipzig 1932, 15–16, 87.
[30] On Nationalism and the Right, without much attention to Antisemitism, see Jeff Eley, *Reshaping the German Right*, New Haven 1980.
[31] Hans Rosenberg, *Grosse Depression und Bismarckzeit. Wirtschaftsablauf, Gesellschaft und Politik*, Berlin 1967, and Fritz Stern, *Bismarck, Bleichröder and the Building of the German Empire*, New York 1977, especially part III.
[32] For more bibliography and details, see my book, *The Rise of German Antimodernism. The urban Master Artisans 1873–1896*, Princeton 1978, esp. Chapter 8.

of clearly anti-liberal economic demands. The prosperity of the third quarter of the century made this combination tenable, though it was always problematic. But with the economic reversal of the 1870s, these men increasingly distanced themselves from liberalism, usually of the left-wing version, to which they had been loyal for decades. The "social" or "reform" parties, practically all Antisemitic splinter groups, often managed to enter into the political gap. They offered an anti-industrial and anti-modern platform, without being temperamentally conservative, aristocratic, or elitist. Later in the century, when the Antisemitic parliamentary representatives joined the conservative block in German politics, they were once more merely reflecting the shift in the electorate. By the late nineteenth century, the established conservative party was striving to appear as a popular movement, belatedly responding to the needs of a new political age. Where the Conservatives could only do a half-job, the *Bund der Landwirte*, using different tactics and aggressively flaunting its Antisemitism, proved far more successful. Adopting nationalism, with its Antisemitic overtones, the conservative forces in Germany managed to attract much of the previously liberal, even left-wing, *Mittelstand* electorate. Antisemitism played a major role in this restructuring of German politics, helping to introduce new social and ideological elements into the traditional German right.[33]

Fourth, and finally, Antisemitism had a unique cultural position in Wilhelmine Germany. It had gradually become *a code* for the overall *Weltanschauung* and style of the right. In a situation of cultural polarization developing in Germany in the late nineteenth and the early twentieth century, Antisemitism became a sign of belonging. The expression of anti-Jewish sentiment, even occasionally by Jews, indicated the adherence to "Germanic culture" and a rejection of everything that stood opposed to it at the other end of the evolving cultural spectrum. Even more: opposition to Antisemitism clearly identified individuals and groups in the camp of democratization, parliamentarianism, and often also with cultural and economic modernism.[34] Indeed, socialists, who were not previously slow in attacking Jews, became increasingly careful with the application of these tactics. Social Democracy may not have been successful in weeding out Antisemitism from among its membership, but its public stand on the matter, from the early 1890s onward, was quite

---

33 See my article: "The social and Political Function of Antisemitism: The Case of the Handicraft Masters," no. 2 in this volume above, and Hans-Jürgen Puhle, *Agrarische Interessenpolitik und Preußischer Konservatismus im Wilhelminischen Reich, 1893–1914*, Bonn 1975.
34 On this aspect of Antisemitism, see "Antisemitism as a Cultural Code," no. 4 in this volume, above.

unequivocal.³⁵ Antisemitism was not merely an element in the overall political worldview of the right in Germany, but became a communication signal within the overall political culture of the Reich. It served a unique function in defining the borderline between the two opposing camps which dominated its public life.

These four specific functions of Antisemitism in the Second Reich gave it its peculiar modern character. Their time-specific nature, however, restrict their significance to the period under consideration. They can be used for understanding the surge of Antisemitism in the postwar years only by adjusting them, often quite radically, to the entirely different circumstances in Weimar Germany. Perhaps more problematic still is the rarely admitted, but easily apparent similarity between the functions of Antisemitism in Wilhemine Germany and in France of the Third Republic. The explanatory power of the foregoing functional analysis for later events is further reduced by the comparison – this time not along a time axis but across the geographical border between Germany and France.

IV. French Antisemitism has received far less attention from historians than its German counterpart. We still have no complementary volume to Robert Byrnes's *Antisemitism in Modern France*, which covers the years up to the Dreyfus Affair; and only a few monographs treat this subject in depth.³⁶ The spread of Antisemitism outside the immediate political sphere and the realm of journalism, in social organizations and trade societies, at the local level and the margins of society, all that is only marginally discussed by French historians.³⁷ General books mention, of course, Édouard Drumont and his astounding public success and tell the story of the Dreyfus case. But one cannot help wondering how slanted the picture of the past has become through the perspective of later events.

It is beyond my competence and not entirely necessary for my purpose to go into the specific details of the French history of Antisemitism. It is sufficient to mention here that since the early part of the nineteenth century Antisemitism in

---

[35] See especially Rosemarie Leuchen-Seppel, *Sozialdemokratie und Antisemitismus: Die Auseinandersetzung der Partei mit den Konservativen und völkischen Strömungen des Antisemitismus 1871–1914*, Bonn 1978.

[36] Among the relevant literature, see Robert Byrnes, *The Prologue to the Dreyfus Affair*, New Brunswick 1950; Pierre Sorlin, *La Croix et les Juifs*, Paris 1963; Zeev Sternhell, *La Droite revolutionaire 1885–1914*, Paris 1978; René Rémond, *La Droite en France*, Paris 1963; Michael R. Marrus and Robert O. Paxton, *Vichy France and the Jews*, New York 1981. (For later publications, see especially Pierre Birnbaum's books).

[37] Nevertheless, due to the French tradition of political geography, studying the geographical dispersion of Antisemitism is better developed in France than in Germany. See the books listed in the note above, and in addition: Stephen Wilson, "The antisemitic Riots of 1898 in France," in: *Historical Journal* XVI, 1973 and his "Le monument Henry: La structur de l'antisemitisme en France 1898–1899," in: *Annales*, March/April 1977, esp. 266–271.

France had developed on both the left and the right, and that on both extremes of the political spectrum it was, in a way, always grafted upon the widespread anti-Jewish, Catholic sentiment. French Antisemitism of the latter part of the century, however, in its form and content alike, can easily be defined in terms reminiscent of the German case: it is characterized by an introduction of new ideological elements, by new organizational experiments, and above all by its particular functions in the public life of the French Republic before the onset of the First World War.

The ideological novelty, on a European scale, indeed, came from the pen of Édouard Drumont. *La France Juive* (1886) won more popularity, and gained more serious treatment in well-placed circles than anything produced by the German Antisemites at the time.[38] In its cultural prestige it could only be compared with Houston S. Chamberlain's *Grundlagen des neunzehnten Jahrhunderts* (Foundations of the Nineteenth Century) (1899), and perhaps with Langbehn's *Rembrandt als Erzieher* (Rembrandt as Educator) (1890). None of these, however, enjoyed the popularity of Drumont's treatise, none such a good press, and none so lenient a historiography. While most of the Antisemitic literature was spurned by the German educated elite, Drumont was discussed in the best Parisian papers, and read, even studied, by some of the outstanding French intellectuals.[39] Nevertheless, Drumont's book suffers from all the shortcomings typical of the works of his German contemporaries. *La France Juive* is a confused, eclectic and boring book. Its popularity was clearly due to the response it had managed to draw from various social elements in France. It had appealed to them all, expressing the whole range of their fears and anxieties, reflecting the general malaise prevalent in these transitional years of the Third Republic.

With the success of Drumont's book there was also a reprinting of some of the French and German Antisemitic "classics," such as Alphonse Toussenel's *Juifs, rois de l'époque* (1845), and Augustus Rohling's *Der Talmudjude* (1873). New Antisemitic writers appeared on the scene, eager to make their fortunes, and pleased to exploit the obviously sympathetic reading public.[40] But the French Antisemitic literature of these years somehow managed to preserve a reputation for remaining

---

38 On Drumont, in addition to Byrnes, *The Prologue*, see Michel Winock, "Eduard Drumont et l'antisemitisme en France, avant l'affaire Dreyfus," in: *Esprit*, Mai 1971, 1085–1106.
39 On Drumont's intellectual influence see also Byrnes, *The Prologue*, 150–154; Sternhell, "National Socialism and Antisemitism: The Case of Maurice Barrés," in: *Journal of Contemporary History* 8, 1973, 46–66; Michael Curtis, *Three against the Third Republic: Sorel, Barrés and Maurras*, Princeton 1959, 203–220; Ernst Nolte, *Der Faschismus in seiner Epoche: Die Action francaise, der italienische Faschismus, der Nationalsozialismus*, Munich 1963, 83–86.
40 Byrnes, *The Prologue*, 91–92.

essentially non-racist. The racist elements in the works of Drumont, Maurice Barrès, and Charles Maurras have all been naturally observed, but for all three, it was repeatedly indicated, the moral, the social, and the cultural aspects of Antisemitism were always of greater importance than the radical-biological perspective. This, however, as I have attempted to indicate, was also the position of the leading German Antisemites. Count Gobineau, it has been recently reasserted, was far better known in France than had been previously assumed; Hippolyte Taine supplied an original French version for social racism; and racial anthropology had some of its main protagonists in France.[41]

Antisemitic political parties, of the kind known from the German experience, did not exist in the Third Republic, but here too the comparison with Germany is illuminating. The *Ligue Antisémitique Française*, while not a proper political party, nevertheless gained an unequaled prominence in France in the late 1890s. It aggressively pushed its candidates in municipal and national elections; and a group of Antisemitic delegates in the Chamber was not very effective, yet easily recognizable. By 1898 an Antisemitic bill managed to receive close to two hundred votes in an early reading, exploiting the hostile atmosphere immediately after the publication of Émile Zola's *J'accuse*.[42] The Ligue's showing in urban constituencies was particularly impressive, and in January and February of 1898 it managed to organize, or at least encourage, some sixty anti-Jewish riots throughout France, many in some of its main urban centers. These became real pogroms only in Algeria, but in France, too, much damage was done and the Jewish population was thoroughly intimidated. The political potential of a populist Antisemitic movement in France was further demonstrated by the Marquis de Morès, operating in the early 1890s, especially in the 1st Paris *arrondissement*, and later by Jules Guérin in the popular press. By the peak year of 1898, the Ligue and its satellites carried on intensive street agitation, organized parades, and tried its hand at all kinds of propaganda.[43]

These were perhaps meager successes, but they were not so entirely unimpressive in comparison with the German performance. In fact, the German parties never managed to attract as much public support as the Antisemitic anti-Dreyfusards did at the turn of the century. One suspects that more complete studies of Antisemitism in French social organizations, among artisans, white-collar employees, shopkeepers, and the professions would have shown a spread of Antisemitic attitudes not unlike that characteristic of Germany at the time. Stephen

---

[41] Sternhell, *La Droite*, Chap. III, 146–176.
[42] Ibid, 236.
[43] On the riots, see especially Wilson, "The Antisemitic Riots," and on the Marquis de Morès: Byrnes, *The Prologue*, 227–250; Sternhell, *La Droite*, 215–230.

Wilson's excellent analysis of the lists of contributors to the Monument Henry, published periodically by *La Libre Parole* in December 1898 and January 1899, suggests that the social composition of Antisemites in late nineteenth-century France was essentially similar to that in Germany, with a somewhat clearer emphasis on elements of the working class and, understandably, on the lower Catholic priesthood. Otherwise, in France too one can identify army officers, small employers, students, and members of the professions as the most highly overrepresented groups among the anti-Semites.[44]

The spread of Antisemitism in Germany might have been somewhat wider than in France. The French movement, however, had had an unequaled one-time peak at the height of the Dreyfus Affair, never to be regained until the Nazi period in Germany and the Vichy period in France.

Beyond the ideological and social-organizational aspects of Antisemitism, all of its functions observed in Germany between 1870 and 1911 reappear when we turn to examine the French case. Antisemitism was an integral component of the new French right-wing nationalism that asserted itself from the early 1880s. In France too the Jew as a foreigner, a non-Frenchman, an outsider, provided a useful symbol of negation of all that was presumably purely authentic and uniquely French, diffused with the special signs of national greatness and promise. Antisemitism appeared, as for instance on the left wing of the Boulangist movement, when an effort was made to enlist the workers and lower-middle-class elements to the support of the Union Générale – obliterating class differences for the sake of a united, glorious France. In Drumont's and Barrès's writings Antisemitism was turned into a major unifying element, and it became an indispensable part of Maurras's "integral nationalism."[45]

France did not face the complex identity crisis which was imposed upon Germany by the Bismarckian unification-from-above. Nevertheless, it was engaged during the latter years of the century in an internal controversy, often real strife, over the meaning of its modern nationalism. Similarly, France did not have to tackle the rapid pace of industrial development characteristic of the German economic growth during the second half of the nineteenth century. But she too was seeking ways to deal with the implications of a new, emerging national market and the unmistakable symptoms of industrial capitalism. Thus, Antisemitism, in France as in Germany, played a role in the channeling of socioeconomic dissatisfaction and resentment engendered by the economic transformations and social restructuring of these years. This is all too well known to be repeated here at

---

44 Byrnes, The Prologue, 261–280; Wilson, "Le Monument Henry," (note 37 above), 271–276.
45 Sternhell, *La Droite*, Chap. IV; Rémond, *La Droite en France*, Chapters 6, 7.

length. Suffice is to mention the surge of Antisemitic sentiments following the collapse of the Union Générale in 1882, and the increasingly Antisemitic tone of the Catholic newspaper *La Croix*, gradually to become the most outspoken mouthpiece for the anti-industrial, anticapitalistic, anti-modern reaction in France. Among the Antisemitic literary stars too, the social theme was and remained prominent throughout. It was Drumont, once again, who gave an early French version to it: "Antisemitism has never been a religious question; it has always been an economic and social question."[46]

Furthermore, the role of Antisemitism in the political transformation of late nineteenth-century France was parallel to its corresponding role in Germany. As an element of new nationalism, it operated with it to "transform from Left to Right a whole combination of ideas, sentiments and values, henceforth considered the birthright of Radicalism."[47] Between 1879 and 1899, explains the historian of the French right, René Rémond, the left-center in French politics moved slowly and by degrees to the right, making for an important change in the political map of the country. While the newly created right mostly used the arsenal of political ideas and ideals borrowed from the tradition of the two empires, only one new element was added – Antisemitism. It was Antisemitism which, in France too, helped reshape the social, not merely the ideological, composition of the main political camps in the country. Finally, French Antisemitism seems to have become in France, as in Germany, a culture code, a sign of belonging. Even if the controversy during the Dreyfus Affair was not primarily a matter of justice versus patriotism, or generally an argument over principles, the struggle itself crystallized the two main blocks in French politics, style, and culture. On the one hand, the anti-republican right was regrouping its forces and testing its muscles. On the other, the republicans were joining hands despite deep internal divisions. The case of the socialists, in France as in Germany, is particularly instructive. In the late 1880s, Antisemitism was still widely diffused across the social and political spectrum of France. *La Revue socialiste* published a series of Antisemitic articles dealing with the Jewish question as late as 1887–89, though it opened its columns to opposite views too. The Blanquist and Proudhonist traditions of the socialist left in France were heavy with Antisemitic material. But as Antisemitism became increasingly an identity card for the new revolutionary, anti-republican right, the socialists began to distance themselves from it. By 1892 their line became clearly opposed to Antisemitism, though their position on the Dreyfus case was still equivocal. It was only in 1898, after the public appearance of Zola on

---

[46] Quoted from Sternhell, *Neither Right nor Left. Fascist Ideology in France*, Princeton 1993 (original in French 1983), 44.
[47] Rémond, *La Droite en France*, 224.

the Dreyfusards' side, and as the specter of the Ligue in the streets of Paris was becoming increasingly alarming, that the socialists came out finally for revision. But from that point onward they seemed to have grasped the overall political, indeed cultural, meaning of Antisemitism, and they acted accordingly.[48] The Dreyfus Affair made this last function of Antisemitism unquestionably clear, in a more overt and outspoken manner than had ever been the case in Germany.

V. Two points of diversity are often mentioned when French Antisemitism is compared with its contemporary German counterpart. First, the fact that the French Jewish population was considerably smaller than the German Jewish one; and second, that France was then, unlike Germany, a republic, traditionally and structurally better equipped to guard against Antisemitism. Other elements may be added, above all, the unique French path to industrialization. But these two do seem to be of special significance. By 1900 the French Jewish community numbered 80,000 members only, while their number in Germany, in proportion to the general population, was five times as large.[49] And after all, the French Republic did come out victorious at the end of the Dreyfus Affair, reasserting its faith in liberty, equality, and fraternity. Though the battle over Dreyfus may have indeed ended as it did despite, and not because of the pressure of public opinion and the press, the very fact of victory imbued nationalists and Antisemites with bitterness and a sense of impotence that seemed never to be erased, even after the upheavals of two world wars. Reversely, it gave the republican forces a consciousness of their responsibility and power, as well as the necessary self-confidence to continue the battle. It certainly gave the French Jewish community a lasting faith in the benevolence of French civilization.[50]

Germany never experienced such a test case, and we shall never know how she would have reacted. But it is instructive to remember that many in Germany at the time of the Affair saw in it a proof of the inferiority of the French system, and even the Jews expressed the concern of the better-situated brothers. Antisemitism in such extreme and overt forms, they believed, was not respectable in Wilhelmine Germany, though it was almost self-evident in mild, latent forms. In the few riots against Jews at that time, in Neustettin (1881), Xanten (1891), and Konitz (1900), the state authorities proved entirely reliable in using troops to provide protection, and the courts handed out stiff sentences to the rioters. In the Reichstag the Antisemites

---

[48] On the Socialists in France, see, in addition to Byrnes and Sternhell, also J.P. Peter, "Dimensions de l'affaire Dreyfus," in: *Annales*, 1961. Compare also: Arendt, *The Origins of Totalitarianism*, 98–120.
[49] Michael R. Marrus, *The Politics of Assimilation: A Study of the French Jewish Community at the Time of the Dreyfus Affair*, Oxford 1971; Paula Heyman, *From Dreyfus to Vichy: The Remaking of French Jewry, 1906–1939*, New York 1979.
[50] Sternhell, *La Droite*, 242; Marrus and Paxton, *Vichy France*, 31–32.

never managed to get their various bills beyond the initial parliamentary stage and were often ridiculed there and laughed at.[51] In his memoirs, Heinrich Class recalled that the *Alldeutscher Verband* had not been Antisemitic until he was nominated its president in 1908.[52] According to a detailed study of the predecessors of the postwar *Schutz- und Trutzbund*, the leadership of the *Verband* had to tread carefully on the Antisemitic issue as late as 1913, because this clearly had no public resonance, even among its prospective members. Only in 1916, with the early war crises, did it openly launch an Antisemitic campaign, reaching its high point in the summer of 1918.[53]

It is also interesting to observe the reactions to Class's 1912 book *Wenn ich der Kaiser wär'*. The book included a comprehensive critique of the government's domestic and foreign policies and an overall plan for an alternative – reformist and imperialist. Some twenty-five thousand copies were printed by the spring of 1914, but there was much criticism of its Antisemitic part. The conservative, right-wing *Reichspartei*, some big-business groups, and even the *Verein deutscher Studenten*, known for its anti-Jewish stand, regarded these demands as unrealistic, immoderate, impossible, though admittedly not undesirable.[54] Somewhat later, the highest government echelons took the chance of reacting to similar proposals, presented as a memorandum by a close associate of Class, one cavalry officer Konstantin Gebsattel. This was a moderate document according to the standards of *Alldeutsche Verband*, and both Chancellor Theobald von Bethmann-Hollweg and the *Kaiser* obviously felt obliged to comment upon it. As to its Antisemitic points, protested Bethmann-Hollweg, it was impossible even "to begin to grapple with such ideas". The Kaiser called these proposals "childish," insisting that all that went against the best interests of the German state, and "would drag us back a hundred years, while at the same time separating us from the ranks of the cultural nations".[55]

Thus, even that leadership, which continuously toyed with ideas of a *Staatsstreich* to solve domestic problems, and a war of aggression to solve international tensions, recoiled from taking actual Antisemitic action, and considered those

---

51 Richard Levy, *The Downfall*, 154–155, 166–172, 206–208.
52 Heinrich Class, *Wider den Strom*, 87–88.
53 Lohalm, *Völkische Radikalismus*, 32–54; Fricke, *Die bürgerlichen Parteien*, 1–26.
54 The book was published under pseudonym: Daniel Frymann, *Wenn ich der Kaiser wär'*. For the reactions see Dirk Stegmann, *Die Erben Bismarcks: Parteien und Verbände in der Spätphase der Wilhelminischen Deutschland*, Köln 1970, 295–304.
55 Hartmut Pogge von Strandmann, "Staatsstreichpläne, Alldeutsche und Bethmaann-Holweg," in: von Strandmann and Immanuel Geiss, *Die Erforderlichkeit des Unmöglichen: Deutschland am Vorabend des Ersten Weltkrieges*, Frankfurt a. M. 1965, 22, 25–26. (the translation is mine).

suggested *"im ganzen phantastisch."*[56] The leadership feared the revolutionary implications of Antisemitism, it is true, but it was also apparently aware of its incommensurability with the most minimal standards of existing civilization. The picture is similar to that disclosed in France: in both countries a widespread anti-Jewish sentiment, a popular demand for Antisemitic literature, and compliance with certain kinds of social discrimination, combined with an avoidance of any practical public anti-Jewish measures. Beyond the socially diffused antipathy toward Jews, the main legacy of prewar radical Antisemitism, in Germany as well as in France, was a written, literary one. From the very beginning Hitler sensed its basic irrelevance to his kind of Antisemitism, and consciously set out to surpass its very premises.

VI. With the possible exception of Adolf Stöcker, the politicians of late nineteenth- and early twentieth-century German Antisemitism quickly moved from the streets and the public rally to the parliamentary halls, where they were drawn into impotent Reichstag speech-making. They dissipated their energy in internal strife and showed no talent for carrying out any of their grandiose schemes. In fact, neither the politicians nor the ideologues of the movement had any real plan of action. Stöcker and Treitschke repeatedly assured their respective audiences that they had no intention of going back on emancipation.[57] Marr and Glagau occasionally toyed with the idea of restrictive legal measures to cut down Jewish influence on the German economy and in Germany's public life. But neither they nor their younger and more practical heirs in the organized Antisemitic movement had any conception of the kind of desirable or feasible action needed to bring such measures about. Among the early ideologues, only Eugen Düring somewhat expanded upon his proposals for the solution to the "Jewish question," and even hinted at the inevitability of physical extermination. But he too buried his suggestions in the last chapter of his Antisemitic book, which was unusually confused even for this "master" of Antisemitic prose. Essentially, Düring was far too pessimistic to busy himself with drawing practical blueprints. No European government, he argued, was in a position to act against the Jews, and no suggested solution could therefore be applied. One was left to wage only a personal struggle, he concluded, a war of "enlightenment and

---

56 Also Strandmann, as the note above.
57 See: Treitschke, "Unsere Aussichten," und "Herr Grätz und sein Judentum", in *Deutsche Kämpfe*, 45ff.; Stöckers speech in: *Verhandlungen des preußischen Abgeordnetenhauses . . . am 20. und 22. November 1880*, Berlin 1880, 126. On the confusion among the Antisemites concerning each and every concrete measure against the Jews, see Levy, *The Downfall*, Chap 7 and Saul Ash "Antisemitic Schemes for Jewish Policy in Germany up to the Nazi Rise to Power," in: *Yad Vashem Studies* VI, [Hebrew], 73–100.

self-defense."[58] He too was primarily busy re-editing his old Antisemitic opus or expanding and attempting new versions of it. Together with other Antisemites, he was thrown back on written matter, attempting to gain as many *converts* as possible among the reading public, not to recruit *soldiers* for an actual battle.

In Wilhelmine Germany Antisemitism was a part of the written culture. But this was a culture of paradoxes. It included the bureaucratic Potsdam style and the romantic style of Wagnerian grandeur.[59] It also gave rise, despite the authoritarianism of the regime and the pressure of its censor, to Theodor Fontane's moderate tone, and to Thomas Mann's reflective elegance. Moreover, this was a culture which served, to use George Steiner's phrase, as "the real homeland of the Jews."[60] Marr, Friedrich Lange, and even Lagarde remained always bitter and frustrated at its margin. Witness the continuous attacks on the Jewish intellectual and literary man, and the diatribes against Heinrich Heine and Ludwig Börne repeated by every Antisemite from Wagner in the middle of the century to Fritsch at its close. The verbal aggression of these men gives the impression of a public ritual: the preoccupation with the same themes, the return to the same historical and personal examples, the hammering of the same complaints. The written comments, added by the contributors to the Monument Henry in France during the Dreyfus Affair were observed to have had the object and the function of a liturgy. Theirs was *"une réaction de type magique,"* serving an end in itself, not meant to lead to further action. Much of the Antisemitic verbiage in Germany of that time was all of the same kind.[61]

Hitler had no use for this verbiage. Already in *Mein Kampf* he extensively explained the superiority of the spoken word over written matter. All world-shaking events, he argued, have been brought about not by *"Geschriebenes,"* but by *"das gesprochene Wort."*[62] His two examples were the exploits of the French Revolution and the effectiveness of Marxism. In both cases he was at pains to show it was oratory and not ideology, propaganda and not ideas, which won the day. In passing, as was often his habit, he poured scorn on the German *"Tintenritter,"* and the highly educated but entirely purposeless *"Schreibseele."* Written matter, always smacking of intellectualism, was despised and ridiculed by him. He himself wrote extensively

---

58 Dühring, *Die Judenfrage*, 113–135.
59 George Steiner, "The Hollow Miracle," (1959), in: *Language and Silence: Essays 1958–1966*, London 1967, 117–132.
60 George Steiner, "The Language Animal", (1969), in: *Extraterritorial Papers on Literature and the Language Revolution*, London 1972, esp. 71–88.
61 Stephen Wilson, "Le monument Henry", 286–287.
62 Munich edition, 1939, 525.

only once, when the speaker's platform was forcibly denied him, and *Mein Kampf* remained, to borrow his own term, a book *"das geredet ist."*[63]

Striving for power, it was Goebbels the speech-maker who quickly became second only to Hitler himself within the Nazi Party. Men like Alfred Rosenberg were considered harmless but useless. Hitler never actually read his *Mythos des 20. Jahrhunderts*, though he claimed to have been versed in the earlier Antisemitic literature. His admiration, however, was saved for the great rabble-rouser of *fin de siècle* Vienna, Karl Lueger, and his Antisemitism was clearly picked up in conversations, in beer halls, and on street corners. He was converted to Antisemitism by the spoken word, and he knew he could best transmit it by the same medium. And in his case the medium was indeed the message.[64]

Nazism was a spoken culture. Its language was all speech, with no literary dimensions, no privacy, no individuality. It was the language of demagogy, of declamations and shouts, with flags flying in the wind and the swastika constantly before one's eyes.[65] It was a culture in which verbal aggression was *not a substitute for action but a preparation for it*. In contrast to the language of Wilhelmine Germany, this was a medium which in all seriousness meant to lead to glorious deed. In his so-called *"grundlegende Rede über den Antisemitismus,"* Hitler sounded his faith in final victory, when *"endlich der Tag kommt, an dem unsere Worte schweigen und die Tat beginnt."*[66] Thus, the spoken word too was merely a tool for action, a practical instrument for bringing it about. Hitler's rhetoric forced a transformation of meaning even upon the substance of Antisemitism. He may have not had a clear plan for handling the Jews if and when he would seize power in Germany, but his Antisemitism was, from the very beginning, entirely and consciously a matter of action. It turned the old written stuff into a new kind of material – explosive, dangerous, leading inexorably to catastrophe. The change came gradually and almost imperceptibly. Contemporaries were easily fooled by it; historians too often ignore it.

The old, tenacious tradition of European antipathy for the Jews no doubt contributed to the choice of the Jews as a target for persecution, and to the preparation of the crowds of onlookers throughout Europe to accept passively the reality of the Holocaust in their midst. The Antisemitism of the pre-1914 years helped

---

63 Ibid, 528–534.
64 On the sources of Hitler's Antisemitism see Phelps, "Hitler's Rede . . .", 390–399; and Joachim C. Fest, *Das Gesicht des Dritten Reiches: Profile einer totalitären Herrschaft*, Part I, sec. 1 and 2.
65 Victor Klemperer, *Die unbewältigte Sprache: Aus dem Notizbuch eines Philosophen. LTI*, (first edition 1946) 3rd edition, Darmstadt n.d., 17–49.
66 Phelps, "Hitler's Rede . . .", 418.

preserve this tradition and adapted it to the modern social and political context. It was as such of great significance in shaping the particular human environment at the time. But the murderous acts of the Nazis were of a different category and sprang from different sources. Their final act of violence must be understood by the specific details of the case, not by reference to some commonly observed pattern of human behavior. Nazism too, I believe, can best be studied through its own dynamism and character, not by reliance upon its "beginnings." Here is how Marc Bloch concluded his chapter on the "idol of origins":

> In a word, a historical phenomenon can never be understood apart from its moment in time. This is true of every evolutionary stage, our own and all others. As the old Arab proverb has it: 'Men resemble their times more than they do their fathers.' Disregard of this Oriental wisdom has sometimes brought discredit to the study of the past.[67]

---

[67] Bloch, *The Historians, Craft*, 35.

6 Antisemitism and Anti-Feminism: Cultural Code or Social Norm

The singular status of Antisemitism in Wilhelmine culture may be better understood when compared to the status of anti-feminism at about the same time.* In 1781, the first and most seminal book on the position of Jews in Prussia, written by Christian Wilhelm Dohm, a "secret" archivist – as his title read – and a foreign affairs adviser in the Prussian state department, was published in Berlin.[1] It was entitled *On the Civil Improvement of the Jews* and immediately became the focus of a lively public debate. A dozen years later, in 1793, another "secret" public servant, later revealed to be Theodor Gottlieb von Hippel, a "war advisor," regional police commissioner, and mayor of the city of Königsberg in East-Prussia, published a book under a similar title, *On the Civil Improvement of Women*. In contrast to the commotion raised by Dohm's book, von Hippel's arguments made almost no mark at the time, and the book's influence was limited to the author's close circle of friends.[2] Even 100 years later, when an active and militant women's movement was already present in Germany, the book remained practically unknown. Yet, despite the radical differences in the reception of the two books, they offer an interesting perspective into a pivotal connection between what was later termed "the emancipation of the Jews" and the processes of "the emancipation of women."

This connection was by no means limited to late-eighteenth-century Prussia. Von Hippel's book, written in the faraway eastern part of the continent, was published almost simultaneously with Mary Wollstonecraft's book, *Vindication of the Rights of Women*, which appeared in London in 1792. A further reminder of the apparently inadvertent application of the identical terms in the discussion of the status of Jews on one hand and the rights of women on the other, along with the international contexts of the debate, may be found in Moses Mendelssohn's almost contemporary translation of a 1656 book by Menasseh Ben Israel, entitled *Vindication of the Jews*. The link and its political significance were visible in the early 1790s in France,

---

1 The complete edition, including responses to various critiques, entitled *Über die bürgerliche Verbesserung des Juden*, was published in Berlin/Stetin 1783. For biography of Dohm, see Ilsegret Dambacher, *Christian Wilhelm von Dohm*, Frankfurt a. M. 1974.

2 On von Hippel's life and work, see *Biographie des königlichen Preuß. Geheimkriegsraths zu Königsberg: Theodor Gottlieb von Hippel, zum Teil von ihm selbst verfasst*, Gotha 1801 (a new printing: Hildesheim, 1977). Also Juliane Jacobi, "Der Polizeidirektor als feministischer Jakobiner T. G. von Hippel und seine Schrift 'Über die bürgerliche Verbesserung der Weiber'," in: *Sklavin oder Bürgerin? Französiche Revolution und Neue Weiblichkeit 1760–1830*, ed. Viktoria Schmidt-Linsenhoff, Frankfurt a. M. 1989, 357–72, and her introduction to the new edition of von Hippel's book, *Über die bürgerliche Verbesserung der Weiber*, Vaduz/Lichtenstein, 1981, ix–xli.

too. The National Assembly had initially been swarmed with petitions and pamphlets urging, if not the full equality of women, at least their right to education and improvement of their legal status. In 1790 an essay by Condorcet concerning the possibility of granting women full civil rights, aroused considerable public attention.[3] At the time, the Assembly was in the midst of deliberating the status of the Jews in France, and in the fall of 1791, indeed, they were granted full citizenship by the revolutionary republic. In contrast, achievements on the women's front were rather meager. No substantial progress in this respect was made anywhere in Europe during the revolutionary era.[4] Practical achievements were not reached until some hundred years later. Nevertheless, the affinity with the Jewish case, the theoretical analogy, and the principal similarities were and remained striking. Indeed, the situation of social groups demanding equality, women and Jews, but also the peasantry and the poor, were often discussed in similar terms and raised similar questions.

Yet this similarity has often escaped the scrutiny of modern historiography. Although von Hippel's and Dohm's works were closely related in many respects, they were seldom treated together by historians.[5] Now, von Hippel was undoubtedly familiar with Dohm's treatise as he set out to compose his own. But, more importantly, it is obvious that both were nourished by the same intellectual milieu that was typical of the Prussian top bureaucrats and both addressed the basic ideas of the European Enlightenment regarding human equality. Interestingly, both also accepted as given the inferiority and inadequacy of the group in question, attributed this inferiority to its history, and believed in the ability of its members to adapt to the needs of the modernizing state with the help of a balanced and progressive education. The principal arguments in these parallel discourses are strikingly similar. Their weaknesses too are typical of the world in which they were conceived.

---

[3] "Essai sur l'admission des femmes au droits de cité," 23 Juillet 1790. Originally published in *Journal de la Societé de 1789*, No. 5.
[4] There is a considerable body of literature on the subject. See Jane Abray, "Feminism and the French Revolution," *American Historical Review* 80(1), 1975, 43–62; Joan B. Landes, *Women and the Public Sphere in the Age of the French Revolution*, Ithaca, NY, 1988. For a useful summary see Gisela Bock, *Women in European History*, Oxford 2002, chap. 2, 82–126.
[5] Some exceptions are Julius Carlebach, "The Forgotten Connection: Women and Jews in the Conflict between Enlightenment and Romanticism," in: *Leo Baeck Institue Yearbook* XXIV, 1979, 107–138; Robert Liberles, "The Historical Context of Dohm's Treatise on the Jews," in: *Das deutsche Judentum und der Liberalismus – German Jewry and Liberalism*, Königswinter, 1986, 44–69; Ute Frevert, "Die Innenwelt der Außenwelt: Modernitätserfahrungen von Frauen zwischen Gleichheit und Differenz," in: *Deutsche Juden und die Moderne*, ed. Shulamit Volkov Munich 1994,75–94. Compare also Ute Planert, "Reaktionäre Modernisten? Zum Verhältnis von Antisemitismus und Antifeminismus in der völkischen Bewegung," in: *Jahrbuch für Antisemitismusforschung 2000*, 31–51.

Just as Dohm's text clearly reveals his ingrained anti-Jewish prejudice, so does von Hippel's book disclose the author's biased attitude toward women.[6] In an earlier work, *On Marriage*, published in 1775, in which he sharply criticized the status of women in contemporary society, Hippel's fundamental ambivalence was equally apparent. Von Hippel not only set exceedingly strict moral standards for women but also repeatedly stressed their inability to uphold them. He argued that women were incapable of acquiring education in "abstract fields" or of creating any work of substance on their own. He may have changed his mind later, perhaps under the influence of the French Revolution, but even then he remained cautious and avoided any topic that proved too embarrassing or radical. Unlike the dry and businesslike Dohm, von Hippel was quite an able, slightly chatty, satirist. This, in addition to the issue at hand, could explain why Dohm's more serious and more practically oriented work opened almost 100 years of intensive discussion on the position of Jews in Germany, while Hippel's finally remained no more than a literary episode.

It was only in the late 1820s, following the first wave of post revolutionary reaction across Europe, that public debate on the legal and political status of groups still deprived of what was considered their "natural rights" was revived. A new term, *emancipation*, was then coined and quickly applied to diverse causes: the status of Catholics in England, the slavery issue, and gradually and ever more frequently to the Jewish Question, too.[7] In fact, within a few years, public attention in Germany was turned to the question of the emancipation of the bourgeois society at large, focusing on its main constituents rather than on its marginal groups. The original sense of the term "emancipation" in the Roman codex denoted a process of gradual "maturing" along with the symbolic legal act, indicating a separation from paternal authority. This sense was now transferred to a broader, more complex context. The Enlightenment as a whole, let us not forget, had already been defined as the process by which man was "leaving his self-caused immaturity" (Kant), and somewhat later the main objective of the time, wrote Heinrich Heine in 1828, was emancipation, "not only of the Irish, the Greeks, the Jews of Frankfurt, the blacks of the West

---

[6] See the Introduction to the 1981 printing of von Hippel's book, *Über die bürgerliche Verbesserung der Weiber*, pp. xlii–xliii.

[7] In the context of women's status, this term was in use earlier, but not as the preferred term. Compare Reinhart Koselleck, "Emanzipation," in: *Geschichtliche Grundbegriffe: Historisches Lexikon zur politisch-sozialen Sprache in Deutschland*, eds. Otto Brunner, Werner Conze, and Reinhart Koselleck, Stuttgart, 1972–1997, vol. 2, 153–197, especially 185–186.

Indies, etc., but of the whole world, and of Europe in particular," that Europe that was finally setting itself free of its age-old iron shackles.⁸

Europe – perhaps, but certainly not the women of Europe. While the debate about the status of the oppressed – Catholics, slaves or serfs, peasants, workers, and even Jews – intensely and almost incessantly engaged public opinion in Europe in general and in Germany in particular during much of the first two-thirds of the nineteenth century, the discussion of women's status was hardly on the agenda, certainly not until 1848.⁹ The spark ignited during the French Revolution was quenched for the time being. During these early years, the debate about women's rights took place only in literary circles, if at all. Romantics of all shades were often eager to sketch the contours of women's uniqueness while others wished to use their "findings" to delineate a woman's separate sphere, uniquely feminine, and ultimately justify her exclusion from public life. Even during the revolutionary months of 1848, the struggle for women's rights never translated into a substantial social or political force. During the "Spring of Nations," bourgeois society, born under the belated sign of the Enlightenment, had to confront its own counter-universalistic, excluding tendencies. It tended to define itself at this point more aggressively, mainly in ethnic terms, searching for ways to form a robust and integrative national society, overriding its fundamental class hierarchy. The Jewish Question seemed symptomatic in this context, but the Women's Question was usually marginalized. Indeed, it was only after the debate about the legal emancipation of the Jews in Germany had been settled, following the passage of the bill governing their status within the liberal framework of the North-German Confederation and later within the Bismarckian Reich and its various states, that the women's movement finally emerged. After modest beginnings, its cause won real momentum toward the end of the nineteenth century. But by then Jews were already fighting another battle. Their legal emancipation had long been completed. To a large extent, at least the men among them now felt that it had fulfilled its promise and enabled them to be successfully integrated in the non-Jewish world. As far as they were concerned, there was only one battle left to fight – the battle against Antisemitism, that "new," post-emancipatory kind of Jew-hating and its diverse manifestations.

---

8 Kant's phrase is taken from the first sentence of his "What is Enlightenment?" (1784), and the quote from Heinrich Heine is from his "Reisebilder," in: *Sämtliche Werke*, Leipzig and Vienna, vol. 3, 275 (my translation).

9 For a brief description of the status of women in the early decades of bourgeois society, see George L. Mosse, *Nationalism and sexuality: Respectability and Abnormal Sexuality in Modern Europe*, New York, 1985, chap. 5, and more fully, in Bock, *Women in European History*, chap. 3. Compare also, Ute Frevert, *Women in German History: From Bourgeois Emancipation to Sexual Liberation*, Oxford 1989 (originally in German, 1986), chap. 2.

Even in this shifting context, despite the years in which the ways of Jews and women so markedly parted in their respective struggles, certain links between them could still be noticed. One hundred years of deliberations, which were at times tumultuous in every respect, fundamentally changed the precise nature of these links, but by no means did they void them. At the turn of the nineteenth century, as at the turn of the eighteenth century before, there was a renewed interaction between the struggle over women's place in society and the struggle over the Jews' place in it. Locating the "other" in *fin de siècle* Germany was still no less problematic than in the past. A great many obstacles were still laid on the path to integration of anyone other than an adult, relatively educated, and well-to-do male in contemporary bourgeois society.

During these years, between the late nineteenth century and World War I, and despite its apparent cohesion and respectability, Germany was, in fact, fragmented and conflicted on many levels. Two rival camps were gradually formed at its margin: the radical left and the extreme right. They were a distinctly modern bloc on the one hand and an outspoken anti-modern bloc on the other. Antisemitism, as I have argued above, was of only secondary importance at the time, but it has gradually evolved into the hallmark of one of the camps, an identifying element of the "rightwing subculture." To be sure, it was never identical to the general nationalistic *Volk* culture that, at the time, was receiving its final contours on the German right, old and new. Nor was it merely one of its aspects. As I have shown elsewhere, Antisemitism had by then attained a symbolic value. Identification with sworn Antisemites and radical Antisemitism in Germany of that time became a tool of self-definition. It marked an affiliation with a certain ideational and political camp. Within the prevailing conceptual environment, Antisemitism helped those who embraced it to diagnose the presumed symptoms of their malaise, to foresee imminent danger, and to explain what often appeared as an inexplicable world. Antisemitism helped to point out everything that was loathed and feared by the prophets of Germany's anti-modern culture.

This picture assumes a society in which blatant Antisemitism, however widespread, was not a norm. In fact, violent attacks against Jews, such as those attached to the spreading of blood libels against them, were considered unacceptable even by the conservative authorities of the day.[10] Reinforced military and police units were dispatched to affected regions to restore order, and the courts were strict in punishing those responsible for the agitation. In the Reichstag, Antisemites were often the

---

[10] For an interesting reconstruction of one of these cases, see Helmut Walser Smith, *The Butcher's Tale: Murder and Antisemitism in a German Town*, New York 2002.

butt of jokes. Responding to an openly Antisemitic memorandum that was submitted to him, Bethmann-Hollweg, who was the chancellor at the time, commented that ideas such as those were best ignored, while the Kaiser noted on his own copy that the whole thing was "childish" and stressed that the anti-Jewish policy that was proposed by the author would "only make Germany regress a hundred years back" and "cut it off from the company of civilized nations."[11] Even that German leadership that was toying with the idea of a coup to rid itself once and for all of the restrictions placed on it by the constitution, a leadership that finally wreaked havoc on Germany by leading it into a war of previously unknown proportions; even that leadership which was never overly sympathetic to the Jews regarded such a radical, action-craving brand of Antisemitism as pathetic fantasy.

I have characterized Antisemitism in Wilhelmine Germany as a cultural code, signifying the radical right. Concurrently, one may regard explicit anti-Antisemitism as characteristic of the oppositional camp on the left, combining all supporters of emancipation, including those who worked to fortify Liberalism and even some who were daring to back a moderate and reformist Social Democracy from the very heart of the bourgeois establishment.

A case in point is the German peace movement.[12] Many of the pacifist leaders expressed themselves openly and aggressively on the issue of Antisemitism, too. It is fascinating to trace the ideological course of such diverse figures as historian Ludwig Quidde or the Viennese Baron von Suttner and his wife Bertha, all of whom were peace activists before World War I. Known as one of the movement's prominent leaders, Quidde first earned a reputation when he participated in the public debate on Antisemitism back in 1881.[13] In an acerbic polemical essay entitled "Antisemitic Propaganda and German Students," he attacked the "new" Antisemitism, explaining it away as yet another manifestation of a raging social crisis that was typical of life under the Imperial system. Ten years later, in early 1891, Baron von Suttner established in Vienna the Austrian Association for the War on Antisemitism, in parallel with the similarly named but considerably larger body

---

11 See Hartmut Pogge von Strandmann, "Staatsstreichpläne, Alldeutsche und Bethmann-Hollweg," in his and Imanuel Geiss, *Die Erforderlichkeit des Unmöglichen. Deutschland am Vorabend des Ersten Weltkrieges*, Frankfurt a. M., 1965, 22, 25–26.
12 See Karl Holl, *Pazifismus in Deutschland*, Frankfurt a. M., 1988; and for a specific emphasis on the Kaiserreich, see Roger Chickering, *Imperial Germany and a World without War: The Peace Movement and German Society, 1892–1914*, Princeton, NJ, 1975.
13 See L. Quidde, *Caligula. Schriften über Militarismus und Pazifismus*, ed. Hans-Ulrich Wehler, Frankfurt a. M. 1977; On Bertha von Suttner, see *Kämpferin für den Frieden – Bertha von Suttner, Lebenserinnerungen, Reden und Schriften*, ed. Gisela Brinker-Gabler, Frankfurt a. M., 1982, and Beatrix Kempf, *Suffragette for Peace: The Life of Bertha von Suttner*, London, 1972 (originally in German, 1962).

operating in Germany at that time.¹⁴ This was shortly before he joined his wife Bertha, a tireless peace activist, in establishing the local chapter of the peace movement. Other pacifists were also known to be active in the fight against Anti-semitism, though the link between pacifism and anti-Antisemitism has not always proven unbreakable. When World War I broke out, almost the entire German Association for the War on Antisemitism (known as the *Abwehrverein*) was swept up in patriotic zeal. Still, some of its leaders continued to be active in the peace movement. Theodore Barth, for instance, a president of the *Abwehrverein* for many years, was and remained a strong supporter of the peace movement. His successor, Georg Gothein, was an unswerving pacifist and member of the Association for International Understanding even before the war. He later openly opposed the German government's annexationist policy, and as a Reichstag delegate repeatedly protested the authorities' abuse of the peace activists.

Thus, by the beginning of the twentieth century, one could discern not only an ideological syndrome typical of the German Right but also a clear ideological syndrome that was characteristic of the left. That syndrome encompassed the liberal-democratic position, which was sometimes pacifist in one form or another and distinctly *anti*-Antisemitic. In its milieu, *anti*-Antisemitism and unrelenting support for the idea of full equality for the Jews were incontestable tenets. As in the mirror image examined previously, here, too, in leftwing culture, these were not necessarily the central issues at hand, but they had powerful symbolic value and an unambiguous identifying role. Antisemitism, on the one hand, and *anti*-Antisemitism, on the other, were both used in marking membership in these two competing camps. For this reason, both acquired a long-standing special status in Imperial Germany. It should be noted that this was made possible because neither Antisemitism nor anti-Antisemitism were ever the norm in Wilhelmine society. In the atmosphere of prosperity in early twentieth-century Germany, both unbridled Antisemitism and an outspoken advocacy of the Jews were the exceptions. They could therefore both serve as indicators of belonging, each marking one of the opposing camps, fighting, so to speak, over the soul of German culture.

But the clearest affinity between these four components – Antisemitism and *anti*-Antisemitism, feminism and *anti*-feminism – even more distinct than the one between *anti*-Antisemitism and feminism – was forged between Antisemitism and

---

14 See especially, Barbara Suchy, "The Verein zur Abwehr des Antisemitismus (I) – From its Beginnings to the First World War," in: *Leo Baeck Institute Yearbook* XXVIII, 1983, 205–239; "The Verein zur Abwehr des Antisemitismus (II) – From the First World War to its Dissolution in 1933," in: *Leo Baeck Institute Yearbook* XXX, 1985, 67–103.

anti-feminism.¹⁵ The proximity of these two components was born during the nineteenth century, parallel to the emergence of nationalism. In a series of pioneering studies, George Mosse argued that German nationalism emerged as "a cult of masculinity."¹⁶ While both men and women could be expected to show genuine patriotism, it was clear to all that they could not be treated as equals in terms of the nation's needs and its political life. After all, women – apparently like Jews – were not endowed with the "moral earnestness" that marked the German man. They could not be regarded as equal partners in the national community. Furthermore, the old argument about a woman's true "essence" that had become familiar since at least the Enlightenment remained relevant well into the twentieth century.¹⁷ It was in the beginning of that century, indeed, when the repercussions of the feminist struggle in England first reached the Continent, and with the debate about women's rights raging in Germany too, that pure masculine exclusivity within the national community was in danger of being jeopardized for the first time. At this junction it seemed to need urgent protection.

Among the clearest theoretical statements on this issue was Otto Weininger's. This young Viennese Jew managed to raise a real, though short-lived, storm with the publication of his book, *Geschlecht und Charakter* (Sex and Character), in May 1903.¹⁸ Weininger focused primarily on the fundamental dualism between the sexes and on feminine inferiority, but he also labored to compare "femininity" with "Jewishness," reiterating older analogies, and suggesting new links between them. The struggle against Judaism and femininity was one and the same, Weininger argued, and his

---

15 See, for example, Friedrich Lange, *Reines Deutschtum: Grundzüge einer nationalen Weltanschauung*, Berlin 1905 [1893], 166. On antisemitism in the context of the struggle for women's rights, see Richard J. Evans, *The Feminist Movement in Germany, 1894–1933*, London 1976, pp. 175–82, and Pulzer, *The Rise of Political Antisemitism*, 221–222. Marion Kaplan discusses the issue from a different point of view in her "Sisterhood under Siege: Feminism and Antisemitism in Germany, 1904–1938," in: *The Jewish Response to German Culture: From the Enlightenment to the Second World War*, eds. Jehuda Reinharz and Walter Schatzberg, Hanover and London 1985, 242–265.
16 Mosse, *Nationalism and Sexuality*, 78–79.
17 See Carole Pateman, *The Sexual Contract*, Cambridge 1994; Sylvana Tomaselli, "The Enlightenment Debate on Women," *History Workshop* 20, 1985, 101–124.
18 See Otto Weininger, *Sex and Character*, London 1906 (originally in German, 1903). By 1904 there were already four editions, by 1914 there were fourteen, and by 1925 it had reached twenty-six editions. Ute Frevert, 'Mann und Weib, und Weib und Mann': Geschlechter-Differenzen in der Moderne, Munich, 1995, 120. Luckhardt devotes the last section of her study to the discussion of this book, see Ute Luckhardt, "Die Frau als Fremde: Frauenbilder um die Jahrhundertwende," in: *Tel Aviver Jahrbuch für Deutsche Geschichte* XXI, 1992, 99–126, here 120–126. Compare also Jacques Le Rider, *Der Fall Otto Weininger: Wurzeln des Antifeminismus und Antisemitismus*, Munich and Vienna 1985 (originally in French, 1982). My discussion is based on a new edition of Weininger's book, Munich 1980, 403–441.

message evoked a range of cultural associations, usually dormant but familiar notes, in the minds of his contemporaries. In retrospect, the popularity that his rather tiresome book had enjoyed in Vienna, a city brimming with levelheaded and incisive minds, is striking, indeed. It was no doubt aided by the fact that the young author committed a very dramatic, or rather melodramatic, suicide shortly after its publication. But the book's unique attraction was not mere coincidence. It was rooted in a much broader context, that of the attitude toward all "others" in Europe in general and in the German speaking countries in particular. For our purpose, of paramount importance is the associative link between Jew and woman that had been forged more than 100 years earlier and was finally being expressed in a most extreme and somewhat perverse manner by Weininger. The German public was in fact busy defining the essence of "otherness" for a long time. The concepts formulated in the process became a cornerstone in the struggle to preserve ethnic as well as masculine exclusivity within the boundaries of the national community. Eventually, the biological-racial explanation was appended to buttress this ideological structure, augmenting the rather intuitive explanations of the Enlightenment with a presumably bona fide scientific theory. The new mix was clearly much harder to resist.

The preoccupation with difference was a stabilizing factor in bourgeois society at the turn of the century. It was in the center of the intellectual as well as the social and political response to the challenge of the modern age. The Enlightenment propagated the creation of a new, open society that was free of any preference or discrimination. Throughout the nineteenth century, various attempts were made to formulate the principles that would permit the use of exclusionary tactics despite this egalitarianism. These were first and foremost conceived in terms of social class, but also in terms of ethnicity, biology, and gender. The colonial-imperialist discourses, as well as the domestic social and local ones, were all affected by such considerations. From the 1860s onward, talk of race had been linked to the *Judenfrage* and, above all, to the attempts to exclude Jews from the mushrooming public sphere of the new bourgeois society. As the struggle for women's rights intensified, the use of biological arguments along with racial theories became central to that struggle, too. It was a weapon designed to neutralize feminine influence and preserve the traditional role of women at the margin of public life.[19]

---

19 Compare George L. Mosse, *Toward the Final Solution: A History of European Racism*, London, 1978, and his *The Crisis of German Ideology: Intellectual Origins of the Third Reich*, New York 1964, 145–166. In addition to Ute Frevert's book, *Mann und Weib, und Weib und Mann*, see Ute Planert, *Antifeminismus im Kaiserreich*, 83–93.

By the late nineteenth century, even those wishing to defend the Jews or support the women's struggle found themselves forced to address the analogy between these two groups. Some even attempted to consider this combination a positive sign, though they were few and far between. Theodor Lessing, for instance, a rather controversial philosopher at the time, known to later generations as the author of *Jewish Self-Hatred*, published in 1910, had written an essay a number of years before under the title "Weib, Frau, Dame" (Woman, Wife, Lady).[20] Upon its publication, it was inevitably regarded as a response to Weininger's book, and the debate over *Sex and Character* may have indeed brought Lessing to publish it at that time. In any case, it was a resolute statement in defense of the link between women and Jews. The moral and intellectual supremacy of these two, ran Lessing's argument, was the result of their ongoing efforts to overcome age-old oppression, suffering and dependence. It was under these dire circumstances that their negative traits were likewise developed, and, as a way of overcoming them, Lessing offered two radical remedies: Feminism and Zionism.

An equally unusual combination of feminism with philo-semitism can be found in the writings of Leopold von Sacher-Masoch, who gave his name to masochism and was notorious at the time for his scandalous essays on the presumably true nature of the relationships between the sexes. Less known is the fact that Sacher-Masoch had always been fascinated with scenes from the Jewish milieu, mainly in Galicia, and with what he considered Jewish life in general. He was particularly captivated by the situation in which an allegedly passive man was permanently preoccupied by study while his wife assumed the active role of a breadwinner, managing the entire household, including the worldly affairs of her own husband.[21]

Comments on the primitive, authentic nature of sexuality that was typical of both Jews and women are also to be found in the writings of Otto Rank, one of Freud's more original and independent disciples. Rank considered the individuals who made up these groups as leading the struggle against the repression of what

---

20 Theodor Lessing, *Weib, Frau, Dame: Ein Essay*, Munich 1910. Compare also Lawrence Baron, "Theodor Lessing: Between Jewish Self-Hatred and Zionism," in: *Leo Baeck Institue Yearbook* XXVI, 1981, 323–340; pp. 330–332 are specifically relevant for this work.
21 On Sacher-Masoch, see Hans Otto Horch, "Der Aussenseiter als 'Judenraphael': zu den Judengeschichten Leopolds von Sacher-Masoch," in: *Conditio Judaica: Judentum, Antisemitismus und deutschsprachige Literatur vom 18. Jahrhundert bis zum Ersten Weltkrieg*, eds. Hans Otto Horch and Horst Denkler, Tübingen 1989, Part II, 258–286; David Biale, "Masochism and Philosemitism: The Strange Case of Leopold von Sacher-Masoch," in: *Journal of Contemporary History* XVII, 1982, 305–323. I also relied here on an unpublished lecture given by Ms. Alison Rose at the Comparative European History Seminar held during the academic year 1991/2 at Tel Aviv University, entitled "Exotic Temptress or Ideal Housewife? The Representation of Jewish Women in Vienna in the Late Nineteenth Century."

he saw as "natural" sexuality. He saw them as having a liberating and therefore essentially positive mission.[22] Less positive analogies appeared in the writings of Hans Gross, a pioneering criminologist, and Georg Groddeck, who was later known in Freud's circle as the "wild analyst" – each from his own singular perspective.[23] In *fin de siècle* European culture, it was possible to find a great variety of attitudes toward the supposed link between women and Jews. Some foresaw and advocated the feminization of society while regarding the Jews as an obstacle in the process. Others, witnessing the budding women's movement, anxiously observed what they saw as a "feminine takeover" and rose to the defense of "masculine rationality" in the face of the inherently feminine irrationality principle. In this "last battle," most of them regarded the Jews as dangerous enemies. In the prevailing atmosphere, only a few were able to formulate a positive connection between women and Jews or to cultivate a line of action supporting both feminism and Jewish equality. At the center of attention were those who overtly expressed their contempt for both women and Jews and viewed them as inferior, the enemies of culture and a threat to the existing social order.

Still, despite the persistent discourse on the affinity between women and Jews, the place of Antisemitism in Wilhelmine Germany was not identical to that of antifeminism. Identification with Antisemitism was indeed common enough in various social milieus of the right, but blatant Antisemitic expressions were typical of its margins only. It was there, and there alone, that Antisemitism had been sweeping and unequivocal. The opposition to women and their demand for equality, in contrast, was more culturally widespread and more generally acceptable. Except for a few radical democrats, everyone seemed to regard them as intruders into public life, in higher education, and in politics. Such views were common among conservatives and liberals, modernists and anti-modernists, anti-socialists and even some

---

22 Otto Rank, "Das Wesen des Judentums" [1905], translated in Dennis B. Klein, *Jewish Origins of the Psychoanalytic Movement*, New York 1981, Appendix C. On Rank, see E. James Lieberman, *Acts of Will: The Life and Work of Otto Rank*, New York 1985, and Esther Menaker, *Otto Rank: A Rediscovered Legacy*, New York 1982.
23 Both, along with others, are discussed in Jacques Le Rider, *Modernity and Crises of Identity*, New York, 1993, 101–146. Hans Gross, who, together with psychiatrist Paul Nacke, established the first periodical in criminology (1898), was from 1905 a professor for "Kriminalstatistik" in Graz. See Franziska Lamott, "Prof. Dr. Hans Gross gegen seinen Sohn. Zum Verhältniß von Wissenschaft und Subjektivität," in: *Wunderblock. Eine Geschichte der modernen Seele*, eds. Jean Clair, Cathrin Pichler, and Wolfgang Pircher, Vienna 1989, 611–619. On Groddeck, see Carl M. and Sylva Grossman, *The Wild Analyst. The Life and Work of Georg Groddeck*, New York 1965.

socialists – men and women alike.[24] Clearly unambiguous was the conservative stance in all its shades; the position of moderate liberals, who now found themselves drifting away from their movement's progressive views, was more complex. But most intriguing was the attitude of the staunch modernists, who were active in Germany's progressive cultural scene and who had devised a way to combine creativity and innovations with an unyielding antagonism to women's emancipation. In late-nineteenth-century Vienna, some of the well-known modernists, such figures as composer Arnold Schoenberg and architect Adolf Loos, held only contempt for anything they saw as "feminine." Perhaps fearful of revealing the feminine aspect of their own personalities, they insisted on keeping their distance from anything they regarded as feminine: the "femininity" of the contemporary decadent style, the materialism and overt simplicity that were considered to be distinctly feminine traits.

From this perspective, George Mosse's thesis in his *Nationalism and Sexuality*, stressing the uniform attitude of Germany's nationalist society to all "others" within it, seems all too encompassing.[25] Mosse's presentation of the conformist facet of the nationalist movement underlines its emphasis on a specific kind of masculinity along with its characteristic repulsion of any kind of "deviation." He argues that, throughout the nineteenth century, the champions of nationalism – many liberals among them – feared feminization and devoted themselves to establishing "bourgeois decency," complete with a puritanical sexual ethos. Not all "others" in this society, however, were treated equally. Homosexuals, indeed, were disqualified from equal membership in the national community by the large majority of those who regarded themselves as its legitimate members at the turn of the century. The opposition to women's equality, while sometimes less vehement, was consistent and shared by the majority. In contrast, the Jews, who in the days prior to 1848 were commonly rejected by the various ideological camps – liberals included – were by now regarded as complete outsiders only by a relatively small Antisemitic minority. In support of his position, Mosse refers to Antisemitic activities of that time: the book by the Frenchman Eduard Drumont, the politics of Herman Ahlwardt', and the publications of Carl Wilmanns and Otto Weininger, of course. However, in comparison with the short-lived popularity of the Antisemitic agitators, authors and politicians, we should consider the large-scale and long-term effects of those who were then preoccupied with matters of sexual identity: Ivan Bloch, the most prominent sexologist in the early twentieth century; Sigmund Freud himself and almost all

---

[24] For examples see Evans, *The Feminist Movement in Germany*, 146–175; Jean H. Quataert, *Reluctant Feminists in German Social Democracy 1885–1917*, Princeton, NJ 1979, and especially Planert, *Antifeminismus im Kaiserreich*.

[25] Mosse, *Nationalism and Sexuality*, especially the conclusion, 181–191.

contemporary psychologists, psychiatrists, physicians, and criminologists.²⁶ From today's perspective, most of the members of this group seem troubled and cautious defenders of bourgeois values, but at the time they were the heralds of a generally progressive and enlightened sanity. Prior to World War I, blatant Antisemitism was shared by a minority on the far right, a marginal minority albeit one that was often loud and, contrary to expectations, eventually very influential. Anti-feminism, in contrast, was an element of mainstream culture, represented equally on both the left and the right, and carring a message that reflected a well-established norm that was shared by the entire spectrum of Wilhelmine society, indeed by much of European society as a whole.

Feminism, finally, was upheld by a small group of men, and a somewhat larger group of women – a tiny and rather inconsequential minority. In addition, its location on the German political scene was much less definable. Only Liberals and Socialists of a very distinct shade supported equal rights for women, while at the same time, a milder and more conservative version of feminism, one that rejected egalitarianism and stressed the unique "essence of femininity," had also emerged. This kind of feminism put special emphasis on motherhood as the ultimate feminine role, motherhood that could serve as a basis for launching an attack on the presumably cold and inhuman nature of modern society. Ideologically and socially, then, feminism, and not only in Germany, lacked a clear and consistent backbone.²⁷ Moreover, it often found itself in rather strange company. While nationalism was indeed designed especially for men, women too could apparently find their place within it. On the eve of World War I, most women's organizations embraced the national verbiage of the time, often with open enthusiasm, and during the war some of them even propagated their own sort of chauvinism. This was by no means a phenomenon limited to Germany. Some of Europe's most prominent feminists climbed on the bandwagon of nationalism at that time.²⁸ This was particularly conspicuous in the case of Emmeline and Christabel Pankhurst, the militant leaders of Britain's Women's Social

---

26 Mosse discusses contemporary sexologists in chap. 2 of *Nationalism and Sexuality*, with an emphasis on the issue of homosexuality. On Freud see mainly the fifth volume of his collected writings, *Sexualleben*, Frankfurt a. M., 1972. A vast body of literature exists on this aspect of his theory. See, for instance, Frank J. Sulloway, *Freud: Biologist of the Mind: Beyond the Psychoanalytic Legend*, Cambridge, MA 1992, especially chap. 8. See also Peter Gay, *Freud: A Life for Our Time*, New York 1988, 501–522 and the bibliographical references, 773–774.

27 See *Maternity and Gender Policies: Women and the Rise of the European Welfare State, 1880s–1950s*, eds. Gisela Bock and Pat Thane, London 1991, and Ann T. Allen, *Feminism and Motherhood in Germany, 1800–1914*, New Brunswick 1991.

28 For a comparative look, see *Behind the Lines: Gender and the Two World Wars*, eds. Margaret R. Higonnet New Haven, CT 1987, and *Borderlines: Gender and Identities in War and Peace, 1870–1930*, ed. Billie Melman, New York 1998, 65–84, 421. See also Susan Kingsley Kent, "The

and Political Union (WSPU). Even before the war, the two were freely borrowing from the nationalist vocabulary, and in 1916 they publicly urged a special feminine contribution to the war effort based on the "natural patriotism" of Britain's women, their highly developed sense of duty, and their proven courage. In that conceptual framework, Germany was conceived of as a particularly despicable masculine nation, and the call for victory over its army was thus made self-evident from a feminist point of view, even an extension of the fight for women's rights. The inclusion of nationalism within the overall feminist syndrome in early twentieth-century Europe occurred just as swiftly and as smoothly as the parallel inclusion of nationalism as a legitimate aspect of socialism. Thus, at no stage was feminism ever the hallmark of one specific political camp or social group. It was much too weak to serve as a signifier of a particular cultural milieu, and it was much too rare to be regarded as a social norm in any contemporary context. Thus it was the belief in emancipation on the one hand and Antisemitism on the other that served as the signposts of the two extreme political cultures co-existing in Wilhelmine Germany. Feminism and anti-feminism were important battle cries but neither of them, each for a different set of reasons, could assume the role of cultural code.

Politics of Sexual Difference: World War I and the Demise of British Feminism," in: *Journal of British Studies* XXVII (3), 1988, 232–253.

7 Readjusting Cultural Codes: Reflections on Antisemitism, Anti-Zionism and the Critique of Israel

Twenty five year ago the Leo Baeck Institute Yearbook had published my essay "Antisemitism as a Cultural Code."[1] I was astonished at the attention it later received, since I hardly had a chance to try it on a live audience before publication and expected only a limited reaction, if at all. My single presentation of this text had taken place in a conference at St. Antony's college in Oxford, and there it drew a rather hostile response from some of the participants. There seemed to be no reason to expect that others would react differently. In the end it was probably the ringing title, based on a variation upon an essay by Clifford Geertz, that contributed to the modest fame of this piece.[2] Concepts based on anthropological and ethnographic research were becoming fashionable at the time in other historiographical contexts too, and the introduction of the term "cultural code" in relation to the problematics of Antisemitism has apparently been timely.[3]

I myself had some grave doubts. I took seriously the critique of the historians, dealing both with German and with German-Jewish history, and have tried on several occasions during the following years to re-examine the validity of this term and work out its implications in a number of different ways.[4] Now, in view of the antiquity of this entire episode, let me begin by recapitulating what still seems relevant to me in the arguments laid out in that old paper and in some of the additional, related work I did thereafter.[5]

At the time, I was working on the so-called modern Antisemitic movement in Germany during the last third of the 19th century. This has been a major focus of research since the end of the Second World War and many historians then – as

---

1 Shulamit Volkov, "Antisemitism as a Cultural Code", essay number 4 above.
2 See Clifford Geertz, "Ideology as a Cultural System," in his *The Interpretation of Cultures. Selected Essays,* New York 1973, 193–233. Geertz, who uses terms such as "cultural patterns" or "symbolic systems", finds the term "code" rather less appropriate. On that see his "Thick Description: Toward an Interpretive Theory of Culture," also in *The Interpretation,* 3–30, especially page 9, where he critically discusses Gilbert Ryle's ethnographic approach and a term he used, "established codes".
3 A more favorable reaction to the term and its potential use was forthcoming after a lecture and publication of a subsequent paper, Shulamit Volkov, "Le Texte et la Parole: de l'Antisemitisme d'avant 1914 a l'Antisemitisme nazi," in: *L'Allemagne Nazie et le génocide Juif,* ed. François Furet, Paris 1982, 76–98. The English translation here, number 5.
4 See "Antisemitism and anti-Feminism", number 6, above.
5 For the relevant bibliography see the original essay, number 4 above.

now – believed that here laid the roots of Nazi Antisemitism and at least the partial explanation for the Holocaust. The novelty of that *modern* Antisemitism, it was generally agreed, was twofold. It allowed the substitution of racial theory, or rather pseudo-theory, for the old religious hatred, and it brought to fruition for the first time the *political* potential of Jew-hating. Both these characteristics, ran the argument, were later exploited to the full by Hitler and his followers.

I tended to minimize the importance of these factors. I thought that racialism was grafted upon old motivations for Jew-hating rather than substituted for them, and that if anything the meager success of the mushrooming Antisemitic political parties at the time could have served to show *the limits* of its recruiting power. Instead, I suggested, Antisemitism has had another function in Imperial Germany. It served as a code, a sign for a much larger and more important phenomenon typical of the time, namely that of anti-modernism. An entire section of German society was by then deeply unsettled by the implications of an advanced industrialism and its concomitant new value-system and life-style, I argued. And apparently, all of the typically anti-modern social elements, and not only in Germany, were at the same time infected by Antisemitism. In their eyes, Jews stood for modernity, for success under its auspices and for the chance of manipulating its advantages for the purpose of destroying all remnants of the old world. Anti-Jewish attitudes were not particularly *important* for most of these people, I argued. But precisely *because* they were marginal to the overall anti-modern worldview, expressing them could serve as a mark of a radical position on other, more important matters. It became a political symbol in the context of the late 19th century; or even more generally: it was becoming a cultural code, indicating the overall adherence to a certain cultural choice.

Beyond its descriptive value, this thesis has had a number of advantages, I thought. For instance, it allowed one to explain the presumably anti-Jewish position taken by some Jews, who belonged to what I saw as the anti-modern camp, and to do so without using the concept of self-hatred, which I have treated then, and still do today, with a great deal of skepticism.[6] It also – perhaps even more importantly – allows one to suggest that Nazi Antisemitism, never indeed merely a code or a sign but a source for a full-fledged program of annihilation, was itself a kind of novelty, considering this background. The change in the *meaning* of anti-Jewish rhetoric's introduced by the Nazis was radical, no doubt, but it was – surprisingly perhaps – not immediately apparent. Many Jews – as well as many non-Jewish Germans – tended to misread Hitler's intentions. *They* were still using

---

[6] See Shulamit Volkov, "Selbstgefälligkeit und Slebsthaß", in: *Antisemitismus als kultureller Code. Zehn Essays*, München, 2000, 181–196.

the cultural tools of a previous era, I argued, not realizing that the language, their very own language, was meanwhile being transformed and its meaning changed. The meaning of Antisemitism has shifted, but it was not easy to perceive the shift or prepare to react upon it.

Furthermore, and crucial in many respects, the cultural code thesis could help explain the open *anti*-Antisemitic line taken by the left, for instance, in pre-World-War-I Europe, especially in Germany and in France. To be sure, any long-term view of Antisemitism could not fail to show an anti-Jewish streak in the various movements on the left. Some historians, such as Edmund Silberner in an earlier generation and Robert Wistrich later on, claimed, in fact, that Antisemitism has always been constitutive to the left, especially to the revolutionary left.[7] And examples could be brought not only from thinkers and ideologues, such as Proudhon in France and Eugen Dühring in Germany, but also from the French socialists' procrastination in defending Dreyfus in fin de siécle France, as well as from the position of most Austrian socialists on a variety of Jewish issues and from the many common asides against Jews in the Social Democratic press throughout the German *Kulturraum*.[8]

Moreover, even the most decent European socialists, entirely uncontaminated by explicit Antisemitism, were hostile to the idea and the ideals of Jewish Nationalism and to any and all forms of Zionism.[9] Nevertheless, beginning no later than the first decade of the 20th century, European Socialists clearly saw the inner bond between Antisemitism and anti-modernism, and were able to diagnose its meaning for Socialism. In France it meant a bond between Antisemitism and anti-Republicanism. In Germany it was the link between Antisemitism and the opposition to everything related to the new world of industrialism and democratization. Because Antisemitism served as a cultural code for a not-always-outspoken posture that was clearly associated with the right, socialists began to feel they had to distance themselves from it, at least publicly. They were careful not to appear as philo-semites – to use a contemporary term – but as a rule, stayed clear from any Antisemitism in the *Öffentlichkeit*.[10]

So far some supporting evidence for my cultural code thesis and at least *some* of its implications. Before I attempt to apply this idea in other, more contemporary

---

7 Edmund Silberner, *Sozialisten zur Judenfrage*, Berlin 1962; Robert Wistrich, *Socialism and the Jews: The Dilemmas of assimilation in Germany and Austria-Hungary*, London 1982.
8 See Rosemarie Leuchen-Seppel, *Sozialdemokratie und Antisemitismus im Kaiserreich*, Bonn 1978, especially chapter 5.
9 See, above all, Shlomo Na'aman, *Marxismus und Zionismus*, Gerlingen 1977.
10 See "The Immunization of Social Democracy against Antisemitism in Imperial Germany", number 3 above.

contexts and examine its present validity, let me say something about the route that had led me to take up this thesis. The cultural code thesis has had two sources, as is so common in historiography: professional and autobiographical, or – better perhaps – personal. Originally it grew out of my early work on the master-artisans in Germany during what we then used to call – after Hans Rosenberg – "die Grosse Depression" (the Great Depression).[11] Indeed, it was easy to demonstrate the instrumental role, i.e. the *function* of Jew-hating within the organizational and political efforts of these handicraft masters at the time. Their deep uneasiness with modernity was all too often translated into an Antisemitic verbiage, though rarely into anything more threatening than that. They were not revolutionaries. They were usually even ready to defend the "system". But they were convinced it had been corrupted. Not Capitalism was their enemy, they argued, but the Jews who had led it to inhuman excesses; not Liberalism as such – but the Jews who misinterpreted and misrepresented it. Not the modern state was responsible for neglecting their interests, but the Jews who always thought of their own interests only. The link between Antisemitism and the fear of modernity was clearly apparent among the men I then investigated.[12]

But it was not only my academic work that led me to seek the possibly symbolic function of Antisemitism in modern society. More important perhaps was my first-hand experience with anti-Zionism on the Berkeley campus during the 1960s and in some of the German academic towns immediately afterwards. By then, Anti-Zionism was clearly a constant theme among members of the so-called *New* Left, including those who considered themselves the revolutionaries of these heroic years. Strangely enough, at least from my perspective, Anti-Zionism was often particularly strong among the Jewish members of this crowd. No doubt, the realization that perhaps not only anti-Zionism but also Antisemitism may be seen as part of a larger, more comprehensive ideological package-deal first occurred to me as I observed my American Jewish friends operating as they did within the various leftwing groupings during these years.

In some ways, of course, their anti-Zionism could merely be considered a continuation of the anti-Zionist position of so many liberal Jews from the inception of this movement. In the prosperous Jewish communities of the West during the early decades of the 20th century, Jews opposing Zionism were surely more common than Zionists. However, after the Holocaust, this "balance of power" shifted, and following the realization of the dimensions of mass extermination of

---

[11] See his influential *Grosse Depression und Bismarckzeit. Wirtschaftsablauf, Gesellschaft und Politik im Mitteleuropa*, Berlin 1967.
[12] See Shulamit Volkov, *The Rise of Popular Antimodernism in Germany. The Urban Master Artisans 1873–1896*, Princeton 1978.

the Jews under the Nazis and the tragic effects of the closed-doors policies of so many countries during and immediately after the war, it seemed no longer bon ton to oppose Zionism – neither principally nor in practice. Both Jews and non-Jews, on the Left and on the Right, proceeded much more carefully now along the lines of the old pro-and-contra-Zionism debate. In fact, it was only after the Israeli victory in 1967, when the existence of Israel seemed secure and its policies of occupation began to draw criticism, that anti-Zionism began to play the role of a cultural code within the ideological set-up of the New Left, both in America and in Europe. Once again we were faced with an ideational package-deal. Its main components were anti-Colonialism, a somewhat vague but often violent anti-Capitalism and a deep suspicion vis a vis the policies of the United States, not only in Vietnam but also, often especially, in various parts of Latin America. In some countries this package also included the emerging ecological argument, so that on the whole, this was no longer the old anti-modern package, though it still had some similarities with it. Moreover, it was no longer located on the Right but on the Left. But despite these all-important differences, here too a particular form of anti-Jewish posture was made to serve as a symbol, an indication of belonging, or a cultural code. The package-deal has been transformed, its social and political focus relocated, but the general mechanism of its operation was similar in many ways.

An additional perspective then helped convince me of the validity of my interpretation. By the late 1960s and the early 1970s, expressions of anti-Israeli, if not always clear anti-Zionism, were sounded ever more frequently from representatives of the so-called developing countries, members of the now seemingly extinct "Third World". Occasionally, such attitudes were based on solidarity with the Arab cause, no doubt. But the general anti-Jewish, indeed Antisemitic twist, given to such political stand could not be missed. Furthermore, it was at this point that the anti-Colonial struggle no longer focused on straightforward demands for independence on the part of the colonized and instead began to display its cultural contours. The overall set of values and norms typical of the Imperialist West and its inherent list of priorities were turned upside down and made into a target for attack. It was an attack on cultural conceit, on disregard for the suffering of non-white peoples, on the traditional paternalism and cultural arrogance of the West. Finally, and through a vague adoption of old Antisemitic claims and suppositions, the proverbial Jew has become a symbol of that West. He stood now for its essence and for all its vice. By attacking him one was finally up in arms against all and every manifestation of the colonizers' culture. Among the colonialists the persecuted were as guilty as the persecutors. Even the most downtrodden among them were no longer privileged. Even they were legitimate targets for hatred. Jewish claim for special consideration because of the Holocaust and its horrendous consequences seemed especially outrageous to spokesmen from the Third World. In view of their own devastation, the Holocaust elicited little sympathy. A combination of opposition to Israel, often while linking its policies to the evils of South-African apartheid, and a reliance on a borrowed, European Antisemitic tradition, became a part of the overall anti-Imperialist syndrome. Antisemitism may not have been particularly important to those applying it, but – once again – it served them well to signify their overall position. Personally, then, it was the case of anti-Zionism among leftwing activists during the late 60s that I had first diagnosed as a cultural code for one or another larger political-intellectual package and that served me for interpreting both contemporary and historical situations. A look at France in the late 19th century, during the Dreyfus affair, offered a fitting historical case-study. It appeared that as the affair became a major public issue, it consolidated on the one side the anti-Dreyfusards, who were part of the general anti-Republican camp in the Third Republic of the late 1890s, and on the other – the Dreyfusards, namely the Republican forces, despite the various controversies that raged among them.[13] A decade earlier, one could still locate Antisemitic attitudes across much of the social and political spectrum of France. In the years between 1887 and 1889, the *Socialist Review*, the official newspaper for the Socialist movement, published a series of Antisemitic articles, though it occasionally gave voice to milder positions, as well. The Blanquist and Proudhonist traditions within the Socialist left in France were heavy with Antisemitic connotations. But when an anti-Dreyfusard and a generally anti-Jewish position became a mark of the anti-Republican camp, French Socialists, much like their German comrades under different circumstances, found it necessary to distance themselves from it. This became particularly evident in the aftermath of Emil Zola's *j'acuse* of 1898 and as the violent message of the Antisemitic League was made apparent in the streets of Paris. Like the Social Democrats in the *Kaiserreich*, the French Socialists too never managed to rid their membership entirely of Antisemitic prejudices, but in public and in their open pronouncements, they left no doubt as to the side they chose to take.[14]

Here too, a position on the so-called Jewish question, not in itself of paramount importance, came to indicate a belonging to a larger camp, signifying loyalty to a larger ideological package deal, a political stand as well as an overall cultural choice. In both Germany and France of the turn of the 19th century, however, it was often unclear whether Antisemitism served as a code for a general anti-modern and anti-Republican stand, or if an outspoken *anti*-Antisemitism

---

[13] See "The Written Matter and he spoken Word," number 5 above.
[14] For this issue see, among the many new books on this subject, Pierre Birnbaum, *The Antisemitic Moment. A Tour of France in 1898*, New York 2003.

fulfilled this role for the modern, emancipatory – and in France the Republican – camp. A decision along these lines, I believe, depends on the prominence of the Antisemitic issue within each context. A position on a certain issue could be considered a code, it seems to me, only if and when it plays a rather marginal role for the men and women concerned. Thus, as I have elsewhere argued, anti-Feminism, another creed of the conservative, anti-modern block in pre-world War One Europe, could not serve as a code, because already by the last decade of the 19th century and the first of the 20th, it was a major issue; neither a sign for something else, nor a code for more important matters.[15]

To sum up, we have so far relied upon two assumptions in trying to interpret Antisemitism – or later on anti-Zionism, too – as cultural codes. The first is that cultural as well as social and political views come in packages, in the form of ideational syndromes. The second – that only relatively minor issues, though of the kind that are common enough in public discourse, can serve as codes, signifying larger, more important syndromes. Much of the criticism that has been voiced against my thesis came from those who objected to one or the other of these assumptions. The first kind of objection, was not usually sounded on theoretical grounds. The fact that people's belief-system has the form of more or less well-integrated compounds or 'syndromes' was rarely contested. Opposition usually came from historians, familiar with the complexity and diversity, especially of Germany during the period under consideration, who claimed that a division of its society into two camps, recognizable by their attitudes to Jews, was an unwarranted simplification. This, moreover, was from the start intertwined with a more comprehensive and perhaps more important objection, related to the validity of the *Sonderweg* thesis in German historiography. My paradigm, the paradigm of a split-society, so to speak, in which two major political camps and two sub-cultures were set against each other, seemed to fit that thesis well enough, despite the fact that I have attempted to apply it not only to Germany. It seemed to support the *Sonderweg* view, according to which social, political and cultural developments, most particularly since the late 19th century, prepared the ground for the later victory of National Socialism.[16] Moreover, this thesis included the claim that it was some shortcomings in the process of modernization and in the way modernity had been received and internalized in Germany that were the sources of its uniqueness vis a vis its European neighbors. The alternative view, originally proposed by Geoff Eley and David Blackbourn precisely at the time I published my "cultural code" paper,

---

15 See the essay no. 6 above.
16 For a critique of my work from this perspective, though without reference to the cultural-code thesis, see Geoff Eley, *From Unification to Nazism: Reinterpreting the German Past*, London 1986, 23–41.

disputed this uniqueness altogether and stressed the bourgeois nature of German society at the time of the *Kaiserreich*, its relative modernity and its similarity to societies in other countries at the time.[17] Accordingly, Germany was pluralistic and diversified, so that a breaking line along issues of emancipation and Antisemitism could not gain the importance of a cultural code. A number of studies by English historians on some of the early 20th century political associations, such as the Navy League and the Pan-German League, argued that Antisemitism had in fact been negligible even among members of the popular right.[18] Later on, some German historians too, above all the late Thomas Nipperdey, took up the same argument and likewise claimed that other, reform-oriented associations, too, though sometimes anti-modern in orientation, were not Antisemitic.[19] Afterwards, Gideon Reuveni, has argued that if consumers' organization rather than producers' interest-groups were to be investigated, Antisemitism would be found even less frequently among their membership.[20] In other words: a variety of other lines of division were more significant for the social world of the *Kaiserreich*, overshadowing the general left-right division, or indeed the Antisemitic versus the anti-Antisemitic camp.

There were, no doubt, other divisions within German society at the turn of the century and there were likewise quite a few cases in which ideological package deals proved unreliable as descriptive characteristics of this society. Some of the better-known individual examples were to be found among artists, such as the poet Stefan George, whose artistic modernity clearly did not match his reactionary social and political views. But artists, after all, are expected to excel in breaking up conventional wisdom, and ideational package deals are – and were – such conventions

---

17 By now the literature on the *Sonderweg* debate is enormous, indeed, but still critical for understanding its origins is Geoff Eley and David Blackbourne, *The Peculiarities of German History. Bourgeois Society and Politics in Nineteenth-Century Germany*, Oxford 1984. The earlier German version was published in Frankfurt a. M. 1980.
18 See Geoff Eley, *Reshaping the German Right*, New Haven 1980, and a wider perspective in "The German Right: How it changed," in his *From Unification to Nazism: Reinterpreting the German Past*, London 1986, 231–253; Roger Chickering, *We Men who Feel most German. A Cultural Study of the Pan-German League*, Boston 1984.
19 See Thomas Nipperdey, *Deutsche Geschichte 1866–1914*, Vol. 2, München 1992, 301–303, and an earlier, but as far as I can see a more balanced view, in: "1933 und die Kontinuität der deutschen Geschichte," in his: *Nachdenken über die deutsche Geschichte*, München 1986, 186–205. Also compare Hans-Günter Zmarzlik, "Antisemitismus im Deutschen Kaiserreich 1871–1918," in: *Die Juden als Minderheit in der Geschichte*, eds. Brend Martin and Ernst Schulin, München 1981, 249–270.
20 See Gideon Reuveny, "'Productivists' and 'Consumerist' Narrative regarding Jews in German history," in *German History from the Margins*, eds. Neil Gregor, Nils Roemer and Mark Roseman, Bloomington 2006, 165–184.

par excellence. Similarly, there were also men on the left who continued to parade their Antisemitism. Vienna at the turn of the century knew quite a few of them.[21] Ideational package deals are indeed rough tools and clearly not everyone succumbs to their spell. Still, on the whole they are very pervasive and extremely powerful. While the Pan-German League had been careful on the Jewish issue for some time, it eventually took on Antisemitism – always central in its Berlin chapter – with a vengeance. The Navy League may have been less than outspoken on that matter, since it was an association representing above all the interests of the upper bourgeoisie – by no means obvious candidates for upholding the cultural views of the anti-modern right. And a variety of reformers, fighting for abolition of alcohol or tobacco, for instance, were probably likewise unlikely to get involved publicly on the Jewish issue, as theirs too was not a typically rightwing agenda – old or new. Furthermore, there were clearly numerous variations within each camp; not just with regard to the Jews. Elements of the Right held different attitudes towards Christianity, to take one example. Despite the prominence of the Junkers within this milieu, to take another, others within it were vocal opponents of the old aristocracy. Material interests too tended to divide members of the same cultural block. Still, on some major issues these people saw eye to eye. Mosse's "German Ideology" seemed crucial to all of them. They heavily relied upon an anti-modern mentality, including a systematic rejection of the tenets of Liberalism, Democracy and Socialism, and they all too often reveled in nostalgic visions of a long lost golden past while having various utopian plans for the future. An antagonistic attitude towards Jews could easily be found among them. It sometime sprang from a deep-seated Christian education; occasionally from some kind of xenophobia or from unease in a situation of real or presumed professional competition. The function of their publicly paraded Antisemitism was the same: to indicate their basic cultural choices, to qualify them in the eyes of their peers, to define them vis a-vis their adversaries.

The second type of criticism directed at the cultural code thesis was in a way merely the other side of the same coin. If some historians of Wilhelmine Germany thought this thesis gave too much weight to the issue of Antisemitism, others felt it underestimated its significance. Such underestimation could pertain to a particular case – in a particular place and particular time – or it could be claimed for the overall development of Antisemitism, from its inception and up to National Socialism. Surely, both these reproaches deserve some consideration. In fact, there is a tradition of sorts, according to which historians of Antisemitism insist

---

21 See Leuschen-Seppel, *Sozialdemokratie und Antisemitismus*, and Wistrich, *Socialism and the Jews*.

on considering all its manifestations as outgrowths of a permanent antipathy towards Jews, based on ancient controversies and conflicting social relationships. Every attempt to disengage a particular case from that linear age-old story is therefore strictly rejected. Let me mention here as an example, Jacob Katz's elaborate attempt to dismiss Eleonora Sterling's interpretation of the 1819 Hep-Hep riots in Germany as "displacement" of hostility and violence from issues of modernization to anti-Jewish rioting. Katz, usually a very open-minded historian, refused to acknowledge such an interpretation. His famous essay on the Hep-Hep riots is an extended effort to reject it, dismissing the significance of contemporary issues and stressing the role played by a continuous European tradition of Jew-hating in this case, too.[22] He was also ill at ease with the cultural code idea. Now, there is no question that the choice of the Jews as targets for violence – actual in the early 19th century and only verbal in its later years – was not arbitrary. It clearly relied on the anti-Jewish sentiment embedded in Christian culture. But a historical view of the manifestations of this sentiment must also consider the particular context in which such sentiments were activated and their particular function at a certain point in time. The fact is, after all, that though Jews were not much appreciated at *all* times, they were actively resented and persecuted only in *particular* places and *particular* times. Beyond acknowledging the persistence of anti-Jewish feelings, it is the historian's role to explain how and why a certain form of Antisemitism characterizes certain societies at certain times.

Still, concentrating upon the function of Antisemitism within a particular historical context and beyond the effect of its permanent existence, while not necessarily detracting from its significance – so I believe – is surely a way of avoiding its over-estimation. We have all gone through what might be called 'the Goldhagen-stage' about a generation ago. It was a reminder of how history could be read backward, by choosing only the supporting evidence for one's thesis. However Antisemitic Germany was during the late 19th century, it was clearly in fact a land of what at that time seemed a uniquely successful emancipation. Contemporary Jews from across Europe who sent their sons – and sometimes even their daughters – to study and live in Imperial Germany were not simply blind or ignorant. Its society embodied for them the potential of existing freely and creatively as Jewish citizens of a modern state. It was not an existence free of Antisemitism, to be sure, but this issue was largely "under control", according to most observers. Let us not forget that the Antisemitism that provoked the emergence of

---

[22] See Eleonora Sterling, "Anti-Jewish Riots in Germany in 1819: A Displacement of Social Protest," in: *Historia Judaica* 2 (1950), 105–142, and Jakob Katz, *Die Hep-Hep Verfolgungen des Jahres 1819*, Berlin 1994, especially 71–88.

Zionism then and there was mainly manifested in Russia of the pogroms and in France of the Dreyfus affair. Yes, no doubt, the cultural code thesis suggests the *relative un*importance of Antisemitism at the time. While it does not deny its existence, it does try to avoid inflating its significance. It provides a perspective on the period under consideration, which is dependent upon its own parameters, seeking to preserve its own "directness to God", to use Ranke's terminology, or simply uphold its own uniqueness.

Before I move forward in time, examining the validity of the idea of cultural code for more contemporary situations, let me first take a small detour, in order to further undermine the claim to exclusivity of those explanations that rely on the age-old heritage of Antisemitism alone. In fact, the historiography of Antisemitism has for many years applied another term that carried with it symbolic connotation and related Jew-hating to particular events, chronologically and geographically, namely – the "scapegoat". The word itself, as is well known, indicates an ancient Jewish ritual, in which guilt is symbolically laden upon a he-goat that is then sent to a no-man's land in the mountains of Jerusalem. By analogy it was often argued that Jews were made to carry blame for various catastrophes, such as a variety of social ills or the plague, primarily during the Middle Ages. Turning against Jews in some of the early-modern episodes seems to have followed a similar pattern too, and even later attacks on Jews, instead of on landlords or on exploiting capitalists, were often interpreted along the same lines. Like the cultural code paradigm, scapegoating too does not stand outside the tradition of Jew-hating, since it is precisely that tradition that qualifies Jews in particular crisis-situations to take the blame. The cultural code model seems to depend on this tradition even more heavily. Being a later phenomenon, it relies not only on the tradition of despising the Jews but also on that of making symbolic use of this hatred in a variety of social and cultural situations. In comparison with scapegoating, the cultural code mechanism is more general, applicable to times of stability, or even of growth and prosperity, not only to days of wrath.

Furthermore, scapegoating is basically a psychological tool, the workings of which is presumably always the same, while coding is a cultural process taking different shapes in different times and places. It may have been born out of the same mechanism in Germany and in France of the late 19th century, but in each case it served a somewhat different purpose. It surely serves different purposes when it is found to be a practice of the right or of the left, and it is a better instrument for historians, because it takes into account both change and repetition. It clearly stresses the *shifting* function of Antisemitism and provides a way of thinking about *difference*, not only about continuity.

Thus, while antipathy towards Jews is to some degree a cultural constant, my model rejects the approach of observing its history as simply cyclical or spiral.

This antipathy, I argue, is neither always the same, nor does it follow a pattern of rising intensity. The nineteen century, accordingly, ought not to be considered a "rehearsal for destruction", nor Nazism the peak of an on-going, linear development. It did build upon "the longest hatred", of course, but finally introduced – as had happened in the past – a radical new variation upon the old theme.

Thus, Nazi Antisemitism was not simply yet another step in the long march towards extermination, but in many important ways an entirely new departure. It was, in any case, a diversion from the path of Antisemitism during the years of Imperial Germany. Only under Nazism did Antisemitism lose its symbolic role and became most emphatically an end in itself. For Hitler, though even for him Antisemitism may not have always been the highest priority, it was in any case a separate, central issue, one that became ever more crucial as his other goals seemed less and less realizable. Under the rule of National Socialism, Antisemitism no longer stood for other issues. It was no longer a sign of belonging to a particular cultural or political camp. The attack upon the Jews has become a major policy matter under Nazism, a goal to be pursued relentlessly, under all circumstances, in peace and in war, in times of victory and in times of defeat. Perhaps here lied an important accompanying danger of Antisemitism used as a cultural code: At a certain point it could lose its symbolic nature and turn almost imperceptibly into a full-scale violent attack.

Is that what we are experiencing today? If indeed the joint anti-Zionist and anti-Israeli language of the Left in the 1960s and 70s served as a cultural code to indicate belonging to the camp of anti-Imperialism, anti-Colonialism and a new sort of anti-Capitalism – has it now lost its symbolic meaning? Is it now a matter of direct and full-scale attack upon the Jews? I do not know. Perhaps. Surely, the context has been transformed. A number of additional elements have meanwhile been added to the ideational package deal that characterized the Left during the 60s: the specter of globalization, for instance, the growing importance of the ecological agenda, and more. And even more important now is the identity assumed between the policies of the United States, always a target for attack, especially from the European Left, and those of the State of Israel. Today, following three decades of conflict in the Middle East – opposition to Israel can hardly be regarded as a code for some other evil. In addition to a more open Antisemitism among xenophobic groups on the Right, the sub-culture of the Left, even of the Center-Left, can no longer consider its position towards Israel a side-issue, ripe to serve as a cultural code. This has become a major concern. The last public opinion poll in Europe documented, in fact, not so much a rising level of Antisemitism, but a rising anxiety concerning the world-wide implications of the Israeli-Palestinian conflict. Our traditional enemies may not need to adjust their position to the new situation, but we may have already passed the moment in which our friends too could use their attack against us as a sign of other beliefs and commitments. We may be approaching the stage in which we really are the target of their resentment, fear and hatred.

Unlike previous occasions, however, this time we are no longer pawns on someone else's Chess game. It is up to us to act. We could take action that would prove our commitment to peace and our concern for the wellbeing of others. We could set out to convince those who were either against us or at the very best were using their opposition to us as a code for their opposition to more important forces, that we understand the severity of the hour. Unfortunately, there seems to be no step taken in this direction. It is apparently easier to blame all others, to complain of Antisemitism or anti-Zionism, to measure incessantly their intensity, but never to take any responsibility for trying to diminish their force.

III **Revisions and Related Themes**

8 Nationalism, Antisemitism and German Historiography

Historians are expected to provide an explanation for important events of the past. Following the Second World War, it seemed as if every event connected with the German past merely served as material for explaining National Socialism – its rise, its methods, and its politics. Moreover, behind these efforts often stood the search for an explanation of the most problematic aspect of the Nazi Regime: its project of exterminating the European Jews. Expectedly, valid objections have been raised by later generations of historians, especially since the late 1970s, arguing that with this manner of thinking German history loses its vitality and is channeled into a one-way street. After all, one was always taught in Germany to narrate events of the past as they really occurred, not merely as a "Rehearsal for destruction."[1] It was time to point out the *multitude of continuities* in German history. However, on this route too, it now seems to me, we have lost direction. Today, no doubt, we might be able to perceive a more complex and versatile course of German history, but we are still unable to explain its most important and most confounding events. The circumstances which culminated in what we often call Auschwitz are as hard to explain as ever. And the reasons for this are not only the enormous proportions of the task and the inexplicable nature of the occurrences, nor the fact that one could not or should not historicize them, but the fact that we have by now revised our former explanations too many times and too radically. To put it simply, I think we have gone over the top.

The discussion about the German '*Sonderweg*' can serve as an example. To be sure, post-war historiography has often exaggerated the singularity of German history. After all, Germany never took a completely different path to modernity. On many counts, German society was not more unusual than other European societies, each unique in its own way. All of them underwent a painful process of industrialization, and throughout this process all restructured their respective economy, experienced social transformations and suffered the consequences of political upheavals. Indeed, throughout the last two centuries, European culture experienced radical changes everywhere across the continent. Germany was no exception. At the end of the 1920s, despite the setback caused by World War I,

---

1 Compare Paul W. Massing, *Rehearsal for Destruction. A Study of Political Antisemitism in Imperial Germany*, New York 1949.

Note: Translated from German by Luis Gruhler.

Germany still managed to achieve a remarkable economic recovery and develop a healthy bourgeois society ruled by parliamentary institutions and a democratic constitution that aroused envy in and out of Europe. As most historians now agree, the Weimar Republic was not doomed to fail. Even the *Kaiserreich* was a state with considerable merits, albeit neither a progressive monarchy like England, nor a democratic republic like France. It was a constitutional state, as impressive as anywhere else in the western world, and as some would argue it was, in fact, a reform-oriented society, enjoying the benefits of a socially-oriented interventionist state, a vigorous bourgeois society, and an active public sphere. Moreover, for its time, the *Kaiserreich* was an economic giant and an undisputed cultural and scientific world-center.

It wasn't even particularly Antisemitic. In the late nineteenth century Jews lived securely among Germans. They were equal citizens by law, disproportionately represented in the middle class, often economically successful and again over-represented in the liberal professions. Some were leading figures in culture and politics. While it is true that since the late 1870s, waves of Antisemitic literature and propaganda disturbed this idyll and the growth of Antisemitic parties constituted an unpleasant novelty, Jews enjoyed support and encouragement, too. For each Treitschke, there was a Mommsen. During the financial crisis of 1879/80, for example, we see that the "Berlin University acted better and more decisively than any German university ever since."[2] In fact, the Antisemitic parties soon proved to be a fiasco. Even within the *Alldeutscher Verband*, for instance, often cited as an extreme example, Antisemitism was "anything but constant."[3] Its president, Heinrich Claß, was forced to restrain his anti-Jewish zeal in order not to alienate potential members and other allies among rightwing associations, such as the anti-Polish *Hakatisten*, the *Flottenverein*, or the *Reichsverband gegen die Sozialdemokratie*, which normally kept away from Antisemitism. "It was considered unacceptable," writes Thomas Nipperdey, and even in the case of radical students' associations, "Antisemitism was never the core of the movement."[4] Certainly, antipathy towards Jews was widespread in all strata of Wilhelminian society. Jews were discriminated against within the top ranks of the civil service and in the Prussian army, and "a clear dissociation between Germans and Jews" was no doubt ubiquitously apparent. Overall, however, "all manifestations of

---

2 As cited in: H.-U. Wehler, *Deutsche Gesellschaftsgeschichte*, vol. 3, Munich 1995, 928.
3 R. Chickering, *We Men Who Feel Most German. A Cultural Study of the Pan-German League, 1886–1914*, Boston 1984, 233.
4 T. Nipperdey, *Deutsche Geschichte 1866–1918. Machtstaat vor der Demokratie*, Munich 1992, 301–303.

hostility against Jews [were considered] rearguard actions of disgraceful prejudice and those who wished to differ had to remain silent in public."[5]

I have also argued against overemphasizing Antisemitism in the pre-Nazi stages of German history. After all, simply listing occasional Antisemitic authors and demagogues during the years of the *Kaiserreich* could hardly explain the Nazis' fury later on. Rather, it was late nineteenth century France that displayed unrestrained Antisemitism. Bloody pogroms took place in Tsarist Russia, not in the German Empire. Instead, Germany, and particularly Prussia, often served as a refuge for Jews fleeing to the West. It served as a model for civic virtues and political freedom for many young, educated Jews from the East.

Additionally, I've argued that Antisemitism in Germany at this time was usually a matter of the written word. Though troublesome, it did not constitute a real danger. And finally, in order to explain National Socialist Antisemitism, one must focus on shorter-term developments. It would be counter-productive to view the whole of German Jewish relations merely from the perspective of its terrifying end.[6]

Others argued even more radically. It was stated, for instance, that "a gradual ebbing of radical Antisemitism" could be observed after the upsurge of anti-Jewish *resentments* in the wake of the first World War.[7] Presumably, the organized Antisemitic movement was "not excessively widespread" and never counted more than 220,000 members, an unimpressive number compared to the organizations on the Left and the Center at the same time.[8] The Antisemitic reservoir during the Weimar Republic wasn't bigger than in the *Kaiserreich*. Although a "subliminal Antisemitism" existed within many civil and political organizations during the Weimar years, and "an Antisemitic undertone . . . notably directed against non-assimilated Jewish groups" wasn't rare, all that did not add up to an effective political instrument.[9] In 1928, it was further argued, German Antisemitism declined and research proves that it wasn't a decisive factor in the Nazis' success. Results from numerous local investigations show that "[t]he larger the party's electoral base would've

---

5 H.-G. Zmarzlik, *Antisemitismus im Deutschen Kaiserreich 1871–1919*, in: *Die Juden als Minderheit in der Geschichte*, eds. Bernd Martin and Ernst Schulin, Munich 1981, 253 f.; and the more complex discussion in: Wehler, vol. 3, 1063–1066.
6 Compare my "The Written Matter and the spoken Word," no. 5 above.
7 H. A. Winkler, "Die deutsche Gesellschaft der Weimarer Republik und der Antisemitismus," in: Martin and Schulin (ed.), 283.
8 H. Mommsen, *Die verspielte Freiheit. Der Weg der Republik von Weimar in den Untergang 1918 bis 1933*, Frankfurt 1990, 308 ff; id., "German Nationalism between the two World Wars," in: *The Crisis of German National Consciousness in the 19th and 20th Centuries* [Hebrew], ed. M. Zimmermann, Jerusalem 1983, 104.
9 Mommsen, *Die verspielte Freiheit*, 308.

become, the less the Antisemitic ideology infiltrated the lower levels."[10] Moreover, it is often emphasized that Antisemitism was crucial for the "internal integration of the National Socialist movement," but "for the majority of society it rather applies that National Socialism gave a boost to Antisemitism rather than vice versa."[11] According to Thomas Nipperdey's authoritative conclusion, Hitler came to power not primarily "due to his Antisemitism, a fact which was mostly and merely (bad enough) accepted."[12] Somewhat later, it could be argued, Goebbels' and Streicher's efforts to initiate a pogrom after the boycott of April 1933 were unsuccessful, and the majority of the people even opposed the "Reichskristallnacht."[13]

Clearly, it is not enough to seek out a linear progression from Luther's Antisemitism all the way to Hitler in order to explain the Nazis' efforts to exterminate all European Jews. But to insist that there was no Antisemitic continuity at all is no less unreasonable. "Antisemitism doesn't belong to the dominant continuities of German history," insists Nipperdey.[14] But if Antisemitism was not a distinct, long-term factor in German history and an ineffective political tool even as late as 1938, how can we even begin to explain the Holocaust? Today's historiography tends to underestimate even the scope of Antisemitism with regards to military and civil bureaucracies, which were directly or indirectly involved in the extermination process, or with regards to the Nazi leadership itself. We hear that the *Endlösung* was not a project planned in advance, based on a clear ideology, but that it developed gradually during the war, as its monstrous methods and gigantic dimensions gradually unfolded. This may be true. But the dilemma reappears now and seems greater than ever. When we link the functionalist interpretation of the *Endlösung* to the claim about the weakness of Antisemitism, we are left without an explanation. Could the extinction of the Jews be solely a result of mixing what was at most a subliminal popular aversion and haphazard campaign of the Nazi leaders?

---

10 Compare O. Heilbrunner, "Wohin verschwand der nationalsozialistische Antisemitismus? Zum Charakter des Antisemitismus der NSDAP vor 1933 und seinem Bild in der Geschichtswissenschaft," in: *Menora. Jahrbuch für deutsch-jüdische Geschichte* 1995, 20. An extensive discussion on this problem there, 15–44.
11 Winkler, "Die deutsche Gesellschaft der Weimarer Republik," 186–187.
12 T. Nipperdey, "1933 und die Kontinuität der deutschen Geschichte," in: his *Nachdenken über die deutsche Geschichte*, Munich 1986, 194.
13 Compare Mommsen, in: Zimmermann (ed.), 108, where he quotes W. S. Allen, "Die deutsche Öffentlichkeit und die 'Reichskristallnacht' – Konflikte zwischen Werthierarchie und Propaganda im Dritten Reich," in: *Die Reihen fest geschlossen. Beiträge zur Geschichte des Alltags unterm Nationalsozialismus*, eds. D. Peukert and J. Reulecke, Wuppertal 1981, 396–411.
14 Compare Nipperdey, *Nachdenken*, 164.

Of course, there are different historiographies on this matter. A number of monographies have tried to outline the history of Antisemitism in Germany, though most of these were written between 1950 and 1970. A concise summary has been published by Helmut Berding.[15] After categorically denying the continuity of Antisemitism, as shown in the citation above, Nipperdey treated this topic rather more subtly in the second volume of his history of the *Kaiserreich*, and Hans-Ulrich Wehler presented his own view in *Gesellschaftsgeschichte*: "The existence of a line of continuity between modern, racist Antisemitism and National Socialism is certainly undeniable," he writes. He then notes that Antisemitism "in the mentality" and "in the vocabulary" of the different political parties and social clubs during the *Kaiserreich*, as well as the "silent discrimination" against the Jews and ultimately even their stigmatization as "*Reichsfeinde*," were all too often the results of manipulation "from above."[16] For him, as for most historians today, Antisemitism was an important but isolated phenomenon, to be covered in single chapters of their books, and only seldom placed in correlation with other concurrent historical issues. As such, it is mentioned in chapters on modernization or economic crises and sometimes in relation to chapters on minorities in general.

In this way, what has followed must remain a mystery: How could such a widespread but relatively harmless, latent sentiment gain so much power and influence as to sustain the Nazis' murderous politics? Perhaps the problem does not lie in a defective analysis of Antisemitism, but rather in an approach that does not embed it in a more complete, many-sided context.

This failure is especially noticeable when one approaches the possible link between Antisemitism and nationalism. Historians usually agree that nationalism is an essentially modern phenomenon, an ideological innovation of the last quarter of the eighteenth and the start of the nineteenth centuries. The French Revolution gave it a powerful impetus, and then, through the Napoleonic occupation of large parts of southern and central Europe, nationalism became more militant, encouraging a mobilization of military force against the French occupation. From the beginning, runs the argument here, nationalism was paired with liberalism. In France, it was an additional manifestation of the demand for popular sovereignty, while in Germany it was mostly connected with reform and liberation from foreign domination. Nationalism could thus sometimes stay neutral or even pro-monarchist. Furthermore, from the very beginning, German nationalism had

---

15 Compare e.g. Eva Reichmann, *Die Flucht in den Haß*, Frankfurt 1956; Paul Massing, *Vorgeschichte des politischen Antisemitismus*, Frankfurt 1959; Pulzer, *Die Entstehung des politischen Antisemitismus in Deutschland und Österreich*, Hannover 1966; Helmut Berding, *Moderner Antisemitismus in Deutschland*, Frankfurt 1988.
16 All quotes from Wehler, vol. 3, 1065–1066, 933.

been supported by the Romantic movement and accordingly, tended to stress a cultural-ethnic concept of the nation rather than its political or civil aspects. Concurrently, it also served important social purposes. In difficult situations, it was most of all an alternative principle of legitimation, the driving force of modernization as well as a remedy against ensuing estrangement.

Furthermore, nationalism could be combined with different political trends and adapted to various cultural environments. While it seemed that at first the link to liberalism was the strongest and politically most effective, the later alliance with conservatism took root as early as the first half of the nineteenth century. In addition, nationalism was always easily combined with different forms of xenophobia – not just in Germany – while xenophobia itself helped define the nation and integrate different or even antagonistic elements within it. Finally, nationalism was easily connected to Antisemitism.

Once again, a brief look at the literature can explain this point. Nipperdey's chapter on nationalism in the first volume of his *Deutsche Geschichte* opens with a discussion of the intellectual and political roots of national ideology in the various German lands and continues with a suggestion to divide nationalism into different types. This is followed by an overview of the developments of nationalism during each period with particular emphases on the "dual objectives of freedom and unity." Nipperdey also discusses the problem of particularism on the one hand and of the nation's frontiers on the other hand.[17] But neither here nor in his by now classic essay, *"Romantischer Nationalismus,"* are the Antisemitic tones mentioned in earnest.[18] Nipperdey explains this omission in a later chapter on "Nationalism and the Nation-State" in *Deutsche Geschichte*. Only after 1871 does he see a "sharper turn of nationalism against minorities," characterized as "new within the process of nationalism."[19] For more details, we are directed to a different chapter, but the connection between nationalism and Antisemitism is never brought up again. Here, we are reminded that Antisemitism along with *"Völkischer Kulturkritik"* were both manifestations of the crisis of modernization and of the German identity. Only then, among the characteristics of the "New Right," is Antisemitism finally mentioned as typical for "radical nationalism," designating the third stage of nationalist ideology after "national patriotism" and so-called "normal nationalism." This last-mentioned type included a "demarcation against inner enemies, now most notably against socialists" and an "increased demand for uniformity and attacks against minorities, most notably against the Poles."

---

17 T. Nipperdey, *Deutsche Geschichte 1800–1866*, Munich 1983, 300–313.
18 Compare T. Nipperdey, "Auf der Suche nach der Identität: Romantischer Nationalismus," in: his *Nachdenken*, 110–25.
19 Nipperdey, *Nachdenken*, 254.

Antisemitism presumably played no part of "normal nationalism" in Germany, even at this late stage.[20]

An additional example could be shown in another standard work of German historiography, namely Hans-Ulrich Wehler's *Gesellschaftsgeschichte*. At the end of his first volume, Wehler devotes an extensive chapter to "The Beginning of German Nationalism," analyzing it as a "response to the crises of modernization, revolution, and foreign domination." Political psychology, he explains, naturally included the well-known socio-psychological mechanism, according to which "the inner coherence and the sense of unity of a large group are increased and strengthened by an antagonism against an external, seemingly dangerous enemy." In the case of Germany, these enemies were France, the French people, and Napoleon, who were bombarded with strings of hateful expressions. Wehler mentions anti-Jewish sentiments in this context only briefly, mainly in relation to the discussion of the historian Christian Rühs and Ernst Moritz Arndt's earlier equation of cosmopolitanism with *"Judensinn."*[21] In a republished essay, "Nationalismus und Fremdenhaß," Wehler promises to cover separately the "constant affinity [of nationalism] to aversion against strangers," but at first he mentioned only hatred against the French, while later on, in discussing nationalism in the *Kaiserreich* after 1871, "hatred against Russians and against England" is suddenly added. Even when analyzing the domestic function of various kinds of *Reichsfeinde*, Wehler does not include the Jews. To be sure, in an earlier book on the *Kaiserreich*, the Jews were classified as convenient *Reichsfeinde* along with "Poles and Alsatians," but Wehler never treats the principled connection between nationalism and Antisemitism.[22]

This *could* have been justified. After all, the Jews were a tiny minority in Germany. The French in the early nineteenth and the Social Democrats in the early twentieth centuries were undoubtedly more dangerous enemies in the eyes of German nationalists. Furthermore, Jews managed to perfect their emancipation in parallel to the persistent Antisemitism around them, gradually entering German society despite it and in so doing often even sharing the prevalent nationalist sentiment around them. In the early years of the new century, Meinecke could therefore discuss the ideology of the German nation-state as if it were entirely unrelated to Antisemitism. Apparently, in the aftermath of the Holocaust, this could no longer be done. Hans Rosenberg opens his chapter on modern Antisemitism in *Große Depression und Bismarckzeit* as follows: "Over the long term, historically no less significant than the rethinking in the Socialist camp . . . was an

---

20 Ibid, 595–609.
21 H.-U. Wehler, *Deutsche Gesellschaftsgeschichte*, vol. 1, Munich 1987, 507–30, especially 522–523.
22 H.-U. Wehler, *Das Deutsche Kaiserreich 1871–1918*, Göttingen 1973, 96–100.

essentially different, emotionally heated, intellectually volitional movement," clearly alluding to the Antisemitic movement. He then quickly adds that "only through the connection with other intellectual, social, political, and economic driving forces and objectives did it become historically relevant."[23] I believe he thereby, as so often, "hit the nail on the head," to use his own choice of words. Thus, the scope of nineteenth century Antisemitism can only be understood in retrospect, and its significance can only be judged in connection with other historical factors. The key point is not whether the brown dictatorship was made possible by "extreme German nationalism rather than ... Antisemitism,"[24] but how both could be intertwined and sometimes even made interchangeable, and how they complemented each other so effectively as to bring about the rule of National Socialism.

Had things turned out differently, one could easily ignore the Antisemitic aspects of earlier German nationalism. Fichte's vicious words on the Jews in his earlier, almost forgotten writings, and Saul Ascher's bitter critique of the great philosopher, calling him *"Eisenmenger den Zweiten,"* might have remained secondary to the main political discourse of their time. Just as little weight could be given to the early nationalism of Ernst Moritz Arndt or Friedrich Ludwig Jahn, who could be viewed as harmless reactionary pacemakers, no more than an expression of Germany's social backwardness. Treitschke's rabid Antisemitism, like that of his predecessors, Christian Rühs and Jacob Friedrich Fries, might have justified no more than a footnote.[25] And even if Ascher's diagnosis in his *Germanomanie* and his attack against the "fanatics," their *"deutschtümelei,"* and their pointless *"judenhass,"* could be dismissed as paranoia, one must still take into account the *consequences* of completely ignoring the Antisemitism of the early *Turnvereine* and the *Burschenschaften*.[26] Dieter Düding admits in his detailed study on "Turner-Nationalism," that the nationalist movement – with its emancipatory direction – never succeeded in getting rid of its "xenophobic element" and its *"Francophobie."*[27] The Heidelberg *Burschenschaftler* were openly *anti*-Antisemitic, but plenty of anti-Jewish hatred existed among the *"Schwarzen"* in Giessen or the *"Unbedingten"* in Jena, enough to justify an excellent analysis

---

23 Hans Rosenberg, *Große Depression und Bismarckzeit. Wirtschaftsablauf, Gesellschaft und Politik in Mitteleuropa*, Berlin 1967, 88.
24 H.-U. Wehler, "Die Gefährdung des Sozialstaats durch Nationalismus und Fremdenfeindlichkeit," in: *Festschrift. G. A. Ritter*, Munich 1994, 787.
25 As in Nipperdey, *Deutsche Geschichte 1800–1866*, 249.
26 Compare W. Grab, "Ein jüdisch-deutscher Spätaufklärer zwischen Revolution und Restauration," in: *Jahrbuch des Instituts für Deutsche Geschichte 6 (1977)*, 131–179, here 165–166.
27 Compare his Book *Organisierter gesellschaftlicher Nationalismus in Deutschland (1800–1847)*, Munich 1984, 139.

of their mentality, like the one from the pen of Wolfgang Hardtwig.[28] Finally, while studying the nationalism of the pre-March era, one must ask why works like Eleonore Sterling's *Er ist wie du*, which extensively discusses Antisemitism in this period, or Uriel Tal's sensitive essay on young German intellectuals in the early nineteenth century received so little attention.[29] Could such a negligence persist in the face of later developments? I have elsewhere discussed German historiographical omissions of the Jewish, or rather anti-Jewish, aspects of the 1848 revolution, too.[30] Once again it could be demonstrated that the *Judenfrage* either did not arouse much interest at this time or that only relevant, positive things could be portrayed within the overall framework of this revolution. In the long run, however, is it really unimportant to treat the way anti-Jewish sentiments and arguments were incorporated into nationalism, even during this heroic, liberal chapter of German history?

Nationalism has always been a syndrome. In its earlier stages, it was devoted to liberalism and emancipation. But as George Mosse has shown, nationalism fit all too well into a certain bourgeois lifestyle, a special sense of honor, a way of male self-display, and a cult of friendship.[31] And in the late nineteenth century, when the link to liberalism was lost, nationalism could easily be associated with monarchy, anti-modern cultural critique, and even imperialism and *Weltpolitik*. Interestingly, in both episodes, a touch of Antisemitism could not be denied. While even this had been problematic for the liberal nationalists in the earlier period, Antisemitism belonged to the *Kaiserreich's* nationalism almost by nature. Nationalism could now count on anti-Jewish sentiments to present the Jew as an inversed image of all things German and thereby define German distinctiveness and identity all the more clearly. Other functions of Antisemitism, in connection to later nationalism, could sometimes be found in the literature, most importantly its general turn to irrationalism, which easily created space for racism and Antisemitism.[32] In various

---

28 W. Hardtwig, "Studentische Mentalität – Politische Jugendbewegung – Nationalismus. Die Anfänge der deutschen Burschenschaft," in: id., *Nationalismus und Bürgerkultur in Deutschland 1500–1914*, Göttingen 1994, 108–148.
29 The later edition of Sterling's book was published under the title: *Judenhaß. Die Anfänge des politischen Antisemitismus in Deutschland (1815–1850)*, Frankfurt 1969. Compare also U. Tal, "Young German Intellectuals on Romanticism and Judaism – Spiritual Turbulence in the Early Nineteenth Century," in: *Salo Wittmayer Baron Jubilee Volume*, Jerusalem 1974, 919–938.
30 Compare Shulamit Volkov, "Reflections on German-Jewish Historiography: A Dead End or a New Beginning?" in: *Leo Baeck Institute Yearbook*, 41 (1996), 309–320.
31 G. L. Mosse, *Nationalismus und Sexualität*, Reinbek 1985, belongs to the very few books which deal with nationalism as a cultural syndrome in both Germany and England.
32 J. Kocka, "The Futility of Progressive Nationalism in the Second Reich," in: *The Crisis of German National Consciousness*, Zimmermann (ed.), 86–87.

national crises, Jews were now the obvious scapegoats and Antisemitism could be seen as a "symptom for the disengagement of the radical, integral nationalism from the liberal's moderate nationalism."[33] However, latent Antisemitism remained long acceptable, even to the moderates. In the Weimar Republic, nationalism was not only common to the far right. During the interwar period, it served as a *"politischer Kitt,"* mediating between anti-Marxism and nationalism.[34]

Investigating Antisemitism within the context of nationalism does not mean that one has to posit an uninterrupted, monolithic tradition of Jew-hatred among German nationalists. Certainly, it is possible to indicate a number of exceptions, not only during the early liberal period of the pre-March years, but even later, during the Wilhelminian period, or the Weimar Republic. Historian Moshe Zimmerman has pointed out Friedrich Naumann's rejection of Antisemitism, even as Naumann propagated his own version of national Socialism before the First World War.[35] After the Great War, members of the *Deutsche Demokratische Partei* did not allow anti-Jewish sentiments to blur their patriotism. But by this time, they were clearly the exceptions that confirmed the rule. From Arndt to Treitschke, from the *Bund der Landwirte* to National Socialism, nationalism helped make Antisemitism acceptable for the majority of Germans. Within the nationalistic syndrome, Antisemitism played a different role in each period and thus gradually became indispensable. While the Nazis' murderous policies cannot be explained by such an analysis, the tacit cooperation and continued apathy of so many other Germans might become clearer by adding this perspective.

---

[33] Compare R. Rürup, "Die 'Judenfrage' in der bürgerlichen Gesellschaft und die Entstehung des modernen Antisemitismus," in: id., *Emanzipation und Antisemitismus*, Göttingen 1975, especially 87–95. The quote is taken from: "Antisemitismus – Entstehung, Funktion und Geschichte eines Begriffes," (together with T. Nipperdey), 108.
[34] In: *The Crises of German National Consciousness*, Zimmermann (ed.), 100.
[35] Compare M. Zimmermamm, "A Road not Taken – Friedrich Naumann's Attempt at a Modern German Nationalism," in: *Journal of Contemporary History* 17 (1982), 698–708.

9 Language as a Locus of Confronting Jews and Judaism in Germany

I. The early 1780s are often seen as the starting point of modern Jewish history in Germany. The first volume of Christian Wilhelm Dohm's *On the Civil Betterment of the Jews* appeared in 1781, followed by a European-wide controversy concerning Dohm's suggestions for reform.[1] In 1782, Kaiser Josef II decreed his Edicts of Toleration for the various provinces of the Habsburg Empire, including one for all Jews throughout the land. These edicts were by no means as clear and as comprehensive as the later civil equality legislation in revolutionary France, but they did signal the onset of fundamental change.[2] In 1783, Moses Mendelssohn published *Jerusalem*, in which he undertook to explain the essence of Judaism and argued for its capacity to adapt to the demands of the modern state.[3] Moreover, at that time, the reform efforts concerning the Jews – supported by a mixture of enlightened principles and calculated *staatsraison* on the one hand, and the apparent willingness of the Jews to enter bourgeois society on the other hand – reached their peak and further justify this periodization. Undoubtedly, choosing this starting point greatly influenced the nature of the following narrative. The double claim, concerning the emergence of an open, "half-neutral" German society and a reformed Jewish community, eager to achieve integration, fit well as the opening chord of the so-called Age of Emancipation.[4]

Interestingly, however, it is possible to draw another historical line from the same starting point. Indeed fact, the history of modern Antisemitism can be shown to start at that same time and thereafter proceed in parallel to that of emancipation.[5] In fact, the first secular opposition to Jewish participation in bourgeois life came as a direct response to the demand for Jewish equal rights. The opposition to Jewish assimilation was most clearly expressed by a well-known and respected expert in Jewish affairs, a philologist and orientalist at the University of Göttingen,

---

[1] Christian Wilhelm Dohm, *Über die bürgerliche Verbesserung der Juden*, 2 vols. Berlin and Stetin 1783.
[2] See Joseph Karniel, *Die Tolerazpolitik Kaiser Joseph II.*, Gerlingen 1986, 378–474.
[3] Moses Mendelssohn, *Jerusalem oder über religiöse Macht und Judentum*, Berlin 1783.
[4] Compare especially Jacob Katz, *Out of the Ghetto; Social Background of Jewish Emancipation, 1770–1870*, Cambridge Mass. 1974, and David Sorkin, *The Transformation of German Jewry, 1780–1840*, New York and Oxford 1987.
[5] See my, "Antisemitismus als Problem jüdisch-nationalen Denkens und jüdischer Geschichtsschreibung," in: *Geschichte und Gesllschaft* 5, 1979, 519–544, or in *Jüdisches Leben und Antisemitismus im 19. Und 20. Jahrhundert*, Munich 1990, 88–110.

Johann David Michaelis.[6] His critical reviews, first of Lessing's play *Die Juden* and later of Dohm's reform plans and Mendelssohn's defense of Judaism, were published in the *Orientalische und Exegetische Bibliothek* in 1782 and 1783. From that point forth, it is possible to reconstruct the tale of Antisemitism beginning with Michaelis, Fichte, and Rühs through Richard Wagner and Treitschke, all the way to racial theory, National Socialism, and the Final Solution. In this way, a second narrative, a counter-tale to that of emancipation, emerges.

The year 1783, moreover, can serve as the starting point of yet a third narrative of German Jewish history. In that year, parallel to the publication of Dohm's book, Mendelssohn's Oeuvre and Michaelis' critiques, the Cotta-Verlag in Tübingen published Johann Gottfried Herder's *Vom Geist der Hebräischen Poesie*. Although this may not have been one of Herder's most important philosophical works, it was – in our context – of fundamental significance. Herder, not yet familiar with the controversy over Dohm's reform suggestions, managed to articulate both his admiration for the ancient Hebrews' poetic talent and his detestation of contemporary Jewry. His cultural and linguistic nationalism allowed him to sing the praise of Judaism on the one hand and brand contemporary Jews as permanent strangers, on the other hand; to make use of Jewish ancient history as a model, while calling the Jews to discard it by joining the higher civilization of modern Europe.[7] Observing matters from his perspective, one could circumvent, perhaps, both the emancipatory and the Antisemitic tales. The discourse over language – ever central to Herder's philosophy – provides another look at the enlightenment and its opponents, fleshing out emphatically its inherent dialectics, as well as its failings with regards to the fate of German Jewry.

II. "Discovery of the true meaning of the Scriptures remained the basic substance of Christian scholarship," writes Frank Manuel in *The Broken Staff: Judaism through Christian Eyes*.[8] During the Reformation, interpreting Hebrew and Aramaic texts, especially the Bible, became a tool in the battle among Christian confessions. But by the end of the eighteenth century, attitudes changed again and European philosophers and philologists began to see the Bible not only as a piece of holy history but as a secular document as well. Famous are the consequences drawn from this

---

[6] Here I relie especially on Anna-Ruth Löwenbrück, *Judenfeindlichkeit im Zeitalter der Aufklärung*, Frankfurt a. Main 1995.
[7] On Herder's concept of Judaism, see especially Liliane Weissberg, "Juden oder Hebräer? Religion und politische Bekehrung bei Herder," in *Johann Gottfried Herder. Geschichte und Kultur*, ed. Martin Bollacher, Würzburg 1994, 191–211, and among the somewhat older literature: Frederick M. Barnard, "Herder and Israel," in: *Jewish Social Studies* 28, 1966, 25–33.
[8] Frank E. Manuel, *The broken Staff. Judaism through Christian Eyes*, Cambrirdge Mass. and London 1992, 7.

step, first by the English deists, as early as the seventeenth century, and then by the French *philosophes* during the eighteenth.[9] Most well-known is still Voltaire's position, which saw in the history of the ancient Hebrews a test-case of barbarism and inhumanity, which disregarded centuries of rabbinic scholarship, and which utterly denigrated contemporary Jewry. There were no dialectics here; Voltaire clearly despised both ancient and modern Judaism.[10]

At the same time, Hebraists of more academic orientations, linguistic scholars more than philosophers, applied secular, scientific methods for other purposes. It was once more Michaelis, who by the mid-eighteenth century endeavored to defend ancient Judaism with the tools of secular rationalism. In his six volume *Mosaische Recht*, he conceived of it in the context of ancient Egypt, stressing nomad conditions, permanently forcing man to battle against nature.[11] His immense knowledge allowed him to maintain the age-old Christian appreciation of Jewish monotheism, thinking now outside the paradigm of religious revelation, and while he initially treated his contemporary Jews with respect, he later became – like Voltaire – convinced of their anachronism, their inability to modernize, their inherent otherness. The Mosaic legal order, he preached with the full authority of his philological and historical scholarship, impelled Jews to live in social isolation. Moreover, their hope of returning to Zion together with their deep-seated national pride accounted, he claimed, for their inability to develop true "love of the state."[12] This is also why, he concluded, they could never be trusted in difficult times and would forever remain outsiders.

Meanwhile, both Robert Lowth in Oxford and Herder in East Prussia developed another approach to biblical studies. In light of the growing interest in myths and in the study of ancient languages and literature, they took a different line of argumentation. Attempting to preserve or, rather restore, the religious significance of the Holy Bible, they preferred to see the text not simply as a compilation of historical documents but also – and especially – as a collection of ancient poetic texts. The Bible was an example of primitive poetry of great aesthetic value, they explained, a reflection of an original, authentic religiosity. The language of the Bible, in its form

---

9 Ibid, 192–221. See also Arthur Herzberger, *The French Enlightenment and the Jews*, New York 1964; Shmuel Ettinger, "The Beginning of the Change in the Attitude of European Society towards the Jews", in: *Scripta Hierosolymitana 7*, 1961, 193–219; idem, "Jews and Judaism in the Eyes of the English Deists," [Hebrew], in: *Modern Anti-Semitism. Studies and Essays*, Tel Aviv 1978, 57–88.
10 On Voltaire see also Peter Gay, *The Party of Humanity. Essays in French Enlightenment*, New York 1964, 97–108 and Jacob Katz, *From Prejudice to Destruction. Anti-Semitism 1700–1933*, Cambridge Mass. 1982, Chapter 4.
11 Johann David Michaelis, *Mosaisches Recht*, 6 vols., Frankfurt a. Main 1770–1775 and enlarged editions 1775–1780, 1780–1793, 1793–1803.
12 Quoted from Löwenbrück, *Judenfeindlichkeit im Zeitalter der Aufklärung*, 158.

and content alike, was all around human, according to Herder, and the spirit expressed in it, the unique genius of a unique people. Although other primitive nations had had their special poetry too, ran the argument, the Hebrew language was the perfect medium for the transmission of true faith and the only language that had managed to preserve "the echo of the divine."[13]

Herder admired not only Hebrew language and poetry; he also sang the praise of the patriarchs. The entire biblical text was, for him, a model for national historiography, penetrated with a deep sense of patriotism and the courage to uphold one's uniqueness and exclusivity. In Herder's eye, humanity was made up of a collectivity of unique nations, each of which was formed and held together by its language and history. To be sure, even Herder realized the difficulty of propagating the principles of universalism while praising particularism. While the unjust living conditions of the Jews in past generations were familiar to him too, of course, there was no place in his vision for a Jewish individuality. "Time will come," he wrote, "when man in Europe would not ask who is Jew and who is Christian, since Jews too would be living according to European laws and contribute to the good of the state." It was, indeed, "a barbaric constitution" that had harmed the talents of Jewish individuals. Unfortunately, however, the Jewish people had lost its vitality, "since it has never reached maturity upon its own land" and could thus never gain "a real feeling of honor and freedom."[14]

Like many other enlightenment figures, Herder could live with this dissonance, even as his kind of nationalism became ever more prevalent, and language, in accordance with his own teaching, turned out to be a chief obstacle to the realization of his utopian universal system.[15] While Jews attempted to enter German society and gain civil equality, Herder's linguistic nationalism stood in their way. According to him, after all, words were "solidly based on a substratum of sensual impressions and reactions," and since human beings have been divided into families, tribes, and nations, their languages bear "the imprint of their varying circumstances and of their distinct identities."[16] Thus, to speak a foreign language meant to live an artificial life, alienated from the spontaneous, instinctive sources of the self. Only one language, added Schleiermacher later, could firmly

---

13 See Manuel, *The broken Staff*, 263–271; also J.G. Herder, *Sämtliche Werke*, ed. Bernhard Suphan, 33 vols., vol. 19, Berlin 1879, 7.
14 Herder, *Ideen zur Philosophie der Geschichte der Menschheit*, Wiesbaden o.j. 437, 316.
15 On this issue see Shulamit Volkov. "Die Verbürgerlichung der Juden in Deutschland als Paradigma," in: *Bürgertum im 19. Jahrhundert. Deutschland im europäischen Vergleich*, ed. Jürgen Kocka, München 1988, vol. 2. 343–371.
16 Here I quote from Elie Kedouri, *Nationalism*, Cambridge Mass. 1993, 57. The Schleiermacher quote is also there. For Arndt see page 63.

be implanted in the individual. Only to this one he belonged, no matter how many he learned subsequently. And while it was Fichte who drew the political consequences of this argument, it was Arndt's definition of the German fatherland as the space "in which only the German language sounds" that later became most popular.

III. But the place of language in German Nationalism depended not only on theoretical constructs. After all, German was the main link connecting the nationally oriented men and women living within the borders of the old Reich. Common literature and wandering theaters, as well as a growing network of journals and newspapers – indeed, the entire substructure of the public sphere – depended on that common language. In other countries of Europe, reformers and revolutionaries were likewise aware of the significance of one shared tongue for internal national communication and the exchange of ideas. During the French Revolution, special inspectors were sent to collect data on the actual usage of the French language in the various French provinces; detailed reports were written and strict laws were legislated so that the entire nation, even in the furthest corners of the land, would be speaking "the language of freedom." Furthermore, regional dialects were considered counter-revolutionary, willfully undermining the unity of the glorious, "one, indivisible nation."[17] To be sure, the efforts to achieve linguistic unity in France were not an invention of the revolutionaries. The French administration under the old regime, in its efforts to achieve the centralization of France, had an intense interest in linguistic unity, and in Germany too, this was an official policy of the various governments, though in themselves they were mostly counter-revolutionary and anti-national.

As early as 1739 in the Landgraviate of Hessen-Kassel, Jews were prohibited from using Yiddish or Hebrew in their business transactions.[18] The Josephine Toleranzpatente prohibited the use of Polish as well, and the special edict for Galicia ordered Jews to learn German within two years.[19] In Baden, the success of the Constitutional Edict of 1809 was evaluated by its influence on the names chosen by local Jews and on their use of German in daily life.[20] This was also central for

---

17 See *Une politique de la langue. La revolution française et la Patois*, edited by Michel de Certeau, et al., Paris 1975.
18 See Jacob Toury, "Der Eintritt der Juden ins deutsche Bürgertum," in: *Das Judentum in der deutschen Umwelt 1800–1850*, eds. Hans Liebeschütz and Arnold Paucker, Tübingen 1977, 139–242, here: 177.
19 For the details see Karniel, *Die Toleranzpolitik*.
20 See Reinhard Rürup, "Die Emanzipation der Juden in Baden," in his *Emanzipation und Antisemitismus. Studien zur 'Judenfrage' der bürgerlichen Gesellschaft*, Göttingen 1975, 37–73, here 49.

the Prussian legislators in drafting the Edict of Emancipation in 1812. It, too, stressed the acquisition of German family-names by the local Jews and declared that in all their public and private documents they must make use of "[either] German or any other living language," stating that all who did not follow this rule were to be considered "foreign Jews" without any "civil rights and freedoms."[21]

The Jews, too, considered language proficiency an important issue. The Berlin circles of *maskilim* (the "enlightened") inveighed against the use of the "corrupt jargon," namely Yiddish, and saw the revival of Hebrew as one of their major projects. Mendelssohn's translation of the Bible presented Jewish readers with a German text parallel to the Hebrew original, such that they could choose between two legitimate versions. Indeed, the translation was conceived as a way of acquainting them with German while also refreshing their Hebrew.[22] The first enlightened Hebrew journal, *Ha-Meassef*, attempted to turn Hebrew into a modern language, suitable for literary and scientific discourse, though the number of its subscribers, never more than 150, testifies to its limited success.[23] Significantly, a later Jewish journal, the *Sulamith*, a mouthpiece of progressive Jewry, appeared in German from the outset and even the Orthodox Hebrew weekly published in Altona, *Die treue Zionwächter*, found it necessary, from the 1840s, to produce a parallel German edition.[24]

In 1781, David Friedländer, a disciple and later associate of Moses Mendelssohn, established the first so-called "Free School" in Berlin. Pupils were to learn a mixture of religious and secular subjects, crowned by intensive learning of proper German.[25] And in other schools, such as in Frankfurt, Breslau, Dessau and Hamburg, learning German was likewise a main subject-matter, even, starting in 1822, in the traditional Talmud-Tora-School in Hamburg. Clearly, German language acquisition was a precondition for the acculturation of the Jewish middle and lower classes –

---

[21] For the text of the edict of 11. March 1812, see Ismar Freund, Die Emanzipation der Juden in Preußen, 2 vols., vol.2, Berlin 1912, 455–459.
[22] See Julius Carlebach, "Deutsche Juden und der Säkularisierungsprozess in der Erziehung. Kritische Bemerkungen zu einem Problemkreis der jüdischen Emanzipation," in: *Das Judentum in der deutschen Umwelt 1800–1850*, 55–94, here 67–76.
[23] Compare Tsemach Tsamarion, "Ha-Meassef", in: *Encyclopaedia Judaica*, Jerusalem 1971, vol. ii, 1161f.; Walter Röll, "The Kassel Ha-Meassef of 1799," in: *The Jewish Response to German Culture. From the Enlightenment to the Second World War*, eds. Jehuda Reinharz and Walter Schatzberg, Hanover and London 1985, 32–50.
[24] See Judith Bleich, "The Emergence of an Orthodox Press in Nineteenth Century Germany," in: *Jewish Social Studies* 42, 1980, 323–344.
[25] On Friedländer see Michael A. Meyer, *The Origins of the Modern Jew. Jewish Identity and European culture, 1749–1824*, Detroit 1967, chapter 2. Compare also *David Friedländer. Lesebuch für jüdische Kinder*, with introduction by Zohar Shavit, Frankfurt a. M. 1990.

Jewish and non-Jewish alike. Unique with regard to the Jews was only the fact that their "jargon," unlike the various dialects spoken throughout the land and despite the increasing influence of Romanticism, never regained respectability. Even the scanty appreciation of the Jews by the historical philology of the early nineteenth century did not extend to the Yiddish. While other dialects were becoming more or less acceptable, Yiddish remained contemptible for most Germans and many Jews. Yiddish was seen as a sign of Jewish inferiority, an inappropriate language for men of morality and *Bildung*, and an obstacle in the efforts to achieve both.

Historian Peter Freimark published an interesting article on this topic in the 1979 Leo Baeck Institute Yearbook.[26] In it, he quoted a piece entitled "The State of our Jewry," published in 1804 in a journal dedicated to the "History, Habits, and Taste" of the time:[27]

> Regardless of how one conceives of this matter, [writes the shocked observer] it is incomprehensible why the majority of our Jews insist on speaking the language of the land in which they live and which is their mother-tongue in such a mutilated form, a form so extremely unpleasant to the ear. And even when they speak purely, without foreign admixture, they do it in such a tone, that it is once again just as unpleasant as that which is generally known as the Jewish dialect.

Still, Yiddish never disappeared from the German-Jewish landscape. It was spoken especially in rural areas and was being brought into urban centers ever anew by migrating Jews from the east, especially from Poznan and Galicia. Local Jews, who invested much effort in acquiring proper German, considered these newcomers a liability. Worse still, Yiddish remained a source of embarrassment. Language was not the only source of their attitude towards the *Ostjuden*, of course, but it came to symbolize the status of those who did not belong and who were bound to remain on the margin as foreigners.[28]

IV. In the process of acquiring German, the status of Hebrew too, even as a ritual and liturgical language, came increasingly under attack. Hebrew's role in religious ceremonies was gradually reduced to a minimum, and in the first so-called "Temple," established in Seesen, Westphalia, under the rule of Napoleon, even

---

[26] Peter Freimark, "Language Behviour and Assimilation. The situation of the Jews in Northern Germany in the First Half of the Nineteenth Century," in: *Leo Baeck Institute Yearbook* 24, 1979, 157–177.
[27] Ibid, 164.
[28] For the relationships between local Jews and newcomers from the east, see Steven Aschheim, *Brothers and Strangers. The East-European Jews in German and German-Jewish Consciousness*, 1800–1923, Madison Wisc. 1982, and Shulamit Volkov, "The Dynamics of Dissimilation: Ostjuden and German Jews," in: *The Jewish Response to German Culture*, 192–211.

the Sabbath-prayers were sometimes conducted in German. Somewhat later, the Reform congregation in Hamburg appointed Isaac Bernays, a prominent Altphilologist, as a preacher, and he held his sermons twice weekly in fluent and elegant German. Leopold Zunz followed suit in Berlin.[29]

This shift, however, became a hotly contested issue when the entire liturgy in some reform synagogues was held fully in German. The Orthodox but also the moderate Reform rabbis of the so-called positive-historical school considered abandoning Hebrew a violation of the first order. Zacharias Frankel left the Rabbinical Assembly in Frankfurt in July 1845 in protest, when it was about to decide merely not to rule on this issue.[30] And while his insistence upon upholding Hebrew grew out of his deep traditionalism together with his cautious nature, no doubt, his arguments relied on Savigny's jurisprudent historicism and on Herder's linguistic nationalism. Like Herder, Frankel believed that Hebrew was particularly appropriate for expressing Jewish religiosity and Jewish devotion. Even more importantly, again according to Herder, he saw in Hebrew a key to the inner life of *Klal Israel*, namely the community of all Jews, across time and space. Nevertheless, Frankel was no Jewish nationalist. He often stressed the true bond between Christians and Jews in their German Fatherland. Hebrew, he promised, would never keep Jews away from their patriotism or from fulfilling their civil duties in Germany.

Despite his opposition to abandoning Hebrew, Frankel delivered his speech at the Rabbinical Assembly – just as he held all his weekly synagogue preaching – in perfect, fluent German. The young members of the *Verein für die Cultur und Wissenschaft der Juden* in Berlin during the 1820s had done the same, just as the later scholars of the *Wissenschaft des Judentums*. They all shared the historical-philological principles that were critical for the study of antiquity at that time and which served to define the emerging national identity in Germany. They were devoted to an extreme version of historicism, and with the help of careful linguistic study, dated the chronology and the various literary strata of biblical texts, together with other Jewish and non-Jewish documents, reconstructing the past as it "really was."[31] Still, rethinking Judaism according to "historical canons of the German universities" meant a deep break with tradition. In addition, they

---

[29] see Michael A. Meyer, *Response to Modernity. A History of the Reform Movement in Judaism*, Oxford 1988, Chapter 1 and 2; Katz, *Out of the Ghetto*, chapter 8.

[30] For his speech at this gathering see *Protokolle und Aktenstücke der zweiten Rabbiner Versammlung*, Frankfurt a. M. 1845, 18–22; on Frankel, especially Ismar Schorsch in his: *From Text to Context. The Turn to History in Modern Judaism*, Hanover and London 1994, 255–265, and passim in other essays.

[31] See Schorsch, *From Text to Context*, 158–176.

felt that Christian scholarship manipulated the Jewish past for its own theological purposes and thus, the resulting Christian narrative no longer had any meaning for contemporary Jews. Although both Christian and Jewish scholars applied linguistic and archeological tools in their studies, they often seemed to have been working at opposing purposes.

V. In any case, the full command of German – with or without the negation of Hebrew, of Yiddish, or both – remained for the entire nineteenth century the chief criterion for Jewish acculturation. German was crucial for the Jews' success, and at the same time the most sensitive locus for criticizing and attacking them. Just as the use of the German language was reserved for those who belonged, so too was "true Bildung" never simply a matter of knowledge or education, nor even a matter of character. And since there had never been full agreement concerning the preconditions for such "true Bildung", it was always possible to criticize *"Verbildung"* or *"Überbildung"*, and to attack, most menacingly, "undeutsche Bildung", a kind of treacherous, faulty *Bildung*, characteristic of Jews.[32]

The lives of Heinrich Heine and of Felix Mendelssohn-Bartholdy serve as good examples for these tactics of exclusion. Both acquired early enough all the elements of bourgeois *Bildung*, including the command of German. Likewise, both were attacked for it: Their culture, it was repeatedly argued, was somehow not real. Heine's language and Mendelssohn's music were nothing but a miserable copy, nothing more than could have been expected of Jews. It was an unknown gymnasium-teacher in Hamburg, one Eduard Meyer, who characterized Heinrich Heine, this time together with Ludwig Börne, as neither Jewish nor German.[33] Others followed suit, claiming that neither the poetry and the prose, nor the art and music produced by Jews were of any value. It was their style that betrayed them; not even their language but their inflection.

The most relevant text is, of course, Richard Wagner's *Das Judentum in der Music*.[34] Having given vent to his repugnance of Jewish external features – unpleasant and foreign – Wagner turned to attack not immediately their poetry nor their music but their language:

> By far weightier, nay, of quite decisive weight for our inquiry, is the effect the Jew produces on us through his speech; and this is the essential point at which to sound the Jewish influence

---

32 For further details, see Shulamit Volkov, "The Ambivalence of Bildung. Jews and other Germans," in: *The German-Jewish Dialogue Reconsidered. A Symposium in Honor of George L. Mosse*, ed. Klaus L. Berghahn, New York 1996, 81–98.
33 See Katz, *Out of the Ghetto*, Chapter 15.
34 First published under a pseudonym in the *Neue Zeitschrift für Musik* 19, 3. September 1850 and then as: Richard Wagner, *Das Judentum in der Musik*, Leipzig 1869.

upon Music. The Jew speaks the language of the nation in whose midst he dwells from generation to generation, but he speaks it always as an alien. As it lies beyond our present scope to occupy ourselves with the cause of this phenomenon, too, we may equally abstain from an arraignment of Christian Civilization for having kept the Jew in violent severance from it, as on the other hand, in touching the sequelae of that severance we can scarcely propose to make the Jews the answerable party. Our only object, here, is to throw light on the aesthetic character of the said results. In the first place, then, the general circumstance that the Jew talks the modern European languages merely as learnt, and not as mother tongues, must necessarily debar him from all capability of therein expressing himself idiomatically, independently, and conformably to his nature. A language, with its expression and its evolution, is not the work of scattered units, but of an historical community: only he who has unconsciously grown up within the bond of this community, takes also any share in its creations. But the Jew has stood outside the pale of any such community, stood solitarily with his Jehova in a splintered, soilless stock, to which all self-sprung evolution must stay denied, just as even the peculiar (Hebraïc) language of that stock has been preserved for him merely as a thing defunct.[35]

Not since Johann David Michaelis had someone formulated this issue so clearly.

Now, it is often mentioned that Wagner, rather strangely, exempted Heine from this kind of attack. Apparently, he found in Heine a strange bed-fellow. No less peculiarly, in an article the poet himself sent from Paris in mid-April 1842, he compared a performance of Mendelssohn's "Paulus" with Rossini's "Stabat Mater," and stated – anonymously, to be sure – that it was impossible not to notice Mendelssohn's faulty sense for true Christianity, a sense that could be gained "neither by learning nor by converting."[36] The Jewish element in the composer's art, Heine, himself a convert, publicly claimed, could never be washed away. It could easily be heard despite Mendelssohn's success and his "undeniable world-fame." All of that, his biographer assures us, had not been a common Antisemitic attack.[37] But it must have had something to do with the public discourse of that time. After all, this argument repeatedly stressed the difference between "true" and "untrue" *Bildung*, between authentic and inauthentic culture, between true *German* art and what could not but remain a second-class copy. To be sure, the main locus of this discourse had been language, not music. It was presumably in poetry and literature that the inadequacy of Jews was so clearly noticed, and Heine himself had certainly had to confront this or similar critiques with regard to his own work. It must have touched a sore point – painful despite his sarcasm and self-irony.

---

[35] I used the English translation by William Ashton Ellis, published 1894 in *Richard Wagner's Prose Works*, vol. 3, p. 7.
[36] Quoted from S. S. Prawer, "Heine's Portraits of the German Jews on the Eve of the 1848 Revolution," in: *Revolution and Evolution. 1848 in German-Jewish History*, eds. Werner Mosse, Arnold Paucker and Reinhard Rürup, Tübingen 1981, 352–383, here 360.
[37] Ibid, 363–366.

With time, this anti-Jewish argument was strengthened through a new kind of linguistic turn. During the second half of the nineteenth century, under the influence of Renan and Gobineau, language became ever more prominent as a sign of belonging.³⁸ Earlier on, the term "Semite" had begun to be applied to ancient languages such as Hebrew, Phoenician, Carthaginian etc.³⁹ Then, in the early nineteenth century, the term 'Aryan' was added to this philological discourse, indicating specific groups, defined by their language as well as by their presumed races, and both terms had entered the social sphere, losing much of their academic specificity. Sustained now by racial theory, philology became a tool in its arsenal. In 1848, Renan published *De l'origine du langage*, stressing the differences between Semites and Aryans,⁴⁰ while half a century later, in 1899, Houston Stewart Chamberlain published the *Grundlagen des 19 Jahrhunderts*, in which linguistics together with ancient history and Christian theology were applied to sustain the most virulent kind of Antisemitism. Scholarly theory came to the aid of daily praxis, defining Jews as foreigners and language as the locus of their estrangement.

Interestingly, since the early nineteenth century, some educated Jews communicated their own unease in using German, specifically when they, in fact, mastered it completely. Rahel Varnhagen, for instance, never tired of trying to prove her love and loyalty to this tongue. It underpinned her interest in literature and particularly her life-long love of Goethe.⁴¹ But language was also the site where her not-belonging could be disclosed most easily. Indeed, for a whole generation of Jews, even when economic success and social integration seemed possible, acculturation remained elusive. At the end of the nineteenth century, Walther Rathenau despaired at what he considered his fellow Jews' embarrassingly faulty German,⁴² and in Vienna, Theodor Herzl was likewise scandalized by their *"Mauscheln."*⁴³ Fritz Mautner, recently converted, announced in his *Sprachkritik* that "the Jew would become

---

38 From among his relevant writings, see Ernest Renan, *De l'origine du langage*, Paris 1848 and *De la part de peuple sémitique dans l'histoire de la civilization*, Paris 1862. Joseph Arthur de Gobineau, *Essai sur l'inegalité des races humaines*, Paris 1853–1855.
39 Compare Thomas Nipperdey and Reinhard Rürup, "Antisemitismus," in: *Geschichtliche Grundbegriffe. Historisches Lexikon zur politisch-sozialen Sprache*, vol 1, Stuttgart 1972, 129–153, here: 130. And see also Frank E. Manuel, *The Broken Staff*, 306.
40 Compare Katz, *Out of the Ghetto*, chapter 11.
41 See Wilfried Barner, *Vom Rahel Varnhagen bis Friedrich Gundolf. Juden als Goethe-Verehrer*, Göttingen 1992.
42 Walther Rathenau, Höre Israel, in: *Die Zukunft*, 6.3. 1897, and later in his *Impressionen, Gesammelte Aufsätze*, Leipzig 1902, 1–15.
43 Theodor Herzl, Mauschel (1897), in his *Zionistische Schriften*, Berlin 1920, 172–176.

a *Volksdeutscher* only when expressions in jargon would sound like a foreign tongue to him, or when he could no longer understand them."[44]

Kafka is in this case, too, the best example. This is what he wrote in a June 1921 letter to Max Brod:

> In this German-Jewish world hardly anyone can do anything but *mauscheln*. This *mauscheln* – taken in a wider sense, and this is the only way it should be taken – consists of a bumptious, tacit, or a self-pitying appropriation of someone else's property, something not earned but stolen by means of a relatively casual gesture.

But despite all that, he goes on, Jews were passionately attracted to this language and literature. Therein laid the tragedy of it all. Most young Jews, who began to write German, Kafka tells us, wanted to leave Jewishness behind them: "With their posterior legs, they were still glued to their father's Jewishness and with their waving anterior legs they found no new ground." Their ensuing despair became their inspiration, too.[45]

This must have had at least something to do with the Antisemitic idiom of the time, which even the Jews internalized. In turn, the fact that Jew, too, were using it only served as food for the Antisemites, forever playing upon the theme of Jewish foreignness and their presumably irreparable otherness.

---

[44] Quoted from Gershon Weiler, "Fritz Mauthner. A Study in Jewish Self-Rejection," in: *Leo Baeck Institute Yearbook* 8, 1963, 136–148, here: 142.

[45] Franz Kafka, *Letters to Friends, family and editors*, translated by Richard and Clara Winston, New York 1958, 288–289.

10 German Jews: The Temptation of Racism

By the late 19th century the term 'race' and its multiple derivatives were ubiquitous in Germany, a recurrent element of both the intellectual and the popular discourse of the day.[1] Its origins are many, stretching back at least to the early modern period and buttressed by eighteen-century fascination with physiognomy, the exploding biological sciences in the 19th century, the growth of modern anthropology, some aspects of philosophy and a certain type of history-writing. It was partly an authentic German creation and partly an import from other European countries; a mixed product of various notions and theories. Significantly, race was by no means strictly or clearly a defined term. It was often used interchangeably with *"Stamm"*, *"Volk"* or even *"Nation"*, and its connotations were not only physical but often, indeed, *primarily* spiritual. However, at least in Germany, one thing seemed quite constant, namely the link between issues related to race and the so-called Jewish Question. From the outset, race served to stress the Jews' "otherness" and their existence as foreigners within German society, never to become a part of the nation, never to be fully integrated or absorbed within it.

To be sure, racial theory was not needed in order to exclude the Jews. After all, they were strangers *par excellence* in European society for generations. It was their *religion* that traditionally set them apart – though never completely apart, and gradually, since the late eighteenth century, their joint *ethnicity* has been added, becoming ever more central in the efforts to keep them apart. In discussing the option of granting Jews equal civil rights and the matter of their so-called emancipation, it was the highly-regarded orientalist Johann David Michaelis from the University of Göttingen, who first formulated the Jews' otherness in strictly *ethnic* terms.[2] Jews originated in the sun-struck region of the Middle East, he explained. In addition to the influence of their unique religion, adopted while

---

[1] The literature on Racism cannot be reviewed here. In my opinion the best general history with an emphasis on Germany is still George L. Mosse, *Toward the Final Solution: A History of Euroean Racism*, London 1978. On the earlier forms of racism, going back to antiquity, see *The Origins of Racism in the West*, eds. Miriam Eliav-Feldon, Benjamin Isaac, and Joseh Ziegler, Cambridge 2009.

[2] From among his relevant writings, most important in many respects is his *Mosaisches Recht*, 6 Vols. Frankfurt a. M. 1770–1775 and enlarged editions 1775–1780, 1780–1793, 1793–1803. Generally on Michaelis, see Anna-Ruth Löwenbrück, *Judenfeindschaft im Zeitalter der Aufklärung. Eine Studie zur Vorgeschichte des modernen Antisemitismus am Beispiel des Göttinger Theologen und Orientalisten Johann David Michaelis*, Frankfurt a. M. 1995, and Jonathan Hess, "Johann David Michaelis and the Colonial Imaginary: Orientalism and the Emergence of Racial Antisemitism in Eighteenth-Century Germany," *Jewish Social Studies*, 6/2, 2000, 56–101.

moving in its desert, their character was forever formed by this harsh natural environment. They could therefore never be a part of the German nation, according to him; they could never become neither peasants nor soldiers, and they could never be expected to develop "true love of the state", as he put it, nor any pride in its accomplishments.[3]

The ethnic argument against Jewish emancipation was often repeated by the participants in the early national movement everywhere in Germany, even among its openly liberal spokesmen. Within that movement, a few always fought for the civil equality of the Jews without any preconditions and as a matter of principle; some argued for their inclusion on economic and utilitarian grounds; most – supported it on the assumption that either before or after granting them equality, Jews would shed their unique group characteristics and become fully authentic Germans, "like us", as the saying went.[4] Later on, by the second half of the century, the most eloquent voice in this camp was doubtlessly the historian Theodor Mommsen. Arguing against Heinrich von Treitschke during the famous – or rather infamous – "Berliner Antisemitismusstreit", this is what he finally had to say about the Jews:[5]

> The entrance into a free nation has its price; the Hanoverians and the men of Hesse, as well as we, from Schleswig-Holstein, are paying it, and we surely feel that in doing so we give up a bit of ourselves. But we do it for the common fatherland. Likewise, no Moses is here to lead the Jews to the promised land again, so whether they sell trousers or write books, it is their holy duty, from their side too and as far as it does not clash with their conscience, to give up their uniqueness as much as they can and tear down all barriers between themselves and their fellow citizens with the outmost determination.

According to Mommsen, Jews were a separate "*Stamm*", one tribe among others, one among many in the German fatherland. With some effort on their part and some help from their friends they could and would, like others, merge into the nation and become true Germans. Their assimilation was in fact part of the nation-building process taking place then and there and it was a joint project with a clear end in sight. It is, indeed, worth remembering this combination of stressing

---

[3] The quote is from Löwenbrück, *Judenfeindlichkeit im Zeitalter der Aufklärung* 158.
[4] The best treatment of this issue is still to be found in Eleonore Sterling, *Judenhaß. Die Anfänge des politischen Antisemitismus in Deutschland (1815–1848)*, Frankfurt a. M. 1969. See also Reinhard Rürup, *Emanzipation und Antisemitismus*, Göttingen 1975, especially 37–73.
[5] See Mommsen's "Auch ein Wort über unser Judentum," reprinted in Walter Boehlich, *Der Berliner Antisemitismusstreit*, Frankfurt a. M. 1965, 227. For a full documentation of the entire controversy see *"Der Berliner Antisemitismusstreit" 1879–1881: Eine Kontroverse um die Zugehörigkeit der deutschen Juden zur Nation*, 2 vols., ed. Karsten Krieger, Munich 2003. Illuminating in this context is Klaus Holz, *Nationaler Antisemitismus. Wissenssoziologie einer Weltanschauung*, Hamburg 2001, esp. 165–297.

"other-ness" and hoping for integration. It was and remained the focus of handling the "Jewish Question" in Germany for the entire period discussed below.

See, for instance, the case of Rudolf Virchow, on the other side of the divide between the famous "two cultures" in the German academic world. Virchow, one time rector of Berlin University, a renowned medical doctor cum biologist, a physical anthropologist and founder of social medicine in Germany, was for many years a *Reichstag* member for the left-liberal Progressive Party.[6] Between 1874 and 1884, that same Virchow conducted the most comprehensive study of the racial characteristics of German school children to date, based on data for some 6,7 million pupils in Germany alone.[7] While it is true that his final aim was to prove that the Germans are a so-called mixed-race, Virchow used the Jews as a separate control group throughout, and concluded in his report, finally published in 1886, that they were noticeably different from the Germans on many counts. Virchow's was a "culturally extended race-concept" that carried no overtly negative connotations and surely did not mean to lead to any restrictive measures.[8] It did, however, give credence to the notion of the biologically determined fate of the Jews and to their permanent apartness.

Thus, even for liberal Germany, racial theory posed a great temptation. Not everyone accepted its claims, but they were widely spread, generally considered legitimate, inoffensive, and in any event worthy of serious consideration. What did the *Jews* in Germany think of all that? From the perspective of our times, the idea of Jews sharing the belief in *any* kind of racial theory seems bizarre and unlikely. However, being so deeply a part of their surroundings, it should come as no surprise that German Jews would sometimes share the assumptions and accept the consequences of racial thinking. Among experts in the field of eugenics, for instance, Jews were not hard to come by. Neither did Jews in Sociology or Psychology shy away from discussing racial types, racial characteristics, or the so-called racial mentalities.[9] They sometimes applied such terms interchangeably

---

[6] There is a great deal of literature on Virchow. See especially Constantin Goschler, *Rudolf Virchow: Mediziner, Anthroologe, politiker*, Böhlau 2002. For the above, Chap. X.
[7] The investigation also included about 2,5 million pupils from Austria, Switzerland and Belgium. See Goschler, 342. Especially on Virchow's anthropological study, see Christian Geulen, "Blonde bevorzugt: Virchow und Boas – eine Fallstudie zur Verschränkung von 'Rasse' und 'Kultur' im ideologischen Feld der Ethnizität um 1900," in: *Archiv für Sozialgeschichte* 40 (2000), S. 147–170, and Andrew Zimmermann, "Antisemitism as skill: Rudolf Virchow's Schulstatistik and the Racial Composition of Germany," in: *Central Euroean History* 32 (1999), 409–429.
[8] Geulen, "Blonde bevorzugt: Virchow und Boas," 169.
[9] For Jewish medical doctors in the field of Eugenics see John M. Efron, *Defenders of the Race: Jewish Doctors and Race Science in Fin-de-Siècle Europe*, New Haven & London 1994. More generally for race in medicine, Sander Gilman's various oeuvres are insightful. For race in the social

with notions related to Volk rather than Race. They often applied these terms interchangeably with notions related to Volk or what we would rather call "ethnicity" today, as Moritz Lazarus did, for instance, in writing about what he came to call "Völkerpsychologie".[10] But the end result was similar. Jewish physical and mental marks were underlined and their capacity for fundamental change, a change that would eventually enable full absorption in German society, was believed to be minimal at best. Clearly, for Jews – theories of race and race theory were more than a matter of intellectual choice. They could not have imagined at that time that their very existence might be endangered by such theories, but they must have sensed the intricacies implied in this discourse as far as they were concerned. They were often enough worried about it, no doubt, but despite all that, could not resist the temptation.

In the historiography, two groups of Jews have been singled out as adherents of some form or another of racialism: Men of the various branches of the medical profession, who found themselves entangled in the racial discourse regardless of their attitude on issues of Jewish uniqueness and/or integration, and Zionist intellectuals, applying racial categories precisely in this context, in order to buttress their views on the required solution to Jewish predicaments, particularly in Eastern Europe. In both cases, it has been shown, Jewish reliance on racial theory was never complete or unambiguous. In his book of 1994, *Defenders of the Race*, John Efron describes the special brand of racial theory practiced by Jewish scientists, one that allowed for a "soft" form of biological determinism, always seeking a proper mix between nature and culture and at the same time reversing the commonly postulated racial hierarchy to place Jews parallel with or even above all other white-skin racial groups; in any case – not below them.[11] George Mosse, in one of his early essays, examined the influence of the Folkish (rather than racial) ideology on German Jews, concluding – in a similar vein – that despite the similarities, "Jewish" racial thinking was of a uniquely humanitarian kind and allowed for a defense of the Jews while stressing the values of pluralism and a common humanity.[12] In both cases, Jewish racial thought is shown to be part of a

---

sciences at the time, see especially, Mitchell B. Hart, *Social Science and the politics of Modern Jewish Identity*, Stanford Cal. 2000, and Amos Morris-Reich, *The Quest for Jewish Assimilation in Modern Social Science*, New York & London 2008.

10 The best example is Lazarus' lecture, "Treu und Frei", in his *Gesammelte Reden und Vorträge über Juden und Judentum*, Leipzig 1887, 57–110.

11 Efron, *Defenders of the Race*, see the conclusion, chapter 7, 175–180.

12 See George Mosse, "The Influence of the Völkisch Idea on German Jewry," in: *Studies of the Leo Baeck Institute*, eds. Max Kreutzberger and Frederik Unger, New York 1967, 81–115. For a more recent interpretation in the same vein, different from mine, see now Yfaat Weiss, "Identity

general discourse but not an indistinct part of it; a special, less offensive variant – at least from today's perspective.

Both Efron and Mosse, whom I have taken here as my examples, acknowledge that thinking in racial categories can be found among liberal Jews no less than among liberal non-Jews, and among those who were neither medical doctors or anthropologists nor Jewish nationalists, especially Zionists. Both, however, treat liberal Jews, bent on assimilation, only in passing. It is, however, putting *these* people in focus, it seems to me, that may allow us to add yet another dimension to what is perhaps a rather familiar tale. We may discover not only the intellectual ambivalence, always present in the case of our protagonists across several decades of their life, but also a pattern of change and development in their thinking, indicating a gradual retreat form racial thinking along the time axis. At first hanging on to race as a tool for clearing up the difficult issue of their identity in the midst of assimilation, many German Jews gradually learned to live as both Germans and Jews, and even to do so with a fair measure of equanimity. This was achieved not only through a process of intellectual enlightenment, pushing away from racial determinism. Nor was it simply the overwhelming effect of rabid Antisemitism that brought home to them its dangers. It was rather the gradual acceptance of their Jewishness, no longer a source of constant anxiety for them. The development of a relatively secure hybrid identity may have in the end provided German Jewry with a comforting sense of security, false sense of security, no doubt, but nevertheless at that time trustworthy, liberating, and empowering.

For the early years, in parallel to Mommsen and Virchow during the late 1870s and the 1880s, I find the attitude of the Neo-Kantian Jewish philosopher Hermann Cohen particularly instructive. Cohen may not have taken seriously the existence of *biologically* separate races by then, but he did take very seriously what he named a race-instinct, *Racengefühl*, or what we would now probably call race-consciousness. We all wished, wrote Cohen, meaning the Jews, that "*we* had all simply had a German, a Germanic appearance, of which we now only possess the climatic side-effects . . ." But since "we" clearly do *not,* "it must be a fundamental consideration, and more than that, [it must be] our holiest desire to accommodate the *Naturton* of the *Volk* into which we want to be absorbed in all its ways. Peculiarities may be considered proper for a while, but we must continue to show our efforts to get rid of them."[13] Cohen too seemed to have had no faith in pluralism. "Members of a Volk have the duty to aspire to a unity of existence

---

and Essentialism. Race, Racism and the Jews in fin de siècle," in: *German History from the Margins*, eds. Neil Gregor, Nils Roemer, and Mark Roseman, Bloomington Ind. 2006, 49–68.
13 See Hermann Cohen, "Ein Bekenntniss in der Judenfrage", Berlin 1880, in: Boehlich, *Antisemitismusstreit*, 126–151. The quote is on 140–141, (underlining in the original).

and consciousness and to cultivate it ever more ardently, more intensively", he wrote. Since the nation was in the process of building a new state, he believed, it must reject any kind of *Mannichfaltigkeit* (plurality), though he must have been aware that some saw precisely in that plurality the source of "true culture".[14] Being a philosopher of religion, Cohen felt that despite all race-issues the task of full integration could still be achieved, especially because of the deep affinity between Judaism and Protestantism. This was what finally enabled Jews and Christians to share in the life of a single community. After all, he wrote, "Much of what we, as modern men, acknowledge now as alive in our Judaism, is Christian light that shone on the old, eternal ground".[15] The *Israelitische Religion*, according to him, had already achieved a merger with Protestantism, a "cultural-historical" unity, anchored deep in "our" spirit, he wrote, and manifested in "a most sincere national intermingling".[16] Race was clearly part of Cohen's vocabulary, though for him, as well as for many of his contemporaries, it was spiritually rather than organically defined, always amenable to change and in the end subordinate to religion – or to culture, if one wished to broaden the relevant sphere.

Some felt ill at ease with such a compromise. Walther Rathenau was thirteen years old at the time of the *Berliner Antisemitismusstreit*.[17] He was the elder son of the legendary *Generaldirektor* of the AEG, Emil Rathenau, and grew up in a family that had only minimal ties with either the Jewish religion or the joint Jewish community-life. Nevertheless, Rathenau was self-consciously Jewish throughout his life, and being a Jew meant for him above all simply living *with* and *among* Jews. One is reminded of Gerschom Scholem's description of the exclusively Jewish company kept by his parents, who – like the Rathenaus – had long abandoned most religious customs, even though *they* might have still had stronger ties to the Jewish community.[18] As a child, Walther was probably not quite aware of the exclusivity of this milieu, but as he became older, especially during his student-days, he began to feel oppressed by the constant presence of Jews around him. In letters to his mother, he commented sarcastically on what he saw

---

14 Ibid, 143.
15 Ibid, 149–150.
16 Ibid, 150.
17 The material used in this essay concerning Rathenau has been collected for my book, *Walther Rathenau. The Life of Weimar's Fallen Statesman*, New Haven 2012.
18 See Scholem's memoirs, *Von Berlin nach Jerusalem. Jugenderinnerungen*, Frankfurt a. M. 1994, especially the first two Chapters, and his essay, "On the Social Psychology of the Jews in Germany," in: *Jews and Germans from 1862 to 1933: The problematic Symbiosis*, ed. David Bronsen, Heidelberg 1972, 9–32.

as their unpleasant habits, the futile hopes attached by some of them to conversion and their disproportional prominence at the university.[19]

Despite all that Rathenau possessed a heightened sense of Jewish belonging, a "Racengefühl" according to Hermann Cohen, to which – truth be said – he had at first attached mainly negative connotations. Responding to this frustration, he then developed a kind of exaggerated pride in being Jewish, a typical *Trotzjudentum*, as it was sometimes called at the time. He rejected conversion, considering it both dishonorable and futile, and developed a habit of outwardly parading his Jewishness, making sure no one could overlook it. Years later, it was Chancellor Bernhard von Bülow who described in his memoirs his first meeting with Walther Rathenau: "He was about forty years old at the time," he wrote, "but looked old, extremely attractive and most elegantly attired. He approached me with a deep bow and said in a resounding voice, with one hand resting on his chest: 'Your Highness, before I am granted the honor to speak with you, I wish to make a statement that is also a confession: Your Highness, I am a Jew . . .'"[20] From the outset, then, there was a fundamental tension in Rathenau's attitude both towards his Jewish self and towards other Jews – far and near.

This can be taken as the psychological background for the publication of his first essay, published 1897, dedicated to the "Jewish Question" and dramatically entitled "Hear, O Israel!"[21] The essay opens with that confession, by then so typical of Rathenau: "I want to profess straight off that I am a Jew," he writes and then provocatively adds: "Does it require justification if I write in a spirit other than that of defending the Jews?" Surely, he immediately attracts our attention; but our unease, too. This opening, to be sure, represented the milder version of the text in question. In an earlier draft, now available in his archive, we read: "Does it require an explanation if I tend towards Antisemitism?"[22]

---

[19] See now the full edition of his correspondence in: Walther Rathenau, *Briefe*, ed. Alexander Jaser, Clemens Picht and Ernst Schulin, 2 vols. (vols. V1 and V2 of the *Walther Rathenau Gesamtausgabe*), Düsseldrof 2006 (hereafter GA).

[20] Quoted in the GA, II, 654, from Bülow's *Denkwürdigkeiten*, vol. 3, Berlin 1931 (all the translations are mine).

[21] The essay "Höre, Israel!" was first published in Maximilan Harden's weekly, *Die Zukunft*, then later reprinted in Walther Rathenau, *Impressionen*, Leipzig 1902, 1–20, but never included in his GS of 1918 or in any later edition. For an English translation I have here used Thomas Dunla's partial text in: http://germanhistorydocs.ghi-dc.org.

[22] Rathenau's *Nachlass* fell into the hands of the *Gestapo* in 1933 and was for long thought lost. It was eventually found in 1991/2 in the Central State Archive in Moscow, including drafts of many of Rathenau's writings, none so revealing as the draft of his "Höre, Israel". On the probable impetus to the writing of this piece see now, Ursula Mader and Peter G. Klemm, "Ad Fontes III!

And, indeed, Rathenau does sound like a full-fledged Antisemite in this piece, like a true *racial* Antisemite. In long passages he laments the fact that all Jews look "frightfully alike", describes their typically "south-eastern" looks, their "unconstructive built, the high shoulders, the awkward feet, the soft round forms", and more. He then offers petty advice on how they should dress up and behave if they were really to achieve that "conscious self-improvement of a race", so as to fit the demands of properly passing. "The goal of the process," he finally explains, "is not [to be] imitated Germans, but Germans in manners and in education."[23]

To be sure, neither acts of self-defense nor cries for help from the authorities would cure the widespread antipathy of non-Jews towards Jews. Here as elsewhere, Rathenau was always uneasy with the anti-defamation campaign of the newly established *Centralverein deutscher Staatsbürger jüdischen Glaubens* and openly against the early stirrings of Zionism in Germany. For him, such joint communal efforts were meaningless, since the metamorphosis required was an intimate matter, involving the greatest efforts and the deepest dedication on the part of every single individual. Baptism, an open option for some, no doubt, was rejected by him out of hand, as we already saw. "Since if half of all Israel converted, nothing but a passionate 'Antisemitism against the baptized' would emerge, bringing about snooping around and insinuations from the one side, hate of the renegades and deceit on the other."[24] It was, in fact, only one year earlier that Rathenau had announced his secession from the Jewish Community of Berlin, but true to his conviction, never followed it up with the expected conversion. At this point he must have still believed that a true "Jewish patriarchy" would soon emerge, "not of property but of spiritual and bodily culture", one that would in time – and note the organic metaphor – "emerge from below, absorbing new nourishment from its roots and in time changing all the stuff that can be transformed and digested."[25] Clearly, no one could be more fitting to join this patriarchy than Rathenau himself.

Oder Was gab den Anstoß zu 'Höre, Israel!'" in: *Mitteilungen der Walther Rathenau Gesellschaft*, no.19, 2009, 7–14.

23 In the original: Jews seem "zum Erschrecken ähnlich", possessing a "südöstlich gestimmte Erscheinung", with "unkonstruktiven Bau, die hohen Schultern, die ungelenken Füße, die weichliche Rundlichkeit der Formen." Their goal must be "die bewußte Selbsterziehung einer Rasse zur Anpassung an fremde Anforderungen," culminating not in "imitierte Germanen," but in "deutsch geartete und erzogene Juden . . .".

24 "Denn würde die Hälfte von ganz Israel bekehrt, so könnte nichts anderes entstehen als ein leidenschaftlicher 'Antisemitismus gegen Getaufte', der durch Schnüffeleien und Verdächtigungen auf der einen, durch Renegatenhaß und Verlogenheit auf der anderen Seite . . .".

25 That "jüdisches Patriziertum" would "durch seine Wurzeln von unten herauf immer neue Nahrung aufsaugen und mit der Zeit alles verarbeiten, was an umwandlungsfähigem und verdaulichen Material vorhanden ist."

"Hear, O Israel!", despite its aggressive, racial language, was perhaps not simply an expression of Jewish self-hatred, as has been so often reiterated both at the time and in later literature. Rathenau was attacking some Jews in order to defend others. But in any event, being Jewish was far from a settled issue for him, and neither did he find peace with regard to more general racial issues. In a long essay from 1904, under the title "On Weakness, Fear and Purpose" (Von Schwachheit, Furcht und Zweck), Rathenau divided humanity into two groups, the Wise and the Strong, and argued that history was nothing but a prolonged fight between them.[26] But though the author's admiration was clearly assigned to the latter, that is the Strong, it was to the qualities of the former, that is to the Wise, that he dedicated most of this essay. Out of fear and on the basis of an inherent weakness arose the need to lie and flatter, he explained, but also to invent, amass property, reach for and exercise power, enjoy human accomplishments and bask in human praise. This, moreover, was the source of human ability to reason, act with alacrity and esprit, even take pleasure in humor. But while all these qualities might be admirable, they could never bring "freedom", as he put it, or true aesthetic enjoyment, neither happiness nor relaxation. These come naturally only to the Strong, Rathenau writes – "these wonderful and secretive ancient people of the North . . . whose fair-haired heads we would so much like to crown with the glory of Mankind."[27]

Rathenau's unabashed use of racial categories, especially his repeated use of physiognomy, is characteristic of his style at the time. It is also closely linked to the Jewish issue, always at hand, even if sometimes in disguise. The Weak and the Wise in his world are clearly the Jews, especially those occupied in commerce and finance, like his father. The Strong and the Happy are the handsome "*Germanen*". His contempt, sometimes even his wrath, is outspokenly directed at those who populated his own life. Even more than in "Höre Israel!", he is here talking of his close relatives and immediate colleagues. The ones he loves and admires apparently remain beyond his reach.

It was a position fraught with ambivalence, and although Rathenau never retracted the views expressed in "Weakness, Fear and Purpose", he was less than completely at ease with them from the start. A week after its first publication, on November 19th 1904, Frank Wedekind, among the few friends with whom Rathenau could argue in depth even on matters of contention between them, sent the author his reactions. Rathenau's reply followed immediately.[28] trying to

---

[26] The essay was first published in *Die Zukunft*, XIII, No. 7, 223–239 and then reprinted in Rathenau's *Reflexionen*, Leipzig 1908, 1–23, as well as in his *GS*, vol. 4, 9–32.
[27] GS, vol.4, 26.
[28] For the letter, written November 21, 1904, and for the quotes below, see GA V1, 712–717.

explain himself, he attempted to answer Wedekind's objections one by one. Against what might appear from the text, he admits, his heart goes to the weak, the fearful and the suffering, since after all, isn't it true, he asks while throwing in for good measure a phrase from Baudelaire, that "pain is the only nobility?" "In confidence", as he then put it, he was willing to admit that genius could only arise from a mixture of the two elements depicted in his essay and it was not simply the reign of the Strong that one ought to strive for. Rathenau was ready to assault the Weak and the Wise, but he recognized that they were there to stay and that in the end they were indispensable.

Thus, two elements determined Rathenau's racial thought. His attitude towards Jews and Judaism on the one hand and his attitude towards those true "Germanen" he could identify around him, namely the Prussian aristocracy, on the other hand. Both underwent deep changes in his mind, almost in perfect parallel. Two trips to Germany's colonial territories in Eastern and South-Western Africa gave the first momentum to his turning away from the heroic "Germanen".[29] And when upon his return the attacks on the Kaiser's "personal regime" and upon the corruption of his Camarilla were at their peak at home, he too was beginning to come out against the feudal, anachronistic leadership of Germany. For a whole century, Rathenau now claimed, Prussia had produced only one real statesman and that too by sheer accident or luck, namely Otto von Bismarck. At the same time, England manages such a feat continuously, he claimed, France – intermittently, and even Austria – often enough. This was not a question of "raw materials", he asserted. After all, Prussia managed to produce first rate leadership in industry and business, which differed from politics "in subject matter rather than in method". In that other sphere "we have experienced true selection" based on talent, merit and achievements, while in politics, Prussia was bound by sheer "Aristocratism", to use his phrase, and by institutional traditionalism that made her no more than a respectable Central-European power, far from what she could have been, considering her "military and cultural predominance"[30] This has now become one of Rathenau's main themes. Within a few years, his adoration of the racially superior "Germanen" has evaporated. One pole of his racial scheme of

---

[29] Rathenau joined the official expeditions headed by the Colonial Secretary at the time Dernburg, first to the German Colony of East Africa and then to South West Africa following the horrific massacre of the Hereros and the Mana tribes, carried out by German army units sent to restore law and order in the territories. For details, including an English translation of Rathenau's two reports, written upon returning to Germany, see, above all, *Walther Rathenau, Industrialist, Banker, Intellectual, and politician, Notes and Diaries 1907–1922*, ed. Hartmut Pogge von Strandmann, Oxford 1985.

[30] See Rathenau's essay, "Politische Auslese" (1912), reprinted in his *GS*, vol. 1, 221–232.

things has collapsed. The ground was set for the next step, namely a revision of his attitude towards Jews and Judaism.

Early signs of such a revision could already be found in his "State and Judaism" of 1911.[31] By then Rathenau was undergoing one of his self-searching periods, in the aftermath of his failures in the public-political arena as well as in some private matters, even in matters of the heart. Under such circumstances, the Jewish issue surfaced almost automatically. The similarities between his posture in 1897 and in 1911 are obvious, but so are the differences. While the piece of 1897, targeted the unassimilated, culturally inferior Jews, according to Rathenau, this time he was turning against the Prussian *state*, its discriminatory practices, its unfairness and the deep injustice it was propagating. To be sure, the hostile and condescending tone of the first essay reappears here too, but the tenor of "Staat und Judenthum" is very different from "Höre Israel!" Now, Rathenau's main effort is to expose the absurdity of state discrimination against the Jews by ridiculing the inconsistency that allowed baptized Jews to be exempt from such discrimination, by stressing Jewish talent and contribution, especially in the economic sphere, and by insisting on their loyalty and devotion to Germany.

On the eve of the First World War, Rathenau was gradually coming to terms with being a Jew, and later on, in the midst of war, the process continued. In June 1917, as his "Polemics about Faith" has been published, he finally seemed to be able to explain what Judaism actually meant for him: a religion without church and dogma, without canonical books, indeed without any supervising human agency, insisting on one thing only, namely the "oneness of God", as he put it.[32] Thus, since the publication of "Höre Israel!" two decades earlier, Rathenau moved slowly but surely into the mainstream of Jewish self-definition at the time. Notice how close this maverick now is to Hermann Cohen's position a generation earlier. He too is now a German patriot of Jewish descent, upholding Judaism as a universal ethical standard, akin to Protestantism, at ease with being a Jew, quite naturally combining it with his German citizenship.

Reconciliation with Judaism – his own brand of Judaism, to be sure – made the race issue far less important to Rathenau. In one of his letters, four months after the publication of the "Polemics", we read the following: "We all know that the German tribes are not all of the same blood, and that even less do they represent the descendants of those Germans [described by] Tacitus . . . I consider all

---

31 This was originally a three parts answer to a call for conversion as the only way of achieving Jewish integration into German society. It was then published together as one of the appendices to Rathenau's *Zur Kritik der Zeit*, Berlin 1912, 219–243.
32 First published separately by the Fischer publishing house and then reprinted in Rathenau's *GS*, Vol. 5, 95–119.

race theories a waste of time und acknowledge only one thing that turns peoples into nations and nations into states: the community of soil, experience and spirit."[33] By now, every mention of his earlier books, both the *Impressionen* of 1902, including his "Höre Israel!", and the *Reflexionen,* in which his views on race and racial theory were set out in print, embarrassed him. The tone of "Höre Israel!" was wrong, he now claims, and since "no one can be changed through cruelty," it was also futile.[34] Later on, in another letter, he adds that "the relatively purest 'Germanentum' . . . is more different from the average German than [that German] is from the average Jew," and his final conclusion at this point was that "in its peak the human spirit is [everywhere] the same."[35]

This was no doubt a radical turn of mind. Thinking about race had been central to Rathenau's search for identity. However, its association with that exaggerated admiration he once felt for the Nordic stock of the Prussian nobility seemed rather absurd to him as he grew older and came nearer to the realities of state and society. Its link with Antisemitism made it no longer acceptable as he was finally able to see in Judaism more than an arbitrary, pre-determined and detested destiny.

Rathenau was not alone in going through this process of change. Observe, for instance, the case of Martin Buber, eventually standing at the opposite pole from Rathenau on the German Jewish ideological spectrum,[36] though to begin with, the two were not so far apart. During the years immediately before the First World War, they have had some social and intellectual contacts, and at *that* time such contacts did not seem – to them or to others – questionable or improbable. Both were by then taking part in the general discourse on Ethnicity, Race and Blood, and both were applying these in their search for the true content of Judaism and the modern meaning of being Jewish. What in Rathenau's language was the gulf between the material world and the human soul was for Buber the distinction between "the world of impressions and influence" on the one hand, and the substance that is "being impressed-upon and influenced", on the other. While for the early Rathenau it was race that defined the real essence of man, Buber chose to speak of blood, that "deep-rooted nurturing force within the individual," as he put it, defining the "deepest layers of our being," "our innermost thinking and

---

33 A letter to Karl Scheffler, GA V2, 1777.
34 See his comments on December 30, 1912, in the GA V1, 1151–1152, and for the quote see the undated report of a conversation with Lore Karrenbrock, in GA II, 788.
35 See the GA V2, 2138.
36 On Martin Buber's life see now Gerhard Wehler, *Martin Buber. Leben – Werk – Wirkung,* Munich 2010, and the older but still useful biography: Maurice Friedman, *Martin Buber's Life and Work,* Detroit 1988.

our will". Blood, Buber insisted, was "the most potent stratum of our being." German culture stood – according to him – for the "world around", while Jewishness defined "the world within" – "die Seele", Rathenau would have said; "Volkseele" was Buber's repeatedly-used term.[37]

During the first decade of the 20th century, the two men, coming from such different backgrounds and entertaining such different ambitions, shared this: they both defined their Jewishness in biological terms but felt that that definition could still be reconciled to their efforts at assimilation. Later on, for Buber – as for Rathenau – this intellectual tangle lost its relevance. When he was composing the introduction to a Hebrew edition of his writings about Judaism, this is what Buber had to say: "A number of years after these things were written, evil men falsified the concept of blood that I had then used. Therefore I hereby declare that in every case in which I used the term blood I did not mean by it the matter of race, which I find nonsensical, but the line of births in a people, the line that fixes its identity."[38] Like Rathenau, Buber too was trying to extricate himself from the racial discourse of his earlier years.

And this was a route taken by others, too. At the turn of the 19th century, many German Jews used racial metaphors and concepts freely and frequently, especially those who, in the face of their far-reaching assimilation, were struggling to come to terms with their hybrid identity. Historian Sander Gilman listed such Jews for us: Freud, for instance, repeatedly applying biological, geneticist, and familiar terms in speaking of his Jewishness; insisting on a "Jewish essence", "a special [Jewish] mental life", even a "Jewish mind"; but then also Kafka, talking of his "negro face", Joseph Roth describing himself as "black", or even the three-generations-back-converted-Jew Hugo von Hoffmannsthal, ruminating over "the stirring" of his "Jewish blood."[39] This was typical fin de siècle, but for most Jews this too was a passing phase. In each case, a variety of elements interplayed in blowing it over; the pressure of racial Antisemitism and the emerging self-confidence of German-Jewish identity were particularly important among them. For some, Antisemitism played the major role. Freud may be a case in point. As has often been stressed, he seemed to have been secure in his Jewishness from the start, and his final rejection of racialism was a consequence of his fight against the anti-Jewish atmosphere around him, particularly against those who tried to brand psychoanalysis as a presumably "Jewish science". As he admitted, the sources of Jewish awareness and Jewish uniqueness remained a mystery to him,

---

[37] See Martin Buber, *On Judaism*, New York 1967, and specifically an essay entitled "Judaism and the Jews", 14–16. The essay is based on a 1911 speech by Buber, first published in *Drei Reden über das Judentum*, Frankfurt a. M 1911.
[38] See the Hebrew edition, published under the title *Te'uda veye'ud*, Jerusalem 1959, 29.
[39] See Sander L. Gilman, *Freud, Race, and Gender*, Princeton NJ 1993, 16–27.

but race eventually was no longer a viable option in trying to explain them.[40] In Buber's case – both elements played a role. He was appalled by growing Antisemitism in Germany, and from what by then seemed a relative safe haven in Jerusalem. The problem of defining his identity must have seemed a thing of the past.[41] I believe the reasons for Rathenau's moving away from racial categories had initially *little* to do with Antisemitism, despite its presence in his life. It had much to do with a process of maturing, through which he was becoming ever more secure in his identity as a Jew.

This was indicative of the overall situation of German Jewry at the time. With few exceptions, those who were to be taken to the slaughter by the Nazis, even men as deeply assimilated as Rathenau, had by then acknowledged and accepted their special, hybrid identity. The age of assimilation-at-all-cost was over. German Jews were more often than not far away from Zionism, but on the eve of catastrophe neither were they simply "regular Germans". In the end, Racism caught up with them, so to speak. Just as they were completing a process of accommodation to being Germans and Jews simultaneously, Hitler and his cohorts were working to reverse this long and painful process of adjustment, acting forcefully now on the other side of the equation. Their vicious Antisemitism intended to make any such accommodation into a total chimera. *They* used racism in order to make possible a radical turn in an opposite direction, a turn towards the abyss.

---

40 Ibid, 28–36.
41 On Buber's position and for the context of his thought, see paul Mendes-Flohr, "Martin Buber as an Habsburg Intellectual," in *Jüdische Geschichte als allgemeine Geschichte*, eds. Raphael Gross and Yfat Weiss, Göttingen 2006, 13–29.

11 Interim Balance: Continuity and Discontinuity in the History of German Antisemitism

Some two decades ago, I received an invitation to participate in a conference on the Final Solution, organized by François Furet in Paris.[1] I was no expert in this field, but the invitation provided me with an unexpected opportunity to develop my thoughts on the history and historiography of Antisemitism; I gladly accepted. Working mainly at that time on German-Jewish history in the nineteenth century, I had felt ill at ease with some of the fundamental assumptions common to research in this field, while vaguely guessing that my objections might prove relevant to the study of later years, too. Thus, though my paper for the Paris conference focused on the *Kaiserreich*, it also touched upon the links between that period and the later era of Nazism. It dealt, in short, with the issue of continuity. I intended its title, "The Written and the Spoken Word" to hint at my theme and suggest my approach. But the historiographical thrust of this essay can only be understood by its immediate context, personal and general alike. After all, explaining historiography requires the same tools as explaining history, and while every historical study aspires toward objectivity and truth, it is also a product of its time and circumstances. Twenty years seems long enough to provide distance and perspective necessary for appreciating all that. Here I would like to come back to the same issues, rethink, re-evaluate, and partly revise my previous position.

By the late 1970's, Nazi Antisemitism had usually been seen as the culmination of previous, age-old hatred of the Jews. In its various guises, one often argued, this hatred was a permanent feature of the psychological and cultural makeup of European society. The "Final Solution," under Hitler's leadership, was planned and carried out as this enduring hatred's most extreme version. It was the climax of a gradual and prolonged process of radicalization. New, perhaps, was the depth and extent of the hatred, its organized form, its effectiveness, and its murderous finality. Otherwise, in terms of worldview or motivation, it was all familiar enough.

On the basis of so much consensus, therefore, differences among historians related more often to the choice of a relevant starting point for the narrative of the Shoah than to its nature or the problem of continuity inherent in it. One could start with the earliest antagonism to Jews in the ancient world or with the onset of Christianity. It was possible to open with Paul, continue through the Church

---

[1] For the full proceedings of this conference see *L'Allemagne nazi et le genocide juif*, ed. F. Furet, Paris 1985. My paper here as no.5.

Fathers and retell the story of anti-Jewish words and deeds through the medieval period. It was also possible to start with the twelfth century, the crusaders, and the first blood libel accusations. Some preferred to begin with Luther and focus on German Protestantism, the rise of nationalism, and the controversies over emancipation. Others stressed secularization or the rise of racial theory.

Most historians finally felt they ought to begin with the onset of what was normally dubbed Modern Antisemitism. Freed from the need to begin at some indistinct, remote past, they could take-off with the early formation of the modern state, as Hannah Arendt did in *The Origins of Totalitarianism*, or, more conventionally, in the mid 1870's with Bismarck's new German Reich. This turning point was preferred by Paul Massing in the early 1950s and Peter Pulzer in the late 1960s. "Post-emancipatory Antisemitism," as this modern variety of the old hatred was called by Reinhard Rürup, flourished against all odds in the atmosphere of mild liberalism and even under the auspices of the proud German *Rechtsstaat*. That starting point, in the late 1870s, signaled according to most historians, the beginning of a new or renewed process, in which ever increasing hatred culminated in the Holocaust. Jewish historians tended to prefer a longer-term continuity, while non-Jews more often opted for the shorter-term.[2] But in all cases, continuity seemed irrefutable. Antisemitism was seen as the one single prerequisite, necessary and sufficient, for explaining the "Final Solution." In the end, the continuity thesis accorded not only with the main school of Jewish history but represented the mainstream German historiography too. It was particularly well suited to the *Sonderweg* thesis, rather dominant at the time of the Paris conference, according to which Nazism had been the outgrowth of a long course of German history. A unique process had brought Germany to National Socialism, while France and England, for instance, steadily marched onward towards Democracy. Not only Antisemitism, in fact not even *primarily* Antisemitism, was here at stake. Scholars dealt with militarism, authoritarianism, and imperialism. I chose to study the overall phenomenon of what I named "anti-modernism."[3] Antisemitism fit only too well into this overall continuity-syndrome, from every conceivable perspective.

Soon enough, however, I too began to feel uneasy with the continuity thesis. Even by the early 1970's I was beginning to observe what role the omnipresent

---

[2] For an extensive discussion of early Jewish historiography on Antisemitism see my "Antisemitismus als Problem Jüdisch-nationalen denkens und jüdischer Geschichtsschreibung," in my: *Antisemitismus als Kultureller Code*, Munich 2000, 88–110.

[3] Shulamit Volkov, *The Rise of Popular Antimodernism in Germany. The Urban Master Artisans 1873–1896*, Princeton N.J. 1978.

notion of 'eternal hatred' played not only in historical scholarship but also in present-day politics in Israel; how it helped preserve the sense that the "the whole world is against us" and even underpinned policies that prioritized short-term security over long-term political considerations. It started to seem too simple, too straightforwardly deterministic, a ready-made answer to some fearfully complex matters.

Let me quickly summarize the ways I had tried to revise this answer. I began by raising a methodological objection. The fact that a certain phenomenon had its origins in the remote past, paraphrasing Ernst Bloch, was no explanation for its actual, modern iteration. Although Jews had indeed been the object of antipathy, prejudice, and discrimination for centuries, this history of hatred still hardly accounted for their systematic extermination by the Nazis at a particular place and time. History, after all, should explain the specificity of events, not merely point out their vague beginnings. In more concrete terms: the permanence of Antisemitism was an insufficient explanation for the Final Solution. Even ferocious anti-Jewish sentiment never barred Jewish life in the diaspora, and occasionally even their more or less full integration in gentile society.

Furthermore, Germany was not the primary site of anti-Jewish sentiments in modern times and could not even be considered particularly Antisemitic in pre-Nazi years. Violent pogroms took place in Tsarist Russia and the Dreyfus Affair, the most outrageous case of public, state-supported Antisemitism in the West, was staged in Republican France. Modern Germany had never witnessed anything of that sort and most Germans, Jews and non-Jews alike, considered such transgressions unthinkable in their orderly, monarchical *Rechtsstaat*.

Finally, in the wake of the Antisemitic waves of the late 1870s through the early 1890s, political parties propagating discriminatory measures against the Jews and an end to emancipation repeatedly proved ineffective and unattractive to German voters. A line of continuous Antisemitic crescendo could hardly be shown during the *Kaiserreich* through to Nazism. Moreover, Nazi ferocity could not be deduced from previous events. In many ways and for many acute observers, its appearance was a stunning surprise.

In addition, my paper in Paris stressed a functionalist approach to Antisemitism, an alternative to the essentialism of previous historiography. In Germany of the late nineteen centuries, I argued, Antisemitism has had a variety of functions, old and new. Socially, it served to divert attention from deep-seated inner rifts. Politically, it spurred a gradual realignment of lower middle-class voters from the Left to the Right. It served as a "cultural code," indicating membership in an anti-modern camp, known for its anti-liberalism, its outspoken anti-socialism, and its monarchic, imperialist worldview. It was a signal of an overall anti-democratic syndrome.

This last point was indeed central to my anti-continuity stand. Relying here on an even earlier paper,[4] I claimed that with the rise of National Socialism, Antisemitism, as practiced during the *Kaiserreich*, lost its previous meaning. For Hitler, hating Jews was no longer a token of some other, more comprehensive set of convictions; he was not merely venting general aggression against them. For him, it was the Jews themselves that posed a concrete and present danger. And this change of perspective, I added, was not easy to diagnose and herein lay the reason for so much blindness on the part of his contemporaries. Most of them continued to think in old categories, while Hitler and his true believers moved onto a completely different path.

But the real source of my unease with the continuity thesis, it seems to me in hindsight, was neither present-day concerns nor my tentatively emerging view of Nazi Antisemitism, but its implications for our view of Jewish life in *pre*-Nazi Germany. This, as the previous essays in this collection demonstrate, was my main research interest at the time. I felt one should not allow an undue stress on the permanence and omnipresence of Antisemitism to reflect back so markedly upon modern German-Jewish history as a whole.

The story of German Jewry since the latter part of the eighteen century is by no means a mirror image of the story of Antisemitism. This history was not simple, continuous or unitary. Since the publication of Christian Wilhelm Dohm's *On the Civil Improvement of the Jews* in 1781, a discussion on the theme of equal citizenship-rights for Jews raged far and wide.[5] For the following eighty years, the issue surfaced repeatedly in Germany's various political centers.[6] There was, indeed, a great deal of opposition to this so-called emancipation – in Prussia and elsewhere, on the Left and on the Right – and much of the opposition was clearly Antisemitic. But while the controversy raged, Jews were, figuratively speaking, emerging out of the Ghetto, abandoning centuries-old life-style of isolation and entering non-Jewish society with a vengeance.

To be sure, they were not always welcome. The multitude of ancient edicts that regulated their life and restricted their activities was not, at first, systematically revoked. Moreover, despite the more open environments of the late eighteen and early nineteen centuries, new prohibitions were still being enacted, magnifying the

---

[4] "Antisemitism as a Cultural Code. Reflections on the History and the Historiography of German Antisemitism," first published in the *Leo Baeck Institute Yearbook* (LBIYB) XXIII, 1978, 25–45. Here no. 4.
[5] The reference is to his *Über die bürgerliche Verbesserung der Juden*, Berlin-Stettin 1781–1783.
[6] The best analysis of this controversy and its effects is Reinhard Rürup, "Die 'Judenfrage' der bürgerlichen Gesellschaft und die Entstehung des modernen Antisemitismus," in: *Emanzipation und Antisemitismus*, Göttingen 1975, 74–94.

dissonance and deepening the sense of injustice. While Jews were now permitted to study at universities, for instance, new rules were introduced to prevent their appointment to academic posts. The interventionist and reactionary Prussian state-machinery, to take another example, viewed suspiciously the initiatives of liberals to form new types of Jewish congregations or reform their religious practices. And with only few and short-term exceptions, the "Community of Bread and Bed," to use Jacob Toury's fitting phrase, continued to be denied even to the well off or the better educated among the Jews.[7] In most cases, Jews could not form intimate relationships with their non-Jewish business counterparts, their Christian neighbors, or their closest political allies. Nevertheless, the growing public sphere in Germany did afford them an ever-wider range of possibilities. Jews were not accepted into *all vereine*, which were flourishing throughout the country, but they were *sometimes* accepted into *some of* them. They could not take up *any* open job in state or city administrations, but they could take up *some*, especially in the growing non-governmental public sphere. Within a couple of generations, they grew from a community of impoverished outsiders into a predominantly urban, prosperous population, successful in almost all walks of life, enterprising, and relatively modern by all standards. They were powerfully attracted to the world of culture and the arts, and their talents, while not always properly appreciated, could no longer be ignored. In politics, too, they were slowly taking their place. Even as early as 1848, Jews were prominent among liberal revolutionaries. Their self-identification as Germans grew and on the eve of the First World War, their status in Germany was more solid than ever and, perhaps with the exception of the United States, seemed better secured than anywhere else in the world.

It is still worthwhile reiterating that despite all their accomplishments, Jews continued to live simultaneously as insiders and outsiders. German society seemed to have decided for formal emancipation and even for a measure of social integration, but somehow this decision seemed inconclusive. At least *some* Germans continued to be openly ambivalent concerning the desired status of Jews living in their midst. Antisemitism may not have become an effective political force, but its social ubiquity should not be underestimated. In my eagerness to state my case, I may have all too hastily passed over some radical Antisemitic expressions in pre-Nazi Germany. While there was no need to dig out new Antisemitic publications or obscure Antisemitic authors to prove Antisemitism was still alive and kicking, it was equally wrong to underestimate its force and ubiquity. The written matter on Antisemitism, I would still argue, was a marginal phenomenon

---

7 Jacob Toury, *Soziale und politische Geschichte der Juden in Deutschland 1848–1871*, Düsseldorf 1977, 123.

in Wilhelmine Germany, but social resentment and popular manifestations of antipathy towards the Jews could easily be felt.

The situation at the time of the Weimar Republic further heightened this fundamental ambivalence. In addition to previous works, Dirk Walter's *Antisemitische Kriminalität und Gewalt: Judenfeindschaft in der Weimarer Republik* (1999) provided a complete account of violent and criminal attacks against Jews during these years. It retells the story of anti-Jewish street rioting since 1919, analyzes the numerous physical attacks on Jewish individuals and institutions, and unfolds a horrifying spectrum of Antisemitic incidents throughout the country.[8] And yet, Peter Gay's previous insistence that Jews felt securely at home in Germany is no less convincing.[9] While Gay may be overreaching when he claims that even the early years of National Socialism belonged in this category, for the Weimar period his analysis seems sound enough. After all, the remaining restrictions on Jewish integration in Germany had been rescinded. A number of prominent Jewish figures took active part in the establishment of the Republic and in the management of its affairs, operating as full-fledged, equal citizens within this newly-constructed state-system. For Jews, Gay claims, living in Germany was often no less than a dream come true. Antisemitism could be felt, but it was considered marginal remnant of the past, a minor fact of life, to be reckoned with – no more.

But counter to Gay's insistence on this ongoing ambivalence even during the early years of Nazism, I would claim that everything changed with the nomination of Hitler to Reichskanzler and the Nazi takeover of all branches of government. This was a new beginning, not merely another stepping stone upon the same, familiar road. Continuity paled against novelty during those days. At least for the Jews, nothing in Germany would ever be the same.

It is rather banal to list the elements that comprised this novelty. Nazi Antisemitism, as is well known, intended from the outset to achieve a full reversal of the process of emancipation. Now, as Reinhard Rürup once commented, even the moderates among the new government officials saw in its abolishment an absolute minimum. In fact, the earlier division between Nazi moderates and radicals in this

---

[8] For general works on Jewish life and Antisemitism during the Weimar Republic see among older works, for example, Donald Niewyk, *Jews in Weimar Germany*, Manchester 1980, and Peter Gay, *Weimar Culture: The Outsider as Insider*, New York 1968. Now especially Michael Brenner, *The Renaissance of Jewish Culture in Weimar Germany*, New Haven & London 1996, Moshe Zimmerman, *Die Deutschen Juden 1914–1945*, München 1997 and Dirk Walter, *Antisemitische Kriminalität und Gewalt. Judenfeindschaft in der Weimarer Republik*, Bonn 1999.

[9] See Peter Gay, "In Deutschland zu Haus. Die Juden der Weimarer Zeit," in: *Die Juden im Nationalsozialistischen Deutschland 1933–1943*, ed. Arnold Paucker, Tübingen 1986, 31–44. And for a more extended and personal standpoint his *My German Question: Growing Up in Nazi Berlin*, New Haven 1998.

respect soon lost all meaning.[10] Racial criteria replaced legal ones in defining individual status, not only within the *Volksgemeinschaft* but also in the life of the new, revolutionary German state. The overall consensus regarding the eventual exclusion of Jews from all walks of life was nowhere and at no time seriously in question after the Nazi seizure of power. Exclusion was an official state-policy. It was an absolute novelty. At least since the onset of the process of Jewish emancipation, no other government had openly made Antisemitism its official doctrine.

Instructive is the position of the governing elite during the Wilhelmine period. John Roehl's biography of Wilhelm II leaves no doubt as to the depth of the monarch's and his entourage's hostility toward Jews.[11] But Roehl too repeats what had been noted by others before, namely that even Wilhelm's outrageously irresponsible government realized it was neither practical nor politically worthwhile to attack German Jews in the open. At the back of Wilhelm's mind, Roehl seems to suggest, some vague notions of Christian decency still played a restraining role. Nothing like the stream of Nazi Anti-Jewish legislation and bureaucratic edicts had ever been remotely considered by the Kaiser's otherwise Antisemitic staff. Under the Nazis, despite their constant reliance on the rhetoric of *Volkszorn*, there could be no doubt as to the source of their Antisemitic policies. In contradistinction to nearly all past cases of Antisemitism, the initiative in Nazi Germany clearly came from above.

Discontinuity is thus easy to establish and recent historiography, indeed, tends to underline it. For some time now, the pendulum has swung in what I could have considered "my" direction. The negative reaction to Goldhagen's book, a few years ago, clearly indicated a rejection of his simplified continuity thesis.[12] I could have felt vindicated. However, something has gone wrong again. My own thesis, so to speak, was being used to argue a case I considered exaggerated and ultimately misleading, and while I naturally had no control over its application, I felt the need to reconsider it.

---

10 See Reinhard Rürup, "Das Ende der Emanzipation: Die antijüdische Politik in Deutschland von der 'Machtergreifung' bis zum Zweiten Weltkrieg," in: *Die Juden in Nationalsozialistischen Deutschland*, 97–111.
11 From the pen of John C.G. Röhl, Kaiser Wilhelm II's biographer, we now have a number of interesting volumes. See especially: *Hof und Staat. Wilhelm II. und die deutsche Politik*, München 1995, and for our purpose see also his "Das Beste wäre Gas!" in: *Die Zeit*, Nov. 25, 1994.
12 Daniel Jonah Goldhagen, *Hitler's Willing Executioners. Ordinary Germans and the Holocaust*, New York 1996. For anthologies of responses to this work see *Ein Volk von Mörder?*, ed. Julius H. Schoeps, Hamburg 1996 and *Hyping the Holocaust: Scholars Answer Goldhagen*, ed. Franklin H. Little, Merion Station Pa. 1997.

The significance of Antisemitism, and not just with regard to the history of National Socialism, has meanwhile been reduced to an absolute minimum.[13] Presumably, this trend took its cue from the controversy between "intentionalists" and "functionalists." Within this context, the former usually held onto the centrality of Antisemitism in explaining the 'Final Solution', while the latter drastically reduced the significance of its role. The former insisted on long-term ideological considerations, the latter on short-term, functional ones. Gradually, in combination with other motive forces, such as the need to uphold a respectable national narrative for Germany for the entire modern period, Antisemitism tended to disappear. It all too often vanished from the tale of Nazism, as well as from the long and "twisted road to Auschwitz." Observe, for instance, the way German early liberal Nationalism is usually described in the literature. Scholars often stressed and analyzed Anti-French attitudes but hardly mention Anti-Jewish trends. Or take the common historical narrative of 1848: steps towards Jewish emancipation were usually mentioned, but the wave of anti-Jewish rural pogroms that swept the country for months during that singular 'year of freedom' hardly ever appears. The Antisemitic wave in the 1870s cannot, of course, be denied or passed over, but anti-Jewish statements, it is correctly argued now, were by then normally followed by counterattacks, and Antisemitic politics eventually proved a complete fiasco. Even among members of the *Alldeutscher Verband*, it has been shown, Antisemitism aroused suspicion, not to speak of the *Hakkatisten*, the *Flottenverein* or the *Reichsverband gegen die Sozialdemokratie*. "It did not seem respectable," wrote Thomas Nipperdey, and even student associations no longer considered it a centerpiece of their ideology.[14] All in all, concluded Hans-Guenther Zmarzlik in an essay on Antisemitism in the *Kaiserreich*, Antisemitic manifestations were considered "rearguard action of scandalous prejudices," and whoever disagreed felt compelled to keep his views to himself.[15] The early years of the Weimar Republic also saw "a gradual ebbing of radical Antisemitism." Its organized formations were not "excessively wide-spread" and could not be politically instrumentalized.[16] Finally, both local and regional studies of National Socialism in the 1920s prove that Germans supported the Nazis

---

[13] I have argued this case more fully in "Nationalismus, Antisemitismus und die deutsche Geschichtsschreibung," in: *Nation und Gesellschaft in Deutschland. Historische Essays*, eds. M. Hettling and P. Nolte, Munich 1996, 208–219. Here no.
[14] Thomas Nipperdey, *Deutsche Geschichte 1866–1918*, Vol. 2, München 1992, 301–303.
[15] H.-G. Zmarzlik, "Antisemitismus im deutschen Kaiserreich 1871–1919," in: *Die Juden als Minderheit in der Geschichte*, eds. B. Martin and E. Schulin, Munich 1981, 254.
[16] The quotes are from Heinrich August Winkler, "Die Deutsche Gesellschaft der Weimarer Republik und der Antisemitismus," in Martin and Schulin, *Die Juden als Minderheit*, 283, and Hans Mommsen, *Die Verspielte Freiheit. Der Weg der Republik von Weimar in den Untergang 1918–1932*, Frankfurt a. M. (2nd edition) 1990, 308.

not because of but very often despite their Antisemitism. In general, it was "National Socialism that gave a fresh impetus to Antisemitism and not the other way around."[17] Even among the Nazi perpetrators of the 'Final Solution', Antisemitism has rarely been a top concern.[18] Its role continues to be mentioned in the literature, but it has been eroded beyond recognition.

This is taking the matter far too far. There is, after all, no way of explaining Nazi anti-Jewish policies without their roots in European culture. Nor is it reasonable to ignore the powerful anti-Jewish sentiment in Germany throughout the modern era when dealing with National Socialism. Even though Antisemitism might tarnish the narrative of liberal nationalism, it cannot be denied. It was not a centerpiece of life in the *Kaiserreich*, but it was never negligible. While it is no solution to let the pendulum swing all the way back and land with Goldhagen, a mature historiography, free from excess and hysteria, must be able to weigh conflicting elements and avoid one-sided interpretations.

Clearly, traditional forms of Antisemitism dictated the choice of the Jews as the enemy from within under National Socialism, and that familiarity was at the root of the general public acquiescence with Nazi policies against Jews. In my enthusiasm to describe the clear break with codes of the past, I underestimated the meaning of tradition both for Hitler himself and for the National Socialist leadership that surrounded him. Even more crucial was the influence of tradition upon the masses of undecided onlookers. But while I am now convinced that we must give more weight to continuity than before, I would like to give my own twist to this reformulation.

I would like to do just that by shortly commenting on one aspect of Saul Friedländer's masterful *Nazi Germany and the Jews*. In the midst of his exposition, Friedländer interjects a chapter on what he calls "Redemptive Anti-Semitism."[19] He begins by sketching the changing position of the Jews in German society and the irritation caused by their quick and successful integration, then analyzes the constitutive elements of Nazi Antisemitism based on a constant repetition of the story of "perdition caused by the Jews" and "redemption by a total victory over them."[20]

---

[17] Winkler "Die deutsche Gesellschaft der Weimarer Republik," 287.
[18] The most convincing case was argued by Christopher R. Browning in *Ordinary Men. Reserve Police Battalion 101 and the Final Solution*, New York 1992. I believe, Goldhagen's efforts to undermine his interpretation have not been successful. For an exposition of his view see Daniel Goldhagen, "A Reply to my Critics: Motives, Causes and Alibis," in: *The New Republic*, December 23 1996, 37–45.
[19] See Saul Friedländer, *Nazi Germany and the Jews*, Vol. 1: *The Years of Persecution, 1933–1939*, New York 1997, 73–112.
[20] Ibid, 99.

There is, however, something else in this chapter that has not received proper attention. Although this is not the way Friedländer might have put it, he actually describes here the composition of an Antisemitic whole that is the sum total of most of its previous iterations. Most significantly, perhaps, is Friedländer's return to the centrality of religious Antisemitism, an anti-Jewish Christian tradition shared by Catholics and Protestants alike. The common notion of a complete replacement of religious by racial hatred has been questioned before too, but it is in Friedländer's text that the theory is finally allowed to fall. Friedländer combines the medieval legend of a secret rabbinical synod, convening periodically to organize the next ritual murder, with the eighteen century conspiracy theory concerning Freemasons and Jews, and finally with the Elders of Zion mythology. He clearly sees more than repetition. It was the additive value of all the previous elements of Antisemitism that impressed him. Let me underline this: secular Antisemitism, moving the focus of hatred from Judaism to the Jews, did not *replace* religious hatred but rather *overlapped* it. No one who has seen Landsmann's film *Shoah* could forget the scene in front of a village church, where local inhabitants found it all too natural that Jews were ostracized and murdered. Jews had, after all, "killed our savior," they explained.

Thus, modern Antisemitism, based on racism, did not *replace* previous forms of hostilities to Jews. For most of the nineteenth century, Antisemites' *spirituality* was at stake in fighting the Jews, not biology.[21] Racism did not obliterate religious hatred, social envy, cultural fears, or national prejudices; it added another layer. In this respect, Nazi Antisemitism was neither a new invention nor a simple repetition of familiar patterns. It was *a new* amalgamation. Previous tradition was central to its content and necessary for its effectiveness. Even that "redemptive Antisemitism," so central to Friedländer's interpretation, had no privileged position within this process. Racism constituted an added layer, significant at the time, suited to the paranoid temper of the protagonists, but by no means a substitute for past notions. Continuity, indeed, plays a major role here. A whole unbroken chain of past hatred, prejudices, and discrimination merged together. More recent additions were closer to the surface, of course, but a very long term collective memory was always at work. The medieval Church claimed Jews were to be protected as "living memory of the letter," but hating them finally produced, by itself, a long, unbroken chain of "living memories."[22] The Holocaust was unthinkable outside this tradition.

---

21 A more extensive discussion of this point in my "The Written and the Spoken Word", 60–62. Here no. 5.
22 On this aspect of the Christian position see now Jeremy Cohen, *Living Letters of the Law. Ideas of the Jews in Medieval Christianity*, Berkeley/Los Angeles/London 1999.

Moreover, continuity is more significant than I have previously admitted not only with regard to the content of Antisemitism and the motivations to act upon it but also with regard to its functional aspects. Considering that changing functions served me before in trying to underline *dis*continuity, it is only fair to state now that this is by no means the whole story. Among the characteristics of Antisemitism at the time of the Kaiserreich was also its function in overcoming the crisis of integration experienced by German society in the wake of Germany's political unification in 1871. At a time of reshaping national identity, defining a clear-cut enemy ultimately proved essential. The task of reconstructing a homogenous nation was clearly central for people such as Heinrich von Treitschke. His public endorsement of the nascent Antisemitic movement in Berlin of the late 1870s cannot be understood outside this context.[23] Later on, most of those who participated in the controversy over Treitschke's anti-Jewish position shared some of his concern for national cohesion. Antisemitism served as one of the tools to counter diversity and internal strife. Neither the *Kulturkampf* nor the struggle against Socialism could be so fruitfully deployed for that purpose. After all, Catholics comprised more than 40% of the population in Bismarck's Germany, and the working classes surely made up well over 60%. Unity couldn't be achieved by excluding such large segments of the population.

But Antisemitism, as a homogenizing instrument in an era of rattled self-consciousness, was available and effective. In a book ambitiously seeking a new definition of Antisemitism, Gavin Langmuir has argued that though a confrontation with Judaism was a challenge built into Christianity from its very beginning, tensions only turned it into open hostility in times of religious strife and creeping doubts, such as the early eleventh century.[24] By the mid-thirteenth, in an atmosphere of radical struggle against Muslims outside Europe and heretics at home, the fight against Jews and Judaism received a bitter impetus. Or, to take another example: During the Reformation, the demands to shake off the constraints of a previous faith often legitimized radical measures and under the circumstances, reformers urgently needed to distinguish the true from the false faith, Christ from the Anti-Christ, God from Satan. Jewish existence once more built up the newly reformed Christian identity. Then, while the religious wars were changing the nature of the overall political system in Europe, the increasingly independent

---

23 I have made this point in my "Antisemitism as a cultural Code," but see now the analysis in Klaus Holz, *Nationaler Antisemitismus. Wissenssoziologie einer Weltanschauung*, Hamburg 2001, especially Chapter III, 165–267.
24 Gavin Langmuir, *Towards a Definition of Antisemitism*, Berkeley/Los Angeles/Oxford 1990. For my exposition of this continuity aspect see the article "Antisemitism," in the 2001 edition of the *Encyclopaedia of the Social and Behavioral Sciences*.

secular state transformed into the seat of a single religion, in which the crown ruled over a homogeneous society of subjects and believers. Exceptions could at best be tolerated, as under some Calvinist governments. At worst, nonbelievers were repressed and expelled, as under Lutheranism and the Counter-Reformation. Of course, the need to achieve homogeneity was felt throughout the Catholic world, leading to expulsions and forced conversions especially in Spain and Portugal during the last decade of the fifteenth century. In the days of Muslim rule on the Iberian Peninsula, both Christians and Jews occasionally suffered as adherents of minority religions, but only under the ambitious government of the re-conquering Christian kings, the position of Jews and Muslims became untenable. A thriving culture, relatively open to the other, was replaced by a demand for uniformity and the merciless elimination of all unbelievers. The notorious Inquisition, indeed, acted primarily against *new* Christians, suspected of secretly upholding their old faith. But even true *conversos* were frowned upon in a Spain obsessed with notions of blood and an early version of racism.

Finally, just as this lens proves useful for explaining events in medieval times, so too does it apply to modern times. The case of the German *Kaiserreich* becomes obvious enough, and even thinking about Nazism may gain from a similar approach. Robert Gellately's book *Backing Hitler* may serve as an example.[25] The book's main concern is the support rendered by the general public in Germany to a variety of brutal National Socialist measures. Handling of the German Jews does receive a special chapter here, since Gellately focuses his attentions elsewhere. Gellately recounts the Nazi persecution of political opponents and especially of social outsiders. Even if his stress on public support for the relevant policies is judged to be unbalanced and only partly proven by the evidence, the following thesis may still reflect an important aspect of National Socialism: A fundamental characteristic of the new regime was the effort to attain a *Volksgemeinschaft*, "based on a maddening logic of sameness, purity, and homogeneity." Leaders and followers alike, accordingly, "got caught up in a murderous game of pillorying, excluding, and eventually eliminating unwanted social 'elements' and 'race enemies.'"[26] And seen from this perspective, Nazism may well be joined to the examples above. Nazi Germany was yet another case of a fragmented society in which a common identity could presumably only be constructed by excluding all others. Jews were pivotal to this project, though they were by no means alone; Jews in particular, but within a more general framework; Jews more than others

---

25 Robert Gellately, *Backing Hitler. Consent and Coercion in Nazi Germany*, Oxford 2001.
26 Ibid, 261–262.

but not only out of some ancient animosity, but for a very well-defined, contemporary purpose.

Another kind of overlap had been here at play. As David Bankier has shown in an earlier work, Antisemitic traditions could be grafted not only upon each other but also upon other pressing needs.[27] The focus must not be the endlessly debated question whether Jews and Antisemitism were more or less predominant as elements of Nazi ideology. These can also be seen as yet another case, typical to the maltreatment of all 'others' in the Third Reich. Gellately is convincing in showing the similarity that marked Nazi treatment of all undesirables. Antisemitism was surely not the only tool in the Nazis' arsenal. In any case, integration and the achievement of social homogeneity were undoubtedly among its main functions.

At this point, the novelty, at least the *relative* novelty, of the entire process unleashed by the Nazis seems to be powerfully fleshed-out again. Following the logic of continuity, we finally come back to the centrality of discontinuity. If, for once, we treat leadership and followers together, including issues of public opinion and the daily behavior of those mythological 'ordinary Germans', discontinuity may regain its preeminence from yet another perspective. Let us omit the factors that enhanced Antisemitism and concentrate on the ones that helped restrain and dampen it. Back in the early Middle Ages, it was often the Church itself that protected Jews. It had its own theological needs, of course, and its own moral standards. In some concrete cases, economic considerations made defending the Jews more important than attacking them. A quick look at attitudes towards Jews in nineteen century Germany shows a similar phenomenon. After a prolonged debate on emancipation throughout the German-speaking countries of Central Europe, one observes with amazement that equal rights to Jews were finally legislated with little or no opposition at all during the latter part of the 1860s. What seemed only a generation earlier a contentious, problematic affair suddenly appeared a matter of practical consensus. Jews were by then no more loved or welcome than before. But liberalism of a certain type, consistent only with an overall emancipation, had triumphed and within the boundaries of a principally liberal state, the existence of second-class citizens was no longer acceptable. With the free choice of occupation and the complete freedom of movement, with free trade and raging industrialization, emancipation became unavoidable. Despite Antisemitic verbiage, even conservatives agreed that emancipation could no longer be stopped. In fact, what characterized attitudes

---

[27] Though his argument is complex and many sided, this is, I believe, the gist of Bankier's argument in David Bankier, *The Germans and the Final Solution. Public Opinion under Nazism*, Oxford 1992.

toward Jews, at least since the enlightenment, was not the relative or even the absolute weakness of Antisemitism but the strength of the countervailing forces. Some of the basic humanistic axioms of the time made official discrimination no longer possible. The economic and financial needs of emerging modern states similarly worked in this direction. The so-called *Radauantisemitismus* was also rejected, not only because of its content but often because of its form and style. It suggested the breakup of law and order, a breach of decency and a stain on Germany's prestige among other civilized nations.

The shift – the novelty if you wish – occurred with National Socialism. Whatever social solidarity there had ever been in Germany evaporated after World War I.[28] Whatever spirit of resistance to inhumanity there had ever been was now dissolved. Only individual acts of decency sometimes shone through this darkness, as German society lost its moral backbone. It was now ready to accept a degree of brutality that, with the exception of actions in the colonial world, would have been previously inconceivable. The thugs of the SA, considered by many to be no more than an unruly mob, now donned the authority of a state which legitimized and endorsed them. The handling of communists and socialists may have been a matter of indifference to many middle-class Germans before, but the degree of open violence exhibited against them would have counted as appalling according to any civilized standards. Gellately's book briefly tells this story in its maddening variety. It has also been recently elaborated in one of Ulrich Herbert's short essays, as well as in Michael Burleigh's mammoth volume on the Third Reich and especially in Michael Wildt's *Volksgemeinschaft als Selbstermächtigung*.[29] Only with the backdrop of that moral collapse can the Nazi policies against the Jews begin to be comprehended.

Permanent features are indispensable but never sufficient as explanations. Our main task as historians, moreover, is to uncover and define the novelties, weigh their effects, and explain their appearance at a unique time and place. There is probably no case where this task is more difficult than the one before us.

---

28 A recent description of this process from a personal standpoint is Sebastian Haffner, *Geschichte eines Deutschen. Die Erinnerungen 1914–1933*, Munich 2001.
29 See Ulrich Herbert, "Vernichtungspolitik. Neue Antworten und Fragen zur Geschichte des 'Holocaust'", in a volume he edited, *Nationalsozialistische Vernichtungspolitik 1939–1945*, Frankfurt a. M. 1998, 9–66, and Michael Burleigh, *The Third Reich. A New History*, New York 2000, especially the Introduction and Chapter 2. Also Michael Wildt, *Volksgemeinschaft als Selbstermächtigung. Gewalt gegen Juden in der deutschen Provinz, 1919–1939*, Hamburg 2007.

IV In the Context of National Socialism

12 Old and New Approaches to the History of National Socialism: The Double Perspective of Jews and Germans

Let me start on a personal note: It seems that throughout my work as a historian I have continuously avoided dealing with the history or the historiography of National Socialism. Looking around, it also seems that this has been a standard practice of many historians of my generation.[1] Recently, having completed a Hebrew book on German Jews in the years up to 1933 – avoiding the Nazi period once again – I began to feel this could no longer be justified. It was time, I felt, to join the ongoing discussion on this chapter of German – and Jewish – history. I started with an intensive reading course in order to catch up, so to speak, and soon found myself comparing what I once read as a student with what was now being written and published on this subject-matter; what I thought I knew about National Socialism, and what has meanwhile been discovered. Of course, there was no way one could catch up with a historiographical corpus of that size – not after negligence of so many years. Even only the essential items are far too many to harness in a single spurt of interest. I could rely, of course, on what I have sporadically read or heard throughout the years. To some degree I could also rely on my experience as a historian in other, related fields. But in the end, all of these tactics hardly made a difference.

In a way, the route I have decided to take began with the debate over Daniel Goldhagen's book.[2] There is surely no need to go over this matter again. But I'd like to take up just one point, relevant for the following argument. Let us disregard for a moment the actual *historical* presentation made by Goldhagen and observe his *historiographical* claims. Goldhagen was apparently convinced that he was breaking a new ground in this respect, too. His book, however, clearly reiterates some of the positions taken by historians of Nazism and the Holocaust in earlier stages on this historiographical route.[3] Thus, the claim that Germans always hated Jews and only willingly complied with Hitler's orders to annihilate them had been among the axioms of early historiography. It fits only too perfectly with

---

[1] See Chris Lorenz, "Border-Crossing: Some Reflections on the Role of German Historians in Recent public Debates on Nazi History," in: *Remembering the Holocaust in Germany, 1945–2000*, ed. Dan Michman, New York 2002, 59–94.
[2] Daniel J. Goldhagen, *Hitler's Willing Executioners. Ordinary Germans and the Holocaust*, New York 1996.
[3] For a summary of these positions, with an emphasis on Jewish historians, see Dan Michman, *Die Historiographie der Shoah aus jüdischer Sicht,* Hamburg 2002, 14–48.

the belief of most victims of National Socialism, most particularly with what might be considered the Jewish *collective memory*. While Goldhagen reformulated most of the older tenets in the acceptable historical jargon of our times, his thesis concerning German Antisemitism could surely not be considered new or original. For the connoisseur, the novelty of Goldhagen's thesis lay in the adjective that he added to his tale of perennial Antisemitism. "Eliminationist" or not, it's ever presence in Germany was hardly questioned by Jewish public opinion. It was not by chance that his book evinced a warm reaction in Israel. Its main thesis was simply considered self-evident.

I was beginning to wonder: Did the image of Nazism undergo any change at all between my student days and Goldhagen's? Could *any* new knowledge make a difference in this field as far as the victims or their heirs were concerned? Is this why Hannah Arendt's book on Eichmann was originally so furiously rejected in Israel – demanding, as it surely did, a fundamental rethinking of accepted positions?[4] Is it why Goldhagen caused such a storm in Germany, though he was practically reiterating what had so often been said before? Did the historiography that was being written especially during the last two decades, working out both details and overall conceptions concerning National Socialism and the Holocaust made any dint at that solid surface of personal *cum* collective memory? Does historiography ever do?

It was a couple of years later, that I had an occasion to extend my skepticism to the more general, non-Jewish milieu and to deeper layers of the historiographical discourse. I was then reading with great interest and much sympathy, I must add, the late François Furet's grand volume on the Twentieth Century, "The Passing of an Illusion".[5] To be sure, Furet's focus is not the history of Nazism but that of Communism. However, his book includes an extensive and interesting chapter comparing the two. It has been noticed before, of course, that the collapse of Communism and the rediscovery of the darker sides of this regime, gave a new lease on life to the concept of Totalitarianism, linking Communism to National Socialism in a variety of ways.[6] Furet's book was a part of this trend. For an overall

---

4 See Steven Aschheim, "Hannah Arendt in Jerusalem" and his "Post-Holocaust Jewish Mirroring of Germany: Hannah Arendt and Daniel Goldhagen," now both in his *In Times of Crisis. Essays on European Culture, Germans, and Jews*, Madison Wisc. 2001, 73–85, 137–143.
5 Francois Furet, *The Passing of an Illusion. The Idea of Communism in the Twentieth Century*, Chicago 1999. The book was originally published in French, Paris 1995. The relevant Chapter is Chapter six, 156–208.
6 For a useful summary of this revival, see Ian Kersahw, "Totalitarianism Revisited. Nazism and Communism in Comparative Persective," in: *Tel Aviver Jahrbuch für Deutsche Geschichte*, XXIII (1994), 23–40.

history of the Twentieth Century, ran his argument, what counted above all was the similarity between Stalinist Communism and Hitler's National Socialism; a similarity, he claimed, manifested in the force of ideology, the role of the two absolute leaders, their will to achieve absolute power over their total states and complete control of the presumably unified and homogeneous society within them. Finally, their lack of any moral constraints.

All this, no doubt, sounds familiar enough. As could be expected, Arendt's book on Totalitarianism was frequently referred to in the notes to Furet's relevant pages. But a further examination of these notes discloses some unexpected facts. Furet's sources for Germany, beyond Arendt's truly insightful, though often historically erratic book, include Hitler's *Mein Kampf*, as well as Rauschning's "Conversations" with Hitler, with no further reservations or comments.[7] It likewise includes a host of other publications from the 1930's, written by some chief actors and some prominent observers: Goebbles on the one hand and Spengler or Thomas Mann, on the other. These are supplanted by a couple of memoirs – of Karl Loewith for instance, and then some later titles, such as Meinecke's "German Catastrophe", E.H. Carr from 1951, and a sprinkling of later titles from the early 60's to the mid 1980's. Thus, although Furet's book was first published as late as 1995, not long before his untimely death, there was preciously little in it of the new historiography. His own correspondence with Nolte in the aftermath of the *Historikerstriet* clearly attests to his general knowledge of the field, but the detailed and professional historiography that was being produced during these years virtually made no impression on him at all. He found the Intentionalists-Functionalists debate futile, and made hardly any use of the new, though sometimes tentative insights, offered by contemporary researchers, often motivated – for better or for worse – by this debate.[8]

Now, Furet was no specialist in the history of Nazism and never claimed to be one. But he *was* a conscientious historian of great integrity. Still, contemporary historiography did not seem to matter to him in this case. Clearly, he too was trying to make a point – one that was vital for *his* political or personal situation. And whatever has meanwhile been unearthed, analyzed or re-conceptualized by an army of historians around him counted for little in this context. It was not, to be sure, as in the case of Goldhagen, the need to reiterate the centrality of Antisemitism or the

---

7 The inverted commas appear in Furet's footnote no. 52, 522. Others, too, continue to use Rauschning's famous *Hitler Speaks*, published in London 1939 and based on a series of presumed conversations with Hitler in 1934. But following the controversy about the authenticity of this book, it has become increasingly unusual to quote him extensively and/or verbatim as Furet did. See *The Passing of an Illusion*, 189–192.
8 See his comments, Ibid, 189.

Holocaust that forced his pen. It was rather the final break with Communism – his *own* life-long illusion – and the compulsion to explain it. But if Furet was not able to free himself of pre-conceptions and if *he* so cavalierly avoided the updating of historical knowledge concerning the matter at hand in order to press his own, personal agenda – can any of us be sure of being free of such charges?

Since the famous debate between Martin Broszat and Saul Friedländer over the so-called *"historisierung"* of National Socialism, we have indeed all become well aware of this danger.[9] This emotionally laden controversy underlined above all the apparent irreconcilability of the victims' perspective with a presumably more accurate German one. The recent disclosures concerning the research activities of some well-known German historians during the early years of National Socialism has no doubt added a new perspective to this older debate.[10] The unavoidable subjectivity of some of the major German participants in this historiographical drama has never been more palpable. But are we to conclude now that the obstacles for a joint, i.e. German-Jewish, fruitful research on Nazism and the Holocaust are insurmountable? Is the historiography of National Socialism *bound* to be directed – presumably like that of other topics, but only more so – by prior notions, haunting memories, and the power of beliefs and ideology? Dan Diner, who has often written about these matters, seems to think so. In a published lecture he gave a few years ago at Tel Aviv University, Diner reasserted his claim that the historiographical situation in this field can only be understood in terms of court litigation: the Plaintiff and the Defendant have such conflicting "worlds of experience", that opposing interpretations are "hardly avoidable."[11] The dominant memories thus dictate the structure of the narrative, the periodization, the relevant time span, the basic approach, the central questions, etc. Diner's is surely a powerful argument, but after all is said and done – is his a true picture of the situation? Are we *bound* to stay within the same controversy forever, due to our so-called "experiences"? Can we not begin, at least, to step out of this predicament?

Perhaps it is my own past, working in the field of German Jewish history and on Antisemitism in pre-Nazi Germany with a number of dedicated German

---

9 The essence of this controversy can be found in Martin Broszat/ Saul Friedländer, "A Controversy about the Historicization of National Socialism," in: *Yad Vashem Studies* 19 (1988), 1–47.
10 See *Deutsche Historiker in Nationalsozialismus*, eds. Winfried Schulze and Otto Gerhard Oexle Frankfurt a. M. 1999, and also Nicolas Berg, *Der Holocaust und die westdeutschen Historiker. Erforschung und Erinnerung*, Göttingen 2003.
11 See Dan Diner, "Varieties of Interpretation: The Holocaust in Historical Memory," in: *Language and Revolution. Making Modern Political Identities*, ed. Igal Halfin, London 2002, 379–391. See also his essay in: *The Third Reich. A historical Reassessment*, [Hebrew] ed. Moshe Zimmermann, Jerusalem 2000, 40–51.

historians,¹² that leads me to believe otherwise. Namely, that German and Jewish historians *can* and in fact *do* – not *always* to be sure but slowly, tentatively, and on a number of important fronts – work together, and that we manage such work in an atmosphere that is nowhere near that of court litigation.

One started after the war with strictly diverging narratives, no doubt. The initial non-German, non-Jewish view of Nazism, the one we can perhaps name "the western narrative" has been succinctly described by Volker Berghahn in a *New York Times* article on May 10, 1992, as follows:

> When British and American soldiers advanced into Hitler's rapidly disintegrating empire in the spring of 1945, they carried with them mental images not only of the murderous dictatorship, but also of a backward Germany, in which democracy and other benefits of modernity had never firmly taken root. As their officers and occupation manuals were telling them, this was a society run by a band of Nazi war criminals with the backing of authoritarian landowners, Prussian militarists and reactionary coal and steel barons, a society that had been swept by an irrational ideology into an orgy of destruction. There was also much serious talk about the peculiarities of the German mind . . .¹³

This description, to be sure, is not strictly identical with some of the early western historiography. But clearly, this "view from the West" fits with Diner's argument: it stresses a long-term perspective, the German failure to modernize, their tendency to comply with orders from above, etc. It also implies, no doubt, a wholesale condemnation. To be sure, none of us, outside Germany, grew up without reading at some point William Shirer's *Rise and Fall of the Third Reich* and no Israeli historian could avoid using AJP Taylor's general text, entitled *The Course of German History*.¹⁴ Both embody all these principles. There is a strong determinism in this historical view, but also surely a convincing compilation of powerful causes to form an unavoidable "one-way road" to catastrophe.

The German perspective was initially very different. It is futile perhaps but still inevitable to go back again to Friedrich Meinecke. The main points of his *German Catastrophe* are only too well known.¹⁵ Nazism was part and parcel of a

---

12 Not least among them is Monika Richarz, the recipient of the Festschrift, in which this essay first appeared.
13 Volker R. Berghahn, "Who is afraid of the Twentieth Century," in: *New York Times*, 10 May 1992, 9.
14 Shirer's book was published in New York, 1960, and became an immediate best-seller. It was quickly translated into Hebrew and appeared in Tel Aviv, November 1961, in the midst of the Eichmann trial. Taylor's book, a general history of Germany since the late 18th century, was written during the Second World War and appeared as early as 1946.
15 *Die Deutsche Katastrophe*, was published in Wiesbaden, 1946. an English translation was published by the Harvard University Press, 1950.

cultural European failure, not merely a consequence of the German past. It was brought about by a combination of some long-term circumstances, no doubt, but mainly by a multitude of short-term ones, and – moreover – by the joint forces of *chance* and *personality*. It was, in Meinecke's view, neither a "historical accident" à la Gerhard Ritter, nor the responsibility of "ordinary Germans", as Goldhagen would have it nowadays. The latter were rather *conquered* by "a band of criminals", "subjugated and intoxicated", "compelled for a limited period to follow a false path", according to Meinecke.[16] Though the so-called "German view", if there ever was one, was perhaps somewhat more complex, this, I believe, is not an unfair summary. To use Dan Diner's categories once again: it is a view stressing the short-term, some mistaken but unnecessary choices, the need to remember Germany's overall cultural heritage and not merely its militarism, servility, Antisemitism or anti-modernism.

Some historians outside Germany always supported this early German version and shared its basic assumptions. Applying the term 'Totalitarianism', for instance, was for much of the immediate post-war period a predominantly American line of argument, meant to anchor the "German Catastrophe" in a European context, seeking to turn it into a general. Modern phenomenon – a potential danger everywhere in the world of the 20th century. 'Fascism' too was clearly not only a German phenomenon and the use of this term likewise militated against a complete and singular German guilt. Some Germans and non-German authors also concurred on the interpretation of a few partial aspects of Nazism. The sociological arguments concerning the "radicalization of the middle", for instance, or the general disregard for Nazi ideology, were issues that for long failed to raise any meaningful controversy.[17] On the whole, however, the gap between the two initial conceptions of Nazi history – the mainly German and the mainly non-German – no doubt seemed deep enough.

I do not intend to follow the history of Nazi historiography since the 1950s in order to present the gradual convergence of these two, presumably distinct

---

16 Ibid, 96.
17 The German "classic" on the significance of the middle class 'desperadoes' in the rise of Nazism is Theodor Geiger, *Panik im Mittelstand*, first published in *Die Arbeit*, Oct. 1931. Later see Heinrich-August Winkler, *Mittelstand, Demokratie und Nationalsozialismus*, Cologne 1972. The earliest English-language analysis along this line is probably Seymour Martin Lipset, *Political Man. The Social Bases of Politics*, New York 1960, esp. Chapter 5, and later David Schoenbaum, *Hitler's Social Revolution. Class and Status in Nazi Germany 1933–1939*, New York 1966. As to the role of Nazi ideology in the early phases of historical writing on National Socialism, see, for instance, Franz Neumann, *Behemoth: The Structure and Practice of National Socialism*, Oxford 1942, written by him in exile, and Alan Bullock, *Hitler: A Study in Tyranny*, London 1953, an early biography that stresses Hitler's power-politics above all ideological considerations.

historiographies. Instead, I would only like to pinpoint a few examples – typical, I believe, and significant. Let me start with the issue of historical perspective. By the 1970s, it seems to me, two lines of agreements were formulated concerning this issue. Both the excessively long-term approach, taken up by Shirer, for instance, or by AJP Taylor, and the excessively short-term one, taken up primarily by Gerhard Ritter have been practically discarded. An exception is probably the history of Antisemitism, and I would later come back to this issue. But in all other lines of research a middle-range approach became the so-called "Orthodoxy". It was the emergence, or rather the re-emergence of the *sonderweg* thesis – both in and out of Germany – that eventually brought about a rapprochement. Despite its familiar presence in the historiographical discourse for over a century, this paradigm had only been sporadically applied for explaining the presumed "origins of Nazism" during the immediate post-world war II years. But by the mid-1960's and then with great energy during the 1970's it became increasingly dominant.[18]

For our present purposes, the *non*-German protagonists of the Sonderweg are somewhat less significant. After Shirer and Taylor, we did have the wave of immigrant German, often German-Jewish authors, who buttressed, indeed, a "middle-range origins-position" as we might want to call it, in various ways: Hans Kohn, working on the German mind – to which probably Berghahn alludes in the passage I have quoted above – stressed romantic nationalism since the early 19th century.[19] George Mosse in his book on the Volkish ideology and Fritz Stern working on the prophets of "cultural despair" focused upon the second half of that century.[20] In a more sociological vein, it was men like Barrington Moore in the United states, following in the footsteps of Thorstein Veblen, who took industrialization as a starting point and attempted to point out the failures of modernization

---

18 One can no longer review the entire literature on the *Sonderweg* thesis. Its chief protagonist, however, has just presented us with his view of National Socialism. See Hans-Ulrich Wehler, *Deutsche Gesellschaftsgeschichte*. vol. 4.: *Vom Beginn des ersten Weltkrieges bis zur Gründung des beiden deutschen Staaten, 1914–1949*, Munich 2003, especially part 8, Chapter VI and part 9, 512–937. For a critical view of using the *Sonderweg* thesis for treating National Socialism, see now George Steinmetz, "German Exceptionalism and the Origins of Nazism: The Career of a Concept," in: *Stalinism and Nazism: Dictatorships in Comparison*, eds. Ian Kershaw and Moshe Lewin, Cambridge 1977, 251–284.
19 Hans Kohn, *The Mind of Germany: The Education of a Nation*, New York 1960.
20 George L. Mosse, *The Crisis of German Ideology: Intellectual Origins of the Third Reich*, New York 1964; Fritz Stern, *The politics of Cultural Despair. A Study in the Rise of the Germanic Ideology*, Berkeley Cal. 1961.

in Germany, while Marxist historians – internationally – had no difficulty producing their own versions of this paradigm.[21]

Soon, however, West-German historians were joining this line of argument. Typical was their initial emphasis on the unique history of the German nation-state, or nationalism. Let me just mention Helmut Plessner's pioneering *Die verspätete Nation*, a work of a man belonging to the older generation, first issued in 1959, and perhaps also a piece like Wolfgang Sauer's "Das Problem des deutschen Nationalstaates", first published in the *Politische Vierteljahrsschrift* 1962, drawing a continuous line between Pufendorf and Bismarck, while hinting at the pathologically unfinished national business that has ended up in the Third Reich.[22] While at this first stage a critical view of German history had been still firmly attached to a relatively long-term perspective, a clear emphasis on nationalism was bound to focus attention ever more clearly on the nineteenth century. And since the late 1960s, indeed, this was reflected in the work done by most members of the so-called 'Critical Historical School' in and out of Germany. From that time onward, the long-term perspective, including Luther, early Prussian militarism and the monstrous Holy Roman Empire of Pufendorf's times practically disappeared from view. The starting-point for social historians, whether in the United States, England or Germany, was now placed sometime between the so-called "revolution that did not happen" in the late Eightennth Century and the pre-world war I debacles of the late *Kaiserreich*. Meinecke's few comments in 1946 on the responsibility of the Prussian–German solution of 1871 were now repeatedly taken up by a whole generation of German – and non-German – historians. Regardless of their precise timing for the opening pages of the study of "origins", one thing seemed clear enough: By the late 60s and early 70s German and non-German historians alike (though of course not *all* German and not *all* non-German historians) used more or less the same chronological framework for dealing with Nazism.

At this stage, however, one serious qualification must be introduced: In works explaining the Holocaust, the gap – especially that deep gap separating Germans and Jews – remained unchanged. Initially, in fact, some of the major

---

21 See Thorstein Veblen, *Imperial Germany and the Industrial Revolution*, New Brunswick 1915; Barrington Moore J. R., *Social Origins of Dictatorship and Democracy*, Boston 1966. On the Marxist interpretations of fascism and capitalism see Pierre Aycoberry, *The Nazi Question: An Essay on the Interpretation of National Socialism (1922–1975)*, New York 1981, Chapters 4 and 9. See also the orthodox view in Reinhard Kühnel, *Formen bürgerlicher Herrschaft*, Hamburg 1971, and an unorthodox one in Tim W. Mason, *Nazism, Fascism and the Working Class: Essays by Tim Mason*, ed. Jane Kalan, Cambridge 1995.

22 Helmut Plessner, *Die verspätete Nation. Über die politische Verführbarkeit bürgerlichen Geistes*, Stuttgart 1959; and Wolfgang Sauer's article, "Das Problem des deutschen Nationalstaates," in: *Moderne deutsche Sozialgeschichte*, ed. Hans-Ulrich Wehler, Cologne 1966, 407–436.

early works on the Holocaust, such as Reitlinger's and Hilberg's, gave little weight to the long-term history of Antisemitism.[23] Its role was rather taken for granted. But by my own experience even much later, questioning the role of traditional Antisemitism as a necessary and sufficient explanation for Nazism in general or the Holocaust in particular still tended to draw fire from almost all who worked in this field, especially in Israel.[24] A short-term perspective is clearly problematic in this area of research, while finding the right balance between the impact of an Antisemitic constant and the novel aspects of the National Socialist fury against the Jews remains to this day an awesome task. But in most other aspects of the study of Nazism, a tendency even to further shorten the relevant perspective has been powerfully at work. With the critique that the Sonderweg-thesis has had to contend with in the last fifteen years, the historiographical preference seems to be decidedly on the shorter term. This, moreover, has had less to do with changing conceptions on causes and origins and more with the actual praxis of historiography. As long as one wrote general overviews – these demanded relatively long introductions on origins. The more precise and monographic works were in the making, the more archival sources have become available, the more detailed research is in demand – the less one argues about such vague, general issues, it seems.

Now, partly following the controversies over time-span and origins and partly in parallel with them, ran another grand split in the historiography of National Socialism, known as that between 'Intentionalists' and 'Functionalists'. Much ink has been spilled over this issue, and as Norbert Frei writes in the last edition of his book, *Der Führerstaat*, it is now often difficult to understand the depth of emotions that were associated with this debate.[25] Nevertheless, it is impossible to proceed without mentioning it in my context, especially since at its height this controversy seemed to have split the historians' community precisely along the lines running between "perpetrators and victims". At this stage it sharply underlined the gap between German and Jewish memory and consequently between German and non-German historiography.[26] However it was over a decade ago that Christopher Browning listed a

---

23 Gerald Reitlinger, *The "Final Solution". The Attempt to Exterminate the Jews of Europe, 1939–1945*, London 1953; Raul Hilberg, *The Destruction of the Eurpoean Jews*, New York 1961.
24 See Shulamit Volkov, "The Written and the Spoken Word," no. 5 in this volume.
25 See Norbert Frei, *Der Führerstaat. Nationalsozialistische Herrschaft 1933 bis 1945*, Munich 2001, 296.
26 This line of division was clearly apparent in the debate between Martin Broszat and Saul Friedländer on the issue of 'historicization'. Surprisingly, however, this is only rarely interpreted as a debate between German and Jewish historians. An important exception is Ian Kershaw, *The Nazi Dictatorship. Problems and Perspectives of Interpretation*, London 1985, Chapter 9.

number of intentionalists who began to "modify their views," like himself, and could easily identify a growing number of "moderate functionalists", too.[27] Ian Kershaw's Hitler-Biography, to take another, clearly major and relatively recent example, is likewise an attempt to go beyond this controversy. Kershaw seems to suggest a combination of a structuralist view of German government under Nazism *and* the centrality of Hitler within it.[28] His monumental oeuvres supports his earlier claim, that in the debate between what he usually prefers to call 'Hitlerists' and 'Structuralists', all things considered, "one would have to conclude that neither model offers a wholly satisfactory explanation, and that some room for compromise is obvious."[29] Finally, in the introduction to the first volume of his book on *Nazi Germany and the Jews*, Saul Friedländer, presumably a leading figure among Intentionalists, states that: "The crimes committed by the Nazi regime were neither a mere outcome of some haphazard, involuntary, imperceptible, and chaotic onrush of unrelated events nor a predetermined enactment of a demonic script; they were the result of converging factors, of the interaction between intentions and contingencies, between discernible causes and chance."[30]

It is thus not only the changing of the generational guard that explains the search for a compromise between the two sides in what had seemed such a deep, fundamental split, but the process of historiographical reflection. It demonstrates the ability of historians – if not *all* historians – to listen to arguments, to observe the documentary evidence, to rethink their position and even to be occasionally convinced by then. At least at this stage, it is no longer a legal battle between Plaintiffs and Defendants. Differences in nuance are bound to remain, but these are unavoidable and not always arise from the gap between different "collective memories".

Now, as a consensual chronological middle-range approach have been reached and the debate between Intentionalists and Functionalists subsided, a new controversy, this time concerning the role of modernization, seems to have taken center stage. This, after all, was *the* major theme in the historiography of the nineteenth

---

27 Christopher Browning, "Beyond 'Intentionalism' and 'Functionalism': The Decision for the Final Solution Reconsidered," in his *The Path to Genocide. Essays on Launching the Final Solution*, Cambridge 1992, 86–121. See the quotes on page 88.
28 See Ian Kershaw, *Hitler. 1936–1945: Nemesis*, London 2000. This is the second volume of his Hitler's biography. For an interpretation of Kershaw's position in this book, placing him between Intentionalists and Functionalists, see Omer Bartov's review essay, "A Man without Qualities," in: *The New Republic*, 3. December 2001.
29 Kershaw, *The Nazi Dictatorship*, 105.
30 Saul Friedländer, *Nazi Germany and the Jews*, 5.

century for decades, whether one focused upon social history or upon economic, political, even upon cultural matters. Thus, studies on National Socialism too were repeatedly concerned with the effects of modernization on Twentieth Century Germany. To begin with, the focus on modernization has helped stress the relevance of a general European context for the understanding of Nazism. Signs of interest in this perspective could be already noted in early works, such as Ralf Dahrendorf's *Gesellschaft und Demokratie* in Germany or Barrington Moore's work in the United States.[31] Meanwhile, the *Sonderweg*-thesis proved likewise dependent on comparison with the rest of Europe, though especially with the so-called West, and the study of modernization soon became its primary focus as well.

This relatively older body of historiography, regardless of ideological differences within it, tended to see Nazism as a response to some sort of failure in the German route to modernity, and the modernity was marked by an unambiguous positive sign by all practitioners of the *Zunft*. It was unproblematically associated with some form of democracy – liberal or social in character, and it was the "losers" in that progressive, triumphant march, ran the argument, that finally came to support the Nazis. They were attracted by the promise of an old-style *Gemeinschaft*, adorned with rural values and conservative utopias. In fact, even studies that attempted to define what seemed modern in National Socialism, as against those that sought to proclaim its backwardness, tended to associate positive connotations with modernity. But matters became far more complicated as attitudes towards modernity were beginning to shift by the 1980s. If modernity was no longer the sum-total of what we were striving for in this world but the source of all our ailing – than its role for the study of National Socialism had to be comprehensively reappraised. If modernity was not identical with greater liberty and equality, with the universal higher values of the French Revolution, with a fundamental process of human improvement; if it was in fact the harbinger of oppressive uniformity and the negation of all "others" – as the post-moderns would have it – then the door was open for reexamining its implications for Nazism, too. Directly or indirectly such a new attitude has gradually influenced the historiography we are dealing with, as can be seen, for instance in Zygmunt Bauman's book on *Modernity and the Holocaust*, and in such older books as Horkheimer's and Adorno's *Dialektik der Aufklärung*.[32] This line of thought, indeed, though never a completely unified one, proved attractive to German and non-German historians alike. Lines of divisions here had little to do with initial personal or collective "world of experiences" but

---

31 Ralf Dahrendorf, *Gesellschaft und Demokratie in Deutschland*, Munich 1965. For Barrington Moore's title see note 21 above.
32 Bauman's book was published in Cambridge 1989, while Horkheimer's and Adorno's volume first appeared in Amsterdam, as early as 1947. It was then reprinted in Frankfurt 1967.

rather with attitudes to the world we live in, with overarching political positions, with matters related to our present rather than to our past.

The issue of Eugenics, to take one concrete example, suddenly became top priority. Eugenics indeed was a general scientific trend, prevalent well beyond Germany's borders; in fact – well beyond the European continent as such. It had a far-reaching implications for Nazi racial policies not only with respect to the Jews, but also as far as the variously handicapped, the mentally-ill, and the so-called 'asocials'. Seen from that perspective, it was not only dark irrational forces that led the hand of the Nazi persecutors but also a full-blown modern science. The attraction of segments within the German academic elite to Nazism had likewise been not merely a collapse before its reactionary and anti-modern aspects, but more often than not a response to the modern, utopian components of the movement's ideology.[33] A step further and we are with the studies of Aly and Heim on the *Vordenker der Vernichtung*. It was only in the context of its revolutionary modernism, so their thesis may now be applied, that Nazism managed to appeal to men like Theodor Schieder and Werner Conze. *Their* intellectual motivation, to be sure, may not have been identical with Hitler's and his crew, but it allowed a far-reaching cooperation with Nazism. Even if one continues to hold that Antisemitism and racial frenzy were more important in deciding the policies of National Socialism and its presumed overall vision than was its modern, technologically oriented worldview, the latter too must have had its share in unfolding the horrors of the narrative.[34]

Here was a major historiographical turn, clearly a result of work done by historians both in England or the United states *and* in Germany. Personal memories and national commitments continue, no doubt, to play a role in deciding the stand of historians on these matters, too. But the important divisions are now *inside* Germany or *inside* England, even *inside* Israel; not between and among historians in

---

33 Path breaking here was Jeffrey Herf, *Reactionary Modernism. Technology, Culture, and politics in Weimar and the Third Reich*, Cambridge 1984. On the modern aspects of Nazism and its attractiveness to various social groups see also Peter Fritzsche, "Planes, Pilots and Patriots: Aviation and German Nationalism," in: *Tel Aviver Jahrbuch für Deutsche Geschichte*, XVIII 1989, 417–438.

34 Crucial to this issue was, indeed, Götz Aly and Susanne Heim, *Vordenker der Vernichtung. Auschwitz und die deutsche Pläne für eine Europäische Ordnung*, Frankfurt a. M. 1995. But for a more balanced view of the relationships between Antisemitism and racial and presumably rational planing as sources of the 'Final Solution' see the essays in: *Nationalsozialistische Vernichtungspolitik, 1939–1945*, ed. Ulrich Herbert, Frankfurt a. M. 1998. In it see esp. the piece by Aly, preresnting his revised views on this issue, 67–96. For a different synthesis see now Christopher R. Browning, "From 'Ethnic Cleansing' to Genocide to the "Final Solution": The Evolution of Nazi Jewish Policy, 1933–1941," in his *Nazi Policy, Jewish workers, German Killers*, Cambridge 2000, 1–25.

these countries. These are splits that are both professional and generational, to be sure, but they are equally relevant everywhere. As Götz Aly began to present a more nuanced picture of the *Vordenker* and a more qualified stand on their actual influence, the deep historiographical controversy that his work initially seemed to arouse gradually subsided. While Robert Gellately, Paul Weindling and Michael Burleigh may not have intended to support him, their studies on the various aspects of the "Racial State' and the history of Eugenics, eventually made at least a partial rapprochement a reasonable option.[35] And while the last word has clearly not been pronounced on these issues, historians on both sides of the old divide are struggling with the same problems, working with the same tools and, one may assume, have the same purpose in mind.

Other unsettled issues, too, are usually discussed today along new dividing lines. The controversy concerning the role of the Gestapo in shaping the Nazi state is a good example. On the face of it, a work that came from the pen of an American historian, such as Robert Gellately, claimed to undermine a long-standing, primarily German view of Germany as a civil society terrorized by the ever-present thugs of an all-powerful police force. It offers to replace this so-called "myth" with a seemingly more sober view of German society "backing Hitler", to use Gellately's later title, more or less in line with Goldhagen's "willing-executioners".[36] But Gellately's work on the Gestapo was not the first to question the presumed "myth of the Gestapo". In fact, the image of a society living under permanent terror and the view of Nazism as embodied in the so-called *SS-Staat* have already been under fire for some time.[37] The studies of *Alltagsgeschichte* as well as research on pubic opinion in the Third Reich have all begun to undermine older views regarding the extent of terror in Nazi Germany. Historians like Ian Kershaw from Sheffield, or David Bankier from Jerusalem, joined German authors,

---

[35] See Robert Gellately, *Backing Hitler. Consent and Coercion in Nazi Germany*, Oxford 2001; Michael Burleigh, *Death and Deliverance. 'Euthanasia' in Germany, c. 1900–1945*, Cambridge 1994; Michael Burleigh and Wolfgang Wieppermann, *The Racial State. Germany 1933–1945*, Cambridge 1991; Paul Weindling, *Health, Race, and German Politics between National Unification and Nazism, 1870–1945*, Cambridge 1989.
[36] In addition to Robert Gellately, *The Gestapo and German Society. Enforcing Racial Policy, 1933–1945*, Oxford 1990, and his later book, *Backing Hitler*, see his essay, "Allwissend und allgegenwärtig? Entstehung, Funktion und Wandel des Gestpao-Mythos," in: *Die Gestapo: Mythos und Realität*, eds. Gerhard Paul and Klaus-Michael Mallmann, Darmstadt 1995, 48–70.
[37] The classic publication is *Anatomie des SS-Staates*, eds. Hans Buchheim, et al., 2 vols., Olten 1965.

such as Reinhard Mann and Americans like Robert Gellately, indeed, in questioning its validity.[38]

Even more importantly, it was the re-evaluation of Hitler's propaganda and the effects of notions such as *Volksgemeinschaft* on ordinary Germans that set up the true context for understanding the combination of fear and consensus that characterized Germany during much of the Nazi era. Present-day historiography clearly prefers the paradigm of the "Führerstaat" to that of the "SS-Staat".[39] A more sophisticated approach to the study of ideology, too, helps explain now the attraction of so many "ordinary Germans" to the Nazi "vision". So, relying on a much wider context than that provided by Gellately, it would be fair to say with Norbert Frei, indeed, that loyalty to the regime together with enthusiastic worshipping of the Führer were more significant at the time than refusal or opposition. It was apparently not only terror that has defined the situation. Thus, while one is still looking for the right balance in this context, too, the search is shared – so it seems – by historians regardless of national belonging and the force of competing "worlds of experience".

In closing I would like to go back to the one area of research in which the effect of memory or experience is still perhaps most apparent: that of the Holocaust. Now, throughout the controversy between Intentionalists and Functionalists, Jewish historians in general and Israeli historians in particular have usually sided with the Intentionalists' approach, including its two main pillars: the primacy of Antisemitism and the centrality of Hitler. On the primacy of Antisemitism, as a necessary if not as a sufficient factor, not much has been changed since the 1980s. But since everyone seems to agree now – most avowed functionalists

---

[38] Like the book cited in the note above, the pioneering work on *Alltagsgeschichte* and German public opinion during Nazism was also a product of the *Institut für Zeitgeschichte* in Munich. See *Bayern in der NS-Zeit. Soziale Lage und politische Verhalten der Bevölkerung im Spiegel vertraulicher Berichte*, eds., Martin Broszat, Elke Fröhlich and Falk Wiesemann, Munich 1977. For an example of another type of *Alltagsgeschichte*, see *'Die Jahre weiß man nicht, wie man sie heute hinsetzen soll'. Faschismuserfahrungen im Ruhrgebiet*, ed., Lutz Niethammer, Berlin and Bonn 1983. Compare: Ian Kershaw, *Popular Opinion and Dissent in the Third Reich: Bavaria 1933–1945*, Oxford 1983; David Bankier, *The Germans and the Final Solution. Public Opinion under Nazism*, Oxford 1992. This lasts an English version of a dissertation, written at the Hebrew University of Jerusalem, 1983. See also: Reinhard Mann, *Protest und Kontrolle im Dritten Reich: Nationalsozialistische Herrschaft im Alltag einer rheinischen Großstadt*, Frankfurt a. M. 1987.

[39] See Frei, *Der Führerstaat, passim* and in the summary, 207–215. Compare also his "Wie modern war der Nationalsozialismus?", in: *Geschichte und Gesellschaft*, 19 Jg. (1993), 367–387, and his essay, "People's Community and War: Hitler's popular Support," in: *The Third Reich between Vision and Reality. New Perspectives on German History 1918–1945*, ed. Hans Mommsen, Oxford 2001, 59–78.

like Hans Mommsen included – that it was a *sine qua non* of the "Final Solution", the argument has now moved to the issue of its actual effect during the critical stages of the Holocaust, namely since the fall of 1941.⁴⁰ All agree now that Antisemitism as a mental preparation for the Holocaust had been critical, and that the choice of the Jews as the Nazis' major racial enemy cannot possibly be explained outside its context. All equally agree, however – or so It seems to me – that other elements, such as the barbarization of the armed forces during the long war in the East and the transplanting of the operations to the faraway Polish zone, away from the watching eyes of the civilian population at home, were of some significance, too. In fact, the overall cumulative effect of various elements and a policy that underwent gradual but consistent radicalization can no longer be disregarded by even the most vehement defenders of Intentionalism.⁴¹ Nazi overall population-control plans, their transfer of ethnic Germans into the borders of the new Reich, and their operations against local Slav elements in the occupied territories – to be later intensified as the war was to be won – all these factors undoubtedly played *some* role. Extreme positions that would disregard Antisemitic racial motivation on the one hand or any other consideration except the ideological imperative are by now rare, indeed.

This fact, though, is not always consciously acknowledged. A recently published book by Yaakov Lozowick, *Eichmanns Bürokraten*, may serve as an interesting case in point.⁴² Lozowick is the chief archivist of *Yad Vashem* – Israel's central research institute, dealing with the history of the Holocaust. His book is based on a Ph.D. thesis, written under the supervision of Yehuda Bauer, the dean of Holocaust studies in the country. He can thus be considered a typical representative of the "Israeli School", if there really is one. Now, the book itself is solidly researched, based on a wide variety of archival sources, but it aspires to be more than yet another historical monograph. It has a deeper message, Lozowick claims, a fundamental, philosophical one. Lozowick, in fact, sets out to disprove Hannah Arendt's famous, perhaps ill-famous, thesis on the "Banality of Evil", by looking closely at Eichmann's colleagues and subordinates. His main point is the inner,

---

40 For a more detailed presentation of this issue see Shulamit Volkov, "Antisemitism as Explanation: For and Against," here no. 13 below. In note 18 there, I refer to Hans Mommsen's essay, "Die Realisierung des Utopischen: Die 'Endlösung der Judenfrage' im 'Dritten Reich'," in: *Geschichte und Gesellschaft*, 9.Jg. (1983), 421–452.
41 The most striking example, it seems to me, is now Dan Diner, "The Irreconcilability of an Event: Integrating the Holocaust in the Narrative of the Century," in: Michman, *Remembering the Holocaust*, 95–107, especially 103.
42 Yaakov Lozowick, *Hitlers Bürokraten. Eichmann, seine willigen Vollstrecker und die Banalität des Bösen*, Munich 2000. The Hebrew edition appeared in Jerusalem 2001. The parts most central to my interpretation are Chapters 3 and 4, 55–120 (of the Hebrew edition).

immanent malice of these men. There was nothing banal about them, he claims, they were the embodiment of evil. For my purposes, however, Lozowick's philosophical reflections are less material than the narrative he unfolds in his book. The men who worked under Eichmann in all corners of the Third Reich, he tells us, were vicious Antisemites and more often than not pathological sadists. In addition, however, they clearly emerge from his book as men characterized by two rather common human traits: blind obedience and personal ambition. They were, by his own account, the typical bureaucrats, working conscientiously and industriously "towards the Führer".[43] They were full of initiative, ready at any moment to fulfill as best they could the general line of policy that was handed down to them from above by Eichmann, their own little *Führer*.

Here, then, is a book that claims to backup one thesis and ends up unwittingly backing up another. It is an extreme case – but by no means a-typical. This book reflects, in its own roundabout way, the openness that characterizes research at *Yad Vashem*, often in contrast to its official verbiage. In 1979, *Yad Vashem Studies* did indeed publish an English version of Martin Broszat's path breaking essay on the "Genesis of the 'Final Solution'", only two years after its original appearance.[44] But in 2001, its publishing house went a step further in translating into Hebrew the collected essays edited by Ulrich Herbert under the title *Nazionalsozialistische Vernichtungspolitik*, including essays by Götz Aly, Dieter Pohl, Christian Gerlach and others. The reevaluation of the narrative of extermination, while embedding it in the overall Nazi policies in the various territories under their occupation has thus been made available to Hebrew readers and is now an element in the educated public discourse of all related matters. The institute's new openness is likewise apparent in the last authoritative volume on the Holocaust published by Yad Vashem, dealing with German Jewry.[45] It is part of the transformation, in which both researchers *and* their readership are now of a different, younger cohort. Cooperation with younger German historians is now an easier matter and it reflects openness and flexibility on both sides.

On the basis of my own experience, I could also add that mixed groups of Israeli students are now more than ever ready to approach the historiography of

---

[43] This is Ian Kershaw's phrase, by now commonly used in the historiography. In addition, see Chapter 13 in Ian Kershaw, *Hitler. 1889–1936: Hubris*, London 1998, and compare his essay, "'Working towards the Führer': Reflections on the Nature of the Hitler Dictatorship," 88–106.

[44] Martin Broszat, "Hitler and the Genesis of the Final Solution", in: *Yad Vashem Studies* 13 (1979), 73–125. The German original was published in the *Vierteljahrshefte für Zeitgeschichte*, 25 (1977), 739–775.

[45] *History of the Holocaust. Germany*, eds. Abraham Margaliot and Yehoyakim Cochavi, 2 vols., Jerusalem 1998.

National Socialism and the Holocaust with a measure of equanimity. Functionalism arouses no moral fury in them anymore. Treating the Holocaust in the context of the war-experience is accepted as self-evident. Talking about persecution of the Jews together with measures against the Sinti and Roma or those defined by the Nazis as asocials, i.e. as part of the overall racial utopia propagated by the Nazis, is accepted at face-value. It may be easier these days to teach a course on such topics in Israel than in Germany or the United States. There are many reasons for this shift. Generational change is surely an important one. Another, no less central, I believe, is the new "world-experience", to return to Diner's vocabulary, of today's Israelis. The "personal memory" of many of them, to say nothing as yet of their "collective memory", is no longer limited to that of the victims. It is infinitely more complex now. Their arsenal of experiences is fundamentally different from that brought to the study of history by their elders, twenty or thirty years ago. But be that as it may, I believe we have passed the stage of litigation. The historiography of National Socialism can no longer be described in terms of legal battle. If at all, it reflects a process of mediation between two sides, an increasingly popular procedure today, an alternative to normal criminal procedure. It is perhaps that process of *"Opfer-Täter-Ausgleich"* that we are here beginning to observe. Personal memories are thereby not erased. Incomprehension and moral rage in facing the horrors of Nazism and the depth of human depravity that this system has brought to light do no disappear. But history, it seems, moves in other spheres, too, and in these, most appropriately, time does not stand still and for once it also brings with it, I believe, an atmosphere of cooperation, a true breath of fresh air.

13 Antisemitism as Explanation: For and against

The historiography dealing with the Holocaust has long been a field of contesting and competing views. One thing, however, seems to have remained constant in all its ups and downs, namely the reliance upon Antisemitism as rationale for the National Socialists' "Final Solution." Various protestations notwithstanding, almost all historians make use of Antisemitism as the single most important element in analyzing the road to Auschwitz – twisted or direct. Clearly, along the main divide characteristic of this historiography, it is the "intentionalists" who place a greater emphasis on Antisemitism. But even the most persistent "functionalists" find it necessary to come back to it in one way or another. Some have tried to relativize its centrality as far as the presumably "regular" Nazi voters were concerned.[1] Others have tried to show that even the chief bureaucrats who directed the Nazi extermination machinery were only marginally concerned with it.[2] But at least in viewing the main protagonists – Hitler himself and his closest associates – Antisemitism always reemerges as the main explanatory mode.

While all this may indeed be indisputable, the relevant arguments often remain rather blurred. Considered self-evident, the pros and cons of this prevailing paradigm are only rarely reexamined. In this essay I would like to try and do just that: rethink the role of Nazi Antisemitism as an ideology leading to the "Final Solution," guiding the hands of the murderers. This is no slight matter, of course. The quantity and the quality of the relevant historiography are immense. As I do not intend to bring into the discussion any new facts, nor present any new documents, I would have to rely on this literature, subjecting it – yet again – to close critical reading, examining it from my own point of view.

I wish to start by pointing out one of the ambiguities that has plagued the use of the term Antisemitism for years. Both colloquially and in professional usage Antisemitism normally refers to at least two different, though of course not unrelated, phenomena. To begin with, it indicates the deeply entrenched traditional hatred of the Jews, that ever-present antipathy towards them, based upon centuries of vilification, going back to pre-Christian times. The term itself, introduced into common parlance in Germany during the early 1870s, was not initially

---

[1] See mainly Ian Kershaw, *Popular Opinion and political Dissent in the Third Reich*, Oxford 1983.
[2] See the various publications of Götz Aly and Susanne Heim, especially: "Die Ökonomie der Endlösung: Menschenvernichtung und wissenschaftliche Neuordnung," in: *Sozialpolitik und Judenvernichtung – Gibt es eine Ökonomie der Endlösung?*, Berlin 1987, 7–90. The controversy surrounding this issue is well represented in *Vernichtungspolitik: Eine Debatte über den Zusammenhang von Sozialpolitik und Genozid im nationalsozialistischen Deutschland*, ed. Wolfgang Schneider, Hamburg 1991.

conceived as a simple synonym for the age-old hatred.³ From the outset it was meant to denote a *new* phenomenon, or at the very least a new version of an old one. For the anti-Jewish propagandists of the Berlin *Gründerjahre* and the anti-Dreifusards in fin-de-siécle Paris, Antisemitism meant more than the familiar, rather naive, rejection of Jewish presence. Instead, it was applied as the proper name to a full-fledged new ideology, a complete worldview, grounded in what was then considered a new scientific theory, proving once and for all the spiritual and racial inferiority of the Jews and the imminent danger they posed to mankind in general and to the unique cultures of Germany or France – as the case may be – in particular. The early *historiography* of Antisemitism, written before World War I, only rarely applied the term. It was mainly concerned with traditional Jew hatred. Antisemitism conceived as a full-fledged ideology began to attract scholarly attention only later. Well into the second half of the twentieth century, so it seems, even Nazi policies towards the Jews were still frequently explained by that common, traditional Jew hating, often mixed with the new ideological mode to a greater or lesser extent.

Daniel Goldhagen's much discussed book is a case in point.⁴ Despite the author's repeated claims to originality, his overriding thesis on the primacy of Antiemitism – "Eliminationist" or otherwise – goes back, with a vengeance, one must add, to the initial paradigm. It offers, in fact, yet another version of that single most common explanation of National Socialism based on Jew hating. This, for Goldhagen, is the alpha and omega of the entire tragic affair. It was out of sheer hatred, runs the argument, that Hitler and his accomplices first decided and then carried out their "final Solution." It is the old hatred, dressed, to be sure, in various modern forms, that set the whole machinery in motion, exploiting for its own murderous scheme the ancient and the all-pervasive animosity against the Jews.⁵ Here Antisemitism turns out to be – more through the repetitive rhetoric of the book than through the force of its argument – not only a necessary but also a sufficient condition for the holocaust; the only factor needed for explaining it. The author apparently believes that his thesis is so amply supported by the evidence and so indisputably manifest that the burden of disproving it lies with his

---

3 On the person who apparently "invented" the term, see Moshe Zimmermann, *Wilhelm Marr: The Patriarch of Antisemitism*, New York 1986.
4 Daniel Jonah Goldhagen, *Hitler's Willing Executioners: Ordinary Germans and the Holocaust*, New York 1996.
5 Ibid, 34–35.

opponents.[6] He repeats the old formulas, supporting it with some new evidence and communicating it with a new jargon. Thus, it seems, he has taken the entire scholarly community by surprise.

Historians, busy reevaluating the sources, engaged in that prolong debate between "intentionalists" and "functionalists" and, some would also say, fighting their own petty ideological or even political battles – normally tended to think that that old familiar paradigm, long since proven inconclusive and, in any case, far too simple for the task at hand, was by now altogether superseded. It had been for long, no doubt, the most prevalent approach, adopted by many independent and fair-minded researchers, practically indisputable among Jewish historians, by no means only by Zionists.[7] In fact, establishing Antisemitism as a permanent factor of Jewish history and as an explanation for much of its turbulence had already been a common practice by the time Zionist thinkers began to formulate their own world view. Since Heinrich Graetz, generations of *liberal* Jewish historians trusted, indeed, that with sociocultural integration on the Jewish side and the enactment of legal emancipation on the non-Jewish side, a new era finally dawned and in it Antisemitism was bound to disappear. But at the same time, they continued to accord great significance to the tradition of Jew hating and to the powerful effects of hostility and discrimination upon their history. They invariably saw in Antisemitism a major constitutive element in the formation and transformation of Jewish life throughout the ages.

Zionists, to be sure, took an even more extreme position. They not only insisted on the centrality of Antisemitism in Jewish history but were also more skeptical concerning the plausibility of its future disappearance. In the aftermath of the pogroms in Russia during the early 1880s, but also in view of the recurring waves of Antisemitism in the presumably enlightened new German *Kaiserreich*, the promise of emancipation lost much of its splendor while the constancy of Jew hating seemed to be compellingly reaffirmed. As in so many other matters, it was Ahad Ha'am who gave the most fitting expression to this mixed historical lesson. In his essay 'Two Masters,' published 1902, he stated that modern society could in fact manage to preserve "pockets of reaction and barbarism" even in an age of "general progress and enlightenment." "It is not impossible," he wrote, "that with time humanism would spread and would indeed include all mankind . . . The

---

6 See Goldhagen's argument, for instance in Chapter 1: "So why is the burden of proof not on those who maintain that German society had indeed undergone a transformation and had jettisoned its culturally borne Antisemitism?", Ibid, 31.
7 For a more extensive discussion, see Shulamit Volkov, "German Antisemitism and Jewish National Thought," in: *Jerusalem Quarterly*, 15 (spring 1980), 53–69.

world will be filled with justice, honesty and mercy . . . only 'except the Jews'."[8] Thus, the paradigm for understanding all present and future anti-Jewish verbiage or policies, even under the veil of progress and modernity, has been formulated; eternal hatred of the Jews was accepted as a historical constant. In itself it required little elaboration. It's very antiquity was its rationale; its origins served as an explanation."[9]

Jewish historiography then developed two parallel models for dealing with Antisemitism: the cyclical and the spiral. The cyclical version saw in Antisemitism a kind of permanent obsession, a pathological antagonism towards Jews, reappearing anew in slightly changing forms "in every generation." Such, for instance, was Leo Pinsker's attitude in his *Auto-emancipation*, as well as Nachum Sokolov's in *Eternal Hatred of an Eternal People*, *both* books published almost simultaneously in 1882.[10] The ideological pioneers of Zionism managed to apply, even at that early stage, a rather elementary version of social pathology cum social psychology to account for the permanence of Antisemitism in all known non-Jewish societies – past and present. More recent examples are likewise easy to come by. Shmuel Ettinger, for instance, followed a similar line.[11] For him it was the stereotype of the contemptible Jew, ever present in Western civilization, that provided the clue for the permanence of Antisemitism. Jew-hating could only fade away temporarily, according to this scheme, reemerging anew through the reemployment of old familiar images. No fundamental change needed to be explained within this scheme. Antisemitism, to use Daniel Goldhagen's argument again, was always there – threatening, violent, and "eliminationist."

The spiral version, in turn, stresses dynamism and escalation instead of permanence and repetition. It argues for a *process* in which Antisemitism has been continuously radicalized, especially during the modern period. From a certain point onward, it contends – be it the early restructuring of the modern European state, to use Hannah Arendt 's familiar prototype, or since the emergence of racism, according to Jacob Katz – Antisemitism underwent a process of radical change,

---

[8] Ahad Ha'am, *Selected Essays*, Philadelphia 1936, 105–106.
[9] See Marc Bloch's discussion in his book *The Historian's Craft*, New York 1953, 29–35. I have more fully developed a critique of this approach to Antisemitism in my essay "The Written Matter and the spoken Word," no. 5 in this volume.
[10] See Leo Pinsker's anonymously published book: *Autoemanzipation. Mahnruf an seine Stammengenossen, von einem russischen Juden*, Berlin 1882, and Nahum Sokolov, *Sin'at Olam le'am Olam*, [Eternal Hatred of an Eternal Folk], Warsaw 1882.
[11] For Shmuel Ettinger's position see especially his *Modern Antisemitism: Studies and Essays*, [Hebrew], Tel Aviv 1978. For an English translation of the first, programmatic article, see "The Roots of Modern Antisemitism," in *Dispersion and Unity*, 9 (1969), 17–37.

becoming ever more aggressive in tone and intention, reaching its final consummation in Auschwitz.[12]

The distinctions between the two models are often blurred. The proponents of both place great emphasis on traditional Antisemitism and vary primarily in the significance they attach to its latter-day transformations and the new types of its legitimation. It is, moreover, often difficult to separate the two approaches. The tension is quite apparent in Goldhagen's book. On the one hand, he repeatedly emphasizes the traditional anti-Jewish animus, presumably typical of German society from time immemorial. On the other, he is determined to show its "evolution." It was "a story of continuity and change *par excellence*," he writes.[13] Nevertheless, Goldhagen's own exposition leaves no doubt as to what is central for him and what he considers no more than an elaboration. It is that pervasive and permanent hatred that explains everything, he reasserts, the original deep-seated antipathy towards the Jews. The rest is only variations on a theme. Goldhagen mainly deals, after all, with personal animosity, with fear and aversion, with malice and vindictiveness. He wishes to explain the acts of individuals, the behavior of Hitler and his "willing executioners". It is not their ideology that interests him but their drive; not their *Weltanschauung* but their passion.

It is instructive to remember, that in the immediate postwar years, it was common among historians to deny the very *existence* of a Nazi ideology. It was fashionable then, even more than now, to compare Nazism with Communism, and the poverty of Nazi ideology therefore appeared blatant, indeed. "National Socialism has no political theory of its own," wrote Franz Neumann as early as 1944, "and . . . the ideologies it uses or discards are mere *arcana Domminationis*, techniques of dominations." "(T)he German Leadership," he added, "is the only group in present German society that does not take its ideological pronouncements seriously and is well aware of their purely propagandistic nature."[14] At that time, emphasis usually fell – as in some of the prewar narratives, too – on the National Socialists' "state of mind," on their instincts and passions rather than on their ideals. Fear of the "other" or the collective force of a common hatred, shared by so many Germans for so long towards the Jews – these, above all, were deemed relevant for explaining the Holocaust. Only since the late 1960s, in fact, with the new interest in nineteenth-century Antisemitism, in *folkish* ideology, and

---

[12] See Hannah Arendt, *The Origins of Totalitarianism*, New York 1955, 11–53; Jacob Katz, *From Prejudice to Destruction: Antisemitism 1700–1933*, and Yaakov Talmon, *The Unique and the Universal. Some historical Reflections*, London 1965, 288–299.
[13] Goldhagen, *Hitler's Willing Executioners*, 53.
[14] Franz Neumann, *Behemoth: The Structure and Practice of National Socialism*, New York 1942, 467.

in racism, and then with the appearance of Ernst Nolte 's *Three Faces of Fascism* and Eberhard Jäckel's *Hitler's Weltanschauung* did the historiography of Nazism seem to have finally matured.[15] It now plunged into a far more sophisticated and better-informed search for causation. It was, in short, seeking new explanations.

Goldhagen's single-minded stress on Antisemitism as an "animus" seemed questionable at the very outset. Indeed, when his book first appeared, it was at first challenged by historians of various schools, who felt that his argument was simply one that had been long discarded. Other shortcomings in his approach also seemed familiar enough. To begin with, his insistence on not comparing German Antisemitism with its manifestations elsewhere across the European continent was rightly deemed unacceptable. Decades of research have established and, after all, beyond any doubt that anti-Jewish attitudes were not unique to Germany and that during the pre-World War I years, though such attitudes had by no means disappeared from the German public sphere, they were not particularly pronounced in that country. Furthermore, Goldhagen's cursory treatment of the complex historical evidence concerning the relationships between Germans and Jews from the early nineteenth century up to the Nazi era – also a thoroughly studied theme in recent years – is likewise inadmissible. Jews were perhaps never as well integrated in German bourgeois society of the *Kaiserreich* as they themselves often wished to believe. They surely encountered Antisemitism often enough, at both the private and the public level. But the prewar years as such could be considered a "rehearsal for destruction" only in hindsight.[16] At the time, despite the clouds on the horizon, these were years of hope and of real and conspicuous progress.

Goldhagen's claims concerning the omnipresence of the eliminationist rage in Nazi Germany have indeed been contested by intentionalists and functionalists alike. Historians from both camps protested the universality of his claims as well as his almost principled lack of differentiation.[17] The controversy soon made it evident that the argument, in fact, did not concern the role of Jew hating as *a background* to the Holocaust. Functionalists, too, usually agree that a pervasive anti-Jewish attitude was a *sine qua non* for the "Final Solution."[18] The historiographic debate lies

---

15 Ernst Nolte's, *Der Faschismus in seiner Epoche* was first published in Munich 1961, and the English translation appeared in New York, 1965. Compare also Eberhard Jäckel, *Hitlers Weltanschauung: Entwurf einer Herrschaft*, Tübingen 1969.
16 Paul W. Massing, *Rehearsal for Destruction: A Study of political Antisemitism in Imperial Germany*, New York 1949.
17 For a collection of responses see *Hyping the Holocaust: Scholars answer Goldhagen*, ed., Franklin Jamlin Littell, New York 1997.
18 See Hans Mommsen, "Die Realisierung des Utopischen: Die 'Endlösung der Judenfrage' im 'Dritten Reich'", in: *Geschichte und Gesellschaft*, 9 (1983/84), 421–452.

elsewhere. It revolves around the role of *ideology*, not around questions of love or hate. One argues about the importance of the Antisemites' *Weltanschauung* and about its absolute and relative impact upon the policies leading to extermination. *Nobody* really denies that there has been (more or less) widespread animosity towards Jews in Germany – before, during, and indeed even after the Nazi era. Despite Goldhagen's combative mood, no one doubts the fact that such a general hostility towards them was a basic *precondition* for the initiation and for the "success" of the "Final Solution." The argument lies elsewhere. Moreover, the critical edge of this historiographic debate seems to have been somewhat blunted with the ebbing of the controversy between functionalists and intentionalists. As early as 1992, Christopher Browning listed a number of "modified intentionalists" like himself, and one occasionally encounters in the literature even some "moderate functionalists."[19] In a reprinting of an article dealing with the debate between what he prefers to call "Hitlerists" and Structuralists, Ian Kershaw has announced that all things considered, "one would have to conclude that neither model offers a wholly satisfactory explanation, and that some room for compromise is obvious."[20] Finally, in the introduction to his book *Nazi Germany and the Jews,* Saul Friedländer summarizes his position by stating that "[the] crimes committed by the Nazi regime were neither a mere outcome of some haphazard, involuntary, imperceptible, and chaotic onrush of unrelated events nor a predetermined enactment of a demonic script; they were the result of converging factors, of the interaction between intentions and contingencies, between discernible causes and chance."[21] This, no doubt, is an admiringly balanced view. According to Friedländer, too, it is not vague intentions or a diffuse "animus" with which we are dealing, but an ideology – a more or less systematic set of ideas that eventually led to the Holocaust. Here, the meaning or place of Antisemitism along the road to Auschwitz is being debated – a far more complex matter. Still, the tendency to oversimplify, perhaps also the urge to follow our intuition and draw a direct line between ideology and action, seems irresistible. After all, Antisemitism as an ideology is easily transformed into the functional equivalent of Antisemitism as an animus, and both can thus be treated as self-evident, straightforward explanation. Neither, I believe, is really fit for the task.

---

19 Christoher Browning, "Beyond 'intentionalism' and 'functionalism': The decision for the Final Solution reconsidered," in: *The Path to Genocide. Essays on Launching the Final Solution,* Cambridge 1992, 88.
20 Ian Kershaw, "Hitler and the Holocaust," in: *The Nazi Dictatorship. Problems and Perspectives of Interpretation,* 3rd ed., New York 1993, 103.
21 Saul Friedländer, *Nazi Germany and the Jews,* vol 1*: The years of Persecution, 1933–1939,* New York 1997, 5. This entire issue is dealt with in essay no. 12 above, too.

In a scholarly reevaluation of the relevant historiographic scene, published in 1985, Dov Kulka stated that only through Antisemitism – as an *ideology*, to be sure – was it all possible "to explain the unexplainable."[22] More recently, in a polemical article in one of Israel's most widely-read dailies, Yehuda Bauer and Ysrael Gutman reasserted that despite all the arguments, "the Archimedean point is the ideology."[23] Here lies, according to them, not only the uniqueness of the Holocaust but also the uniqueness of the National Socialist system as a whole. Accordingly, one does not need to *explain* much beyond it. It is, once again, "the origins that explain," to return to Marc Bloch's critical formulation. It is the very existence of the Antisemitic ideology, in a rather intensified form and with some particular and peculiar details that seems to reduce the mystery of the Holocaust. In his much-quoted speech in Berlin, "50 Years After," the Swiss philosopher-historian Walter Hofer proclaimed that it was "simply incomprehensible how the claim can be made that the National Socialist racial policy was not the realization of Hitler's *Weltanschauung*."[24] But after all, is it not precisely this link, between *Weltanschauung* and policy, that we ought to explain? Is it not that process of "realization", apparently so unrelenting and so ruthless, that is the extraordinary fact about the Nazis and their accomplices?

In dealing with this matter, it is apparently all too easy to forget that long-established historical lesson, namely that ideologies are never simply *realized*, that they are never just *put into practice*. The common model of background and events, preparation and performance – this familiar two-tier structure, in which the first always explains the second – has been repeatedly proven flawed. Turning theory into the cause of praxis, moving between ideas and action on some sort of a one-way road, has never been a satisfactory exercise. It is a fine construct of our narrative skill but a dubious practice of historians. In fact, no full-fledged utopian ideology (Antisemitism – eliminationist, redemptive, or otherwise – included) has ever been available "in advance," so to speak, as a simple program for political, economic, or social action.

Examples are easy to come by. The locus classicus of this methodological issue is, no doubt, the controversy over the relationships between the philosophy of the Enlightenment and the French Revolution. The issue received some highly

---

[22] Otto D. Kulka, "Major Trends and Tendencies in German Historiography on National Socialism and the 'Jewish Question' (1924–1984)," in: *Leo Baeck Institute Yearbook*, 30 (1985), 234.
[23] Yehuda Bauer and Ysrael Gutman, "The Archemedean Point Is the Ideology," [Hebrew] in: *Haaretz*, April 16, 1998.
[24] Walter Hofer, "50 Jahre danach. Über den wissenschaftlichen Umgang mit dem Dritten Reich," in: *Geschichte in Wissenschaft und Unterricht*, 34 (1983), 14, cited and translated by Kershaw, *The Nazi Dictatorship*, 84.

sophisticated treatment in recent literature, but Alfred Cobban's brilliant essay of 1965 is always a pleasure to quote from.[25] It opens with a memorable passage from Taine: "When we see a man . . . apparently sound and of peaceful habits, drink eagerly of a new liquor, then suddenly fall to the ground, foaming at the mouth . . . we have no hesitation in supposing that in the pleasant draught there was some dangerous ingredient."[26] Cobban then recalls the testimony of Edmund Burke, who believed that the revolution was caused by the spread of enlightened ideas, and ends with Michelet and Lamartine, who saw in the philosophy of the eighteenth century "the code civil and religious liberty *put into action* in the Revolution by the People." Even Louis Blanc, "for all his socialist ideology," still saw the "revolutionary struggle as one of conflicting principles," and so finally did most of the later socialist historians.[27] Nevertheless, Cobban is not intimidated. He goes on to demolish the entire edifice, mercilessly probing the presumably self-evident link between ideas and praxis, exposing its problematic nature and closing with a characteristically frank indecision: "The influence of the Enlightenment cannot be disregarded in any history of the French Revolution . . . but the revolutionaries did not set their course by its light in the beginning, nor did they steer the ship of state into the haven of the Enlightenment in the end."[28]

Among the many examples demonstrating the intermingling of ideology and practice, the case of nationalism is singularly instructive. It is particularly pertinent as an analogy for Antisemitism, not only because of the imminent historical link between the two,[29] but also because in both cases one could distinguish between a widespread *sensibility*, an "animus," to be sure, and a mature *ideology*. It is generally agreed that some form of initial national awareness as well as few budding political institutions relying upon it were present in a number of European societies long before the French Revolution. Clearly, a vague national consciousness preceded the formulation of a national worldview and full-fledged modern national ideologies. The history of both England and France abound with examples of that prolonged interaction between theory and practice, characteristic of the development of modern

---

25 Alfred Cobban, "The Enlightenment and the French Revolution," in: *Aspects of the French Revolution*, London 1968, 18–28. For the more recent literature, see, e.g., Keith Baker, "On the problem of the Ideological Origins of the French Revolution," in: *Modern European Intellectual History. Reappraisal and new Persectives*, eds. Dominick LapCara and Steven L Kaplan, New York 1982, 197–219, and Roger Chartier, "Enlightenment and Revolution, Revolution and Enlightenment," in: *The Cultural Origins of the French Revolution*, Durham N.C. 1991, 3–20.
26 Cobban, "The Enlightenment and the French Revolution," 18.
27 Ibid, 19–20.
28 Ibid, 28.
29 For the historians' neglect of this link, see my, "Nationalismus, Antisemitismus und die deutsche Geschichtsschreibung," translated into English in this volume, no. 8. above.

nationalism. It is, however, usually argued that Germany represented a different model, one in which nationalism *as an Idea* preceded its realization; one in which a clear ideology has more or less simply and directly been put into practice.[30]

But though an embryonic national consciousness can surely be detected, at least among members of certain social strata even in pre-Napoleonic Germany, and though a national discourse gradually evolved there during the first half of the nineteenth century – this, too, I believe, never reached the stage of containing a blueprint for action. Fichte's *Reden an die deutsche Nation*, often quoted with great aplomb, is a good example. In fact, the *Reden* contain no clear ideological design and are instead suffused with universal ideals, as much as with some early sense of nationalism, no doubt. They were later used for a variety of contradictory political purposes, but at the time they mainly gave voice to the frustration of the occupied and contained no orderly draft for solving any immediate or general problem. Likewise, the political ambitions of the early nineteenth-century *Burschenschaften*, were drowned in a romantic rhetorical idiom – a far cry from any well-conceived *Weltanschauung* or ideology. And the revolutionaries of 1848 had no clue as to what kind of national unity they were aiming at. Neither, of course, did Otto von Bismarck when he finally took office as the Prussian Chancellor in September 1862. Bismarck's policy making is a prime example for the complex nature of the relationships between political intentions and performance. The fact that he had been often credited with fulfilling the dreams of the German national movement at the time neither means that he *intended* to do so, nor that his *Kaiserreich* had ever been the true realization of these dreams. The quick ideological adjustment eventually made by the German liberals, moving from a vocal opposition to his policies to a warm support of all his vagaries, was only a fitting counterpart to his own equivocation. It was only later on, with the actual establishment of the new Reich, its scope and its particular type of regime, that Bismarck's solution seemed to many – though never to all – the realization of their previous vision. But, in any case, this only happened *in retrospect*. The German national ideology took its *concrete* shape – and a temporary one at that – not prior to or in preparation of the consolidation of the Reich but in *parallel* to this process and perhaps only after it had been achieved.[31]

---

[30] The literature of this issue is immense and has been growing in recent years. The classic argument, however, was formulated by Friedrich Meinecke in his *Weltbürgertum und Nationalstaat*, Munich 1908.

[31] For years after its establishment, the Kaiserreich – split from Austria – was far from being internally unified – politically, socially and religiously. See, for instance, David Blackbourn, *Class, Religion and Local politics in Wilhelmine Germany*, New Haven 1980; Helmut W. Smith, *German Nationalism and Religious Conflict*, Princeton 1995; and Alon Confino, *The Nation as a local Metaphor*, Chapel Hill N.C. 1997.

This, to be sure, is *not* an attempt to resurrect a simplified, reductionist Marxism, according to which material circumstances explain any form of consciousness. What we are forced, yet again, to confront in all the available examples, but in a most convincing way, finally, in the case of National Socialism, is the *tangled web* of in*teraction between ideology and praxis*. It is not some kind of "ideological falsehood," to use Bauer and Gutman's phrase, that can explain the "Final Solution," even if the hopes of "getting rid" of the Jews did in fact constitute a powerful motive force for its realization. Neither was an Antisemitic blueprint suddenly drafted and executed following some concrete events in occupied Poland or in Russia between 1939 and 1942, as has sometimes been suggested. Antisemitism – both as a general sentiment and as a vague but powerful ideology – had been there before, but its effectiveness came from the chances of implementation, and these became evident only with the onset of the military campaign in the east. It was not the prevalent anti-Jewish sentiment as such, nor the grand redemptive schemes that so captured the imagination of Antisemites since the days of the Bayreuth Circle, which finally directed the hands of the executioners. It was rather a version of it all that suddenly became *feasible*, almost "easy to carry out" then and there, under the particular conditions at the Russian front in the fall and winter of 1941. At the background of the systematic terror and discrimination practiced by the Nazis against the Jews for some eight years, plans of extermination were now finally turned into reality, bolstered by a virulent Antisemitism that had acquired a dynamic of its own and became yet another major force to be reckoned with in those days.

This argument is, of course, not mine and is by no means unknown in the literature, but for some reason it normally remains unacknowledged. Observe, for instance, Eberhard Jäckel's essay, "Der Weg zum Mord an den Juden" (The path toward the murder of the Jews). Despite his protestations concerning the preeminence of Hitler's deep-seated racism, the constant interaction between ideology and practice clearly emerges from his day-to-day review of Nazi policies during the critical moments just before and just after the beginning of Barbarossa. At that time, Hitler himself "probably did not yet know how it should all continue."[32] He still hesitated, according to Jäckel, as late as August 1941, while Heydrich and Goebbels, who were apparently pushing forward, did so "in an effort to win favor and gain power more than out of sheer hatred."[33] In any case, the fortunes of war and the circumstances surrounding it were most intimately linked to the decisions concerning the "Final Solution."

---

32 Eberhard Jäckel, "Der Weg zum Mord an den Juden," in: *Hilters Herrschaft*, 112.
33 Ibid, 120.

Another example of ostensibly stressing the primacy of ideology while in fact describing a much more complex interaction between theory and practice can be found in Omer Bartov's two books on Hitler's army.[34] Bartov labors to show the deep impact of that peculiar blend of anti-Bolshevism and racism upon the soldiers on the Eastern Front. At the same time, however, he describes the far more complex situation that existed. Bartov repeatedly stresses the effectiveness of Nazi indoctrination, but what emerges from his overall description is the *interplay* of ideological indoctrination and inhuman conditions at the front – not the primacy of one over the other. Finally, this is also apparent in Saul Friedländer's latest book. While the author opens by proclaiming that his main explanatory tool would be the "redemptive Antisemitism" typical of the Nazi leadership, the strength of his argument lies – to my mind – elsewhere.[35] It lies in the *complex, incremental* character of his narrative concerning the treatment of the Jews under National-Socialism; in the way in which he so pertinently describes their gradual exclusion from German society, their debasement and dehumanization supported by a mixture of emotions, ideology, opportunism, and political circumstances.

Let us once again quickly review the arguments concerning the fateful months between October and December 1941.[36] Hitler was relatively silent concerning the Jews since about January 1941. His diatribes against them vigorously recur around mid-October and by mid-December he was daily concerned with the logic of their extermination. His generally combative oratorical style during these months may perhaps be explained by the overall military situation both at the Eastern Front and elsewhere upon the global theater of war. It was by then quite obvious that victory against the Russians could not be achieved before winter, and that counter-offensive on the Moscow front could not be avoided. In addition, the American entry into the war was imminent, and resistance was becoming ever more violent, especially in the West.

But the context of Hitler's anti-Jewish outbursts surely included other factors, too. It was during these very weeks that action against the Jews everywhere in Europe escalated to new heights. The first "Table Talk" entry against them is dated October 21, followed by further outbursts on October 25 and November 5,

---

34 Omer Bartov, *The Eastern Front 1941–1945. German Troops and the barbarization of Warfare*, New York 1986, and his *Hitler's Army, Soldiers, Nazis, and the War in the Third Reich*, Oxford 1992.
35 Friedländer, introduction to *Nazi Germany and the Jews*, vol 1, 3.
36 See Saul Friedländer, "Ideology and Extermination: The immediate Origins of the Final Solution," in: *Catastrophe and Meaning. The Holocaust and the Twentieth Century*, eds. Moishe Poistone and Eric Santner, Chicago 2002, 17–33. Compare the essays by Jäckel, Browning, and Kershaw quoted above.

and by speeches and private utterances during the rest of November and throughout December. Organized extermination began either at the same time or perhaps even somewhat earlier.[37] Following Heydrich's briefing of the higher SS and police officers on July 2, 1941, sporadic killings by the *Einsatzgruppen* occurred along the entire front. They seem to have escalated during August and September. On 29–30 September over thirty-three thousand Jewish men, women, and children were killed at Babi-Yar near Kiev. By that time "full-scale genocide had already been embarked upon by the *Einsatzgruppen* in the Soviet Union,"[38] and active preparations for full-scale extermination were taking place elsewhere, too. The expulsion of Jews from Berlin began on October 1, 1941. Between October 16 and November 2, nine trains from various towns in Germany arrived at Lodz. Twenty-one other "transports" came from Prague, Vienna, and Luxembourg. Additional trains were intended to reach Riga but finally arrived at Kovno, where Jews were immediately murdered at a nearby site on the twenty-fifth and twenty-ninth of November. Killing of the ghetto inhabitants in Minsk was already taking place somewhat earlier at the beginning of November; by the end of the month it was occurring in Riga as well. The first experiments in gassing were performed at the same time.

Hitler's Antisemitic rhetoric, then, did not precede these events but occurred simultaneously with them. Clearly, the Nazi leadership made sure that the Führer's basic attitude regarding the "Jewish Question" was known to all involved. Hitler's own outbursts encouraged them and drove them on. But his ideological obsessions were fed by the increasing tempo of the killing – not only the other way around. The web of cause and effect in this case is probably impossible to disentangle. But seen in this light and regardless of its explanatory power, Nazi Antisemitism can no longer be treated as the only *cause* for other events, an omnipresent *motivation* at the background of the Holocaust. After all, it, too, needs explaining: Antisemitism is *part of the enigma.* Beyond its wild, redemptive, utopian visions, Antisemitism – like other ideologies – was not only shaping events but also affected by them, intensified or watered down in response to them, reformulated and redirected in relation to them.

In view of this complexity, only those narratives that manage to substitute the question *how* for that of *why* seem to get at least *near* an explanation of the Holocaust – the ones that endeavor to reconstruct the devilish interplay of action and ideas, that linger on the particulars, that insist on giving us even the most minute details. Nine out of Friedländer's ten chapters in the second volume of his book

---

37 See the chronology in Kershaw, *The Nazi Dictatorship*, 100–107, and in Yehoyakim Cochavi, "The last stage in the history of German Jewry," in: *The History of the Shoah: Germany* [Hebrew], vol. 1, Jerusalem 1993, 348–400.
38 Kershaw, *The Nazi Dictatorship*, 103.

deal with the actual course of events, with *how* the Germans behaved and *how* the Jews suffered; with the daily interaction between the thoughts and actions of both victims and perpetrators.[39] And in reading these chapters, one does feel that the mystery begins to unravel. The transition between mere Antisemitic verbiage and "*die Tat*," to use Hitler's own phraseology, that is between that famous anti-Jewish animus and/or ideology on the one hand and the actual praxis of discrimination and ever-increasing abuse on the other begins to make sense. A similar sensation of an almost unexpected insight is solicited by the detailed description of events during the period between 1939 and 1941 provided by Christopher Browning in his studies of Nazi resettlement policies and the ghettoization of the Jews in Poland.[40] The chapter on German Jewry between 1938 and 1943 in the newly published two-volume collection of Yad Vashem written by Yehoyakim Cochavi achieves equally impressive results.[41] Moreover, even Goldhagen's horrifically descriptive chapters on the camps and the death marches occasionally provide such rare moments of cognition.[42]

"The degree of influence to be attributed to ideas is an unresolved question in respect of all great historical movements," writes Alfred Cobban.[43] Marx's effort to dispose of this difficulty by treating ideas as mere reflections of social class interests has long been tremendously attractive, mainly for its simplicity and its inner coherence. But it clearly won't do. No case demonstrates the weakness of this approach more than that of Nazism. Max Weber's converse thesis, giving priority to doctrine and belief, has ultimately proven equally reductionist. And, alas, all the variations and combinations of these two approaches failed to produce theoretically satisfying solutions. Historians, luckily perhaps, are not expected to overcome such fundamental hurdles. It is as part of the practice of our craft that we must come to terms with them, each time anew. We should therefore – so I believe – loyally stick to our minute narration, continue to put our trust in the details, and beware of too easily crossing the line between explanation and that which must be explained. Doing just that still constitutes a major challenge.

---

39 The only exception is Chapter 3, "Redemptive Antisemitism", 73–112.
40 Browning, *The Path to Genocide*, Chapters 1 and 2, 3–56.
41 See Cochavi, *The History of the Shoah*, 235–400.
42 See Goldhagen, *Hitler's Willing Executioners*, part 4 on the camps and part 5 on the death-marches.
43 Cobban, "The Enlightenment and the French Revolution,", 20.

14 A Comment on Brutal Antisemites and Brutal Antisemitism

Review of Jonathan Littell, *Les Bienviellantes (The Kindly Ones)*

One could criticize Jonathan Littell's *The Kindly ones* as far-fetched, pornographic, and even boring. However, the question is not only what is *written* in the book but also how one *reads* it. I, for one, have not read the book with an eye to the author's failures and inaccuracies. I assumed at the outset that in writing fiction, even when one attempts to recreate historical situations, as Littell does here, accuracy is secondary. To be sure, a text ought to include sufficient historical details to anchor it in time and place, but no more. While accuracy is necessary in writing history, it is not a literary criterion. What the author tells us need not even be possible in the real world. His is a poetic truth, so to speak, a psychological and hypothetical one.

Thus, in approaching Littell's 900-page novel, I was curious to see what a novelist could add to the ongoing attempts of historians to answer the most intriguing and unsettling question in the history of Nazism, or perhaps in the history of the twentieth century: How did some apparently normal people turn so quickly and so completely into ruthless, uninhibited murderers. In the historiography of the period one calls this riddle the "the perpetrators' question." The question underpins all attempts to explain Nazism. For years, the so-called "intentionalist" historians, focusing on ideology in general and Antisemitism in particular, insisted that it was simply the conglomerate of anti-Jewish ideas and sentiments that best accounted for the motivation of the perpetrators, the ways they acted and the reasons so many accepted their brutal behavior. The murderer that these historians usually described was full of Jew hatred, "a true believer" in racial theory à la Nazis and convinced of the absolute supremacy of the Aryan man over all others, in particular the Jews. This prototypical Nazi would have been certain of the poisonous effect of the Jews on the world and on everything dear to him. He would have been acting out of deep-seated passionate hatred. In contrast to this hateful, passionate type, the "functionalists" drew a different portrait of the Nazi murderer. For them, he could either be a cold-blooded and effective bureaucrat or a disciplined "little man," acting in complete amorality, fulfilling orders blindly and automatically. There were many variations of these types, of course, but principally, they all lie more or less within this range. And in the end, though we have collected so many details about the processes leading to the Holocaust and about the various forms of its execution in the various parts of Europe, we know relatively little about individual perpetrators. It is not that we lack proper documents.

Yet what we do have is too often contaminated by lies and the efforts to evade punishment. Nor was it because we have not tried hard enough, but rather because we have left out some options that were apparently beyond our comprehension, outside the range of our methodology as historians.

What, then, could an author, who tries to get into the murderer's boots, so to speak, add to expert historians of this period? Could we perhaps solve that unspeakably horrible "perpetrator's question" with his help?

Jonathan Littell's *Les bienveillantes* (Paris 2006), indeed, introduces a radically different murderer's type into our discussion, Obersturmbannführer Max Aue. At first, it seems that we are being shown the usual small bureaucrat, basically a normal, even decent person, who is being transformed into a monster through years of Antisemitic brain-washing and the experiences of barbarization on the Eastern front. Had this been all that Littell describes, his account might, seem serious and reliable, but ultimately not add much to our knowledge or understanding. But as we read on, we soon realize that Littell proceeds in an entirely different direction. He presents us with a murderer, who is as far from conventional or normal as possible. His hero turns out to be a man drenched in sexual fantasies and unimaginable visions. He is a figure with apparent schizophrenic traits, living in more than one reality, hopelessly entangled in them all. Moreover, he is clearly atypical, an unreliable figure, representing no one. Naturally, while historians look for representative figures, this is no literary requirement. On the contrary, the theory about murderers as normal people suffers a devastating blow in this book; our murderer moves in other spheres. His story is that of a deformed individual, beginning with his erotic relationship with his twin-sister through to his compulsive relations with his mother, and finally his brutal sexual life. He is neither a typical German, born and educated in France, nor a normal SS officer, fulfilling a series of special duties and connected to the highest Nazi elite. In short, there is nothing normal about him.

What does Littell achieve by choosing such a figure? To begin with, he prevents readers from identifying themselves with his hero, even though Littell offers numerous indications in the text that suggest an affinity between himself and his protagonist. Still, it is hard to feel empathy with Max Aue, an aesthete who reads Plato and Flaubert in the trenches and drinks fine wine at his leisure – when he is not participating in brutal, senseless murder. His surrealistic private life story further underlines his uniqueness and squashes any measure of empathy towards him. At the end of the novel, he even murders his best friend, the only person who continued to keep him company even beyond the war-time years. The story leaves us with revulsion and horror. Nevertheless, while this is no doubt an important point, I assume it is not the only reason for Littell's preoccupation with this side of Aue's biography.

One could argue that these are merely pornographic interludes, intended to relieve the boredom of long battle-scenes and bureaucratic haggling. The violence is meant to attract readers by adding sensational drama, full of body-juices and drenched in kitsch. Perhaps, though I have no insight into the author's intentions. But I tend to read here something else, namely an attempt to return to an element that has gradually been lost in treating Nazism: that of the perpetrator, who lives in a world full of irrational myths, pathological hatreds, and dark impulses.

In the two decades after the war, some historians had attempted to take this route. Some tried their hand in writing psychological biographies of Hitler; others tried to analyze the psychology of the Nazi movement as a whole. These efforts, however, too often ended in grand generalizations that were impossible to substantiate. Eventually, this research line has been abandoned. The stress on ideology and on a functioning bureaucracy, culminating in murderous action, seemed to make psychology redundant. The sickly aspects were replaced by more rational, more easily explainable motives. Nazi modernity blurred what we knew of their anti-modern drive; Himmler's belief in a mix of irrational myths and occult mysticism remained a subject-matter of what most historians considered dubious literature; the various homoerotic tendencies disclosed by segments of the Nazi elite and given rein in years of fighting on the front were left to the footnotes. Rightly so, perhaps. Historians were, in any case, undecided. Saul Friedländer, for instance, who warned us against the accumulating kitsch-effect of ruminating over these themes, insisted in later writings on the combination of cool rationality and a hallucinatory, pathological world that had insistently reemerged in the study of National Socialism. But in the end, hardly anything of all that remains in present-day historiography.

Littell reminds us of this side of the picture. He exaggerates, of course, as is so often the case in literature. But his exploration of the more familiar rational, though cruel, bureaucrat vis-à-vis the fanatic and mentally deranged executor is thought-provoking, both with regard to the individual Nazi perpetrator and with regard to the movement as a whole. The book gives us no tool to decide between the two. But we are urged to consider this alternative again, this time in a new light. Possibly, we would never be able to decide between the two. However, it would be a mistake to dismiss the whole issue as irrelevant.

15 Revisiting Friedländer on Nazi Antisemitism

Hatred of the Jews is a phenomenon of non-Jewish society. Still all Jews are being affected by it to a greater or lesser extent. Saul Friedländer's early life was practically determined by it. Immediately after the German occupation of Czechoslovakia, having finally realized the danger of Nazi antisemitism, his parents decided to leave their home in Prague and found refuge in Vichy France. Being pursued there, too, by both the German occupiers and the local police force, the Friedländers finally decided to cross the border to Switzerland, not before they bravely took leave of their only son, for whom they found a safe haven in a Catholic seminary in Montluçon, near Néris les Bains, in the heart of France.[1]

A couple of years later, soon after the end of the war, the fate of his parents, perished in Auschwitz after they had been caught by the Swiss police and handed over to the Nazis, was revealed to the young Friedländer by a friendly priest. In a nearby church, Father L. tried to explain to the precocious 13-year-old what had happened to them. "And so, in front of this obscure Christ," recalled the adult Friedländer, "I listened: Auschwitz, the trains, the gas chambers, the crematory ovens, the millions of dead . . ."[2] The effect was staggering: "For the first time," he later confessed, "I felt myself to be Jewish . . . whatever this term meant in my mind."[3] At that time – and apparently later, too – he could not explain, not even to himself, the source of his "need of return, a return toward a decimated, humiliated, miserable group."[4] Likely an intuitive response to the incomprehensible evil involved in his parents' deaths, it irreversibly changed his life. Soon thereafter, he left behind his until then extremely devout Catholicism to become a Jew again, and then a fervent Zionist and a loyal – though always critical – Israeli.

Antisemitism, however, continued to haunt him. Back in Paris in 1953, after an eventful five years in the newly established State of Israel, Friedländer realized, as he recorded in the second volume of his memoirs, that "the Jewish state, which should have saved the Jews from a monstrous paroxysm of antisemitism, came too late." Now it contributed "not only by its misguided policies, but by its very existence, to the surge of a new/old antisemitism."[5] Thus, in the old/new Europe that was trying to reconstitute itself after the war, Antisemitism – once

---

1 See Saul Friedländer, *When Memory Comes*, New York 1979. The original French version of the book was published by Edition du Seuil in 1978. Here, I have used the Other Press English edition of 2016. On Friedländer's life in Néris les Bains, 47–57.
2 Ibid, 138.
3 Ibid.
4 Ibid, 139.
5 Saul Friedländer, *Where Memory Leads: My Life*, New York 2016, 36.

again – kept resurfacing. Even during his stay in faraway Sweden, Friedländer unexpectedly encountered a violent outburst of Antisemitic rage that, as a budding historian, he could not but interpret, even then and there, as "something present in [the] cultural background, something still widely present all over Europe."[6] And later, too, as a novice scholar, the theme came up again and again, although it took time to take center stage. In fact, it took years of psychoanalytical treatment before Friedländer was finally able to confront the topic in a rational way, and even include it in his academic work.

We will never know, of course, what really transpired in those many hours of psychoanalysis in Genève of the late 1960s, but in 1971, Friedländer – now well-versed in the psychoanalytical literature of the time, as he later observed – published his one and only book dedicated to Antisemitism: *L'antisémitisme nazi: Histoire d'une psychose collective* (1971). It was soon followed by another book, once again originally written in French and then translated into English under the title *History and Psychoanalysis: An Essay on the Possibilities and Limits of Psychohistory* (1978).[7]

A number of reasons combined to cause the relative obscurity of these two books. Although applying psychoanalytical tools to the study of National Socialism was not entirely a novelty at the time,[8] Friedländer's stress on antisemitism as a collective *"craze"* was daring from the perspective of both historians and psychoanalysts.[9] Moreover, the author himself, though at first enthusiastic about this approach, has had his own doubts. Twenty years later, he still felt that "[t]he two studies led me on a road I should not have taken; they were simplistic."[10]

Be that as it may, Friedländer *did* touch in these early works upon some important and neglected aspects of Nazi antisemitism. In them, he treated the link between the image of the Jew as "the most enduring symbol of Evil known to Christianity" and the "myth of the Jew" in modernity, which "allows the society in question to distinguish Good from Evil, the Pure from the Impure, what is itself and what is 'other.'" This link is clearly established in these texts, sociologically and psychologically, while historically "[t]he biographies of some twenty notorious Antisemites," recalls Friedländer, "most of whom lived in the nineteenth and

---

6 Ibid, 51.
7 The original book was published in Paris by Edition Seuil in 1975 and in New York by Holmes & Meier Publishers in 1978.
8 In the essay mentioned in the next paragraph, Friedländer provides a partial list of relevant publications (see his footnote 17); in his *History and Psychoanalysis: An Inquiry into the Possibilities and Limits of Psychohistory*, New York 1978, 45–48.
9 For this phrase, see Saul Friedländer, *History and Psychoanalysis*, 92.
10 *Where Memory Leads*, 130.

the beginning of the twentieth centuries, seem in fact to indicate a correlation between a fanatical hatred of the Jews and various personality disorders."[11] And these, together with more widespread problems of collective identity and "the high frequency of the authoritarian family context," as he explains, had a particularly powerful effect "in a crisis-ridden Germany."[12] Free of the psychoanalytical jargon and various adjacent sidelines, all these insights would often reappear in his later work.[13]

It was in the spring of 1975 – a period later described by Friedländer as "difficult,"[14] and just as he began to explore his youthful memories – that he was invited to hold a lecture, to which he gave the title "Some Aspects of the Historical Significance of the Holocaust."[15] This lecture, soon developed into a massive essay as ambitious as any of his early works, was an important milestone in his thinking about Nazi antisemitism. Incidentally, however, recounting the events of his life during that stormy time, Friedländer does not even mention this extraordinary lecture/essay, although in it he expanded for the first time upon three questions that would later preoccupy him repeatedly, namely: how to identify the motivations behind the exterminatory drive of the Nazis; how to explain the passive position and occasional collaboration of the "bystanders"; and how to describe the attitudes of the Jews themselves within this context. Having proceeded to discard as partial and insufficient all the various interpretations known to date concerning Nazi Antisemitism, beginning with the ones that stress the economic factors and listing sociological, political, and ideological studies, Friedländer finally comes up with the claim that what was missing in all these explanations was an additional dimension, that "of the utterly irrational impulse, of some kind of insanity."[16]

"It is not the killing as such that is considered pathological," he explains, "but the *obsession* with the Jewish danger which motivated the killing, the various *phantasms* that initiated the uncompromising drive towards first the expulsion of the Jews, and then their extermination." Friedländer then proceeds to indicate the analytically required further steps: first, the need to generally explain the expansion of this pathology to wider strata of the population, beyond the Nazi elite;

---

11 All the quotes in this paragraph are from *History and Psychoanalysis*, 92–94.
12 Ibid, 94–95.
13 For a particularly late example, see "Erlösungsantisemitismus: Zur Ideologie der 'Endlösung,'" in: Saul Friedländer, *Den Holocaust beschreiben*, Göttingen 2007, 28–53.
14 See the reference in the next footnote, 160.
15 It was first published in the *Jerusalem Quarterly*, 1, (1976): 1–50. I quote from a later edition: *Perspectives on the Holocaust*, vol. 1, Berlin and New York 1989, 138–161.
16 Ibid, 145.

and second, to particularly discover the link "between the pathology and the bureaucracy, that is between the Antisemitic obsessions of a leading group and their implementation within the huge organizational framework of the 'Final Solution.'"[17] Some comments on the state of the masses in Germany following World War I, namely "the emotional regression" experienced by them, as well as "the weakening of rational controls," which in turn opened "the widest fields of influence to the minority of the extreme Antisemites," seem to suffice for solving the first problem. The second, however, is far more difficult, and it is here that Friedländer reaches out beyond the mere pathology of a minority to the *rationally* construed *ideological* tenets of Antisemitism that had presumably permitted normal bureaucrats to join the fanatics and eventually carry out the Holocaust.

Later, it would be this strand of Antisemitism, namely the racial ideology on its various components, that would preoccupy Friedländer, especially as he was writing the first volume of *Nazi Germany and the Jews*.[18] But the 1980s were still years of intense preparations. Earlier visits to Germany produced Friedländer's *Reflections on Nazism: An Essay on Kitsch and Death*, not directly dealing with the past, but rather, perhaps for the first time, with problems of memory, specifically with attitudes to National Socialism in the popular culture of that time.[19] It took a prolonged and more intimate confrontation with Germany of these years, by then a country more fully aware of the Shoah, experiencing "an exponential growth of sustained scholarly attention to the subject," according to Friedländer, before he would take on the subject of National Socialism in general and Antisemitism in particular once again.[20] During these years, he was often involved in debates with German colleagues or witnessed their debates with each other. The exchange of letters between himself and Martin Broszat could, indeed, well represent this stage.[21] In his memoirs, Friedländer describes in detail his personal and professional experiences during these years, and concludes the relevant chapter with the following comment: "My stay in Berlin convinced me to turn entirely to the history of the Holocaust. The debate with Broszat pointed to some of the questions I needed to deal with."[22]

---

17 Ibid, 147.
18 See vol. 1, *The Years of Persecution, 1933–1938*, New Yor 1997, and vol. 2: *The Years of Extermination, 1939–1945*, New York 2007.
19 See *Reflections on Nazism: An Essay on Kitsch and Death*, New York. The original appeared in French in Paris 1982.
20 On these years in Germany, see part III of *Where Memory Leads*, 191–226.
21 For the English translation, see Martin Broszat and Saul Friedländer, "A Controversy about the Historicization of National Socialism," in: *Yad Vashem Studies*, XIX (1988), 1–47.
22 *Where Memory Leads*, 226.

These, however, were not the only questions Friedländer had to confront. In fact, by then all historians were made to face the challenge of post-modernism. Accordingly, the very possibility of establishing "historical truth" was questioned and the practitioners of the historian's craft were forced to develop a heightened sensitivity to theory, to the traditional narrative style one had often rather automatically applied, and to a long-established trust in documentary evidence.[23] Friedländer, on his part, was searching throughout these years for the right way to narrate the Shoah: ". . . how to define the Nazi regime, how to interpret its internal dynamics, how to render adequately both its utter criminality and its utter ordinariness, or, for that matter, where and how to place it within a wider historical context."[24]

To be sure, he had by then established himself as the main voice among the so-called intentionalists, convinced of the centrality of Hitler's Antisemitic drive and the importance of his racist ideology in dictating the policies of the regime. With time, however, he was no longer as insistent as some of his colleagues, and – as in the case of psychoanalysis – tried to introduce more "nuancing," as he often claims, here and elsewhere.[25] In the introduction to the first volume of *Nazi Germany and the Jews*, published in January 1997, Friedländer states that "[t]he crimes committed by the Nazi regime were . . . the result of converging factors, of the interaction between intentions and contingencies, between discernible causes and chance. General ideological objectives and tactical policy decisions enhanced one another and always remained open to more radical moves as circumstances changed."[26]

In any case, Antisemitism remained at the core of his interpretation. Describing the early stages of Nazi persecution of the Jews in Germany after Hitler's accession to power in 1933, he takes a respite in Chapter Three of his book to explain what he now calls "redemptive antisemitism." It is a brilliant chapter, though unlike the rest of the book, which already relies – just as vol. 2 of this comprehensive work would later even more emphatically do – on description and quotes, this chapter is a more conventional historical text. It begins with four introductory sections, telling the story of German Antisemitism from the late eighteenth century onward and only as he reaches the second half of the nineteenth century does Friedländer

---

[23] For Friedländer's singular way of confronting this challenge, see the volume he edited, *Probing the Limits of Representation: Nazism and the "Final Solution"*, Cambridge Mass. and London 1992, especially his own Introduction, 1–21.
[24] *Nazi Germany and the Jews*, vol. 1, 1.
[25] See, for instance, his comment on the evaluation of Antisemitism by Donald L. Niewyk, mentioned in *Nazi Germany and the Jews*, vol. 1, 110.
[26] Ibid, 5.

introduce the figures that constituted the Wagnerian "court" of Bayreuth, "that meeting point of German Christianity, neo-romanticism, the mystical cult of sacred Aryan blood, and ultraconservative nationalism" – in other words, the inventors of "redemptive antisemitism."[27]

This, presumably *new* form of Antisemitism, later constituted the pillars of Hitler's worldview, he claims, in which redemption could be achieved only by freeing the world – mentally as well as physically – from Jews and Judaism before they take over and destroy everything: the race, the *Volk*, the nation.

Beginning in section V, Friedländer follows Hitler step by step through all his Antisemitic pronouncements, from the *Hofbräuhaus* in Munich on August 13, 1920 until his access to power on January 31, 1933. Here he resists the temptation to analyze Hitler in terms of individual pathology, but the psychological "lead," as he calls it elsewhere, does crop up occasionally and appears even between the lines. Thus, he recounts the tenets of Hitler's ideology that joined eugenics and racial anthropology with "the mythic dimensions of the race and the sacredness of Aryan blood," and finally also with "a decidedly religious vision, that of a German (or Aryan) Christianity," all woven together into "what can be called 'redemptive Antisemitism.'"[28]

There are two other characteristics of Friedländer's way of handling Antisemitism in this chapter that are worth mentioning. First is his repeated stress on traditional Christian Antisemitism. ". . . [I]n dogma, ritual, and practice, Christianity branded the Jews with what appeared to be an indelible stigma," he writes, explaining that "perhaps the most powerful effect of religious anti-Judaism was the dual structure of the anti-Jewish image inherited from Christianity." On the one hand, the Jew was a despised pariah, the reviled witness of the triumphal onward march of the true faith. On the other hand, he was powerful and demonic, "the potent and occult emissary of the forces of evil."[29]

This dualism characterized redemptive Antisemitism, too. On the one hand, the Jews were "a kind of bacilli which had to be eradicated at all costs"; on the other, they were "a culture-destroying race," powerful and demonic, "aiming at world domination."[30] Christian anti-Jewish dogma together with other elements of traditional Antisemitism never disappear from Friedländer's overall view of Nazi Antisemitism.

Secondly, from the outset, he always makes sure to provide us not only with details about Antisemitism, but also with the true facts – as opposed to the

---

27 Ibid, 87.
28 Ibid, 86–87.
29 Ibid, 83–84.
30 Quoted from Friedländer's earlier essay, "Some Aspects of the Historical Significance." 147–148.

Antisemitic exaggerated ones – about Jewish life in Germany and elsewhere. These mainly serve to point out some supportive evidence for the Antisemitic claims and give the chapter an air of objectivity, but in fact they add up to more than that. Chapter Three, indeed, moves constantly between the phantasms about Jewish influence and power in the minds of the Antisemites and the real, actual influence of the Jews, especially in German society. Thus, for instance, section II of this chapter opens with a description of the prominent role of the Jews in banking, culture, the press and book publishing; in Austria-Hungary and other parts of Europe – as he stresses – no less than in Germany.[31] And section IV provides a full view of the role of exceptionally numerous Jews in revolutionary Europe during and after World War I.[32] Friedländer then even succinctly explains the *reasons* for the presence of so many Jews among the revolutionaries of that time. Only afterwards does he go on to discuss the Antisemitic "view of things," culminating in a review of the *Protocols of the Elders of Zion*. This is an interesting and convincing move, but from here it would not be easy to come back to what he himself had often stressed, namely that "whatever the Jews did or did not do, they could not alter the fact of antisemitism as such."[33]

The focus on Antisemitism, Friedländer explains, "should not lead to a skewed perception of the German scene – and particularly of the situation of the Jews in Germany before 1933."[34] It is part of the "historically relevant background." Still, the proximity of the two narratives forces him to tread a narrow path and it is interesting that in his later writings on Nazi Antisemitism, Friedländer does not take up again this sort of double-line. Jewish life in pre-Nazi Europe hardly plays any role in the second volume of Friedländer's book; neither does it appear in the essays he continued to write afterwards. In fact, while in this second volume he mainly chronicles the events and does not directly engage in explanations, the additional essays serve him as a platform to do just that.

A good example is an essay of 2007, available now in German translation.[35] Accordingly, the insistence of Hitler and his associates on capturing every single Jew – in eastern Europe and in the west, in the north and in the south – men, women and children, sending them all to their death, does require, after all, at least some kind of explanation. As usual, Friedländer begins by discarding previous efforts to do so, with special stress on the ones that attempt to link modernity and its typical "instrumental reason" to the Nazi project of extermination. Friedländer

---

31 *Nazi Germany and the Jews*, vol. 1, 77–80.
32 Ibid, 90–94.
33 See the essay quoted in note 15 above, 159.
34 See *Nazi Germany and the Jews*, vol. 1, 105.
35 See "Erlösungsantisemitismus: Zur Ideologie der Endlösung," n. 13 above.

insists: Neither modernity nor material interests, nor all kind of strategic calculations could explain the Holocaust; only the apocalyptical anti-Jewish faith of the Nazis that had always directed their action, ever since the mid-1920s to the fall of 1941 and beyond. It is then in the Führer's explosions during December 1941, parallel to the United States' entry into the war, that we find him announcing the crucial battle against that "satanical" coalition of forces blocking his victory now ever more effectively, and making the future battle all the more critical: The final battle against the joint power of plutocracy and worldwide Bolshevism – itself nothing but a plot concocted, as always, by the Jews.

Still, and the impressive line of reasoning in this essay notwithstanding, Friedländer's greatest accomplishment in writing about Nazism and the Holocaust lies not in explaining but rather in finding the right *tone* for chronicling it.[36] Throughout the second volume of his opus magnum, he remains distant and objective, but above all careful to uphold our sense of sheer disbelief in confronting the facts. "Beyond all theories," Friedländer summarizes elsewhere, "we may *intuitively* grasp . . . the peculiar evil of National Socialism and the quintessential core of the events that we call the Holocaust, the extermination of the Jews of Europe."[37]

Perhaps now the circle has been completed. It is the awe, the astonishment, and the disbelief that his great two volumes book manages to preserve, and finally, too, a kind of intuition that plays the main role in grasping the events, just like it did so many years ago, somewhere in the heart of France, when the young Friedländer was listening to Father L. in front of that "obscure Christ," describing "Auschwitz, the trains, the gas chambers, the crematory ovens, the millions of dead . . . ."[38]

---

36 Briefly on this unique approach, see Saul Friedländer, "An Integrated History of the Holocaust: Possibilities and Challenges," in: *Years of Persecution, Years of Extermination: Saul Friedländer and the Future of Holocaust Studies*, London and New York 2010, 21–29, esp. 25–26.
37 This was the final sentence of Friedländer's lecture at Royal Holloway, University of London, entitled "Mass Murder and German Society in the Third Reich: Interpretations and Dilemmas," held on March 6, 2001. See: *Hayes Robinson Lecture Series* n. 5, 25 (my underlining).
38 As in note 2, above.

16 Historiography in the Loop: Explaining Nazi Antisemitism

Clearly, it is no longer possible to provide a complete overview of the historiography dealing with Antisemitism, nor is it even possible to master that section of the available literature dealing with what is usually called *"modern* Antisemitism" in Germany. This theme, with all its aspects and variations, has been studied very intensively.

By the end of the 1960s, while I was working on my doctoral dissertation, only marginally concerned with Antisemitism, the literature on this topic seemed rather meager. One could rely on the first part of Hannah Arendt's *The Origins of Totalitarianism*, on Eva Reichmann's and Paul Massing's path-breaking publications, and perhaps even Leonora Sterling's slim but important volume of 1956, *Er ist wie Du,* later to be simply entitled *Judenhass*. A further effort would have disclosed Martin Broszat's doctoral dissertation, completed as early as 1952 under the supervision of Theodor Schieder in Köln, documenting Antisemitism in pre-Nazi, modern Germany. Finally, Peter Pulzer's seminal work on Antisemitism in Germany and Austria first published in 1964.[1]

To be sure, the study of Antisemitism was not the only one that seemed neglected at the time. Other, often related research themes, were likewise in an embryonic stage. But while for the study of National-Socialism, the turning point from occasional to intensive research occurred as early as the mid-60s, the history of Antisemitism, following the gradual shift of interest in the direction of studying the Shoah, received its real impetus only in the late 1970s. It was in the winter of 1982 that a review essay I wrote on two Hebrew volumes dealing with Antisemitism appeared in *Zemanim,* the Hebrew language journal of the Tel Aviv University School of History, where I had by then been teaching for almost a decade.[2] Taking a long-term perspective, it is interesting to examine the transformation

---

1 See Paul Massing, *Rehearsal for Destruction. A Study of Political Anti-Semitism in Imperial Germany,* New York 1949; Eva Reichmann, *Hostages of civilization. The Social Sources of National Socialist Anti-Semitism,* London 1950 Hanna Arendt, *The Origins of Totalitarianism,* New York 1951; Martin Broszat, *Die antisemitische Bewegung im Wilhelminischen Deutschland,* Diss. Köln, 1952; Eleonore O. Sterling, *Er ist wie Du. Aus der Frühgeschichte des Antisemitismus in Deutschland 1815–1848,* München 1956; Peter G.J. Pulzer, *The Rise of Political Anti-Semitism in Germany and Austria,* New York 1964.
2 See essay no. 1 in this volume.

of this historiography, the changing context of the relevant scholarly discourse, and where we stand today with respect to these issues, in Israel and elsewhere.³

And let me state at the beginning: When taking this long-term perspective, it now seems that we simply move in circles. Thus, for instance, the position of Shmuel Ettinger that I had criticized at the time, seems more convincing than ever today, and what had appeared anachronistic at the time is once again considered innovative, central to the main interpretative line. In his introduction, Ettinger had explained that Antisemitism must be seen as a phenomenon, which started so far back in antiquity that even early Christianity could make use of earlier forms of Jew-hating and anti-Jewish attitudes. Thus, it was then that the "negative stereotype of the Jew," he writes, became "a cultural asset of Christian Europe." For hundreds of years, this stereotype was being formed and reformed, and while some of its characteristics moved to the background, the final image was deeply "anchored in the consciousness of the European man, especially the educated."⁴

Ettinger, a leading scholar of Jewish History at the Hebrew University, placed great emphasis on the element of permanence and continuity in the history of Antisemitism. Changes in place and time, in society, in economy and politics only renewed and strengthened negative stereotypes, he argued, and gave them new justifications. To be sure, there were moments in which Antisemitism was in retreat, hidden in latent layers of consciousness or pushed aside by other trends of thought, as for example during the second half of the seventeenth century. However, it appears that modern man, trying to find his way through a mass of information, was in particular need of stereotypes and thus the influence of those stereotypes became ever stronger. Modernity merely strengthened the force of the negative Jewish stereotype, Ettinger claimed, and increased its effectiveness.⁵

Being a meticulous historian, Ettinger devoted much of his efforts to a description of external circumstances that influenced this process of mental fixation, but as he himself stated, "[even considering] the importance of historical circumstances, it is impossible to underestimate the spiritual tradition of Antisemitism and the Jewish stereotype."⁶ Finally, Ettinger asserts, "[t]he Germans slaughtered the Jews more than once in history in the years 1942–44. They did it

---

3 Th date of this essay is 2011.
4 For the last two quotes, see Shmuel Ettinger, *Modern Anti-Semitism. Studies and Essays*, [Hebrew] Tel Aviv 1978, 19.
5 See for the seventeenth century, Ettinger in ibid, 29–55 and then later in the same volume the essay, "On the permanent and the changing Elements in contemporary Antisemitism," 209–221, here 212.
6 Ibid, 216.

also in 1096 and 1348."[7] Despite its apparent changes, Antisemitism followed a constant thread as it repeatedly reemerged. Not only up to the point of total extermination but also afterwards; not only in Europe but also in the Arab world; not only in the central and western parts of Europe but also in its most eastern reaches; not only in Tsarist Russia, but also in the Soviet Union.

Many found – and still find – Ettinger's position convincing. The same thesis has been expressed in the historical literature both before and after him. The thesis of continuity holds sway over many reflections about Antisemitism, with important consequences for research and even politics. It has many opponents, too. Thus, as I came out against this line of argumentation, I was by no means alone. Most of the historiography that was being written outside Israel was on my side, so to speak. Without negating continuity, historians since the 1960s stressed change and novelty, innovation and breaks. For me, it was the transition from the known tradition of hatred and exclusion to the brutal acts leading to total extermination that represented a complete break with the past. Drawing one continuous line between anti-Jewish manifestations of hatred or even acts of violence from the remote past all the way to the Holocaust, or comparing medieval pogroms and the Nazi project of extermination, seemed a source of confusion rather than a way of reaching meaningful insights.[8] Beyond noting the elements of continuity, I believed the role of the historian was to find the differences and the novelty in each historical epoch. In our case, we were charged with explaining the turn of this age-old hatred, with which Jews had lived for generations, to the murderous rage of the Nazis and their so-called Final Solution. Insisting on continuity did not allow for an explanation of the break made possible by their rise to power. In the ongoing controversy among historians concerning change and continuity, I held that one ought to stress the novelty and handle with suspicion the familiar continuity thesis. At the same time, it was becoming common, at least outside Israel, not only to stress the novelty of Nazism but also to place considerable importance on pre-Nazi *modern* Antisemitism and thus break up the line of continuity from the pre-modern to the modern world. At that time, Jacob Katz, another prominent historian at the Hebrew university in Jerusalem, insisted on the transition from *religious* to *racial* Antisemitism, which he used for both periodization and interpretation. It was a generation later that Saul Friedländer

---

7 Ibid, 217.
8 To the best of my knowledge, it was Hannah Arendt, in her book *The Origins of Totalitarianism* that formulated this point. See there, 3–10. For a critique of the misleading comparison that the so-called Pogrom of November 1938 with the various pogroms throughout Jewish history, see Shulamit Volkov, "The *Kristallnacht* in Context. A view from Palestine," in *Leo Baeck Institute Yearbook*, XXXV 1990, 279–96.

diagnosed the crucial turning point in the discourse of the Bayreuth circle, defining what he then preferred to call *"redemptive* Antisemitism." At the same time, Daniel Goldhagen chose the late nineteenth century and described a prelude to Nazism characterized by the emergence of what he preferred to name *"exterminatory* Antisemitism."[9]

Taking for granted the existence of Antisemitism in modern European society as a whole and particularly in Germany, the issue of continuity gradually lost some of its urgency. Antisemitism remained a central, indeed *necessary*, element in explaining Nazism and accounting for its policies against the Jews. But then, during the controversy between intentionalists and functionalists, matters related to the role of Antisemitism during the Shoah suddenly resurfaced. Functionalists, to be sure, never denied the importance of Antisemitism altogether, but they did prefer to place the emphasis elsewhere. The intentionalists, on the other hand, centered Antisemitism – a full-fledged ideology – throughout their arguments. In fact, they often insisted on its significance not only for comprehending Nazi policies towards the *Jews* but for analyzing the Nazi phenomenon as a whole. By now, as we have long since realized, the line dividing the two positions has lost much of its sharpness. The growing distance from the events and the entry of new generations of historians into the arena brought about a noticeable rapprochement of the two warring camps.[10]

At first, it seemed that the more meaningful step in this direction was taken by the intentionalists. No later than the mid-90s, even some of the most dedicated spokesmen of their position were ready to take a less extreme stand. For instance, Saul Friedländer seemed by 1997, with the appearance of the first volume of his *Nazi Germany and the Jews*, to have found a comfortable middle-ground.[11] Although we may wonder whether his representation of the functionalist position is fair and whether the balance he claims to have achieved is in fact upheld in his book, it is clear that Friedländer acknowledged the need to move beyond the initial controversy. In his case, I believe, it indicated a move from theory and methodology towards a special kind of thick description, giving voice to perpetrators and victims alike. While the functionalists, it appears, were merely required to clarify their

---

[9] For the examples mentioned here see Jacob Katz, *From Prejudice to Destruction. Anti-Semitism 1700–1933*, Boston 1982, especially Chapter 21, 215–228; Saul Friedländer, *Nazi Germany and the Jews*, part 1: *The Years of Persecution, 1933–1939*, New York 1997, especially Chapter 3, 73–112, and Daniel J. Goldhagen, *Hitler's Willing Executioners. Ordinary Germans and the Holocaust*, New York 1997, the entire first part.

[10] In more details see my "Antisemitism as Explanation", no. 12 in this volume.

[11] See Friedländer, *Nazi Germany*, part 1, 5.

positions regarding the issue of Antisemitism, the intentionalists had to integrate new elements into their argument to remain comfortable.

Antisemitism, ran the rough consensus of the post-debate years, was a necessary *but insufficient* element for explaining Nazism. And in the aftermath of what we may call "the Goldhagen affair," at least members of the *Zunft* seemed to agree that while Antisemitism in Pre-Nazi Germany had been endemic, it had never been as prevalent or as all-powerful as Goldhagen suggested. Moreover, while during the *Kaiserreich*, for instance, Antisemitism was always countered by the forces of emancipation and integration, its Nazi version was far more radical than previous anti-Jewish sentiment, unexpectedly violent, obsessive, and, indeed, exterminatory.

But this, I would now like to argue, was only a temporary truce. Belonging to the same generation as Friedländer, Yehuda Bauer seems to reaffirm the centrality of ideological Antisemitism in explaining not just the extermination of European Jewry but the overall course of Nazi history. Other factors, he insists, may be able to explain "the how" of National Socialism, but only Antisemitism can explain "the why."[12]

Interestingly, the stress on Hitler and on ideology, the hallmarks of intentionalism, has also been reaffirmed by some relative newcomers to the field. In the 4th volume of his 2003 *Gesellschaftsgeschichte*, Hans-Ulrich Wehler takes on a decidedly intentionalist position, despite what may be considered his overall structuralist approach.[13] He placed the onus of explanation on Hitler's charismatic leadership and then on the force of his two major ideological goals – defined, indeed, four decades earlier by Eberhart Jäckel in his *Hitlers Weltanschauung* of 1969. These are the acquisition of *Lebensraum* in the East and a *Judenrein* Reich, a space empty of Jews. For Wehler, to be sure, it is radical nationalism that tied together these elements, not Antisemitism, but the two always went hand in hand, even if not always openly and not always to the same degree.

A number of years ago, Hans-Ulrich Wehler visited Israel and held the 2008 Stern-lectures in Jerusalem. My colleague Steven Aschheim and I used this opportunity to interview him for the Israeli historical journal *Historia*.[14] In responding to our repeated questioning, Wehler finally stated that "in order to explains the

---

[12] This in a lecture he held on April 14, 2008 at the Reichman University, Herzlyia, Israel, under the title "Kristallnacht, Krieg und Shoah". I thank Prof. Bauer for providing me with the text of his lecture.
[13] See Hans-Ulrich Wehler, *Deustche Gesellschaftsgeschichte, 1914–1949*, vol.4: Munich 2003, part VIII, 542–593 and the entire part IX, especially 842–913.
[14] The full interview appeared in *Historia*, no. 23, 2009, 5–22. The following quotes in this paragraph are taken from this interview.

extermination of the Jews, one needs the history of Antisemitism since the late nineteenth century." Otherwise, one could not understand why thousands of bureaucrats and officers of the Wehrmacht and of the SS agreed to take part in Hitler's irrational project and execute it in such a systematic and efficient way. In principle, if not in detail, Wehler acknowledged the importance of an Antisemitic tradition for explaining the Holocaust, though he shied away from applying its long-term perspective.

A renewed stress on Hitler and on ideology, including Antisemitism, could also be observed in the writings of some younger historians. Ulrich Herbert may be taken as an interesting example. Let me use some of his comments in a long press interview, given to *Die Welt* on 27 January, 2005.[15] Herbert first reduced the position of the intentionalists to the belief in the existence of a *Hitler-Befehl* together with a precise plan for exterminating the Jews. He then announced that the arguments relating to this point are futile, and finally – when asked to comment on the "main forces that brought about the extermination" – stated that "now we concentrate especially upon aspects of *Weltanschauung*," proceeding to stress its dual components in the case of National Socialism, namely *Lebensraum* and Antisemitism. But in fact, it was precisely this stress upon ideology, made up of a combination of Jew-hating and east-bound imperialism, that was the main element of the intentionalists' paradigm. Furthermore, Herbert now reinforces another aspect of their paradigm, namely the stress on Hitler's personality, and then, relying upon his own biography of Werner Best and on Michael Wildt's mammoth and hugely instructive *Generation des Unbedingten*, he reconstructs the mental world of higher SS officers, showing that it was deeply rooted in the Antisemitic milieu of the late Kaiserreich.[16]

Two other aspects of Antisemitism have now reappeared in the literature, impinging not only on the matter of continuity in general, but also on that all-important, well-established dividing line we have learned to stress between modern and pre-modern Antisemitism. These are firstly the new, or rather renewed interest in *religious* Antisemitism, especially among Catholics, during much of the nineteenth century and into the twentieth; and secondly, the renewed interest in the more violent manifestations of Antisemitism, both during the Kaiserreich and during the years of the Weimar Republic.

In fact, signs of reasserting the significance of religious Antisemitism, as against the so-called modern and racialist Antisemitism, could be detected in the

---

15 The translation from the German is mine.
16 See Ulrich Herbert, Best. *Biographische Studien über Radikalismus, Weltanschauung und Vernunft, 1905–1989* Bonn 1996, and Michael Wildt, *Generation der Unbedingten. Das Führungskorps des Reichssicherheitshauptamtes*, Hamburg 2002.

historiography earlier, too. Significantly, it was once again Friedländer, who gave a new weight to "the survival of traditional religious Antisemitism."[17] While he continued to distance himself from the view that modern Antisemitism was nothing but a new garment for the same old religious hatred, he contended that it had been above all religious education that provided "a vast reservoir of almost automatic anti-Jewish reactions" for many Germans, and that the notion of "outsider" applied by modern Antisemites to Jews had its deep, perhaps ineradicable, roots in Christianity.[18] The claim for the basic modernity of Antisemitism since the 1870s notwithstanding, Christianity, after all, had laid the ground for the view of the Jew as anti-Christ, a "potent and occult emissary of the forces of evil," a necessary building block for all later conspiracy theories, such as the ones appearing in the *Protocols of the Elders of Zion*.

Around the same time, it was Olaf Blaschke in *Katholizismus und Antisemitismus* who placed religious Antisemitism at the center, rather than the margin, of Catholic life in the Kaiserreich.[19] Even earlier, Zvi Bachtach, in Tel-Aviv, had directed our attention to Catholic Antisemitism, reminding us that some twenty years before, Uriel Tal, in Jerusalem, still had to struggle in order to show even the mere existence of *non*-religious or even *anti*-religious Antisemitism in the "Second Reich."[20] Within the historiographical context of these days, Antisemitism had been considered primarily religious. Jacob Katz, too, concentrated on the transition from religious to racial Antisemitism in pre-Nazi Germany.[21] Today, it seems, the pendulum swings in the other direction.

A similar tendency to pit tradition against modernity is apparent in the resurgent emphasis on yet another form of Antisemitism, namely its violent, brutal form. Against the familiar image of the Weimar Republic, in which emancipation had been completed and Jews were free at last of all restrictions, Dirk Walter's study of *Antisemitic Criminality and Violence* between 1919 and 1933, exposes the *Radauantisemitismus* on the far Right at that time, placing it in the context of the general use of force at the time and analyzing its motivations and excesses. These, if we follow Walter's thesis, apparently prepared the ground for worse things to come, when spontaneous aggression against Jews "from below" joined

---

17 Friedländer, *Nazi Germany and the Jews*, vol. 1, 82–83.
18 Here and the following in Ibid, 83–84.
19 Olaf Blaschke, *Katholizismus und Antisemtismus im Deutschen Kaiserreich*, Göttingen 1999.
20 See Zvi Bacharah, *From Cross to Swastika* [Hebrew], Tel Aviv 1991, and Uriel Tal, *Christians and Jews in the 'Second Reich'. A Study in the Rise of German Totalitarianism* [Hebrew], Jerusalem 1969, especially Chapter 5, 175–234. Tal's book appeared in English at Cornell University Press, 1976.
21 Compare note 9, above.

the meticulously planned aggression against them "from above."[22] Even more interesting is Michael Wildt's book, dealing with the years 1919–1939 and thus entwining the presumably non-violent years of the Republic with the Nazi years, prior to the Second World War. The elements of continuity are essential here, even though Wildt's main topic is the violence applied in the process of constituting the so-called *Volksgemeinschaft*.[23]

But perhaps even more typical for the historiographical turn of recent years are works on violent Antisemitic episodes before World War I. Suddenly, religion and violence joined together to create a picture of Antisemitism in the modern age that is uncannily similar to the one known to us from the Middle Ages. In fact, the dividing line between the old European Antisemitism and the modern one has long been a contested issue. For me, Antisemitism in the *Kaiserreich* had been limited to the "written word." The Antisemitic *act*, I argued, had been considered illegitimate in pre-Nazi Germany.[24] True, there were exceptions, including the Hep-Hep riots of 1819 and the 1848 Revolution, which included both progressive efforts directed at the emancipation of the Jews and a series of violent, bloody pogroms. Moreover, today we have exact information regarding blood libel cases not only in faraway Damascus or in the Steppe of Ukraine but in the heart of Germany, the exemplary imperial *Rechtsstaat*.[25]

By the year 2002, at least four new volumes dedicated to what has been termed an "exclusionary violence" have become available. I find particularly impressive Helmut Walser Smith's book, carrying the tempting title *The Butcher's Tale*, in which he analyzes the ritual murder accusations in the West-Prussian town of Konitz during the spring of 1900.[26] The book offers a detailed description of the relevant events and presents us with an example of a violent, religiously motivated, traditionally anchored kind of popular Antisemitism, only slightly related to modern racialist literature or to the political activism of the new,

---

22 See Dirk Walter, *Antisemitische Kriminalität und Gewalt. Judenfeinschaft in der Weimarer Republik*, Bonn 1999.
23 See his *Volkgemeinschaft als Selbstermächtigung. Gewalt gegen Juden in der deutschen Provinz 1919 bis 1939*, Hamburg 2007.
24 See "The Written and Spoken Word," no. 5 in this volume.
25 For the riots in 1819, see Jacob Katz, *Die Hep Hep Verfolgungen des Jahres 1819*, Berlin 1974. There are now some additional works on the pogroms of 1848. See Stephan Rohrbacher, *Gewalt im Biedermeier. Antijüdische Ausschreitungen in Vormärz und Revolution (1815–1848/49)*, Frankfurt a. M. 1993. On the Damascus blood libel affair of 1840, inclding a useful discussion of blood libel cases in the modern world, see Jonathan Frankel, *The Damascus Affair. Ritual Murder, Politics and the Jews in 1840*, New York 1997.
26 The full title is *The Butscher's Tale. Murder and Anti-Semitism in a German Town*, New York and London 2002.

Antisemitic political parties at that time. Walser Smith, however, goes further. In a prolonged excursus in the middle of his book, he recounts the story of ritual murder accusations from the time of the First Crusade all the way to the Konitz affair. He makes his point forcefully: this was a history of some 900 years, in which Jews were repeatedly associated with murdering Christian children, a tradition replete with folk-tales and fantasies, a tradition that withstood enlightened good-will and continued to surface even within the modern Imperial German state.[27] Clearly, powerful continuities were here at play, continuities not to be lightly disregarded when the story of modern Antisemitism and its Nazi climax is being told and retold.

Now, as the tension around the fierce controversies of the past seems to have calmed down, and as we are able to view them from a certain distance, we can also observe two main lines of historiographical development. First, extreme positions tend to be replaced by more moderate and compromising attitudes, as is, indeed, true in many other cases in which traditional approaches confront various kinds of revisionism. And the second, that the pendulum, which at first seemed to suggest a balance-point closer to newer approaches and to what had seemed the less-conventional interpretations, swung back in the direction of older, familiar formulations.

Maybe it is nothing but an indication that adjustments have not yet been completed. But it does leave us curious as to the next turn of the relevant historiography. It has often been said that while it is difficult to predict the future, it is even more difficult to predict the past. This remains true for the case before us, too.

---

27 Ibid, 91–135.

Epilogue

Germany after 1945 or the Return of Cultural Code

During the reign of National Socialism in Germany, Jews were first excluded from all spheres of social, political and cultural life in the Third Reich, then transported to the East and murdered there, together with their local brethren, by shootings in the woods and by gas in concentration camps. Those who managed to remain in Germany were being hunted even during the very last days of the war. At the end, some fifteen thousand Jews survived in Nazi Germany. Elsewhere, those who wished to return from exile or the few who were liberated from the Nazi extermination and labor camps were often unable to return to their pre-war homes. Some 1,200 Jews were killed in Poland immediately after the war. Throngs of refugees, mostly Jewish, streamed westward, finding shelter in Germany, of all places.

Thus, despite all their efforts, the Nazis did not manage to achieve a *Judenrein* Germany. Instead, their country became refuge for more than 250,000 men, women, and children, exhausted and penniless, making up approximately as many Jews as had lived in Germany on the eve of the war. These surviving Jews, together with the rest of the German population, were trying to recover from various traumata and painful war-losses while they were daily suffering from hunger, cold and lack of shelter. Interestingly, even at that early point in time, the Allies were already investigating attitudes of the Germans towards democracy and towards the Jews now living in their midst. Following years of Nazi rule, anti-Jewish policies and vehement Antisemitic propaganda, they unsurprisingly found out that democracy was suspect and that Antisemitism had not disappeared. At first, most people claimed they knew nothing of the mass murder in the east and considered Allies' reports grossly exaggerated. Later, while few openly defended Nazi policies against the Jews, most still felt "it was good to break their power."[1] Furthermore, in addition to old Antisemitic clichés, Germans now voiced new concerns, including fear of reprisals and resentment against accusations by individual Jews, by local or international Jewish organizations and by the four occupying powers ruling their country.

---

[1] Office of the US Military Government, report (19.11.1945), quoted in Frank Stern, *The Whitewashing of the Yellow Badge. Antisemitism and Philosemitism in postwar Germany*, Oxford 1992, 88. The first part of this epilogue relies on chaps. 11 and 12 in my book, *Deutschland aus jüdischer Sicht. Eine andere Geschichte vom 18. Jahrhundert bis zum Gegenwart*, Munich 2022.

While the Soviets practiced a strict policy of extinguishing any Nazi influence in their zone, the western Allies applied a policy of selective denazification. At the end of 1945, the chief Nazi leaders were either dead or brought before the International Military Court in Nuremberg. However, the efforts at *general* denazification proceeded slowly and with only limited success. It aroused a great deal of resentment and in many cases only facilitated the whitewashing of the Nazi stigma off minor offenders. Within a few years, most of the imprisoned Nazis were freed and many were allowed to reassume their bureaucratic posts in the west-German judicial and political system.

Still, the occupying forces were determined to introduce new moral standards to the public discourse in their respective zones and Antisemitism served them from the start as an important measurement of their success or failure. By the end of 1945 and the beginning of 1946, a number of newspaper articles, dealing with what they continued to call "the Jewish Question," also seemed to sense the meaning attached by the occupiers to the relationships between Germans and Jews. These became "a touchstone for the sincerity of democratic convictions," the *Tagesspiegel* explained, a kind of litmus test.[2] A few years later, in the summer of 1949, the U.S. High Commissioner John McCloy, a guest speaker at the first inter-regional meeting of representatives of the reestablished Jewish communities in Germany, used similar language: "The fundamental reason that prompted me to come here," he emphatically stated, "is the world-significance of the relationships of the new Germany to the Jews and of the Jews to the new German community . . . It will, in my judgment, be one of the real touchstones and the test of Germany's progress toward the light."[3] Thus, with the fall of Nazism, Antisemitism as a cultural code seemed to have returned.

In the early 1950s, during the official negotiations on matters of financial restitution, the same John McCloy urged Konrad Adenauer to make public his opposition to Antisemitism and to accept responsibility, if not collective guilt, for the fate of Jews under the Nazis and for urgent Jewish needs at the present. Inside Germany, anti-Antisemitism signified support for democracy at large, for progress and for human rights. Antisemitism signified the opposite syndrome. The symbolic mechanism that was here at play was similar to what I have diagnosed in some of the essays in this book for the years of the *Kaiserreich*.[4]

---

2 *Der Tagesspiegel*, 5.12.1945.
3 Quoted in Stern, *Whitewashing*, 297–298. This same meeting and McCloy's speech are being also discussed by Michael Brenner in the book he edited, *Geschichte der Juden in Deutschland von 1945 bis zur Gegenwart*, Munich 2012, 146–147. In what follows I often rely on the articles in this volume.
4 See my articles, nos. 4. and 5. above.

Meanwhile, the ever growing enmity between West and East, representing both the struggle between two world-powers and the competition between two over-arching ideologies, greatly intensified. While the foreign politics of the two German states were largely being dictated by the interests of the two superpowers, the two German states were left to concentrate on their internal affairs. In the East, the powerful Stasi apparatus was being built, and meanwile the West experienced what was dubbed a *Wirtschaftswunder*, that is a miraculous economic recovery. But Antisemitism, strangely enough, belonged both in the foreign and in the domestic spheres. For a number of years, the Soviet Union dictated an anti-Jewish campaign in all of the Central European countries under its control, while in the West, a decent attitude towards Jews and readiness to respond to their individual and collective demands for reparations were considered a prime precondition for integrating the *Bundesrepublik* in the Western world. Its relationships with France and the other major European countries, its full acceptance as an ally of the United States and its eventual membership in NATO – all seemed to depend upon it.

However, while the political elite in West Germany seemed to have internalized the significance of an anti-Antisemitic stance for its *foreign* affairs, it did not manage to control Antisemitism *within* its borders. Repeated waves of Antisemitic incidents were being registered during these years. On January 16, 1960, Adenauer, this time on his own accord, broadcasted via radio and television his deeply-felt indignation vis-à-vis the resurfacing of Nazi slogans and swastika signs on Jewish graves and synagogue-walls up and down the country. To be sure, he might have been particularly worried about the effect of these events on foreign public opinion. But since many other government officials, mostly conservative CDU members like himself, also publicly expressed their concern, one could cautiously claim that the political elite, despite its mingling with ex-Nazis in and out of government, reacted apprehensively to open Antisemitism.

Shortly afterwards, as Adolf Eichmann was forcefully brought from Argentina to trial in Israel, old wounds were being even more painfully opened. The so-called Auschwitz-trials, between 1963 and 1965, were attended by hundreds of school classes and the proceedings were broadcast countrywide. Jews were now standing witness to Nazi crimes; sometimes they even played the role of plaintiffs. But on the agenda stood not only, not even particularly, Antisemiitism as a code but simple, brutal Antisemitism too, often of the Nazi type, as real and as poisonous as ever. It was, in fact, only a generaion later, towards the end of the 1980s, that some statistical investigations began to register a gradual reduction of this latter kind of open Jew-hatred. Figures for what was defined as "hard-core Antisemitism" made up by then as few as 6% and it could even be claimed that Antisemites, Neo-Nazis and others, were finally on the defensive.[5]

While this has been shown to be primarily true for Antisemitism on the Right, Antisemitism of another variety was occasionally becoming more vocal and ever more worrying, this time on the Left. At first, it could be argued, using the concept of cultural code, that as a rule, critique of the Israeli occupation of Palestenian territories served the Left as an indication of its comprehensive anti-Colonialism.[6] In itself it was *not* Antisemitic. To repeat my argument in some of the essays in this book: precisely because Antisemitism was not a recognizable component of the leftwing political syndrome, it suited so well the role of a signifier. Clearly, leftwing Israel critique was not – and is not – *identical* with Antisemitism. But at the same time, it does present us with a fundamental dilemma: Is *every* critique directed at Jews or at Jewish Israelis a hidden manifestation of Jew-hating? And if this is not always the case, when is it – if at all?

To be sure, Antisemites often deny hating anyone. One is reminded of the first outspoken Antisemite in Imperial Germany, the Protestant Court-Priest Adolf Stöcker, who insisted as early as 1879 that "[w]e hate no-one . . . we also do not hate the Jews; we respect them as our fellow-citizens and love them as the Folk of the prophets and Apostles, of which our Savior had emerged." He only objected to their "Mammon-spirit" and to their desire "to become masters of Germany."[7] Similarly, though he respected their religion and shared their "ancient, holy memories," Heinrich von Treitschke, a highly respected historian at the Berlin University, found himself turning and twisting, too. He merely objected to that "German-Jewish mixed-culture," which the Jews apparently wished to substitute for "our thousands-years Germanic civilization."[8] There is a long tradition of Antisemites, going back to the Church fathers, who insisted on having no prejudice against the Jews, only justified complaints. They enumerated justifications for criticizing, despising, even hating them, and often claimed to be merely concerned with their "improvement".

Such an attitude has also been attributed to the so-called Jewish Self-Haters. Figures like the young Walther Rathenau in Berlin or Otto Weininger, Karl Kraus, and Egon Fridell in Vienna were listed under this title in a 1930 book by Theodor Lessing. Since then, this characterization has had a brilliant career in public debates among Jews, including in Israel's post-1967 political controversies. By then

---

[5] For the most useful summary of these statistics, see Werner Bergmann and Rainer Erb, *Antisemitism in Germany. The post-Nazi Epoch since 1945*, London & New York 2017, esp. 1–21.
[6] For the following discussion see my essay no. 7. in this volume, above.
[7] See Adolf Stöcker, *Das moderne Judenthum in Deutschland, besonders in Berlin. Zwei Reden in der christlich-socialen Arbeiterpartei*, 2. ed. Berlin 1880, 4–20.
[8] Reprinted in *Der Berliner Antisemitismusstreit*, ed. Walter Boehlich, Frankfurt a. M. 1965, 10.

there were reasons enough to object to the inflationary use of the adjective "Antisemitic," and it seemed absurd that anyone who dared criticize the Israeli government and its policies in the occupied territories would immediately be branded as Antisemite.[9]

Does this also apply in the case of leftwing critique of Israel in present day Germany? After all, such criticism seems to originate from empathy with the sufferings of the Palestinians and from opposition to what appears as continuing injustice imposed upon them by the Israelis. While prior complaints about Jewish greed or immoral behavior were based on long-standing prejudices and invented mythologies, contemporary critique is based on facts, reported by reliable journalists and confirmed by international eye-witnesses. At the same time, while the right of the Palestinians to voice their complaints and express their point of view in discussing the so-called Middle East conflict is surely undeniable, there is something unique in handling these issues in Germany. Here, even a suspicion of Antisemitism is often considered unacceptable, and the almost imperceptible sliding from critique to Antisemitism has not been unknown in the ongoing debates.

During the entire post-1945 period, it was of paramount importance for the construction of a decent *Erinnerungskultur* (Memory Culture) first in West-Germany and later in the united country to exclude Antisemitism from the public sphere, from all official occasions, from all printed matter and from every spoken word. In living memory is the scandal caused by the joint visit of Kanzler Kohl and President Reagan to the military cemetery in Bitburg, where both Wehrmacht soldiers and Waffen-SS men are buried side by side. A couple of years later, a speech held by the President of the *Bundestag*, Philip Jenninger, on the fiftieth anniversary of the 1938 November Pogrom, again caused a public uproar. These incidents already showed the sensitivity of the public in Germany to manifestations of Antisemitism, but it was when such manifestations were joined to matters of free speech or the freedom of artistic expression, that had brought about furious reactions, even earlier. A memorable case took place in Frankfurt am Main, as local Jews objected and, in fact, stopped the staging of Rainer Werner Fassbinder's play *Der Müll, die Stadt, und der Tod* (Garbage, the City and Death) in the city theater. Further conflicts erupted in relation with an exhibition, presenting the role of the *Wehrmacht* in carrying out the "Final Solution", or in relation to various forms of commemoration of the Holocaust, such as the introduction of *Stolpersteine* along the streets of various German towns or the construction of a Memorial for the Murdered Jews in Berlin.

---

9 See my "Selbstgefälligkeit und Selbsthaß: Die deutschen Juden zu Beginn des 20. Jahrhunderts," in: *Geschichte in Wissenschaft und Unterricht*, 1986, no.1, 1–13 (Originally in Hebrew in: *Zemanim*, IV no. 14 1984, 28–41). A later version can be found in my book, *Germans, Jews and Antisemites. Trials in Emancipation*, Cambridge 2006, 33–46.

In 1998, Martin Walser's acceptance speech for the Peace Prize of the German Publishers' and Booksellers' Association caused a heated controversy, yet again touching upon matters of free speech on the one hand and the need to preserve public decency in arguing such issues, on the other hand.

Germany has been trying to come to term with its past throughout these years. Some of its politicians and many of its public intellectuals were ever more intensely engaged in preserving a liberal-democratic *Öffentlichkeit* for the modern, powerful, influential and internationally respected *Bundesrepublik*. What made similar disputes more bitter during the last decade or two was the ever more urgent need to allow more "space", so to speak, for Palestinian and pro-Palestinian voices precisely within such an *Öffentlichkeit*. At this point in time, it was *more* rather than *less* open critique of Israel that seemed to have indicated Germany's robust liberalism and its firm belonging to the international community of democratic states. Occasional interventions of Israeli officials, trying to delegitimize these voices, only heated the argument, and eventually, various German authorities felt compelled to intervene. In January 2019 the federal government established the post of an Antisemitism-Commissioner and a few months later, the *Bundestag* decided to define the BDS movement, calling for a boycott of Israeli goods and a ban on its participation in international events, Antisemitic. The decision was based on criteria formulated by the International Holocaust Remembrance Alliance (IHRA), chaired by the renown Israeli Historian of the Shoah Yehuda Bauer. However, soon other Israeli intellectuals, together with artists and scholars from the United States and Germany, protested what *they* saw as illegitimate attacks on free speech and the unfair use of the accusation of Antisemitism. This, in fact, was a debate about the coded meaning of anti-Israel critique within the German context. It had little to do with the Middle East conflict. In Germany, some insisted such critique was an expression of hidden Antisemitism, while for others it still stood for anti-Colonialism and signified progressiveness and the support of 'open society'.

In the end, it was, indeed, the ease with which anti-Israel critique could slide into Antisemitism that made things so complicated. The controversy over the oral and written texts of the African philosopher Achille Mbembe is a good example. In some of his pronouncements, he seemed to have left behind the *symbolic* function of the anti-Colonial Israel critique, used by the Left since the 1960s, and allowed himself to introduce hateful language towards Jews of the kind that could not but be problematic, especially – though surely not only – in Germany. There were grounds to object to the continuation of his festive speeches and prize-winning ceremonies. In other cases, too, the danger of sliding from the symbolic to the concrete in applying anti-Jewish language or anti-Israeli critique, was equally apparent. And this danger seems always to be there. Some tend to exaggerate its significance; some to underestimate it. In any case, the discussion is no longer limited to supporters or opponents of the Left. It is now carried out by the mainstream, specifically among historians.

Two interesting sidelines recently accompanied this discussion. *First* was a renewed interest in *defining* Antisemitism. After all, much has happened since the term had been invented and became widespread in Germany of the late 1870's, almost 150 years ago. During that time, it has been used extensively in both scholarly and public discourse, while defining it remained difficult throughout. The American historian David Engel suggested dropping it altogether, but his passionate plea for that radical solution received only limited support from colleagues, experts in the field.[10] Perhaps this concept's intuitive and easily understood sense, as well as its continuous application by contemporaries, contribute to its staying power. At any rate it seems, to me at least, that a revolution in our terminology is unlikely to occur and in any case would not be of much use. We would still have to decide each case on its own, and even then we might often remain undecided.

Secondly and more interestingly, historians renewed the controversy concerning the relationships between Antisemitism and Racism and it then also leaked into the daily press, in and out of Germany. The discussion now includes reviewing the presumed *uniqueness* of Antisemitism in comparison with other cases of genocide, primarily in the colonial world, bringing into the open the subtext of competition among victims on a worldwide scale.[11] On both counts the debate has taken a rather ahistorical turn. Clearly, Antisemitism has a separate and unique history. This remains true even in times of increased awareness of other cruelties, mainly those typical of Colonialism and apparent in the various expressions of Racism in contemporary society. In fact, both Antisemitism and Racism ought to be studied with a view to their unique history and since both are morally reprehensible, they must be equally fought against and resisted.

Now, while historians are arguing these issues, Germany as a whole is still repeatedly disturbed by expressions of Antisemitism as well as Racism, especially on its political Right. Resentment of the *Bundesrepublik*, still alive in the eastern parts of the united country and felt even among Germans who never experienced life in the DDR, is joined to the not-yet-extinguished xenophobia everywhere else in the country. In times of increased immigration and the constant confrontation at home with foreign cultures and customs, the Right seems to flourish as never

---

10 See, unfortunately only in Hebrew, the extensive discussion of Engel's suggestion in the collection of essays: *Antisemitism. Historical Concept, Public Discourse*, eds. Scott Ury and Guy Miron, appearing as vol. LXXXV, 1–4, of the quarterly *Zion*, Jerusalem 2020.
11 For all major contributors, see *Historiker streiten: Gewalt und Holocaust – die Debatte*, eds. Susan Neimann and Michael Wildt, Berlin 2022.

before. Germany has indeed become home to hundreds of thousands of refugees from Syria and Afghanistan, many of whom were long subjected not only to anti-Israeli but also to outright Antisemitic propaganda. Nevertheless, their presence in Germany has had only marginal effect on issues related to the intellectual discussion of Antisemitism, though it sometimes leaves its mark on the atmosphere in schools and on the streets of Germany's large urban centers.

In present-day Germany, both on the Left and on the Right, Antisemitism continues to stand for more than Jew-hating. It is still a clear code, perhaps indeed a *cultural code*, for negative attitudes towards democracy, equality, and human rights in general. Its strength or weakness serve as a measure for the ability of German society to judge reality without prejudice and without delusion. Even though the Right has been lately strengthened in some European countries even more conspicuously, Germany – after all – is expected to be far more watchful in this respect. Memory of its past sets higher standards for this country. Thus, terror attacks against Jews, such as the Halle synagogue shooting on Yom Kipur, October 2019, deeply unsettle both Jews and non-Jews. Though there are always voices that attempt to minimize the danger, I consider it too early to feel confident.

But this is primarily a history book. The studies and essays collected in it are meant to illuminate the past. However, like every historian, I may be allowed to hope that they will also be of some value in correctly evaluating the present.

Acknowledgements

No. 1. "More on Antisemitism and the Study of Antisemitism," [Hebrew], here under the title "What's wrong with the Study of Antisemitism: Two Reviews and two unanswered Questions," from *Zemanim. A Historical Quarterly*, winter 1982, 77–81.

No. 2. "The Social and political Function of Antisemitism: The Case of the small Handicraft Masters," from *Sozialgeschichte Heute. Festschrift für Hans Rosenberg zum 70. Geburtstag*, ed. H.U. Wehler, **Vandenhoeck & Ruprecht Göttingen** 1974, 416–431.

No. 3. "The Immunization of Social Democracy against Antisemitism in Imperial Germany," from *Juden und jüdische Asepkte in der deutschen Arbeiterbewegung*, Beiheft 2, Jahrbuch des **Instituts für Deustche Geschichte**, Tel Aviv 1977, 63–81.

No. 4. "Antisemitism as a Cultural Code. Reflections on the History and Historiography of Antisemitism in Imperial Germany," from the *Yearbook of the Leo Baeck Institute* XXIII, **Oxford University Press**, Oxford 1978, 25–45.

No. 5. "The Written Matter and the Spoken Word: On the Gap between pre-1914 and Nazi Antisemitism," from *L'Allemagne nazi et le génocide juif*, ed. by F. Furet, Paris 1985; translated in *Unanswered Questions: Nazi Germany and the Genocide of the Jews*, ed. F. Furet, **Penguin Random House**, New York 1989, 33–55.

No. 6. "Antisemitism and anti-Feminism," [Hebrew], from *Zemanim, A Historical Quarterly*, 1993, 134–143. An English translation was printed in Shulamit Volkov, *Germans, Jews, and Antisemites. Trials in Emancipation*, Cambridge 2006, 129–144.

No. 7. "Readjusting Cultural Codes: Antisemitism, anti-Zionism and the Critique of Israel." from *The Journal of Israel Studies*, vol. 25, no. 1, **Taylor & Francis**, March 2006, 51–62. (*https://www.tandfonline.com/*)

No. 8. "Nationalism, Antisemitism and German Historiography," [German] from *Nation und Gesellschaft in Deutschland. Historische Essays. Hans Ulrich Wehler zum 65. Geburtstag*, ed. Manfred Hettling and Paul Nolte, **C.H. Beck Verlag**, München 1996, 208–220.

No. 9. "Language as the Site of confronting Jews and Judaism," [German] from *Jüdische Intellektuelle und die Philologien in Deutschland. 1871 bis 1933*, eds., Wilfried Barner and Chrish König, **Wallstein Verlag**, Göttingen 1998, 223–238.

No. 10. "German Jews and the Temptation of Racism", from *Expanding Persectives on the Holocaust. Lessons and Legacies,* eds. Hillary Earl and Karl A. Schleunes, **North Western University Press**, Evanston Ill. 2014, 211–228.

No. 12. "National-Socialism: The Double Perspective of Jews and Germans," from *Jüdische Welten. Juden in Deutschland vom 18. Jahrhundert bis in die Gegenwart*, eds. Marion Kaplan and Beate Meyer, **Wallstein Verlag**, Göttingen 2005, 457–465.

No. 13. "Antisemitism as Explanation: For and against", from *Catastrohe and Meaning. The Holocaust and the Twentieth Century,* eds. Moishe Postone and Eric Santner, **Chicago University Press** 2003, 34–48.

No. 14. A book review from the Israeli daily *Haaretz*, [Hebrew] August 18, 2008.

No. 15. "Revisiting Friedländer on Nazi Antisemitism", from a special issue of the *Journal of Holocaust Research,* **Taylor & Francis**, 2023, vol. 37, no.1, 50–56. (*https://www.tandfonline.com/*)

No. 16. "Historiography in the Loop: Explaining Nazi Antisemitism", [Hebrew] from *Zion*, vol. 76 no.3, 2011, 369–379.

www.ingramcontent.com/pod-product-compliance
Lightning Source LLC
Chambersburg PA
CBHW020226170426
43201CB00007B/332